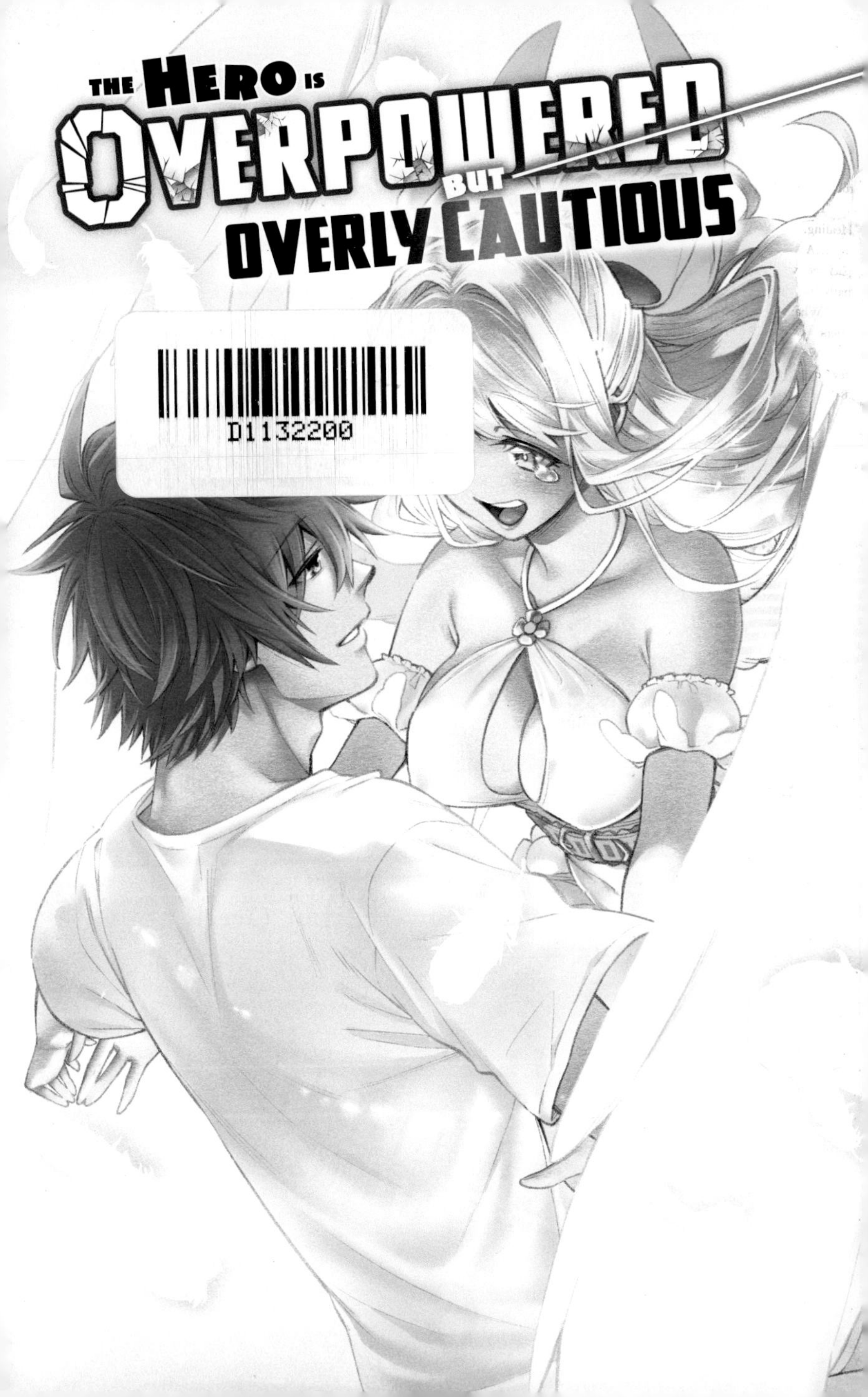
THE HERO IS
OVERPOWERED
BUT
OVERLY CAUTIOUS

CONTENTS

THE HERO IS OVERPOWERED BUT OVERLY CAUTIOUS

6

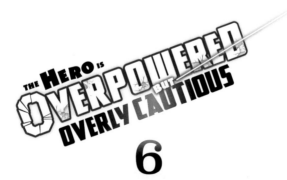

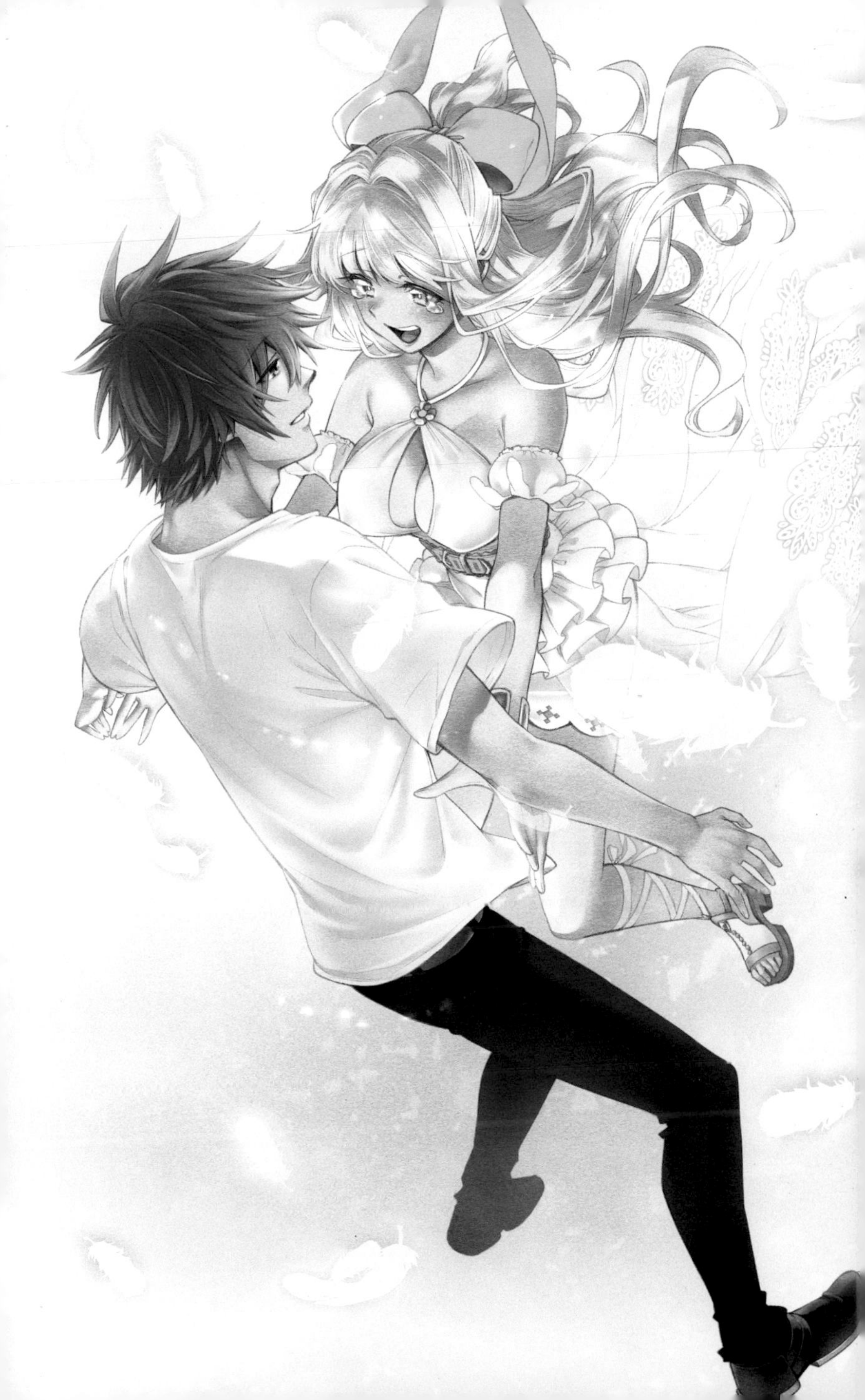

The Hero Is Overpowered but

Overly Cautious

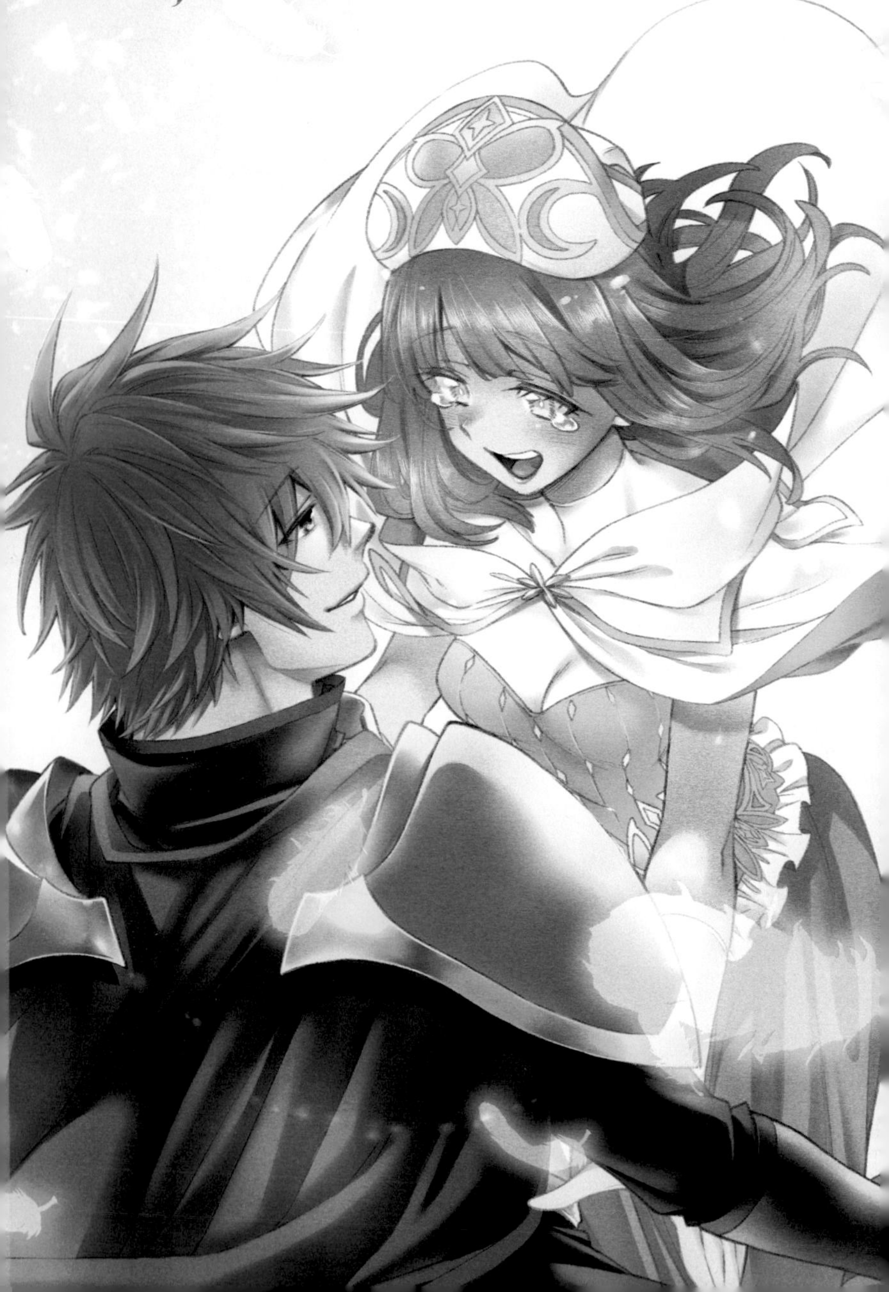

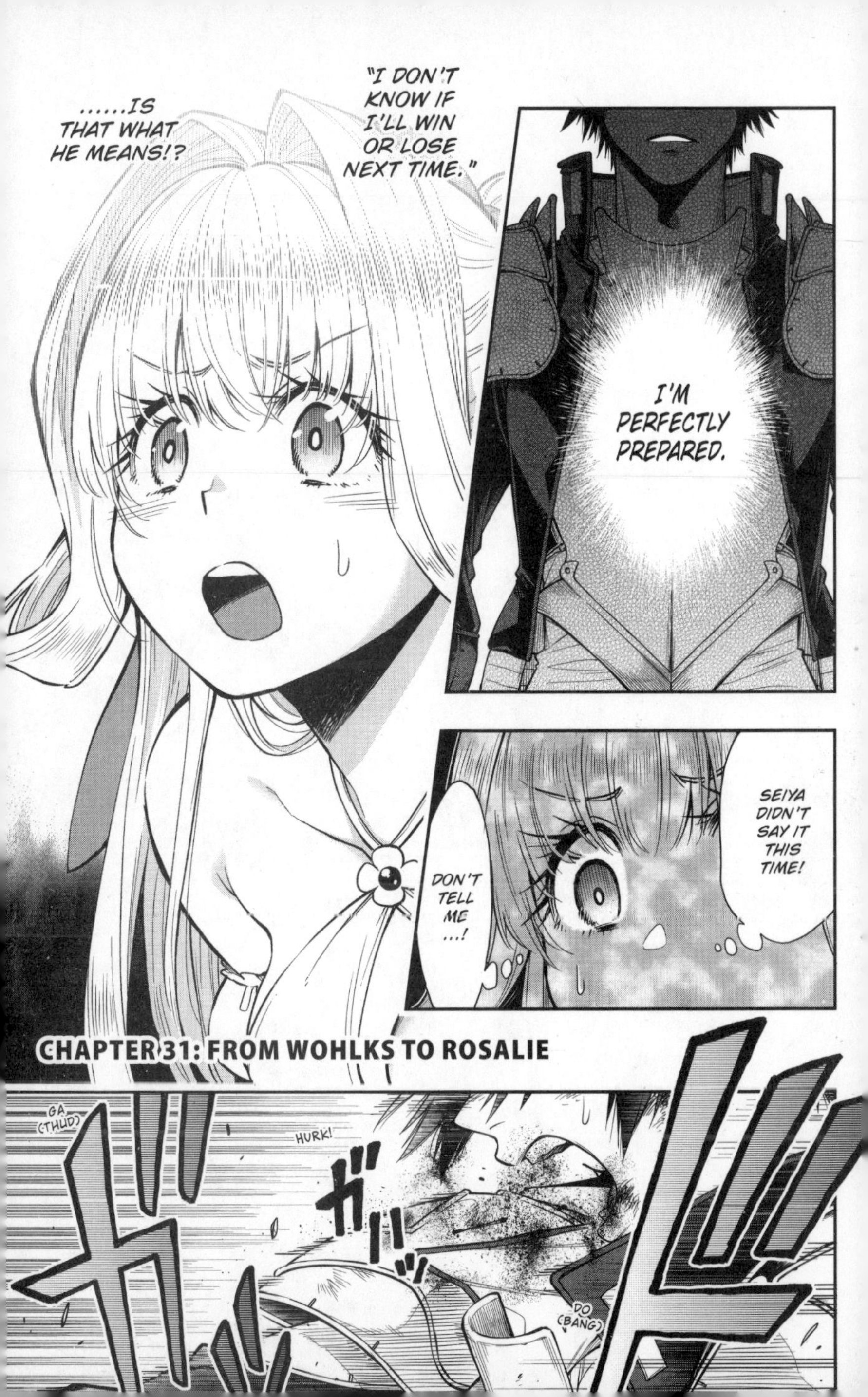
I'M PERFECTLY PREPARED.
SEIYA DIDN'T SAY IT THIS TIME!
DON'T TELL ME ...!
"I DON'T KNOW IF I'LL WIN OR LOSE NEXT TIME."
......IS THAT WHAT HE MEANS!?
CHAPTER 31: FROM WOHLKS TO ROSALIE
DO (BANG)
HURK!
GA (THUD)

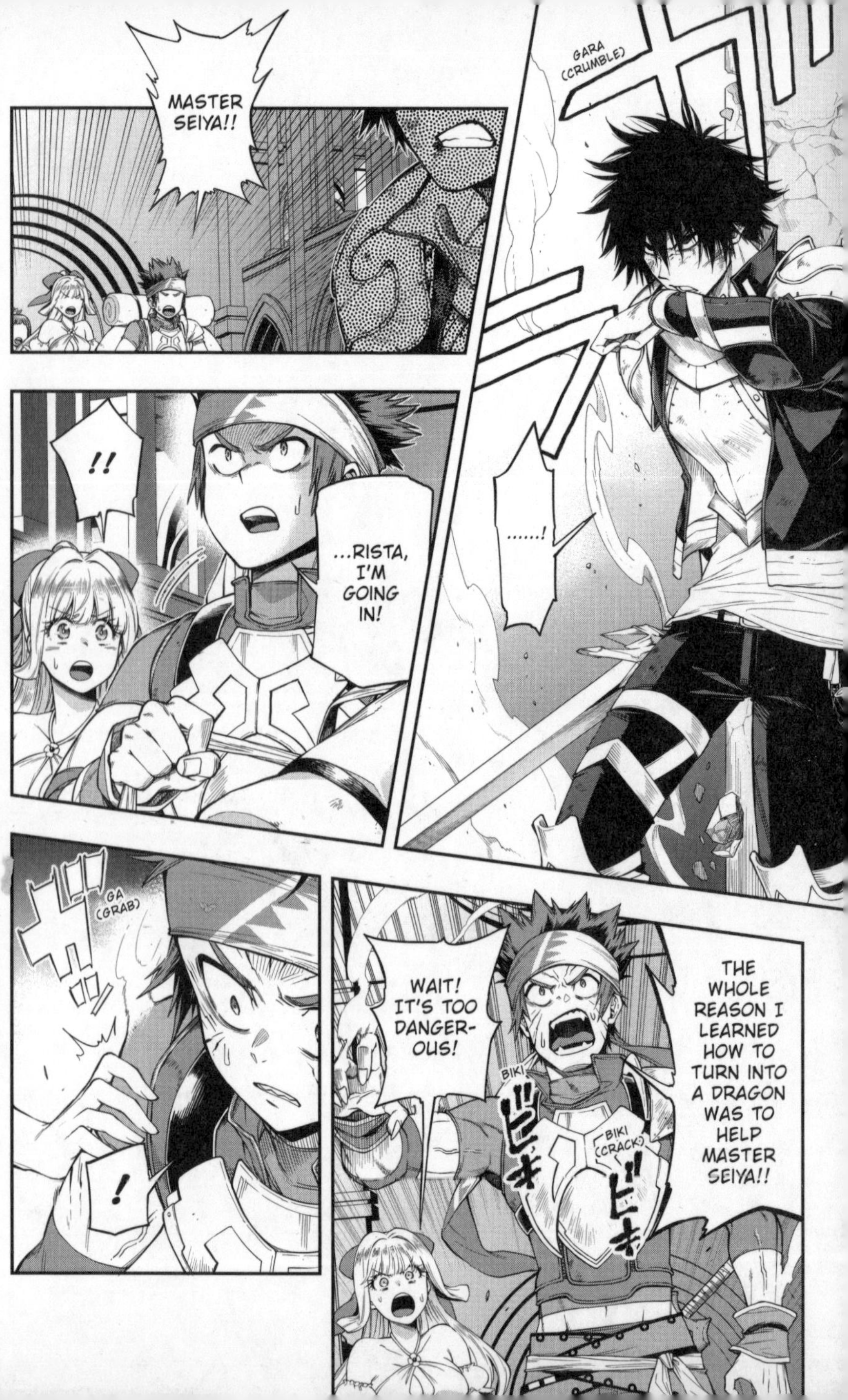
GARA (CRUMBLE)
......!
MASTER SEIYA!!
!!
...RISTA, I'M GOING IN!
WAIT! IT'S TOO DANGER-OUS!
BIKI
BIKI (CRACK)
THE WHOLE REASON I LEARNED HOW TO TURN INTO A DRAGON WAS TO HELP MASTER SEIYA!!
GA (GRAB)
!

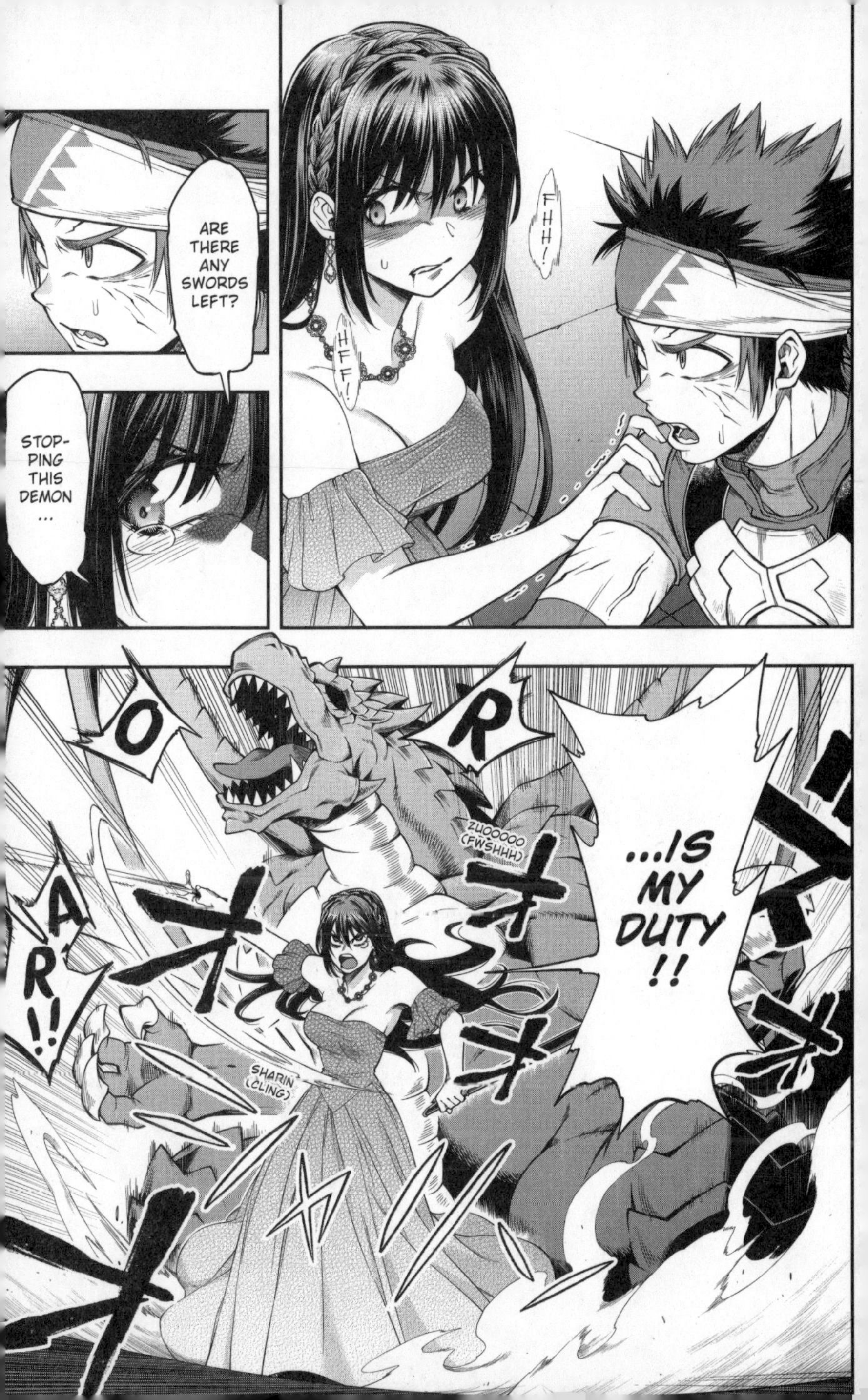
FHH!
HFF!
ARE THERE ANY SWORDS LEFT?
STOP-PING THIS DEMON ...
...IS MY DUTY!!
ZUOOOOO (FWSHHH)
ROAR!!
SHARIN (CLING)

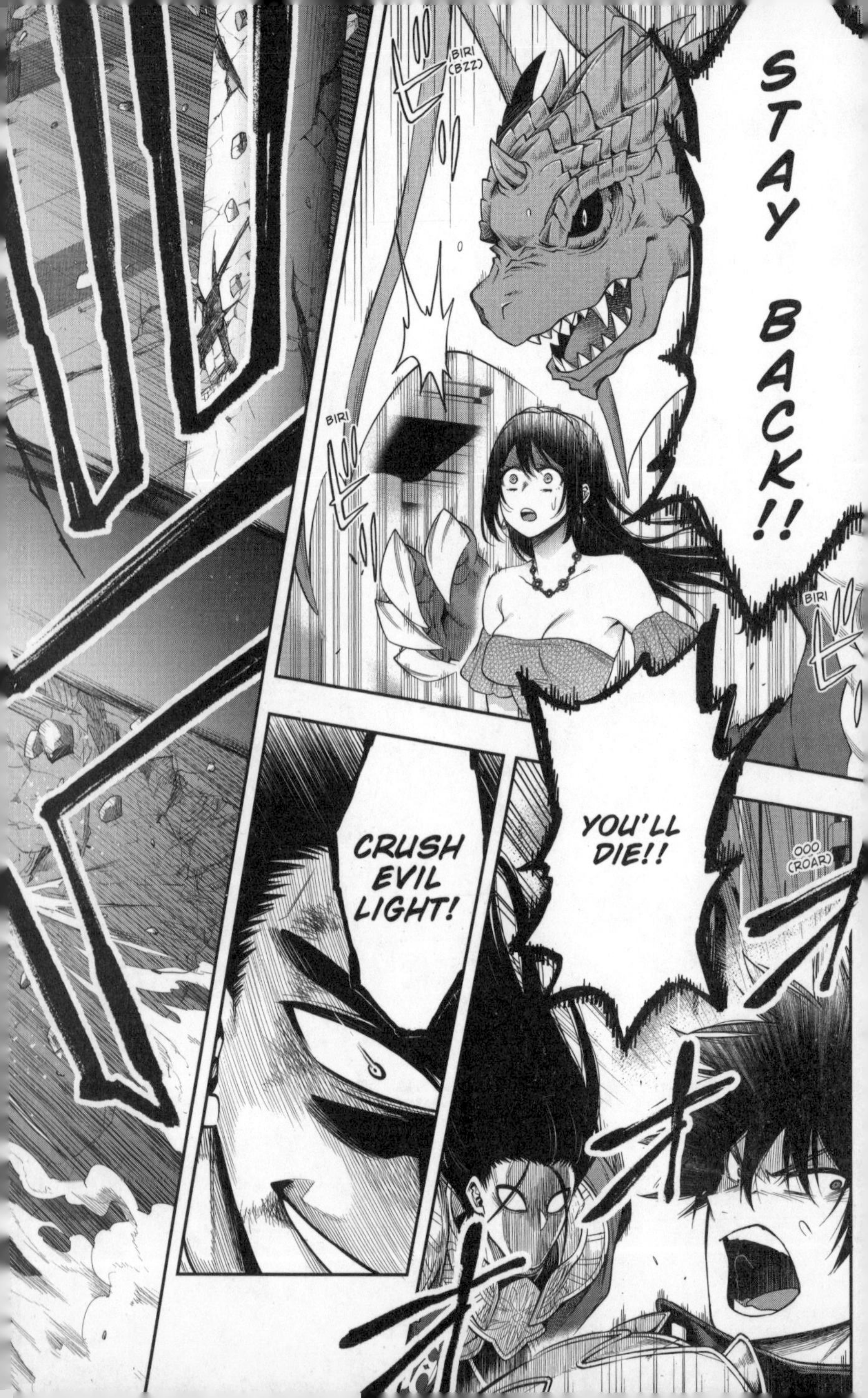
STAY BACK!!
BIRI (BZZ)
BIRI
BIRI
YOU'LL DIE!!
OOO (ROAR)
CRUSH EVIL LIGHT!

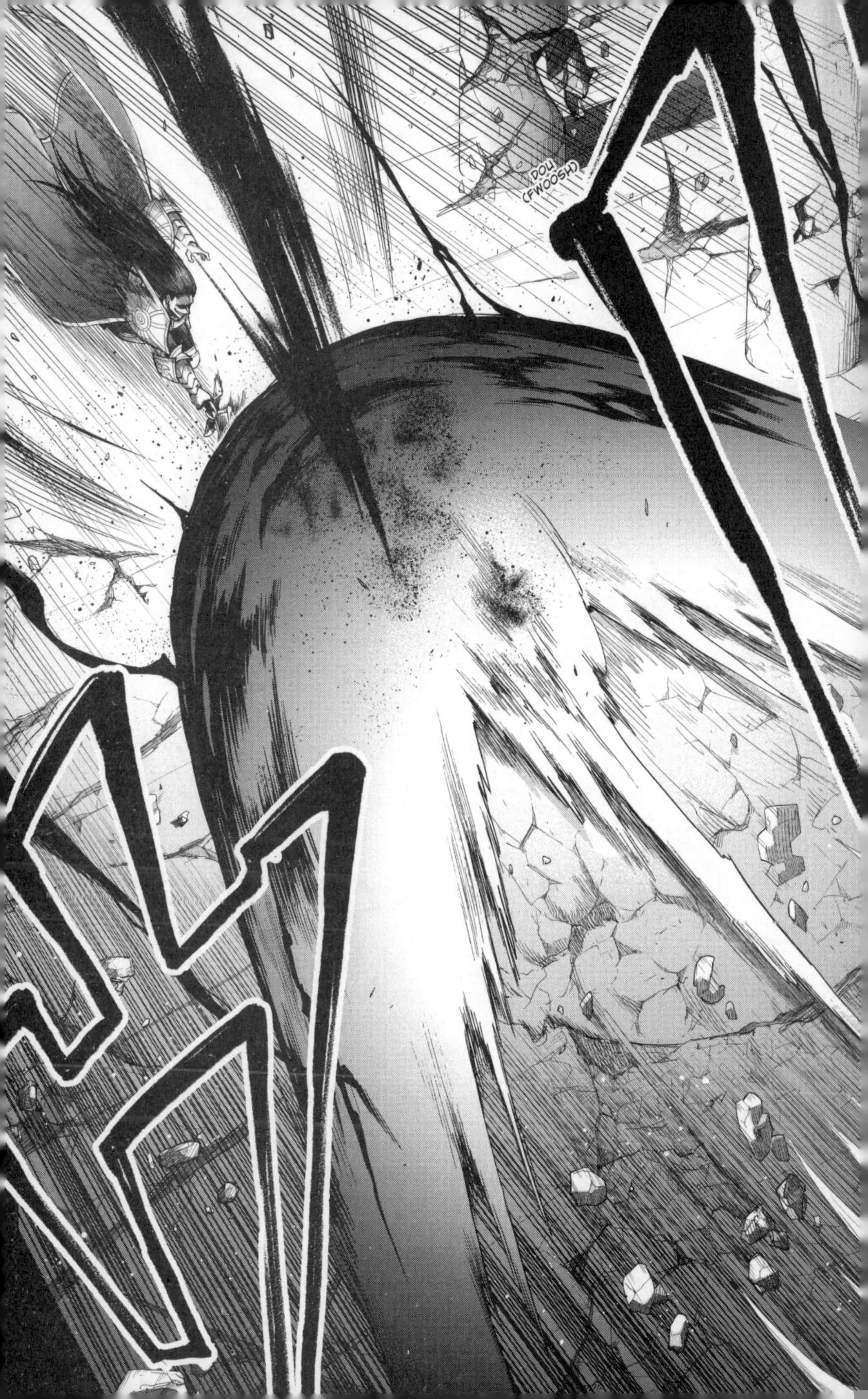
DOU
(FWOOSH)

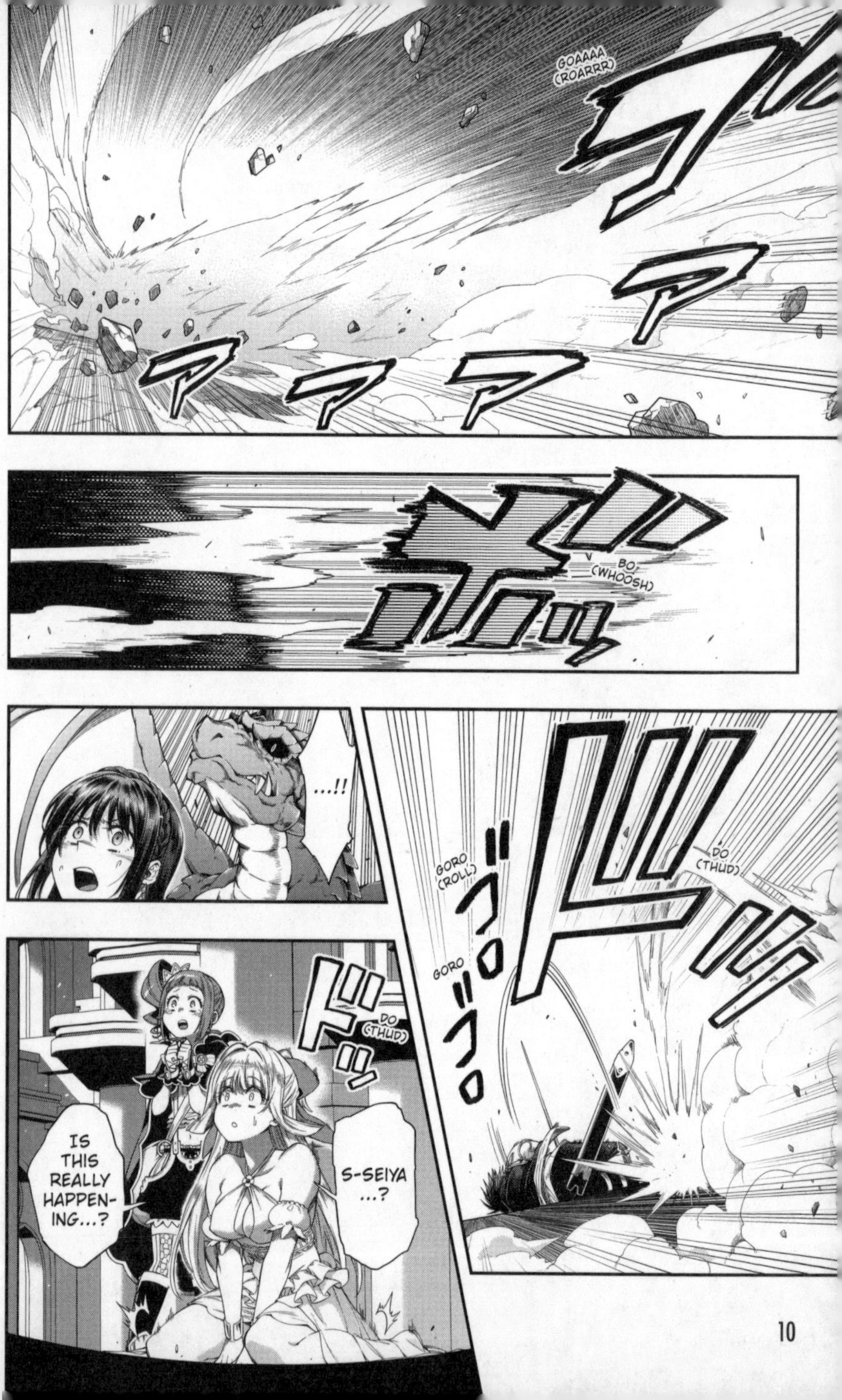
GOAAAA (ROARRR)
BO (WHOOSH)
DO (THUD)
GORO (ROLL)
GORO
...!!
DO (THUD)
S-SEIYA ...?
IS THIS REALLY HAPPEN-ING...?

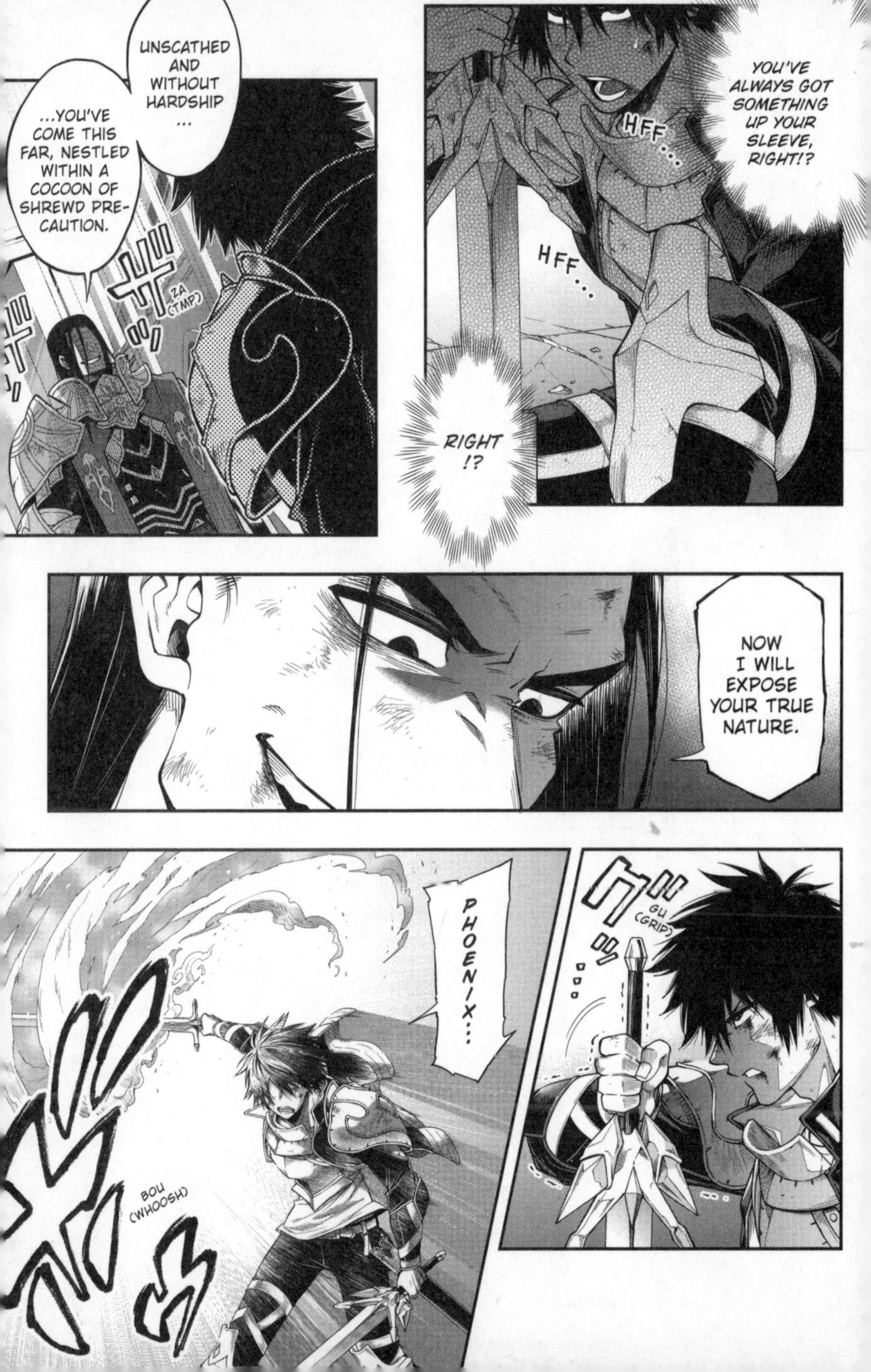
YOU'VE ALWAYS GOT SOMETHING UP YOUR SLEEVE, RIGHT!?
HFF...
HFF...
RIGHT!?
UNSCATHED AND WITHOUT HARDSHIP...
...YOU'VE COME THIS FAR, NESTLED WITHIN A COCOON OF SHREWD PRE-CAUTION.
ZA (TMP)
NOW I WILL EXPOSE YOUR TRUE NATURE.
GU (GRIP)
PHOENIX...
BOU (WHOOSH)

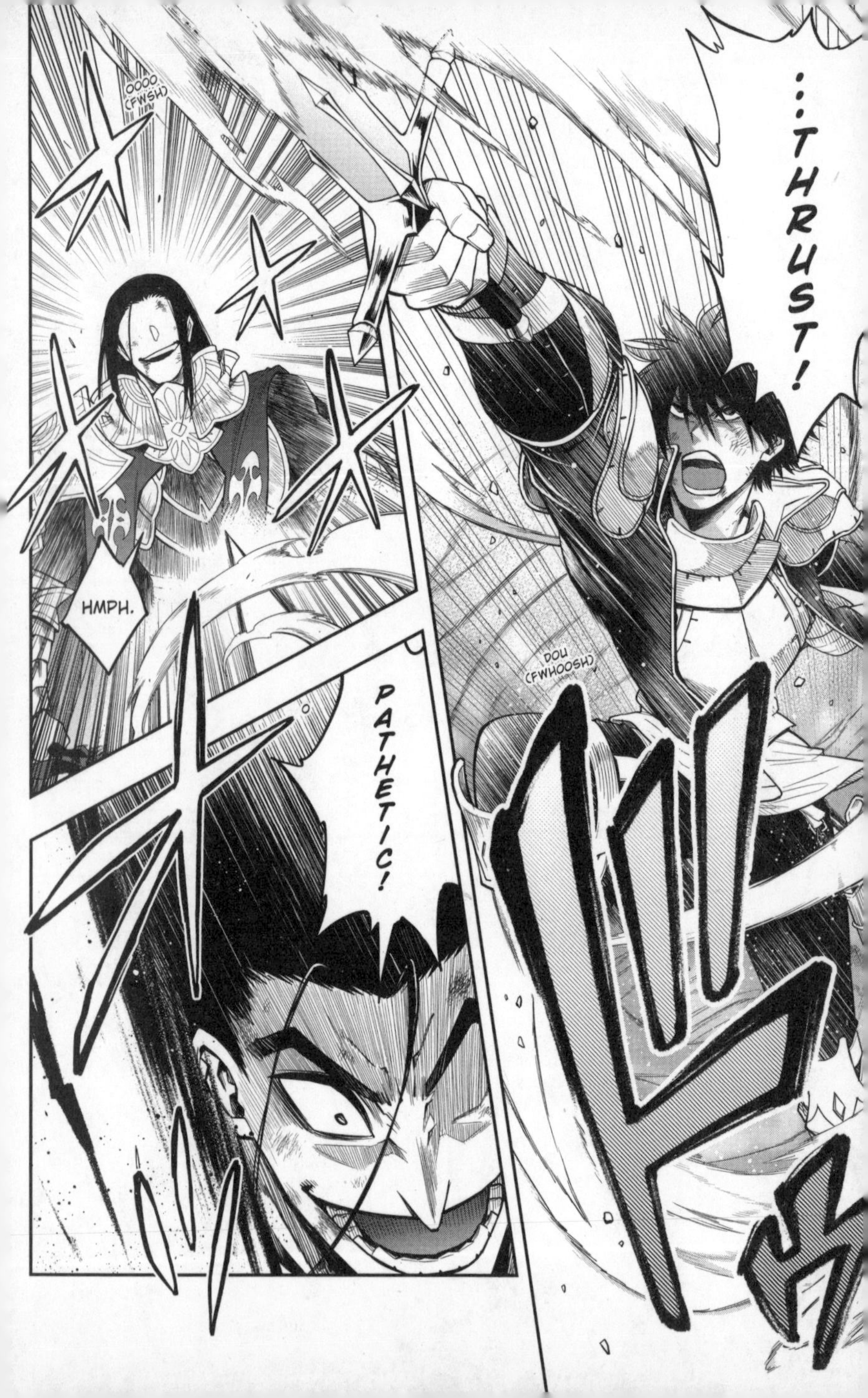
...THRUST!
DOU (FWHOOSH)
OOOO (FWSH)
HMPH.
PATHETIC!

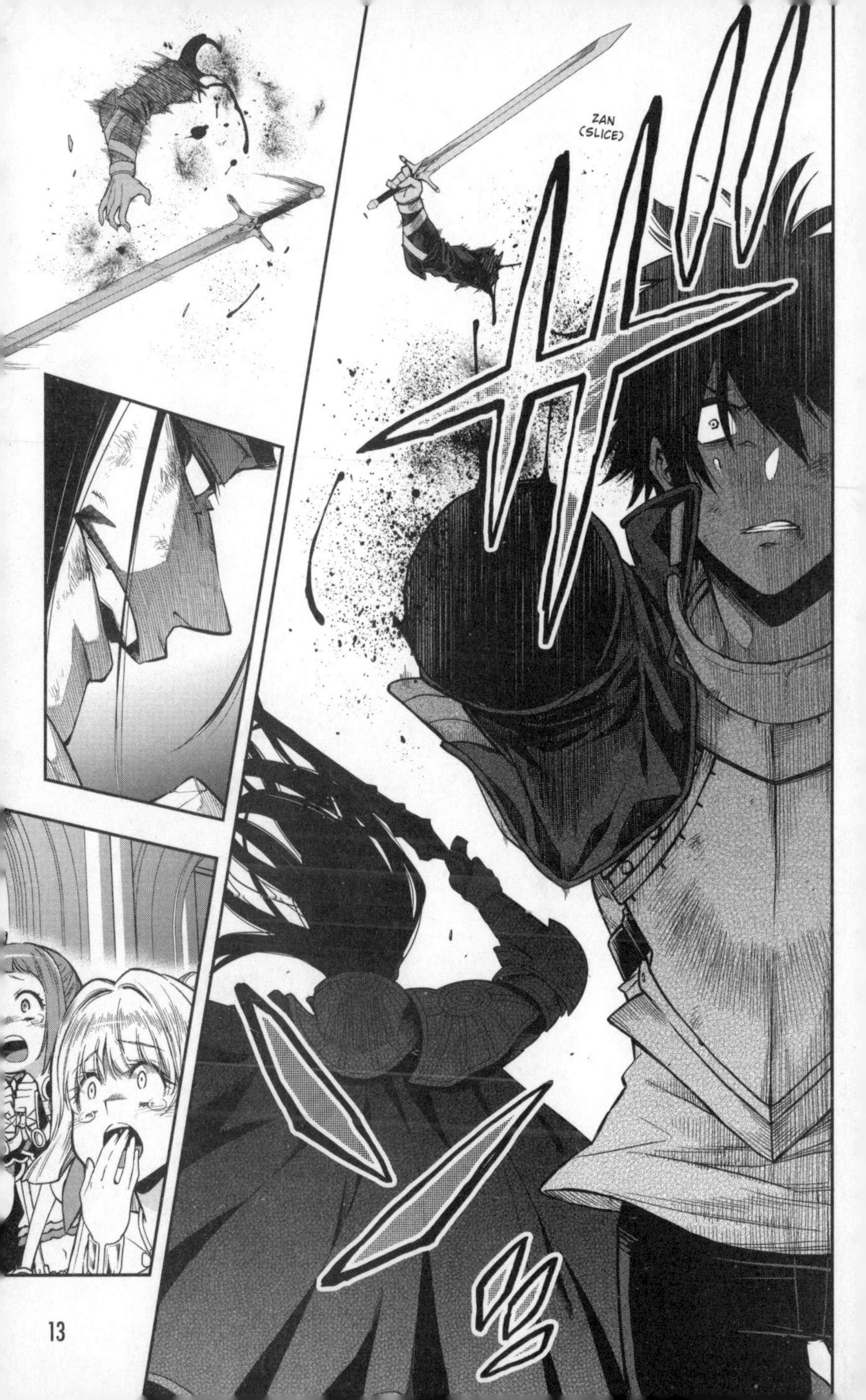
ZAN
(SLICE)

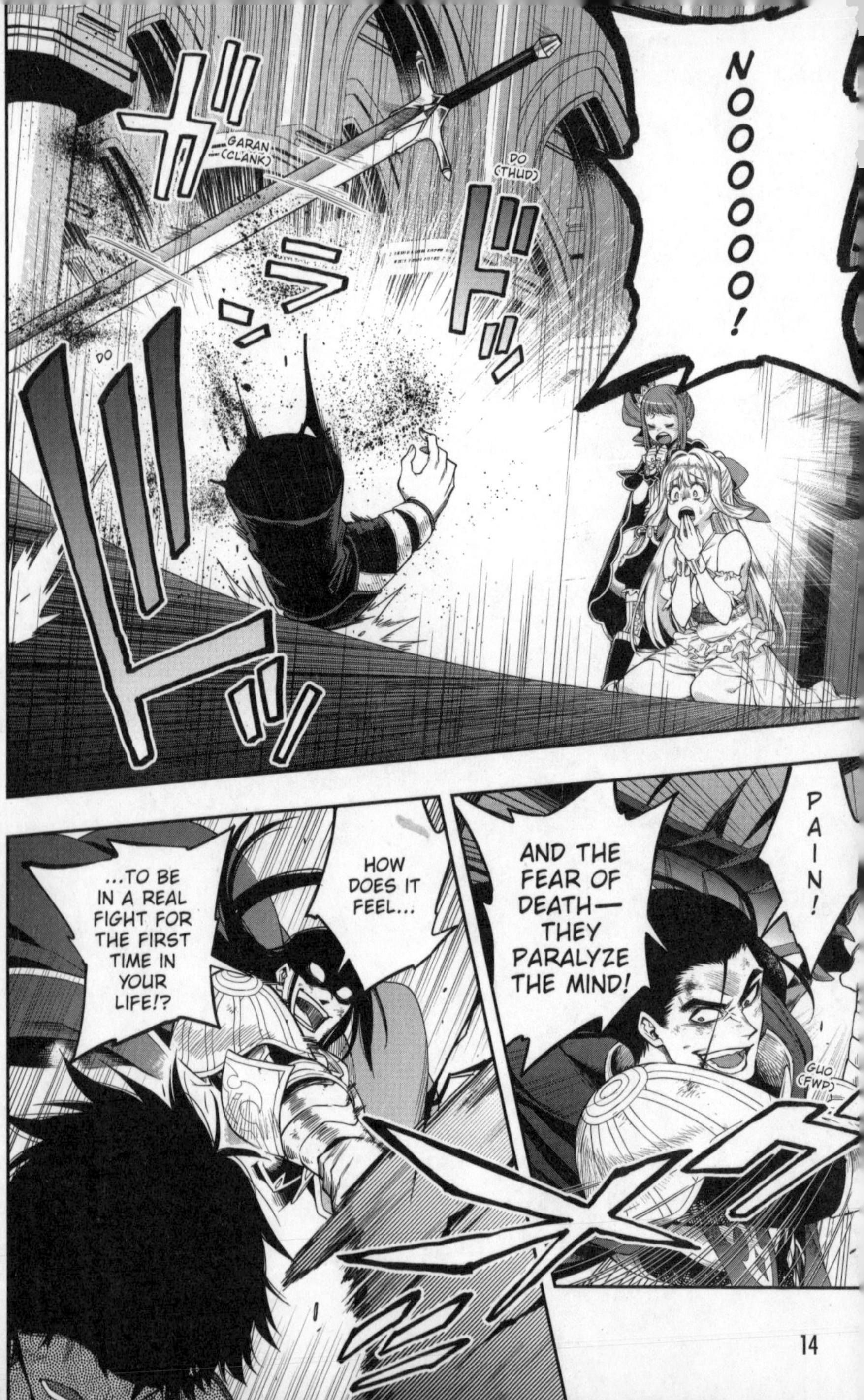
NOOOOOOO!
DO
(THUD)
GARAN
(CLANK)
DO
PAIN!
AND THE FEAR OF DEATH— THEY PARALYZE THE MIND!
GUO
(FWP)
HOW DOES IT FEEL...
...TO BE IN A REAL FIGHT FOR THE FIRST TIME IN YOUR LIFE!?

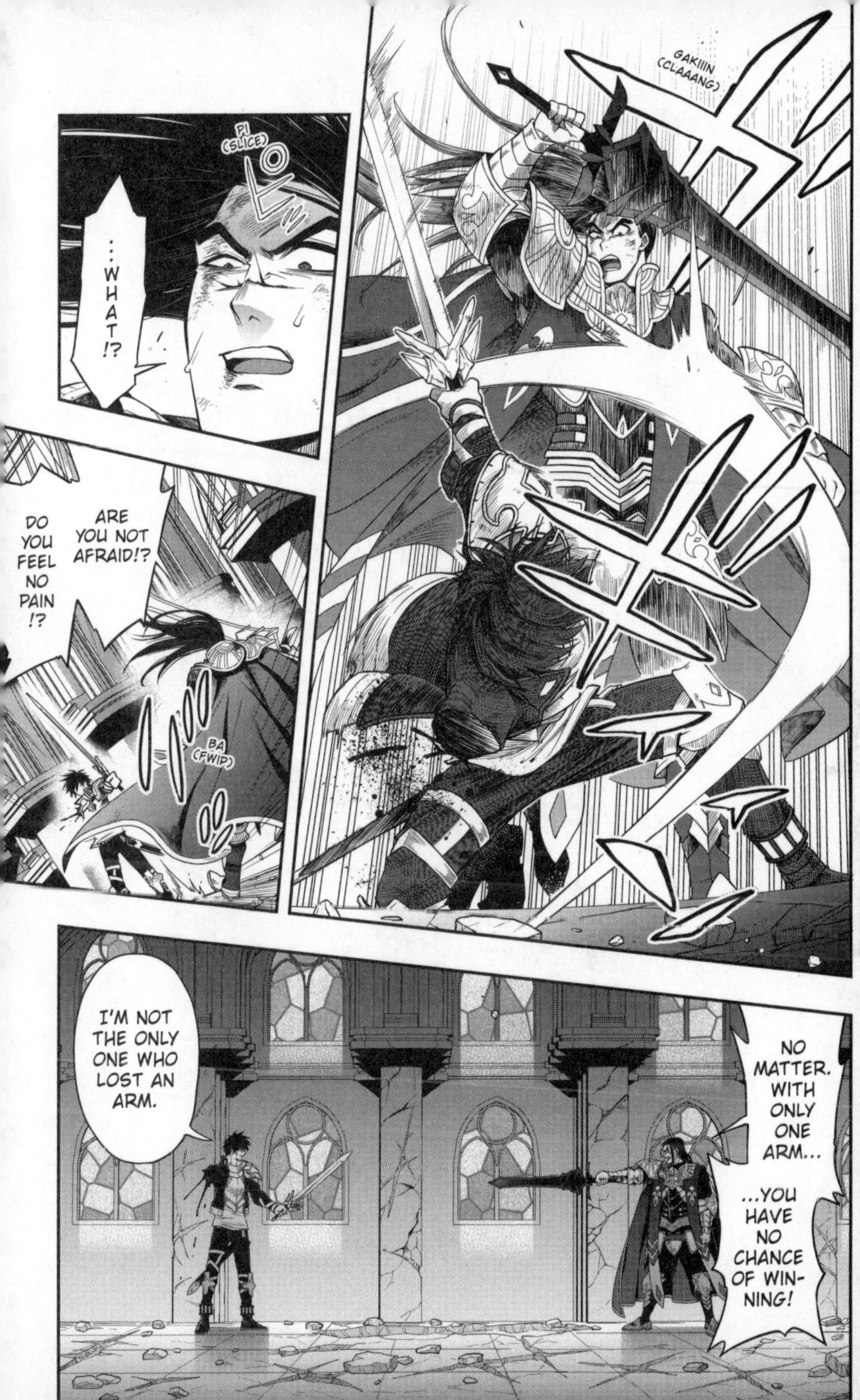
GAKIIIN (CLAAANG)
PI (SLICE)
...WHAT!?
ARE YOU NOT AFRAID!?
DO YOU FEEL NO PAIN!?
BA (FWIP)
NO MATTER. WITH ONLY ONE ARM...
...YOU HAVE NO CHANCE OF WIN-NING!
I'M NOT THE ONLY ONE WHO LOST AN ARM.

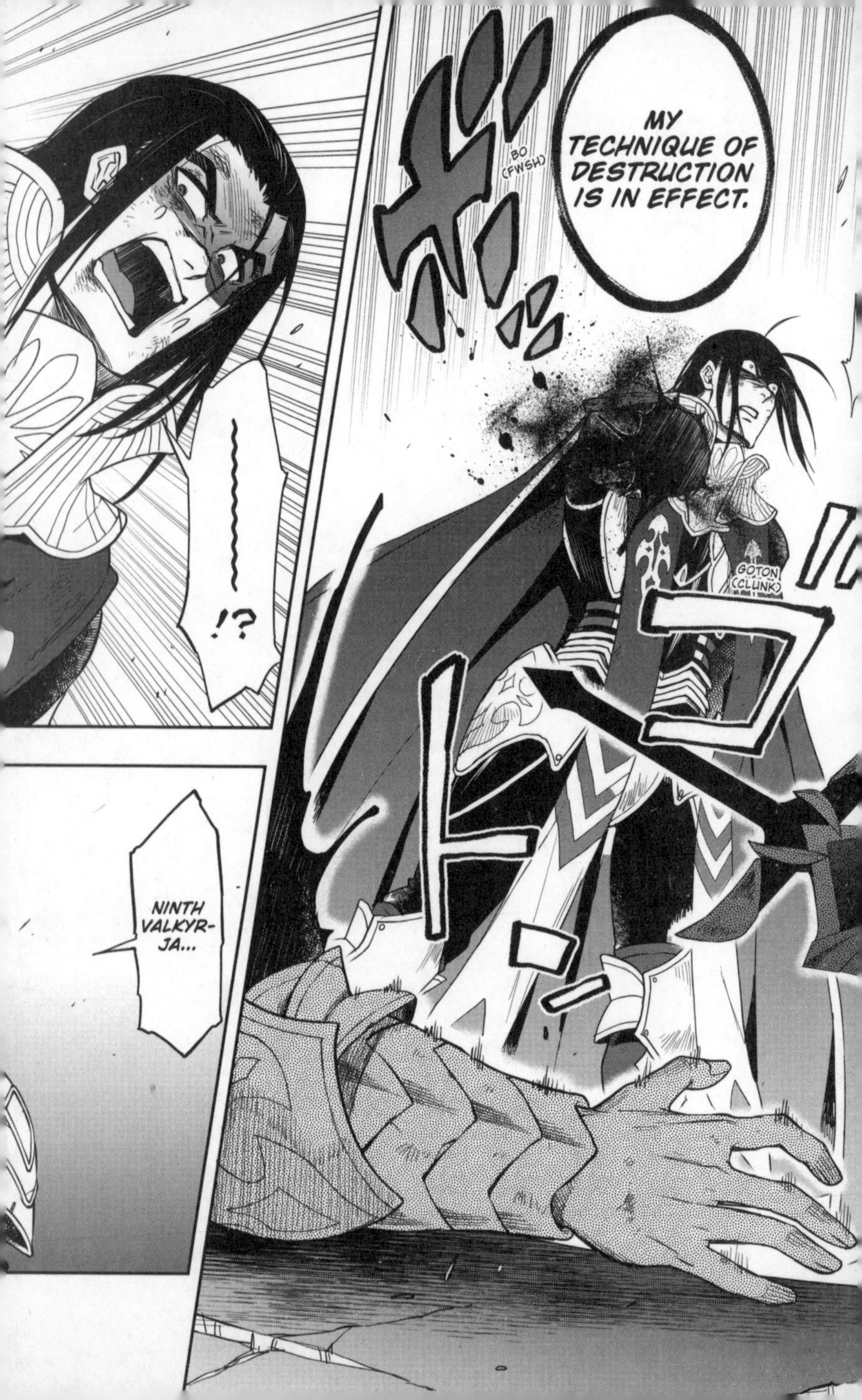
MY TECHNIQUE OF DESTRUCTION IS IN EFFECT.
BO (FWSH)
GOTON (CLUNK)
......!?
NINTH VALKYRJA...

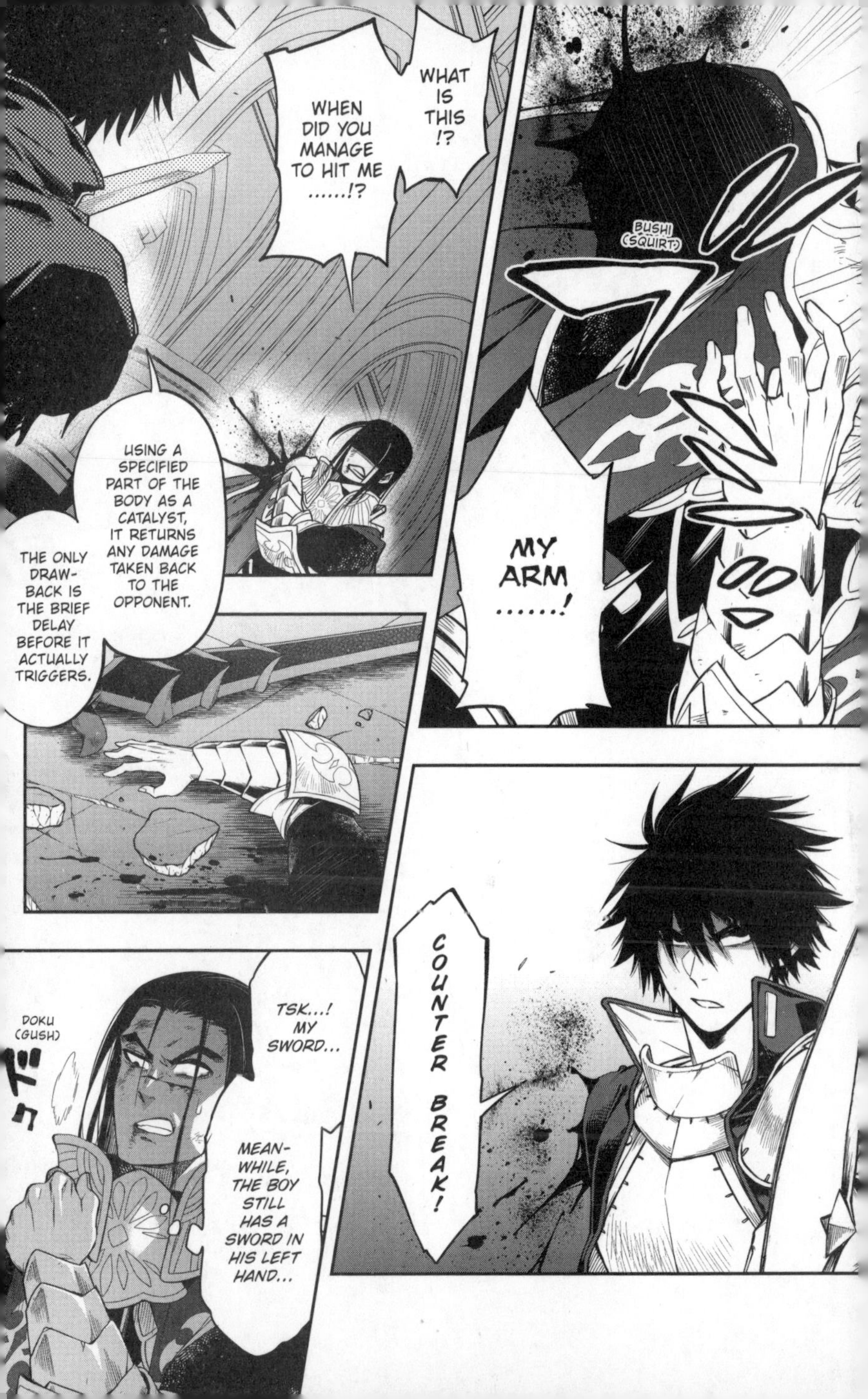
BUSHI (SQUIRT)
MY ARM ......!
WHAT IS THIS !?
WHEN DID YOU MANAGE TO HIT ME ......!?
USING A SPECIFIED PART OF THE BODY AS A CATALYST, IT RETURNS ANY DAMAGE TAKEN BACK TO THE OPPONENT.
THE ONLY DRAW-BACK IS THE BRIEF DELAY BEFORE IT ACTUALLY TRIGGERS.
COUNTER BREAK!
TSK...! MY SWORD...
DOKU (GUSH)
MEAN-WHILE, THE BOY STILL HAS A SWORD IN HIS LEFT HAND...

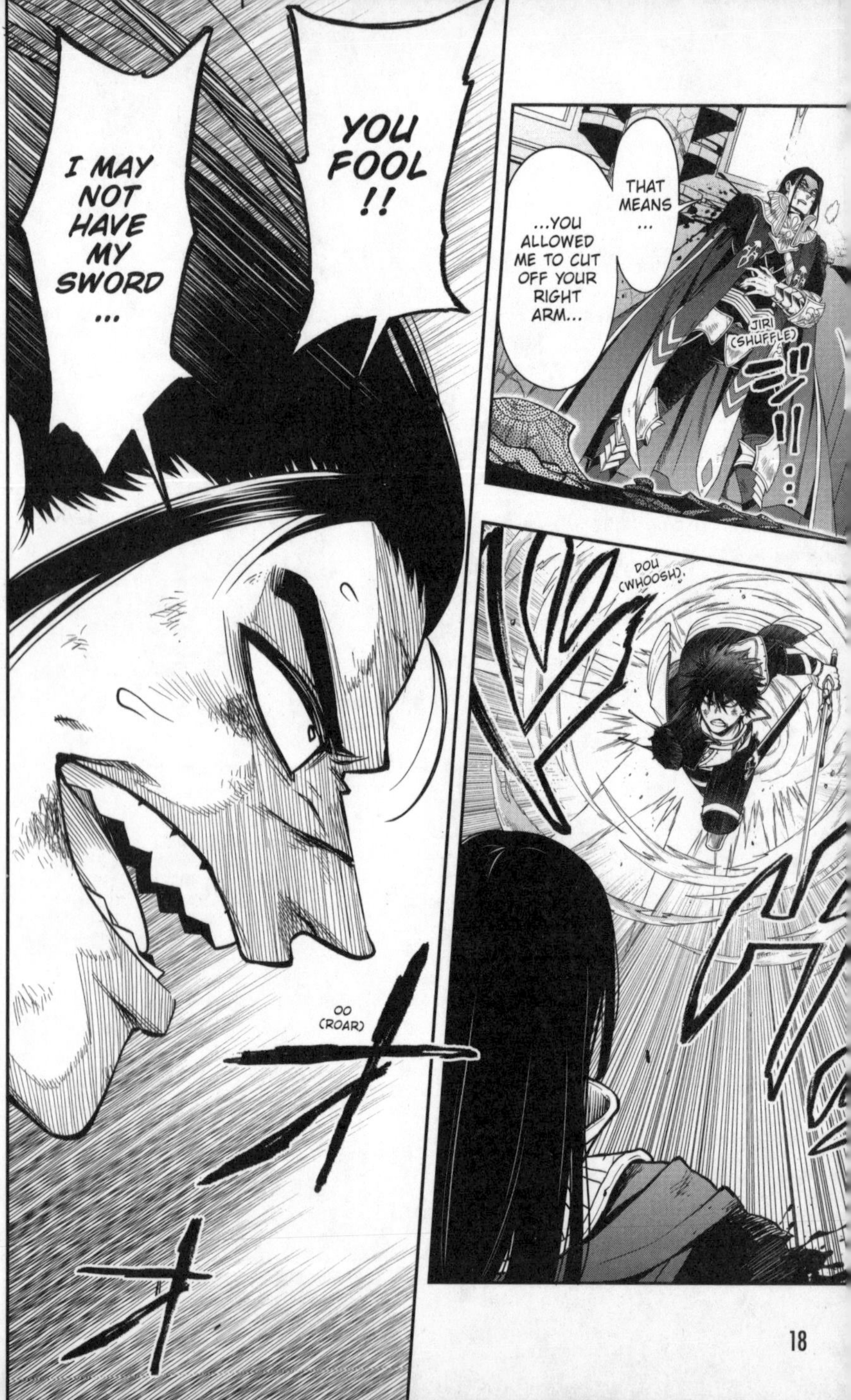
THAT MEANS ...
...YOU ALLOWED ME TO CUT OFF YOUR RIGHT ARM...
JIRI (SHUFFLE)
DOU (WHOOSH)
YOU FOOL !!
I MAY NOT HAVE MY SWORD ...
OO (ROAR)

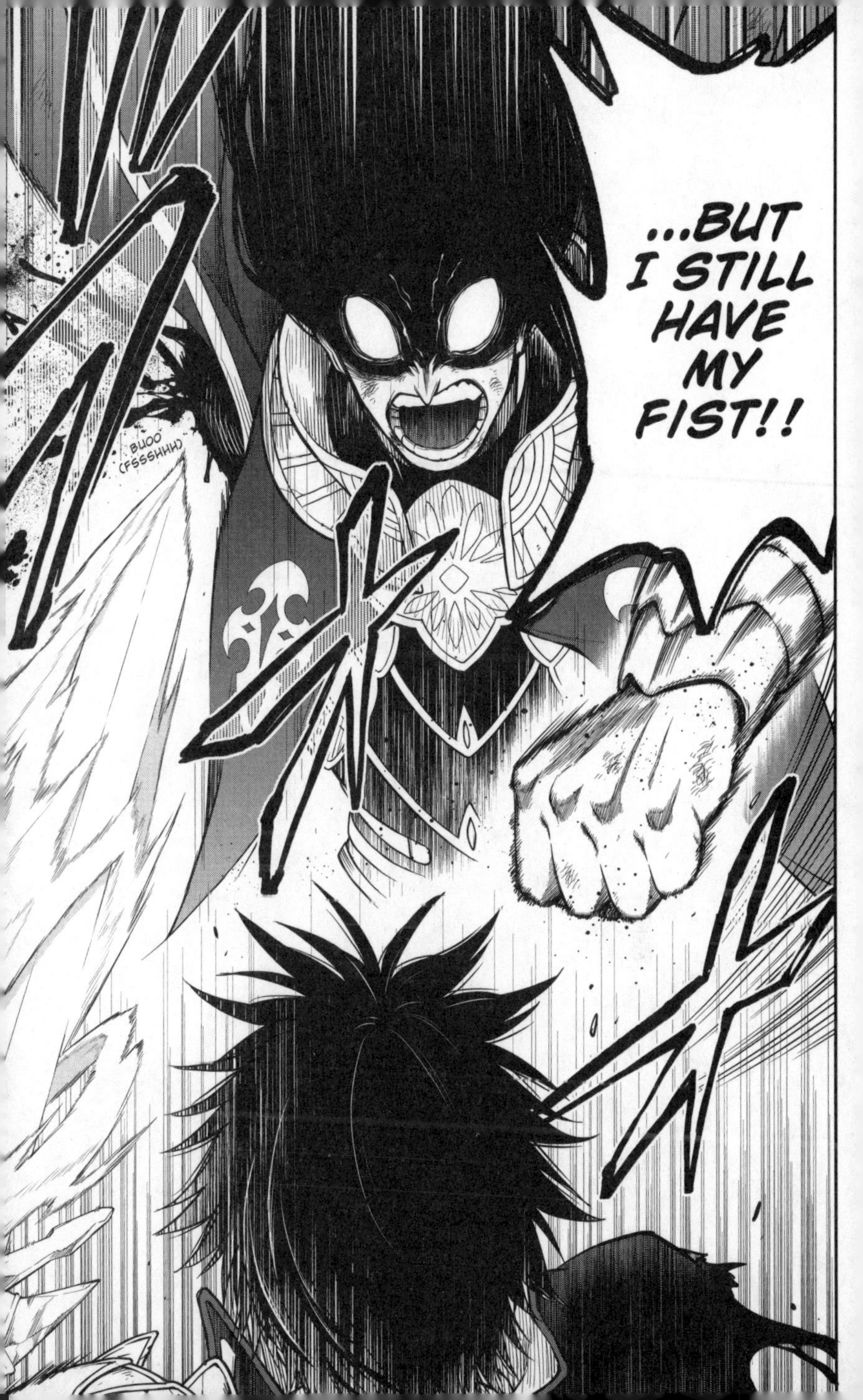
...BUT I STILL HAVE MY FIST!!
BUOO (FSSSHHH)

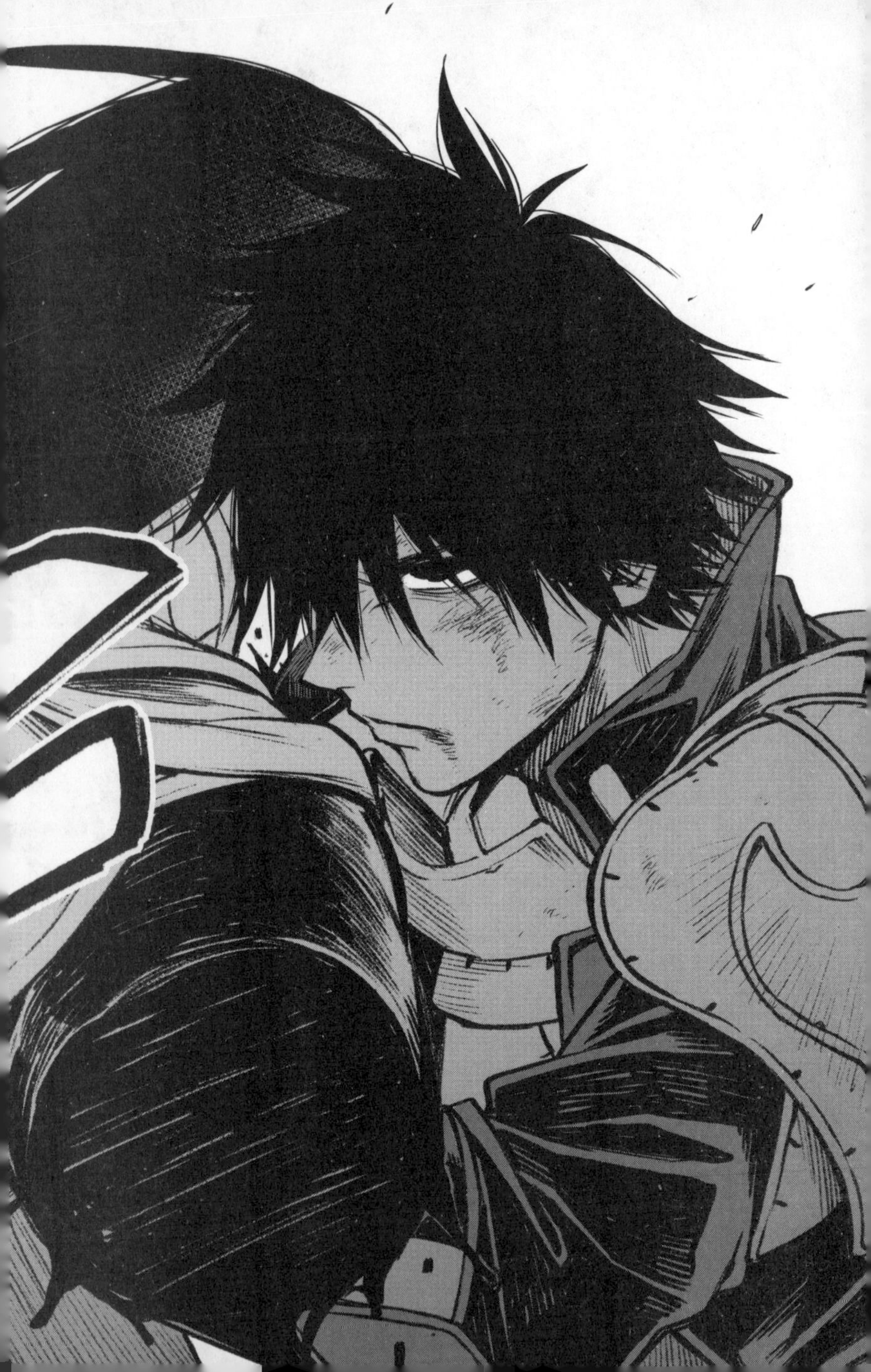

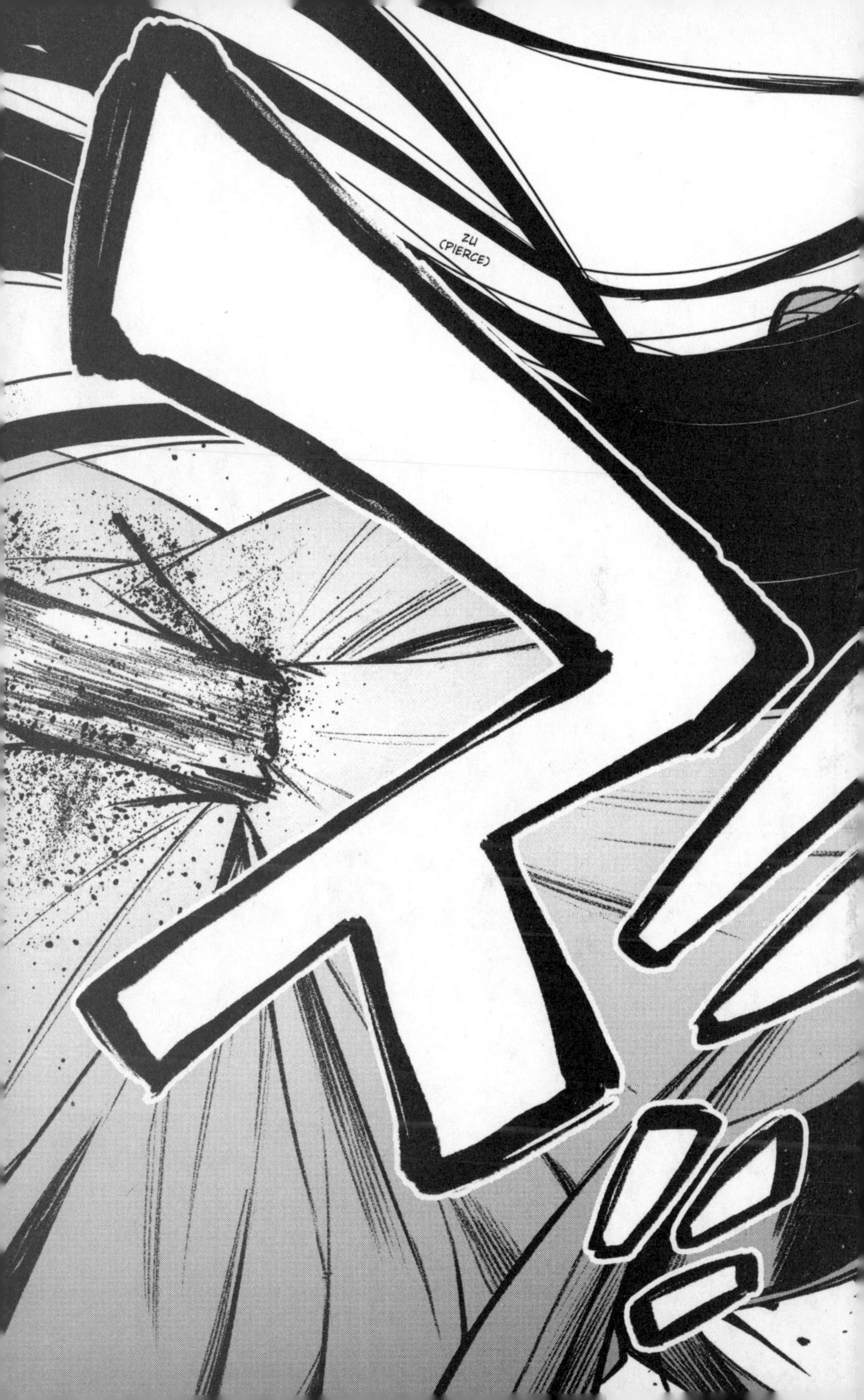
ZU
(PIERCE)

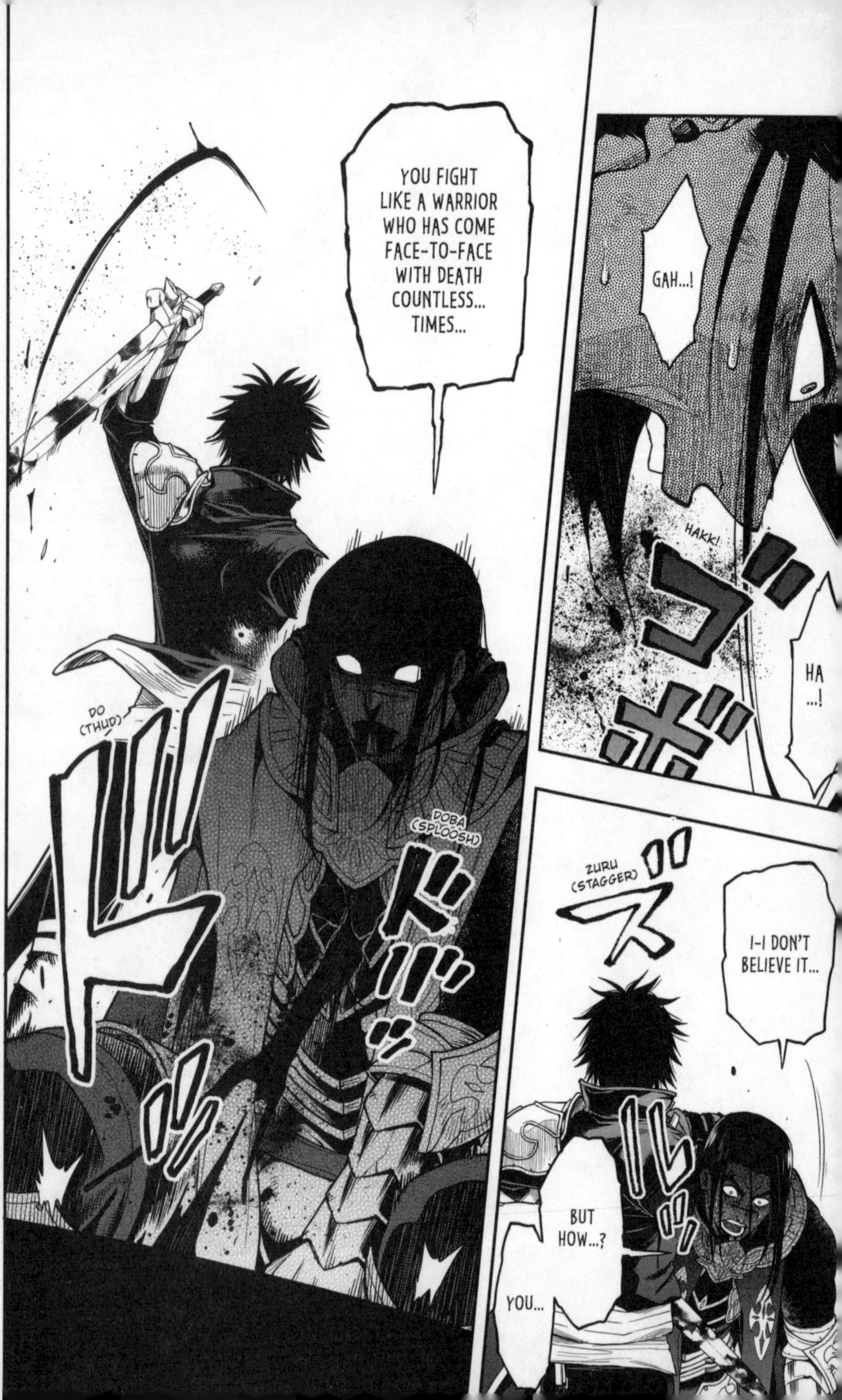
GAH...!
HA
...!
HAKK!
I-I DON'T BELIEVE IT...
ZURU (STAGGER)
BUT HOW...?
YOU...
YOU FIGHT LIKE A WARRIOR WHO HAS COME FACE-TO-FACE WITH DEATH COUNTLESS... TIMES...
DO (THUD)
DOBA (SPLOOSH)

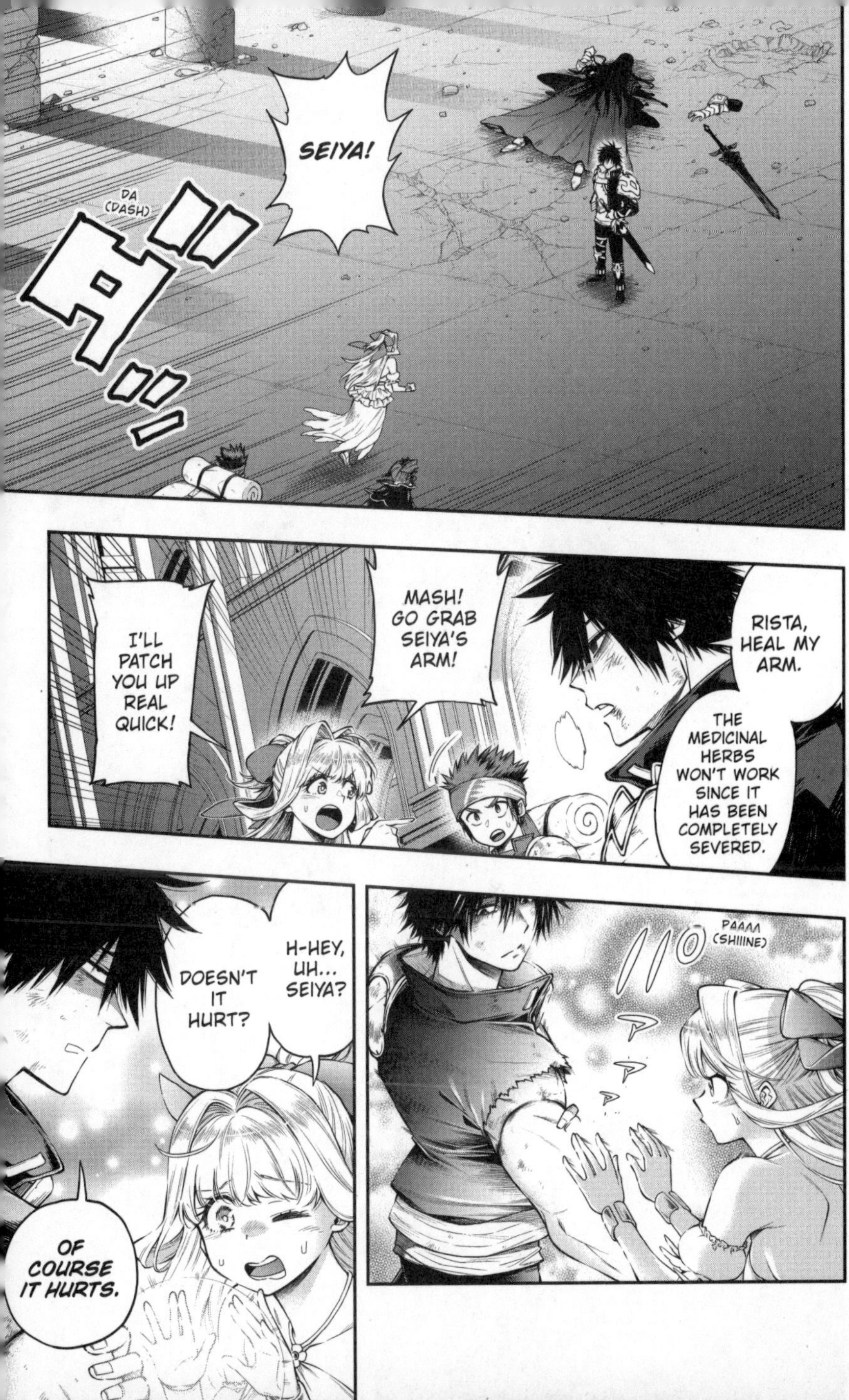
SEIYA!
DA (DASH)
RISTA, HEAL MY ARM.
THE MEDICINAL HERBS WON'T WORK SINCE IT HAS BEEN COMPLETELY SEVERED.
MASH! GO GRAB SEIYA'S ARM!
I'LL PATCH YOU UP REAL QUICK!
PAAAA (SHIIINE)
H-HEY, UH... SEIYA?
DOESN'T IT HURT?
OF COURSE IT HURTS.

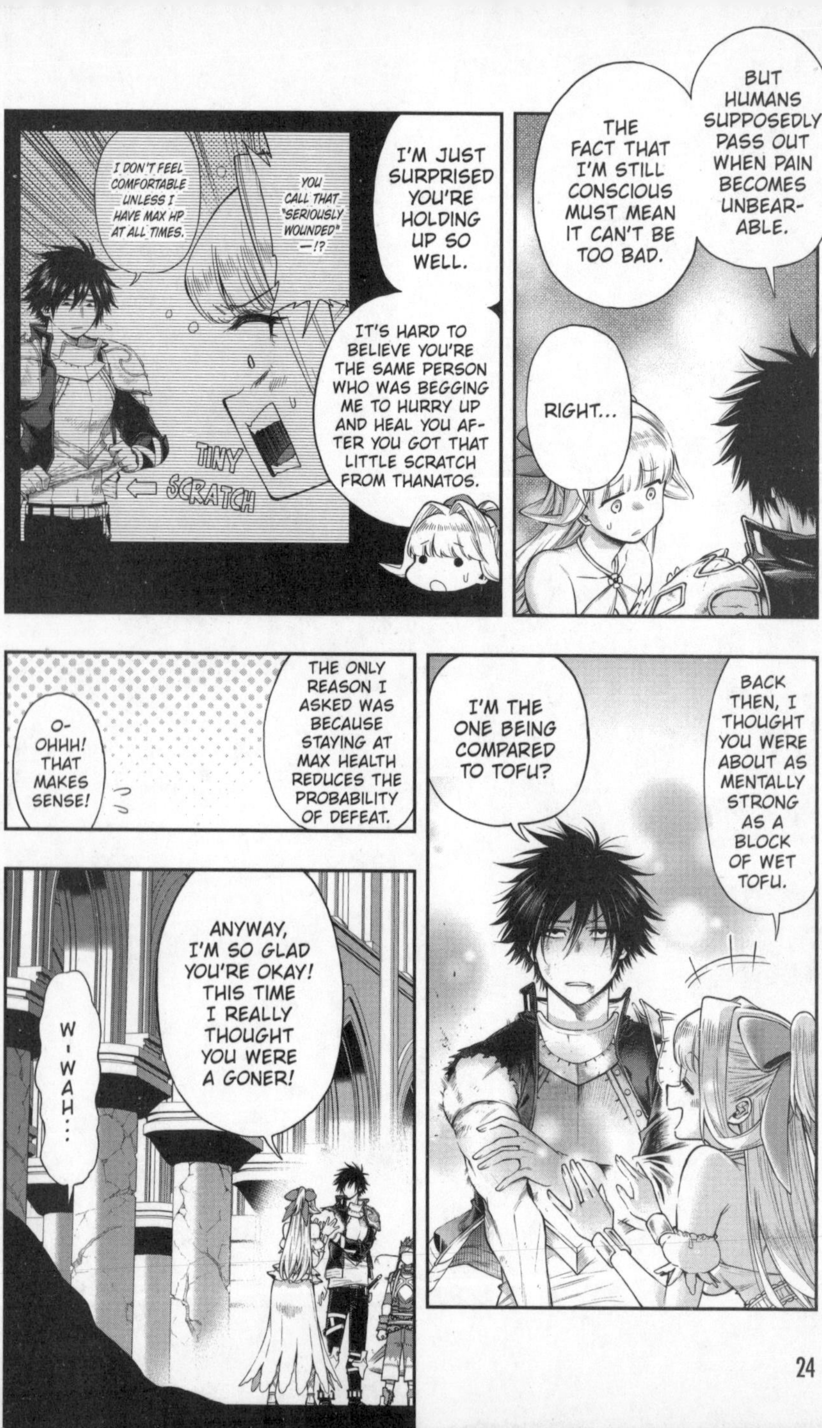
BUT HUMANS SUPPOSEDLY PASS OUT WHEN PAIN BECOMES UNBEARABLE.
THE FACT THAT I'M STILL CONSCIOUS MUST MEAN IT CAN'T BE TOO BAD.
RIGHT...
I'M JUST SURPRISED YOU'RE HOLDING UP SO WELL.
IT'S HARD TO BELIEVE YOU'RE THE SAME PERSON WHO WAS BEGGING ME TO HURRY UP AND HEAL YOU AFTER YOU GOT THAT LITTLE SCRATCH FROM THANATOS.
YOU CALL THAT "SERIOUSLY WOUNDED" —!?
I DON'T FEEL COMFORTABLE UNLESS I HAVE MAX HP AT ALL TIMES.
TINY SCRATCH
BACK THEN, I THOUGHT YOU WERE ABOUT AS MENTALLY STRONG AS A BLOCK OF WET TOFU.
I'M THE ONE BEING COMPARED TO TOFU?
THE ONLY REASON I ASKED WAS BECAUSE STAYING AT MAX HEALTH REDUCES THE PROBABILITY OF DEFEAT.
O-OHHH! THAT MAKES SENSE!
ANYWAY, I'M SO GLAD YOU'RE OKAY! THIS TIME I REALLY THOUGHT YOU WERE A GONER!
W-WAH...

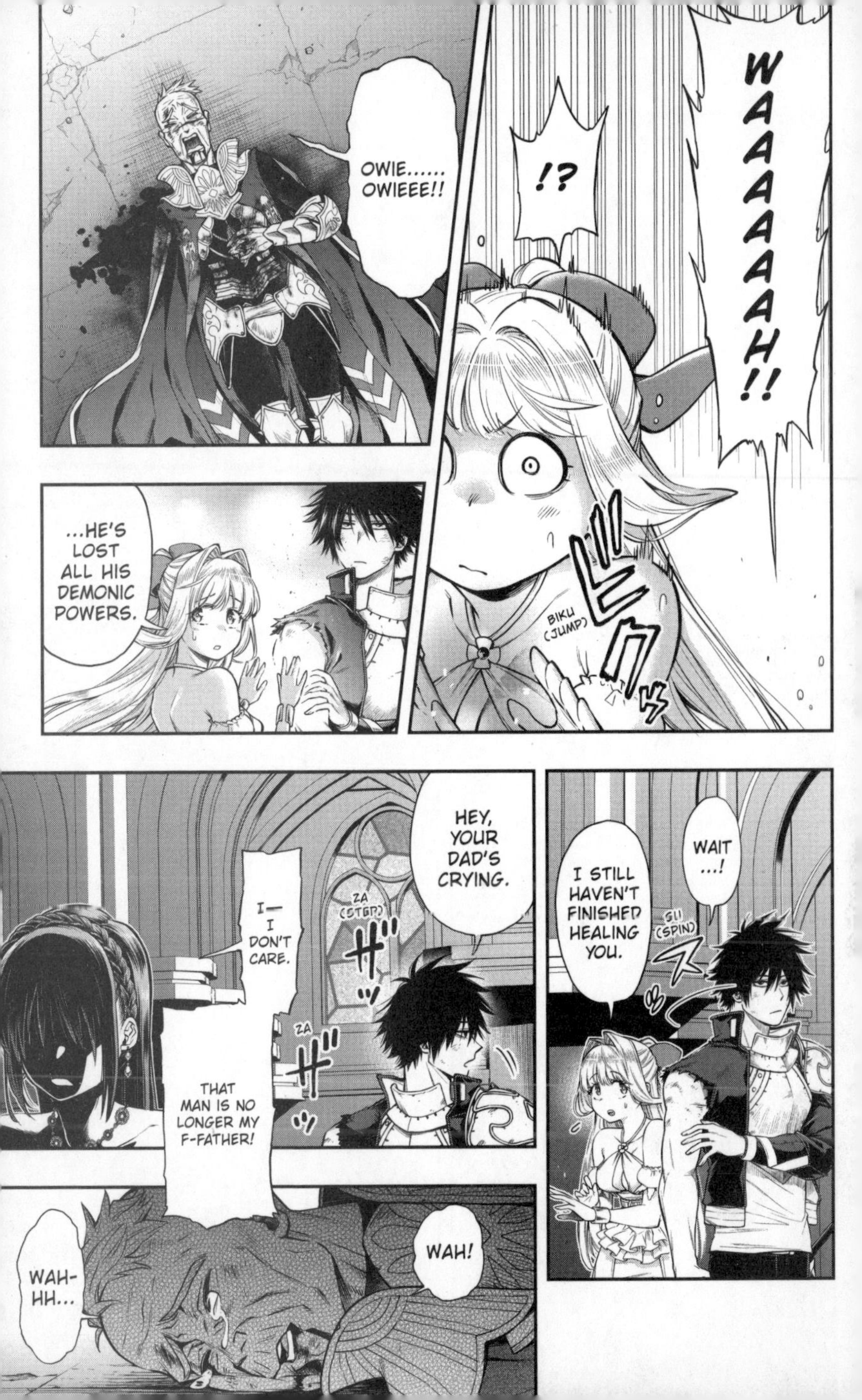
WAAAAAAAH!!
!?
BIKU (JUMP)
OWIE...... OWIEEE!!
...HE'S LOST ALL HIS DEMONIC POWERS.
WAIT ...!
I STILL HAVEN'T FINISHED HEALING YOU.
SU (SPIN)
HEY, YOUR DAD'S CRYING.
ZA (STEP)
I— I DON'T CARE.
ZA
THAT MAN IS NO LONGER MY F-FATHER!
WAH!
WAH-HH...

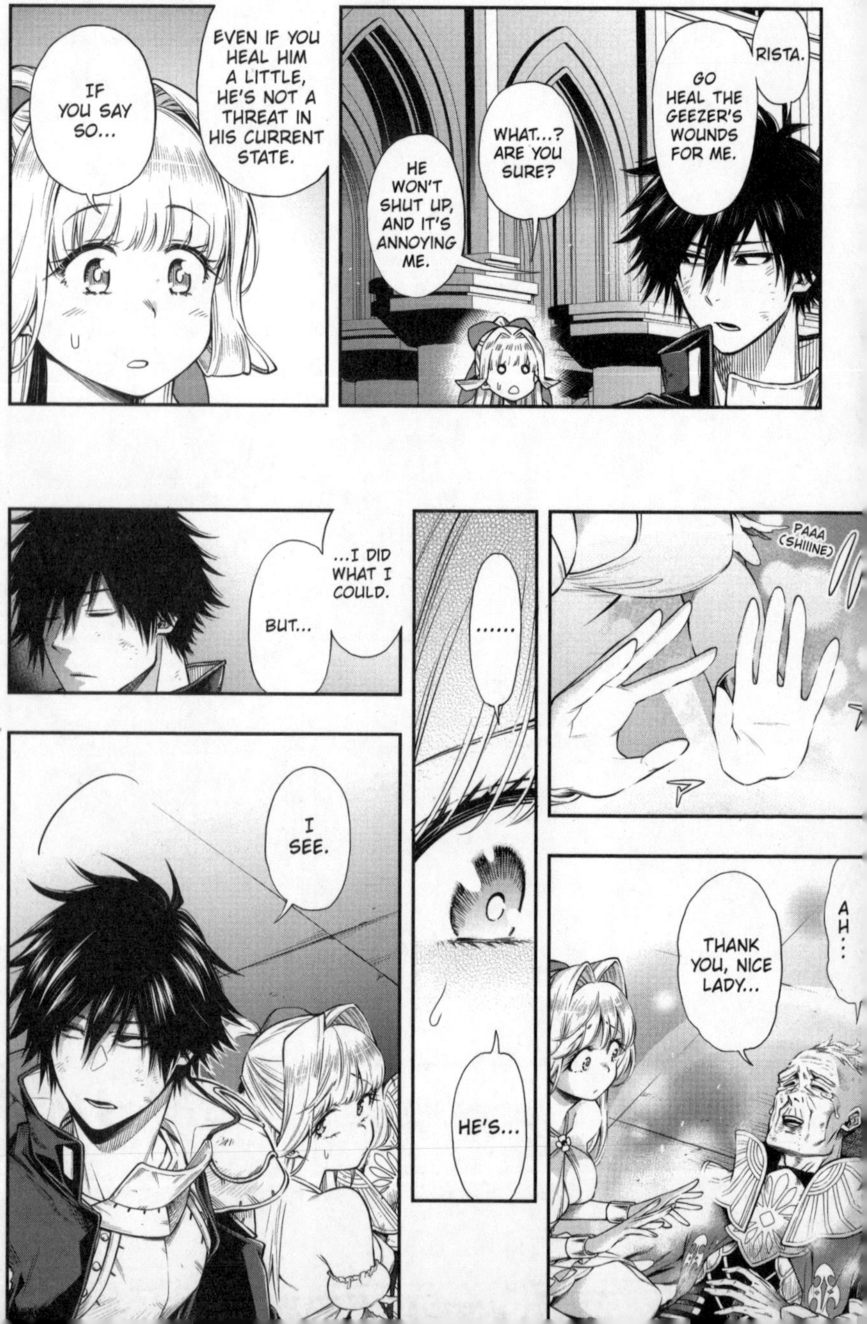
RISTA.
GO HEAL THE GEEZER'S WOUNDS FOR ME.
WHAT...? ARE YOU SURE?
HE WON'T SHUT UP, AND IT'S ANNOYING ME.
EVEN IF YOU HEAL HIM A LITTLE, HE'S NOT A THREAT IN HIS CURRENT STATE.
IF YOU SAY SO...
PAAA (SHIIINE)
AH...
THANK YOU, NICE LADY...
......
HE'S...
...I DID WHAT I COULD.
BUT...
I SEE.

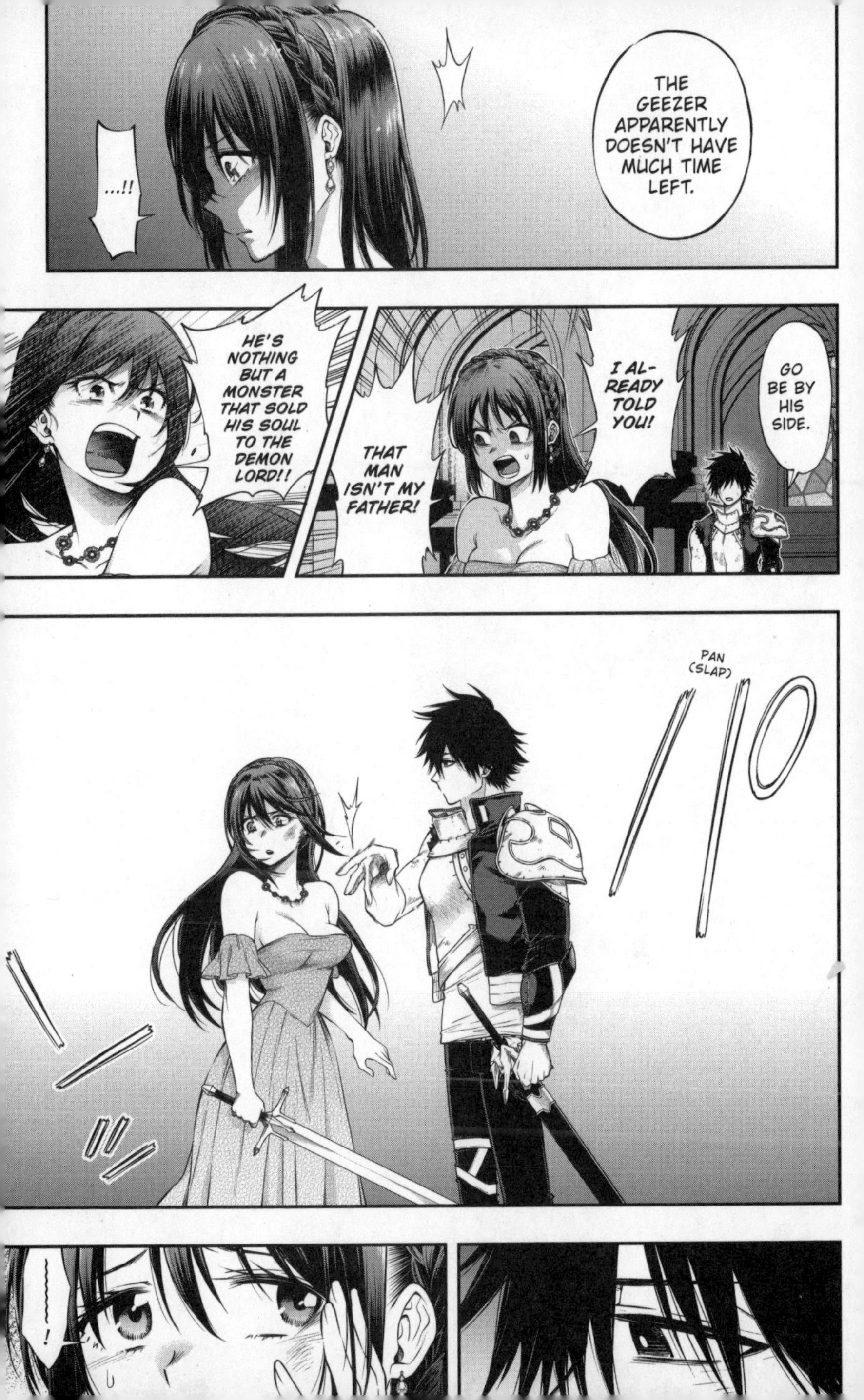
THE GEEZER APPARENTLY DOESN'T HAVE MUCH TIME LEFT.
...!!
GO BE BY HIS SIDE.
I ALREADY TOLD YOU!
THAT MAN ISN'T MY FATHER!
HE'S NOTHING BUT A MONSTER THAT SOLD HIS SOUL TO THE DEMON LORD!!
PAN (SLAP)
~!

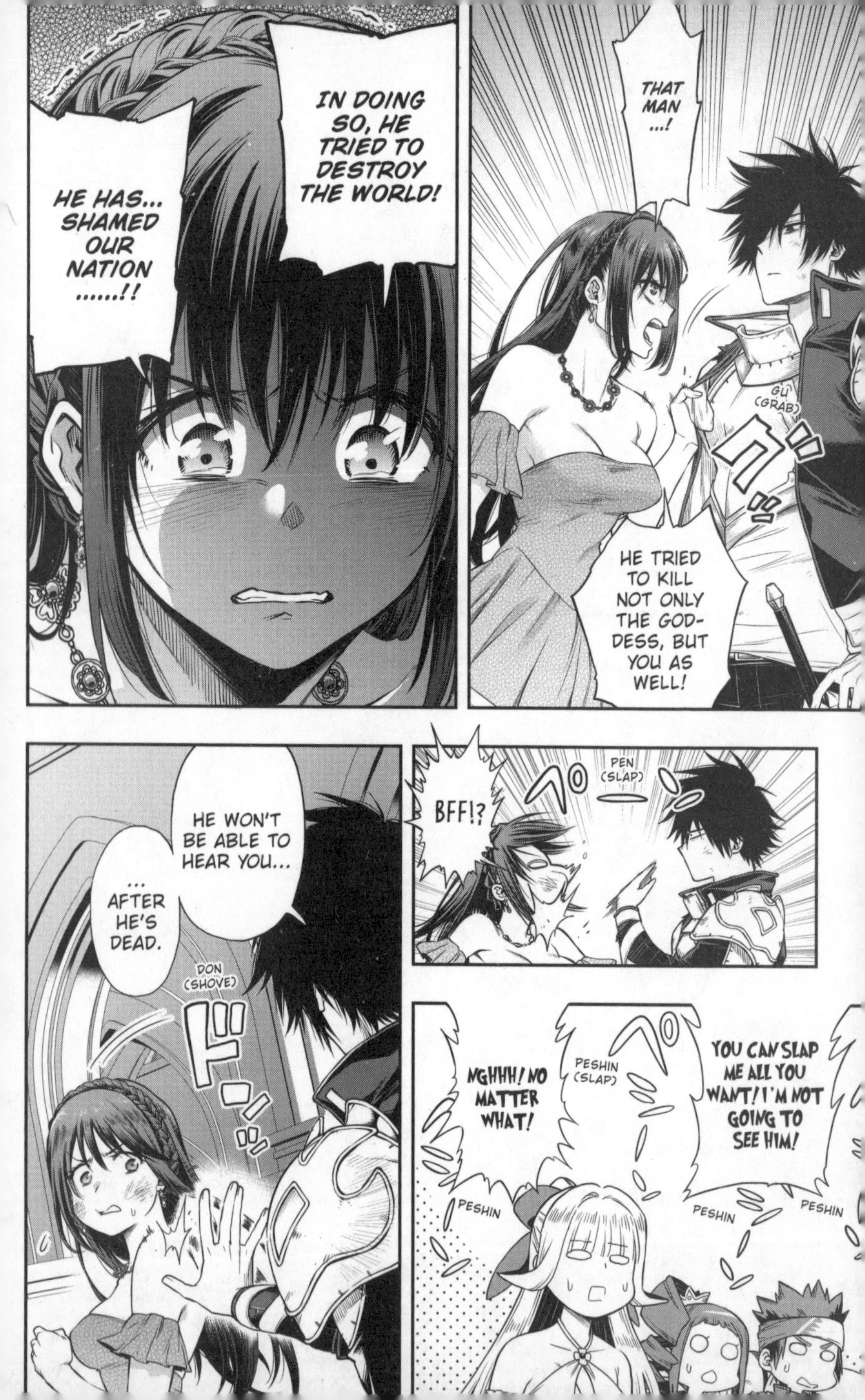
THAT MAN ...!
GU (GRAB)
HE TRIED TO KILL NOT ONLY THE GOD-DESS, BUT YOU AS WELL!
IN DOING SO, HE TRIED TO DESTROY THE WORLD!
HE HAS... SHAMED OUR NATION ......!!
PEN (SLAP)
BFF!?
YOU CAN SLAP ME ALL YOU WANT! I'M NOT GOING TO SEE HIM!
PESHIN (SLAP)
NGHHH! NO MATTER WHAT!
PESHIN
PESHIN
PESHIN
HE WON'T BE ABLE TO HEAR YOU...
... AFTER HE'S DEAD.
DON (SHOVE)

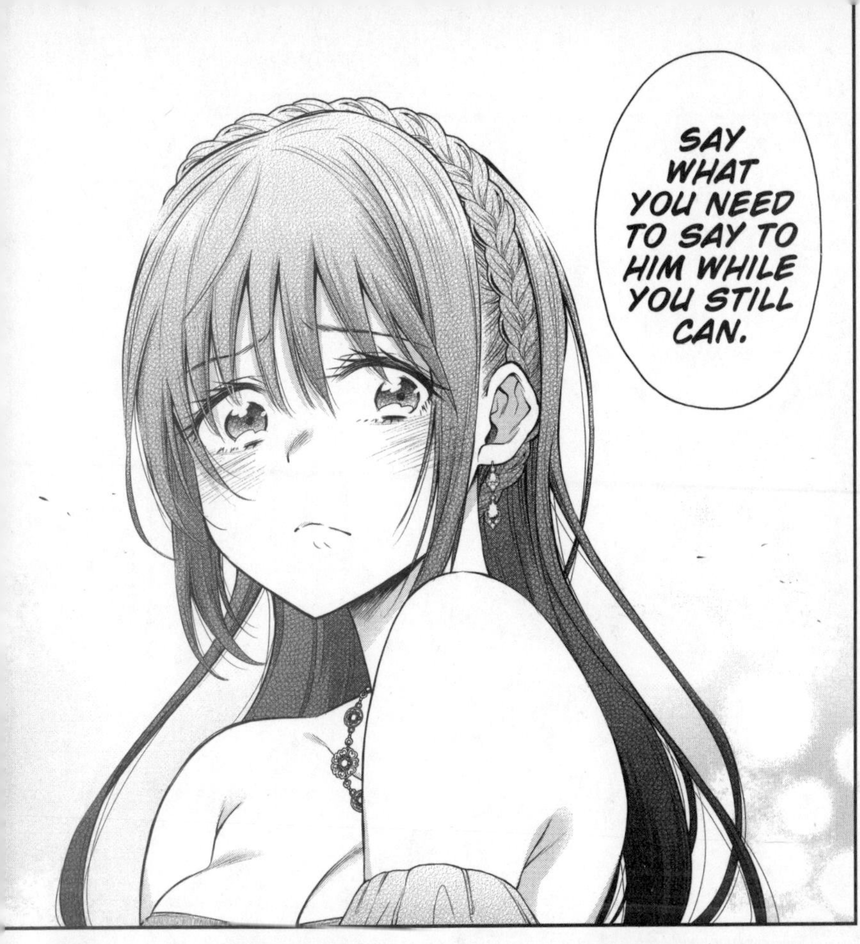
SAY WHAT YOU NEED TO SAY TO HIM WHILE YOU STILL CAN.
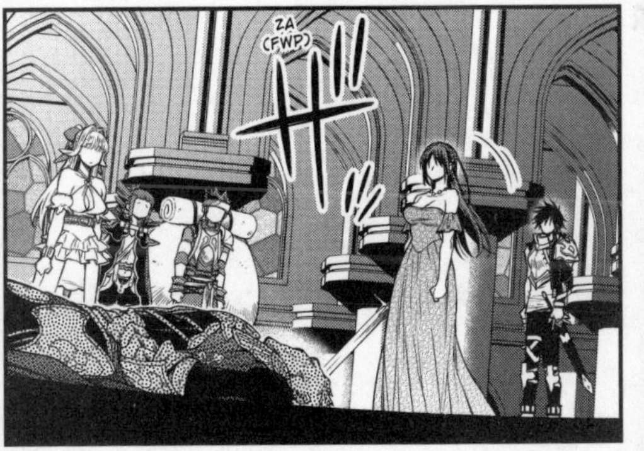
ZA
(FWP)
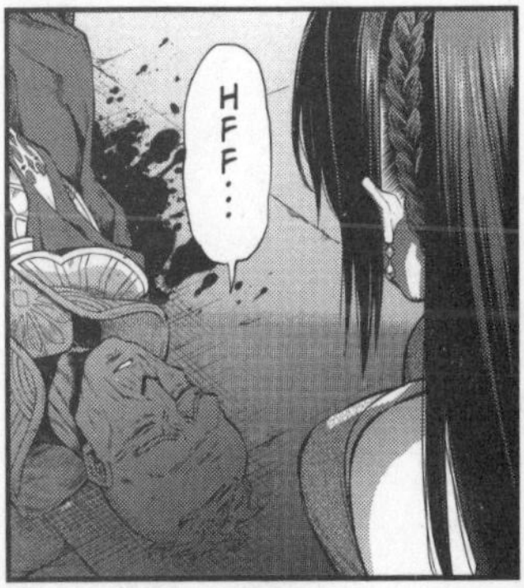
HFF...

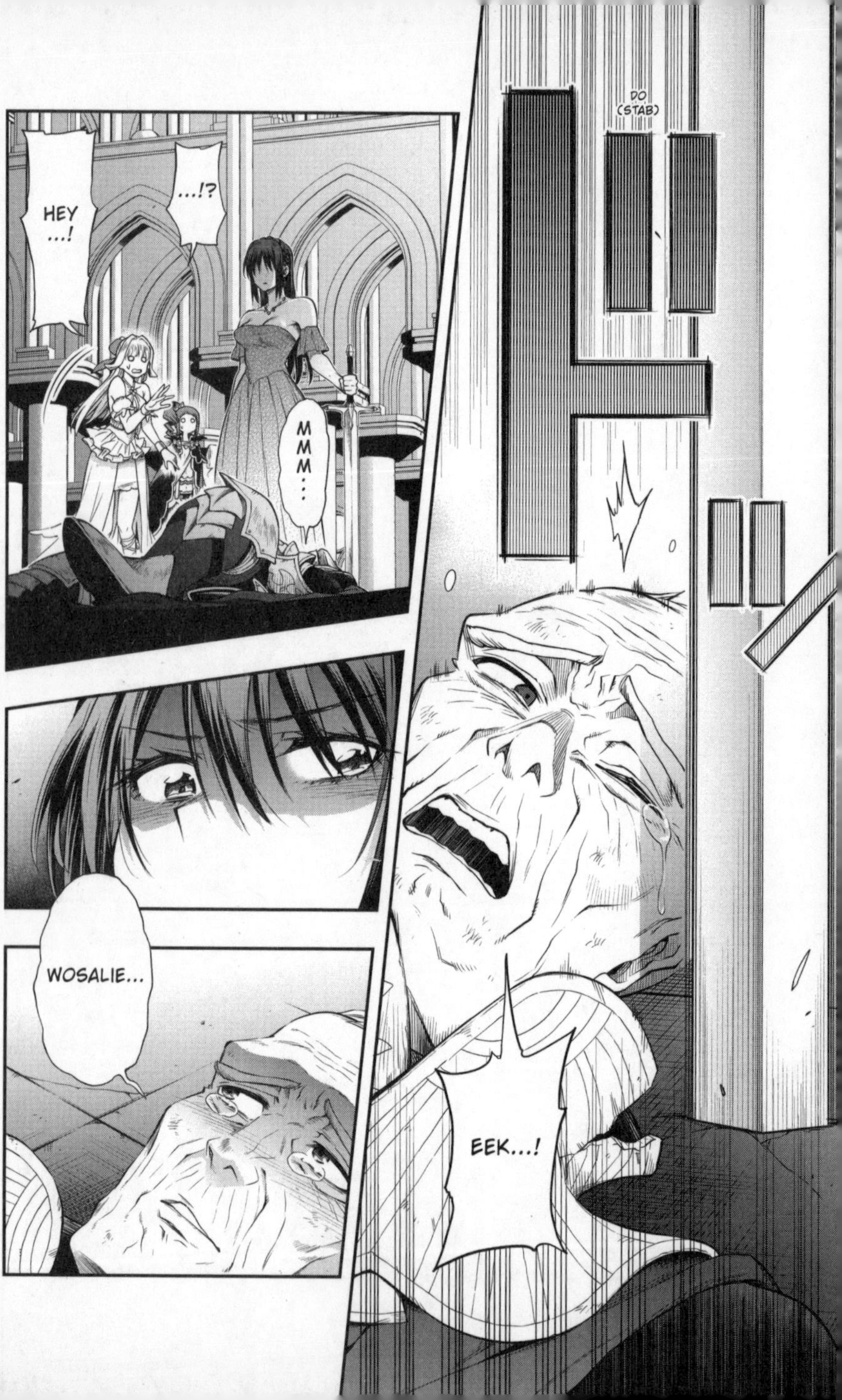
DO
(STAB)
EEK...!
...!?
HEY ...!
MMM...
WOSALIE...

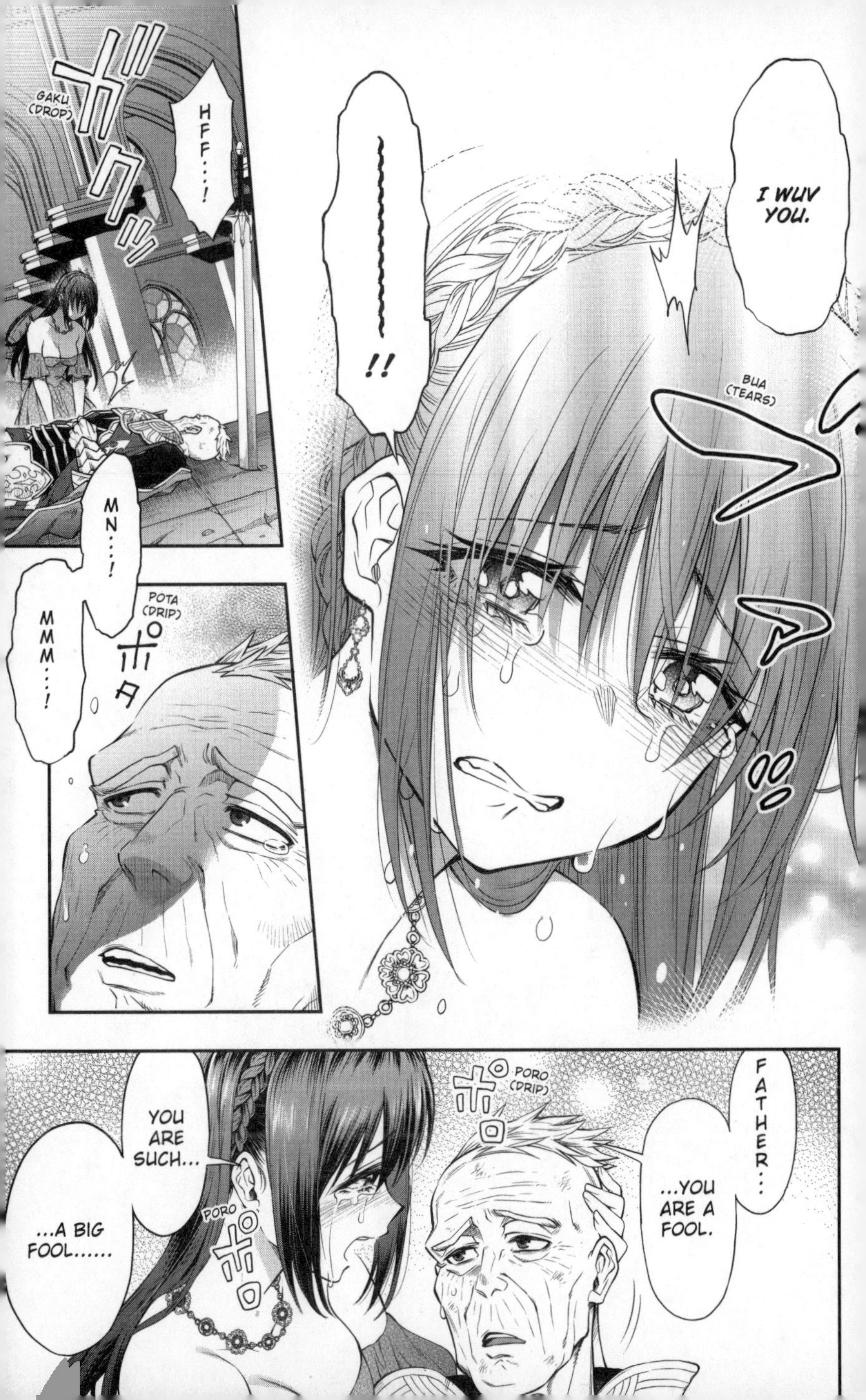
I WUV YOU.
BUA (TEARS)
——!!
GAKU (DROP)
HFF...!
MN...!
MMM...!
POTA (DRIP)
FATHER...
...YOU ARE A FOOL.
PORO (DRIP)
YOU ARE SUCH...
PORO
...A BIG FOOL......

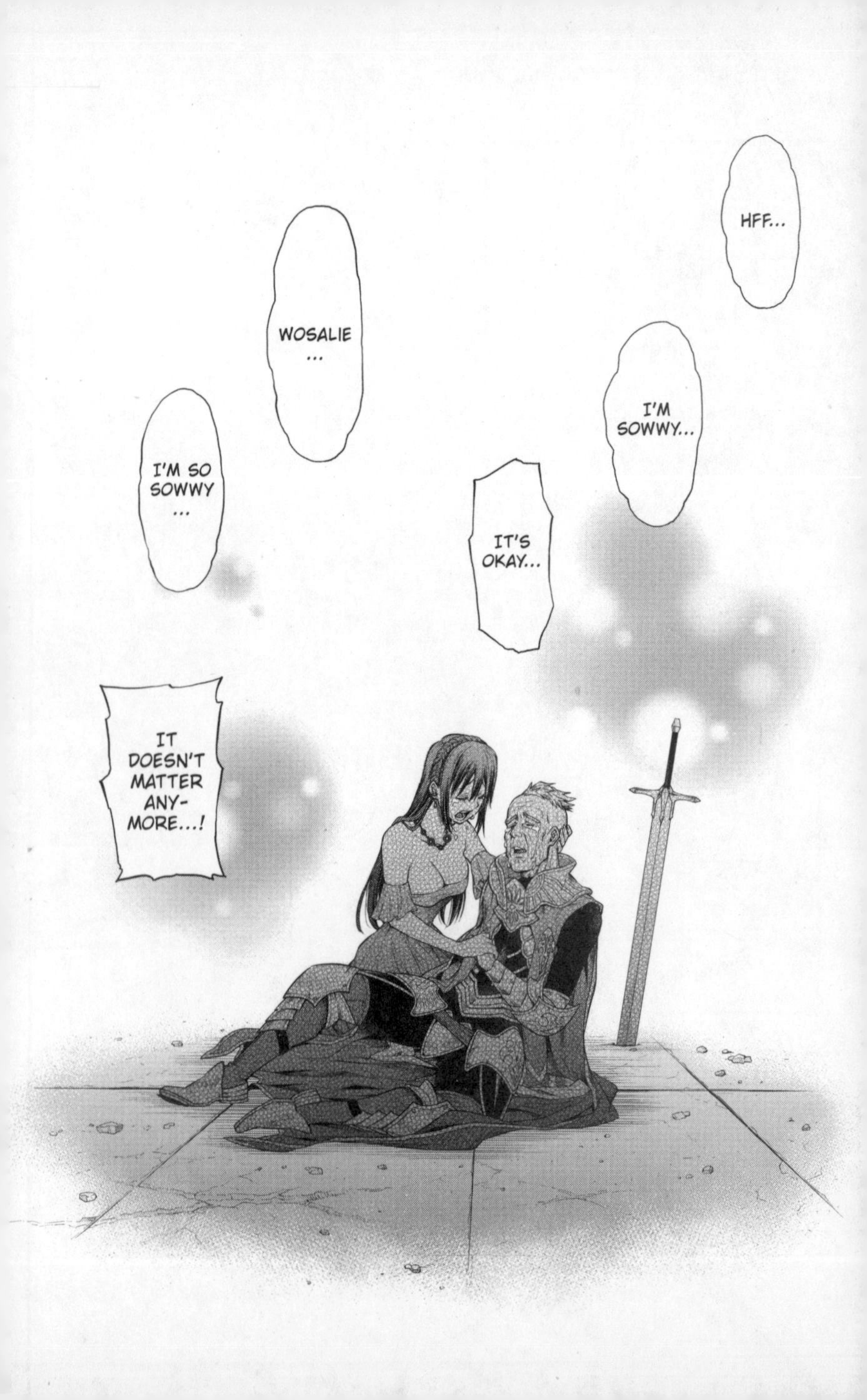
HFF...
I'M SOWWY...
WOSALIE ...
I'M SO SOWWY ...
IT'S OKAY...
IT DOESN'T MATTER ANY-MORE...!

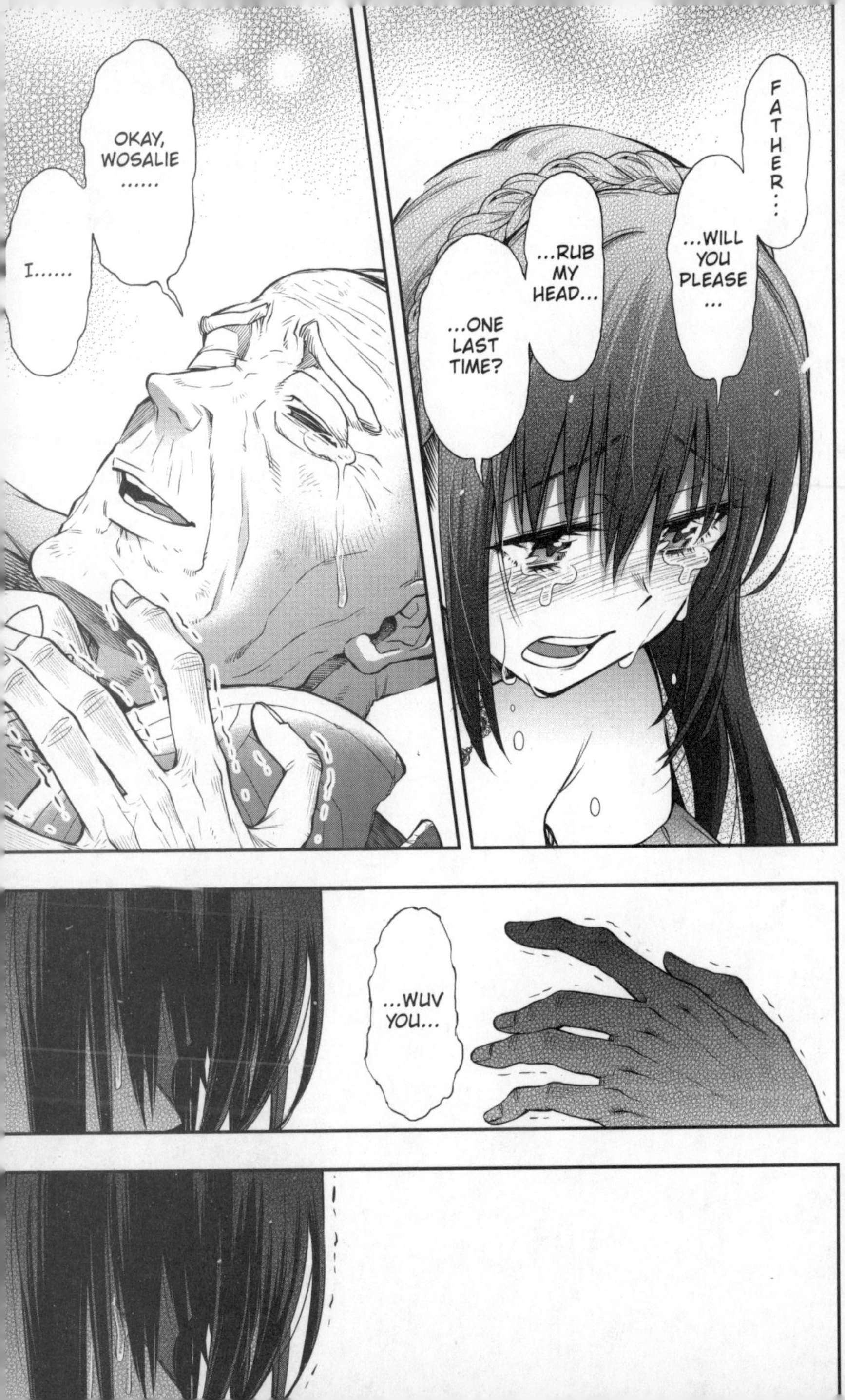
FATHER...
...WILL YOU PLEASE ...
...RUB MY HEAD...
...ONE LAST TIME?
OKAY, WOSALIE ......
I......
...WUV YOU...

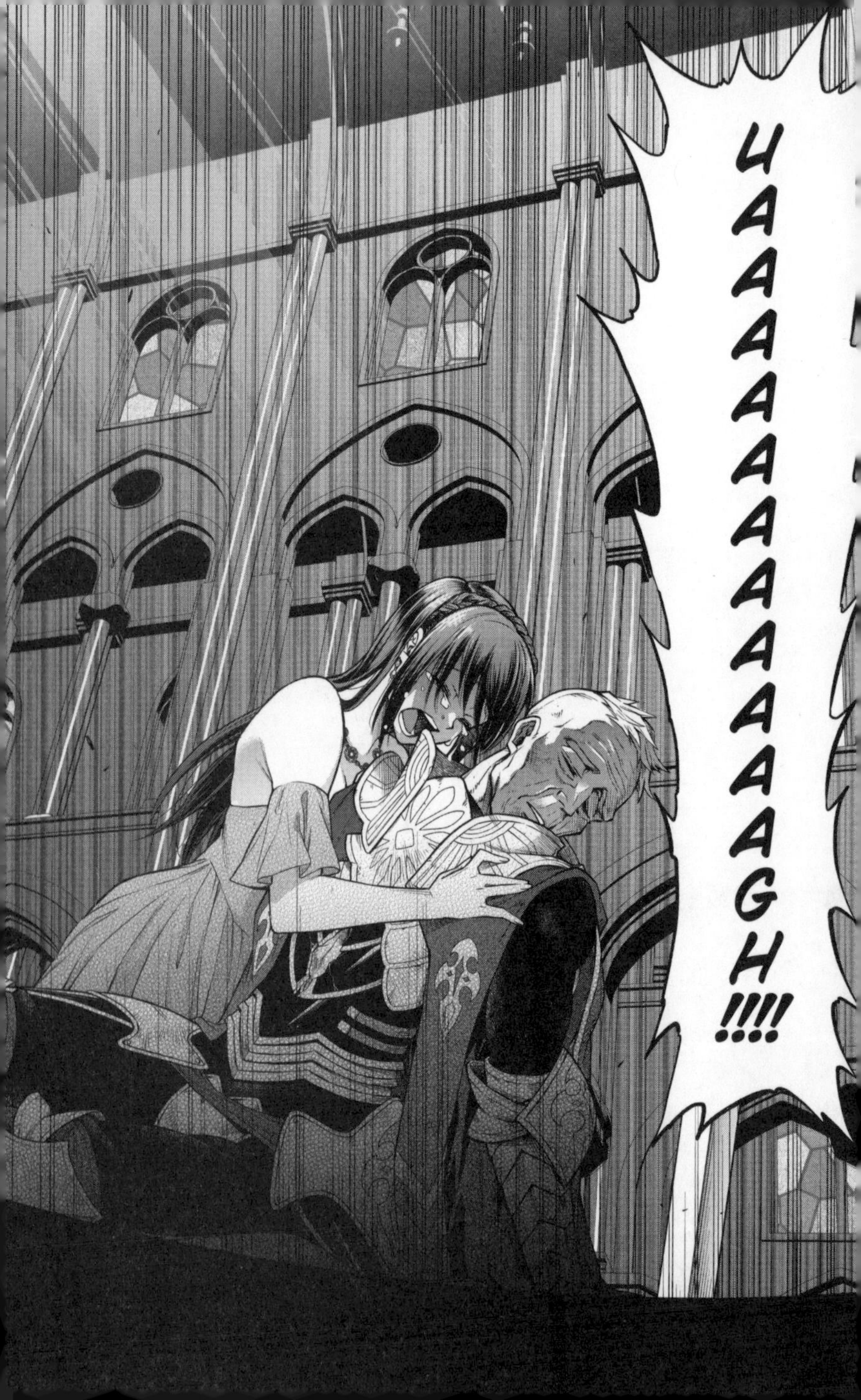
UAAAAAAAAAAAGH!!!!

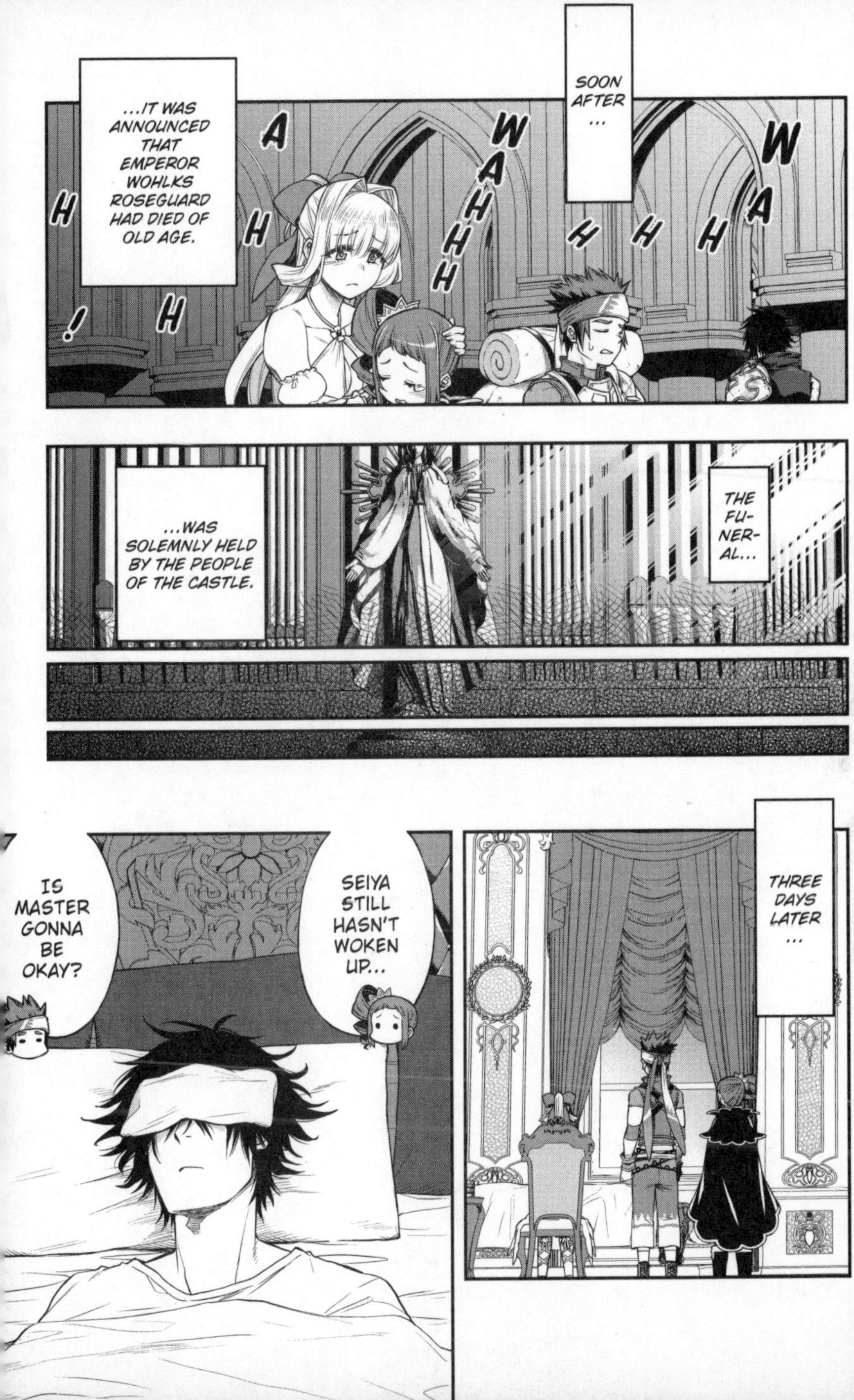

SOON AFTER...
...IT WAS ANNOUNCED THAT EMPEROR WOHLKS ROSEGUARD HAD DIED OF OLD AGE.
WAHHHH
WAHHHH
AHHH!
THE FU-NER-AL...
...WAS SOLEMNLY HELD BY THE PEOPLE OF THE CASTLE.
THREE DAYS LATER...
SEIYA STILL HASN'T WOKEN UP...
IS MASTER GONNA BE OKAY?

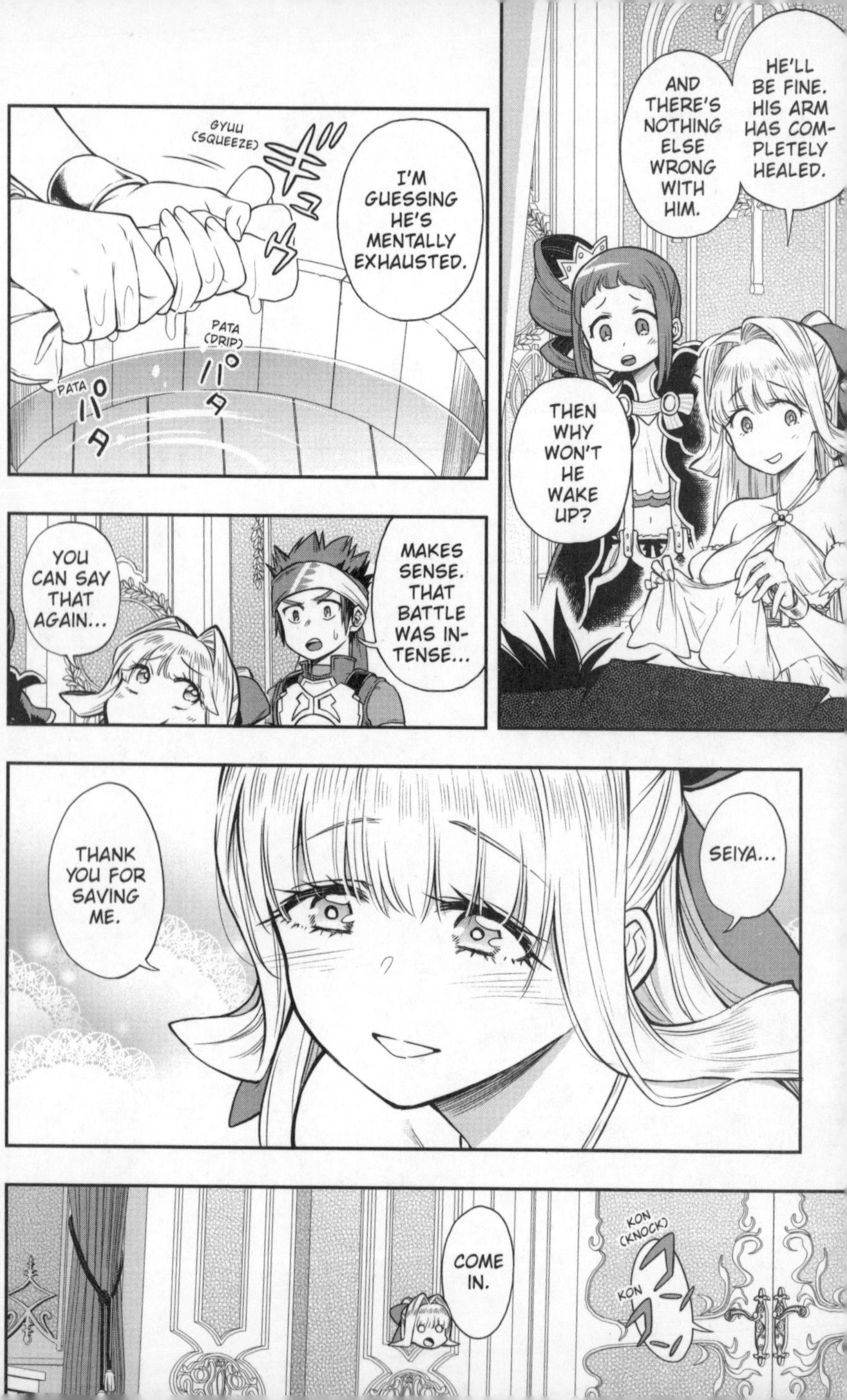
HE'LL BE FINE. HIS ARM HAS COM-PLETELY HEALED.
AND THERE'S NOTHING ELSE WRONG WITH HIM.
THEN WHY WON'T HE WAKE UP?
I'M GUESSING HE'S MENTALLY EXHAUSTED.
GYUU (SQUEEZE)
PATA (DRIP)
PATA
MAKES SENSE. THAT BATTLE WAS IN-TENSE...
YOU CAN SAY THAT AGAIN...
SEIYA...
THANK YOU FOR SAVING ME.
KON (KNOCK)
KON
COME IN.

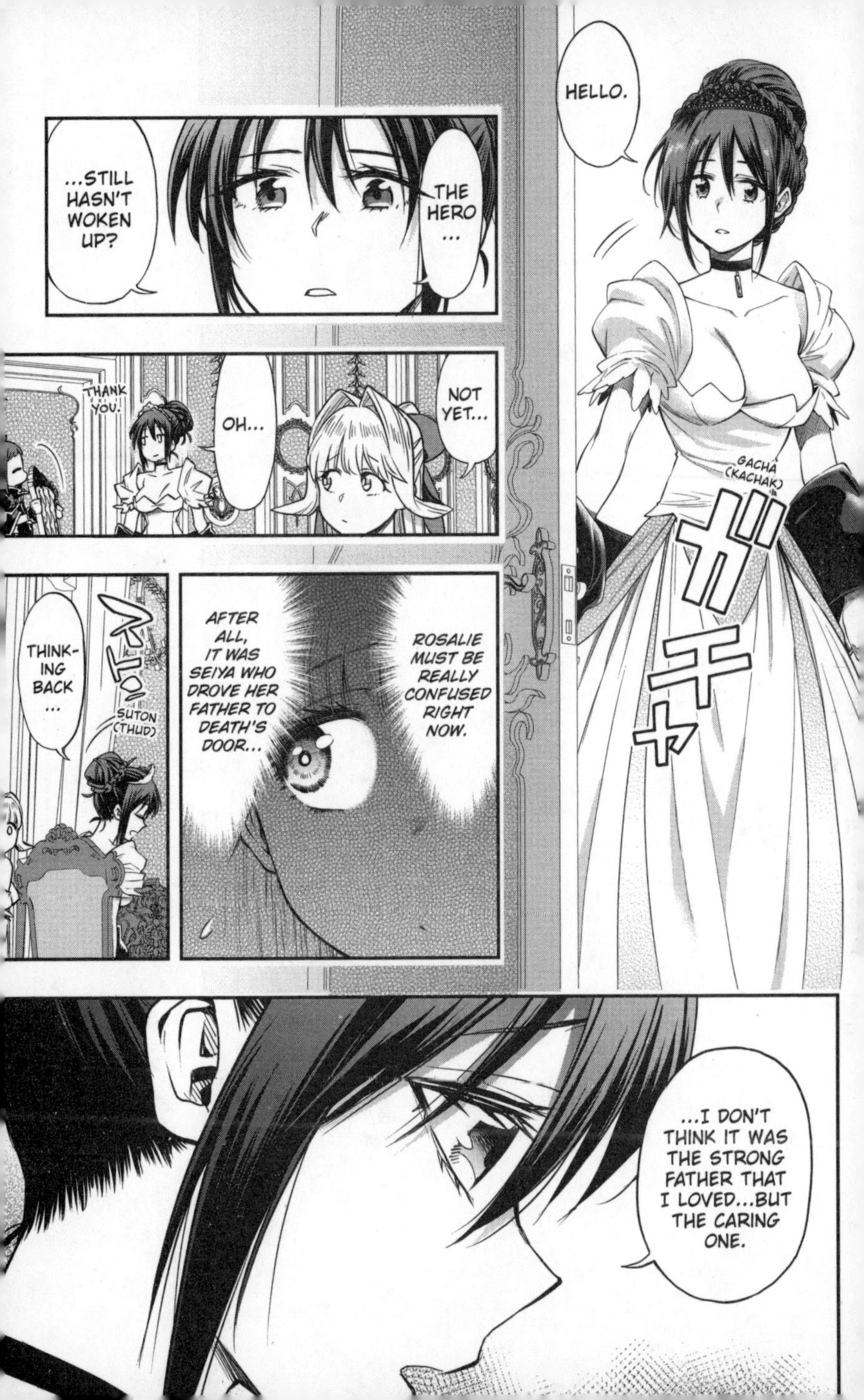
HELLO.
ガチャ
GACHA (KACHAK)
THE HERO...
...STILL HASN'T WOKEN UP?
NOT YET...
OH...
THANK YOU.
ROSALIE MUST BE REALLY CONFUSED RIGHT NOW.
AFTER ALL, IT WAS SEIYA WHO DROVE HER FATHER TO DEATH'S DOOR...
ストン
SUTON (THUD)
THINKING BACK...
...I DON'T THINK IT WAS THE STRONG FATHER THAT I LOVED...BUT THE CARING ONE.

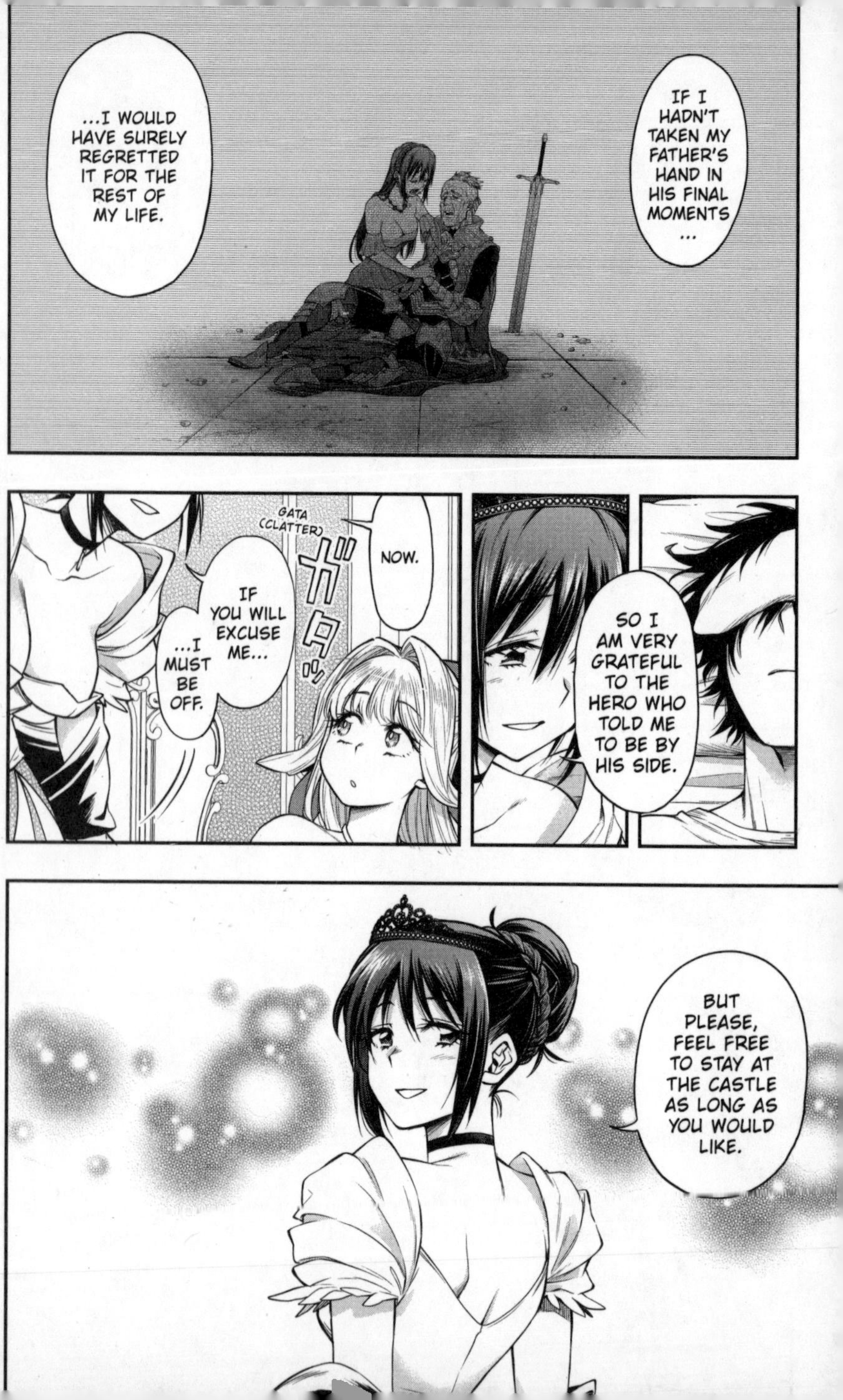
IF I HADN'T TAKEN MY FATHER'S HAND IN HIS FINAL MOMENTS...
...I WOULD HAVE SURELY REGRETTED IT FOR THE REST OF MY LIFE.
SO I AM VERY GRATEFUL TO THE HERO WHO TOLD ME TO BE BY HIS SIDE.
NOW.
GATA (CLATTER)
IF YOU WILL EXCUSE ME...
...I MUST BE OFF.
BUT PLEASE, FEEL FREE TO STAY AT THE CASTLE AS LONG AS YOU WOULD LIKE.

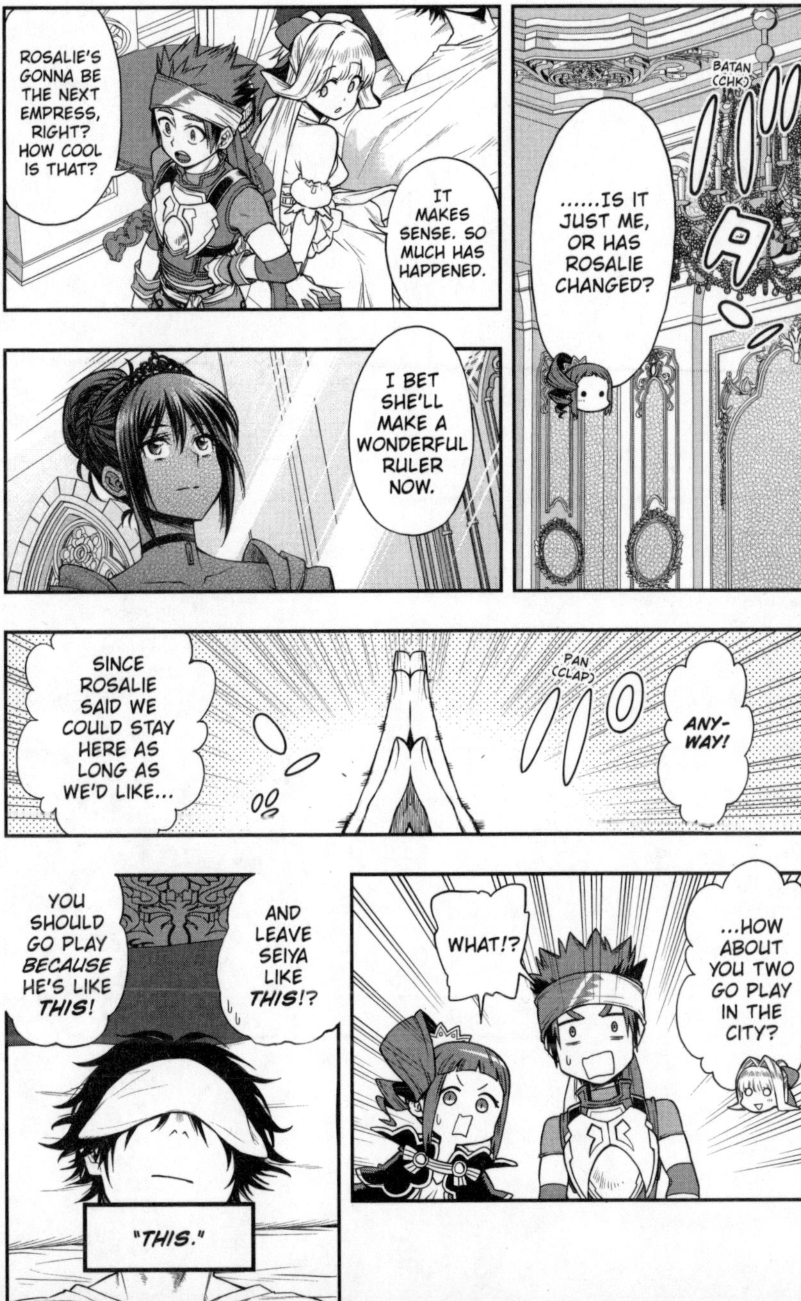
BATAN (CHK)
......IS IT JUST ME, OR HAS ROSALIE CHANGED?
ROSALIE'S GONNA BE THE NEXT EMPRESS, RIGHT? HOW COOL IS THAT?
IT MAKES SENSE. SO MUCH HAS HAPPENED.
I BET SHE'LL MAKE A WONDERFUL RULER NOW.
ANY-WAY!
PAN (CLAP)
SINCE ROSALIE SAID WE COULD STAY HERE AS LONG AS WE'D LIKE...
...HOW ABOUT YOU TWO GO PLAY IN THE CITY?
WHAT!?
AND LEAVE SEIYA LIKE *THIS*!?
YOU SHOULD GO PLAY *BECAUSE* HE'S LIKE *THIS*!
"THIS."

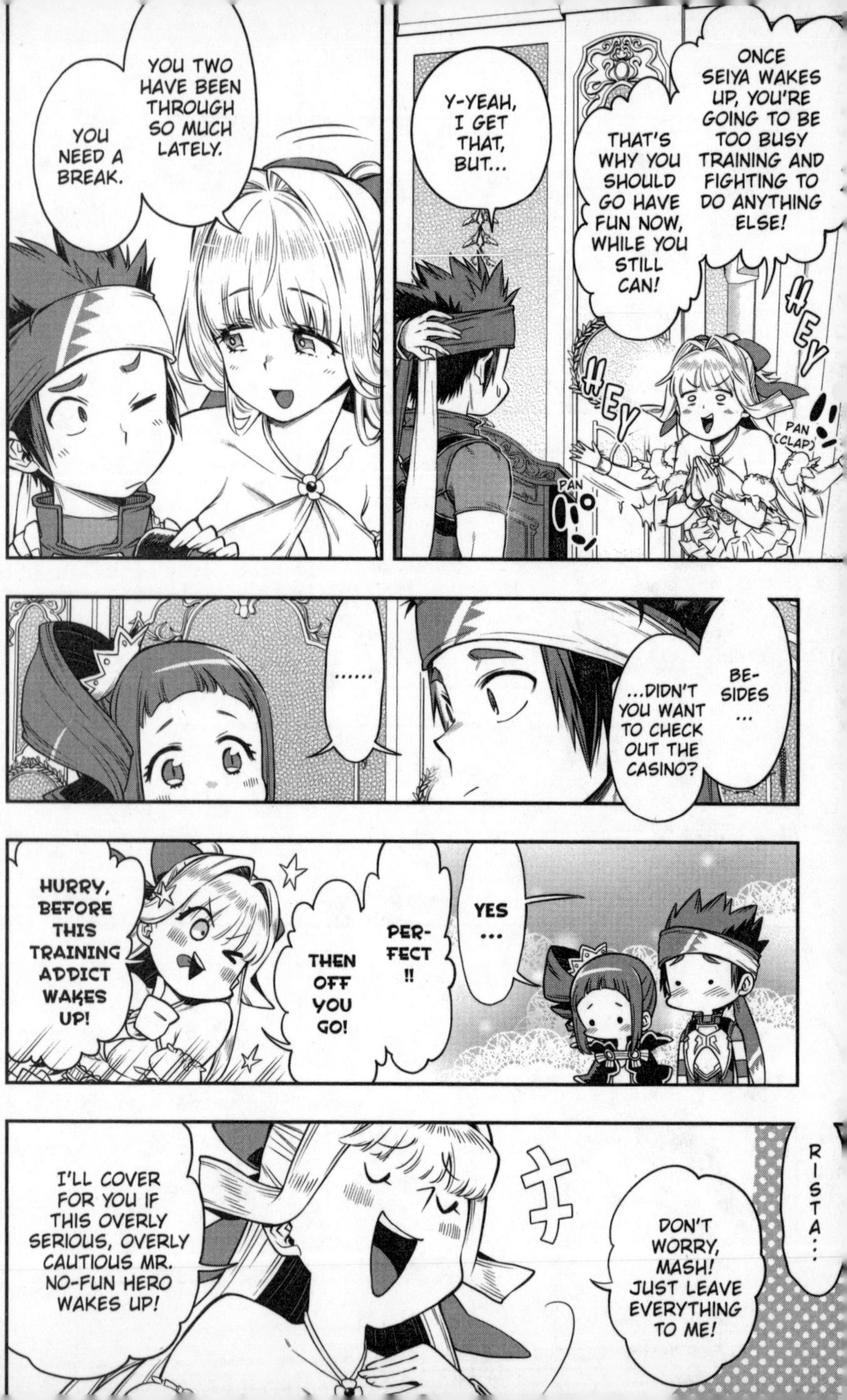

ONCE SEIYA WAKES UP, YOU'RE GOING TO BE TOO BUSY TRAINING AND FIGHTING TO DO ANYTHING ELSE!
THAT'S WHY YOU SHOULD GO HAVE FUN NOW, WHILE YOU STILL CAN!
HEY
HEY
PAN (CLAP)
PAN
Y-YEAH, I GET THAT, BUT...
YOU TWO HAVE BEEN THROUGH SO MUCH LATELY.
YOU NEED A BREAK.
BE-SIDES...
...DIDN'T YOU WANT TO CHECK OUT THE CASINO?
......
YES...
PER-FECT!!
THEN OFF YOU GO!
HURRY, BEFORE THIS TRAINING ADDICT WAKES UP!
RISTA...
DON'T WORRY, MASH! JUST LEAVE EVERYTHING TO ME!
I'LL COVER FOR YOU IF THIS OVERLY SERIOUS, OVERLY CAUTIOUS MR. NO-FUN HERO WAKES UP!

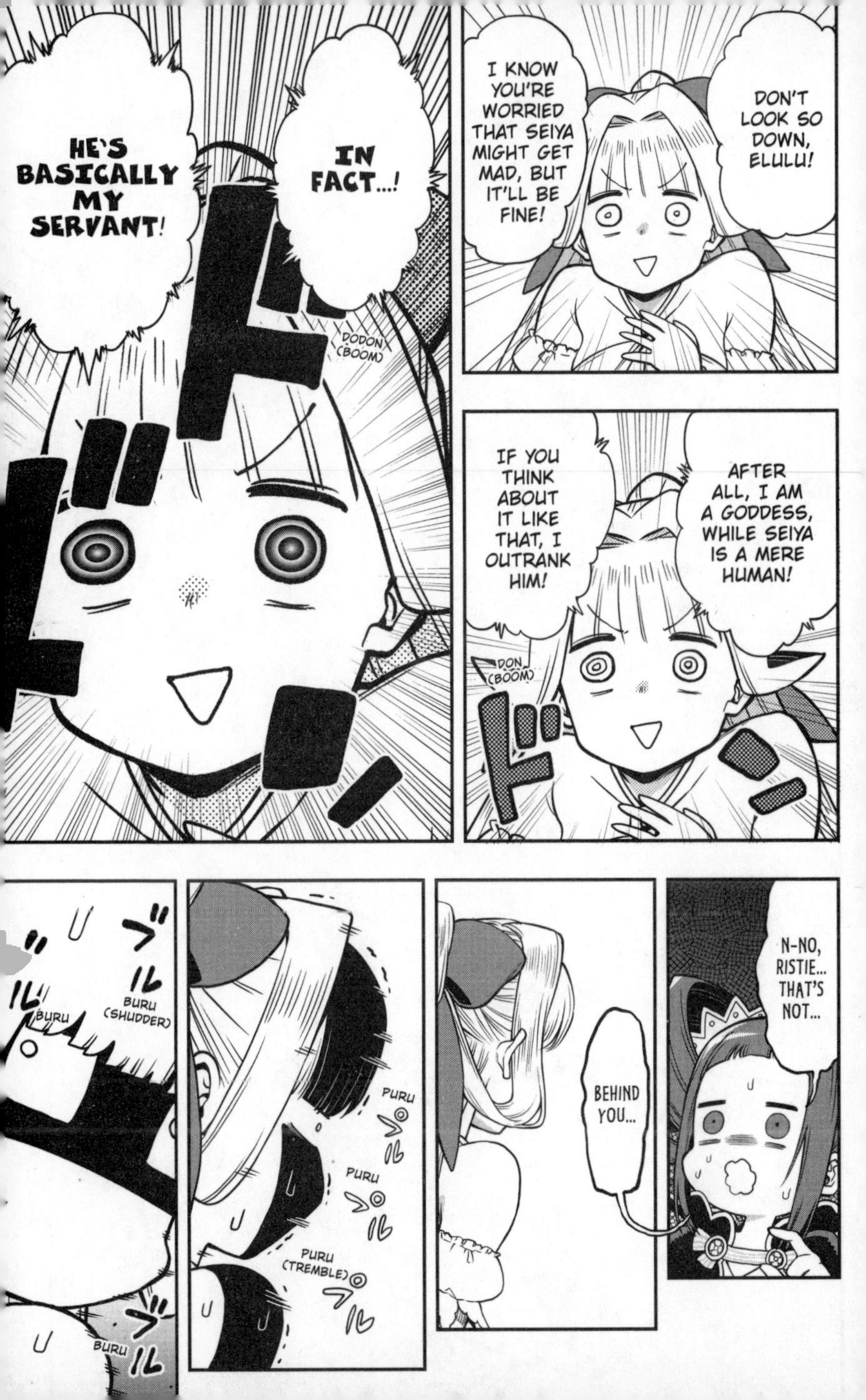
DON'T LOOK SO DOWN, ELULU!
I KNOW YOU'RE WORRIED THAT SEIYA MIGHT GET MAD, BUT IT'LL BE FINE!
AFTER ALL, I AM A GODDESS, WHILE SEIYA IS A MERE HUMAN!
IF YOU THINK ABOUT IT LIKE THAT, I OUTRANK HIM!
DON (BOOM)
IN FACT...!
HE'S BASICALLY MY SERVANT!
DODON (BOOM)
N-NO, RISTIE... THAT'S NOT...
BEHIND YOU...
PURU
PURU
PURU (TREMBLE)
BURU (SHUDDER)
BURU
BURU

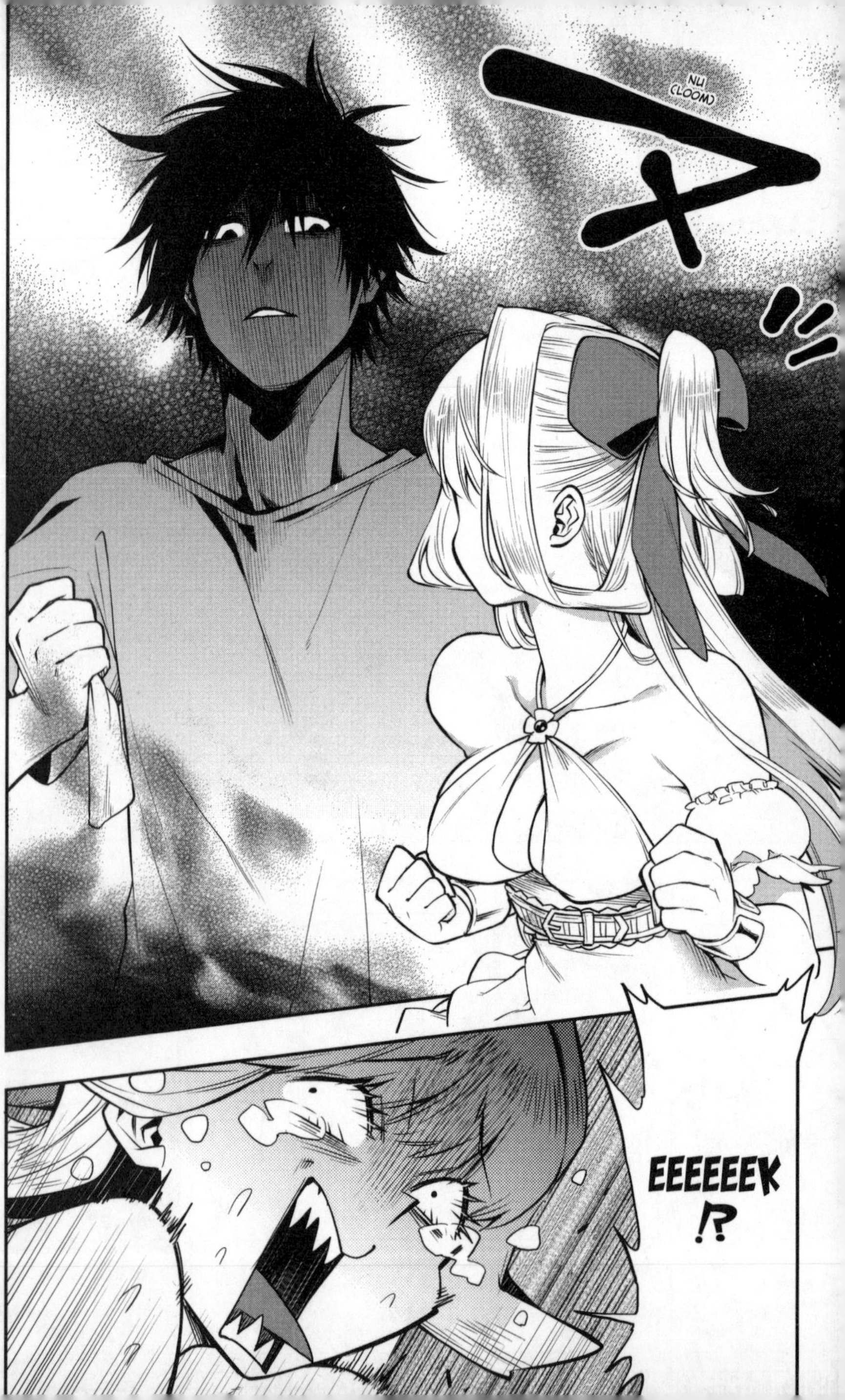
NU (LOOM)
EEEEEEK !?

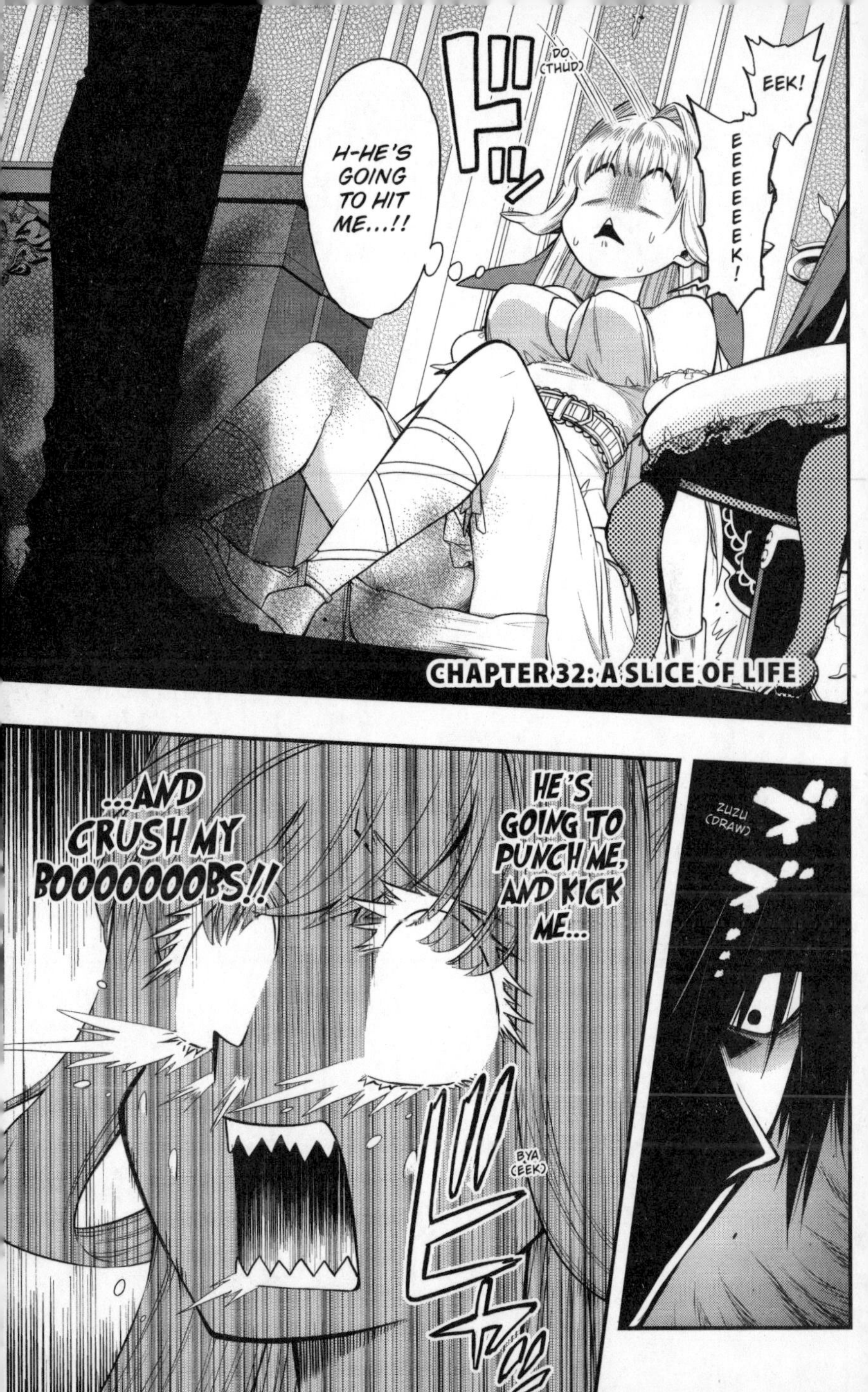
EEK!
EEEEEEEK!
DO (THUD)
H-HE'S GOING TO HIT ME...!!
CHAPTER 32: A SLICE OF LIFE
ZUZU (DRAW)
HE'S GOING TO PUNCH ME, AND KICK ME...
...AND CRUSH MY BOOOOOOOBS!!
BYA (EEK)

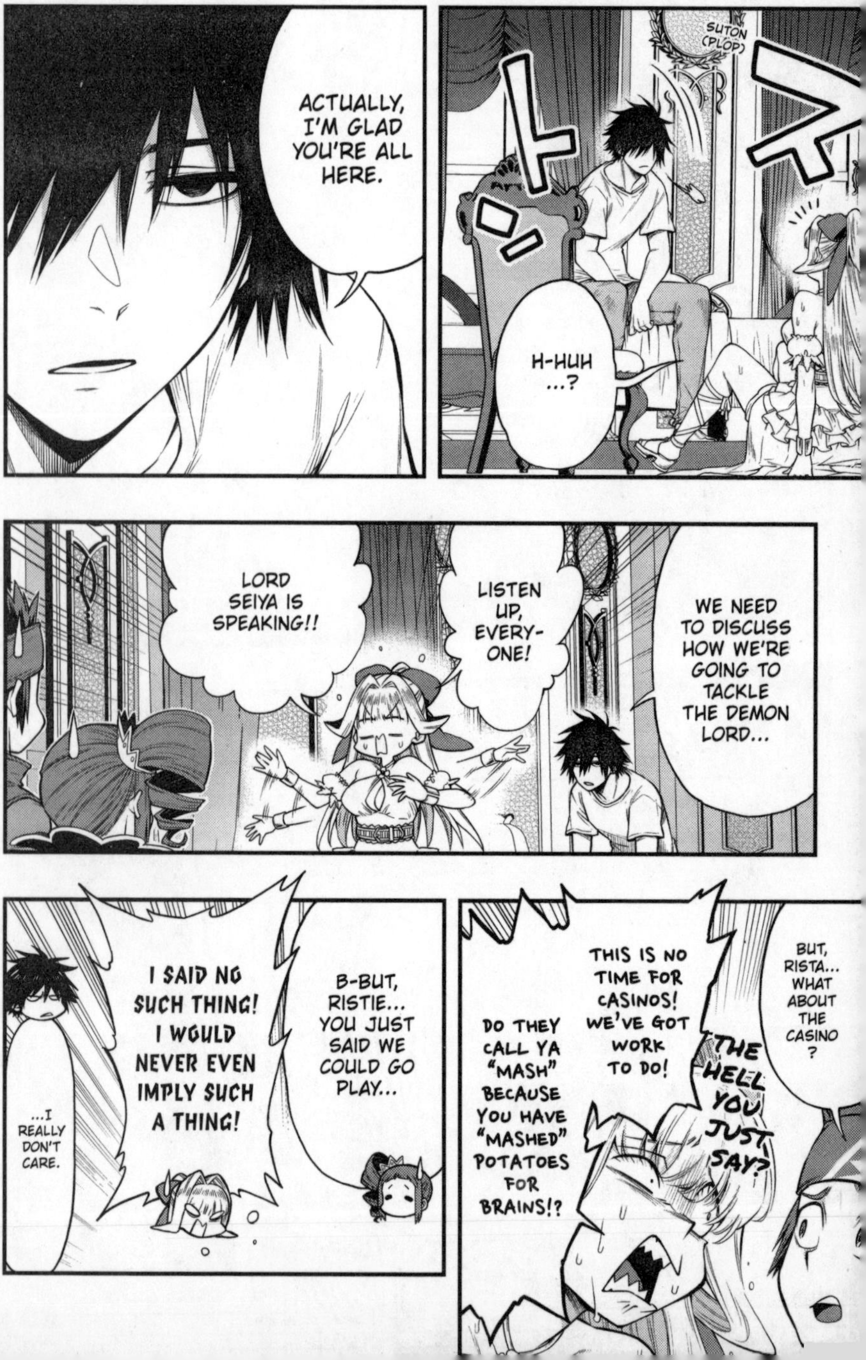
SUTON (PLOP)
H-HUH ...?
ACTUALLY, I'M GLAD YOU'RE ALL HERE.
WE NEED TO DISCUSS HOW WE'RE GOING TO TACKLE THE DEMON LORD...
LISTEN UP, EVERY-ONE!
LORD SEIYA IS SPEAKING!!
BUT, RISTA... WHAT ABOUT THE CASINO?
THE HELL YOU JUST SAY?
THIS IS NO TIME FOR CASINOS! WE'VE GOT WORK TO DO!
DO THEY CALL YA "MASH" BECAUSE YOU HAVE "MASHED" POTATOES FOR BRAINS!?
B-BUT, RISTIE... YOU JUST SAID WE COULD GO PLAY...
I SAID NO SUCH THING! I WOULD NEVER EVEN IMPLY SUCH A THING!
...I REALLY DON'T CARE.

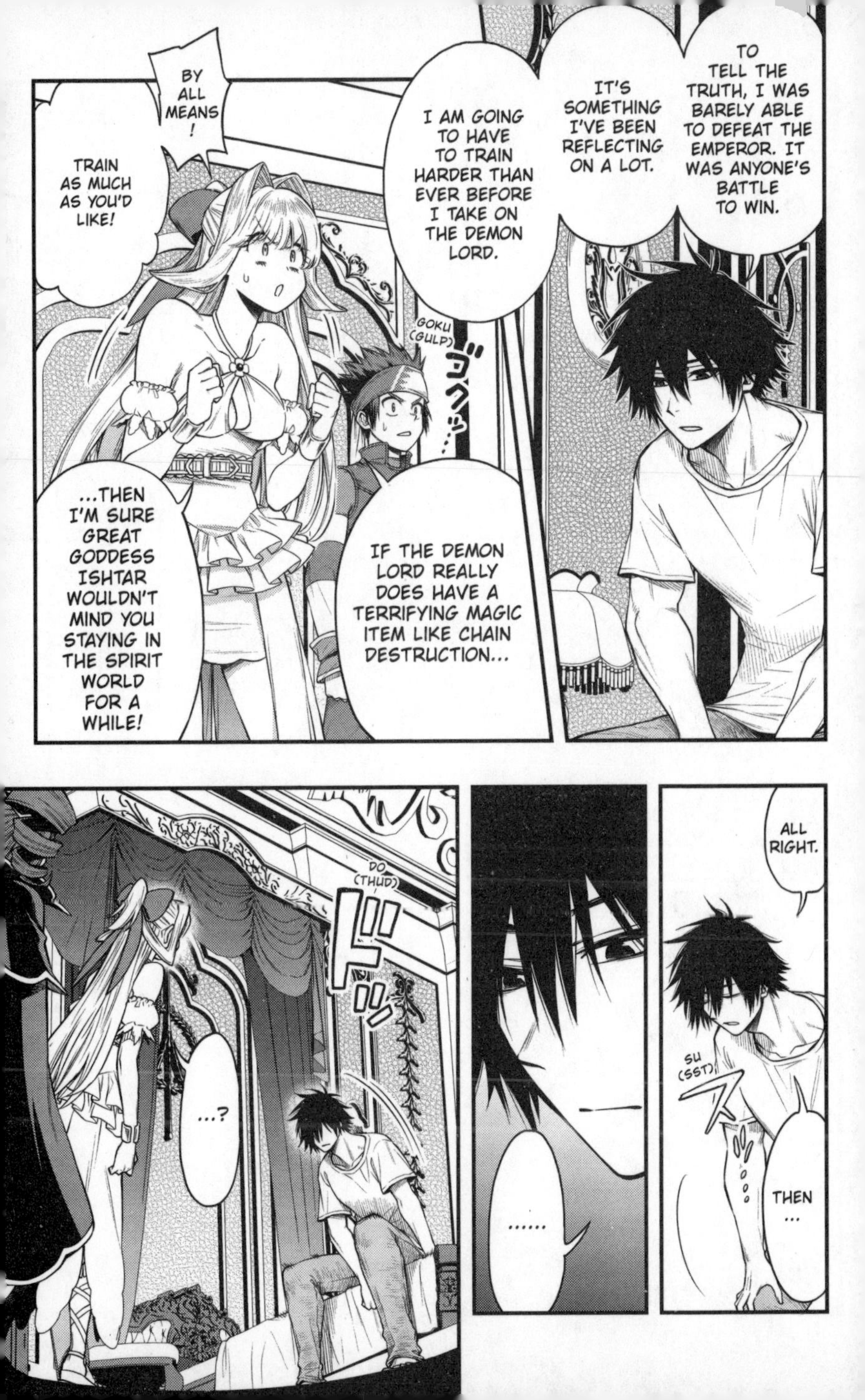
TO TELL THE TRUTH, I WAS BARELY ABLE TO DEFEAT THE EMPEROR. IT WAS ANYONE'S BATTLE TO WIN.
IT'S SOMETHING I'VE BEEN REFLECTING ON A LOT.
I AM GOING TO HAVE TO TRAIN HARDER THAN EVER BEFORE I TAKE ON THE DEMON LORD.
BY ALL MEANS!
TRAIN AS MUCH AS YOU'D LIKE!
GOKU (GULP)
IF THE DEMON LORD REALLY DOES HAVE A TERRIFYING MAGIC ITEM LIKE CHAIN DESTRUCTION...
...THEN I'M SURE GREAT GODDESS ISHTAR WOULDN'T MIND YOU STAYING IN THE SPIRIT WORLD FOR A WHILE!
ALL RIGHT.
SU (SST)
THEN...
......
DO (THUD)
...?

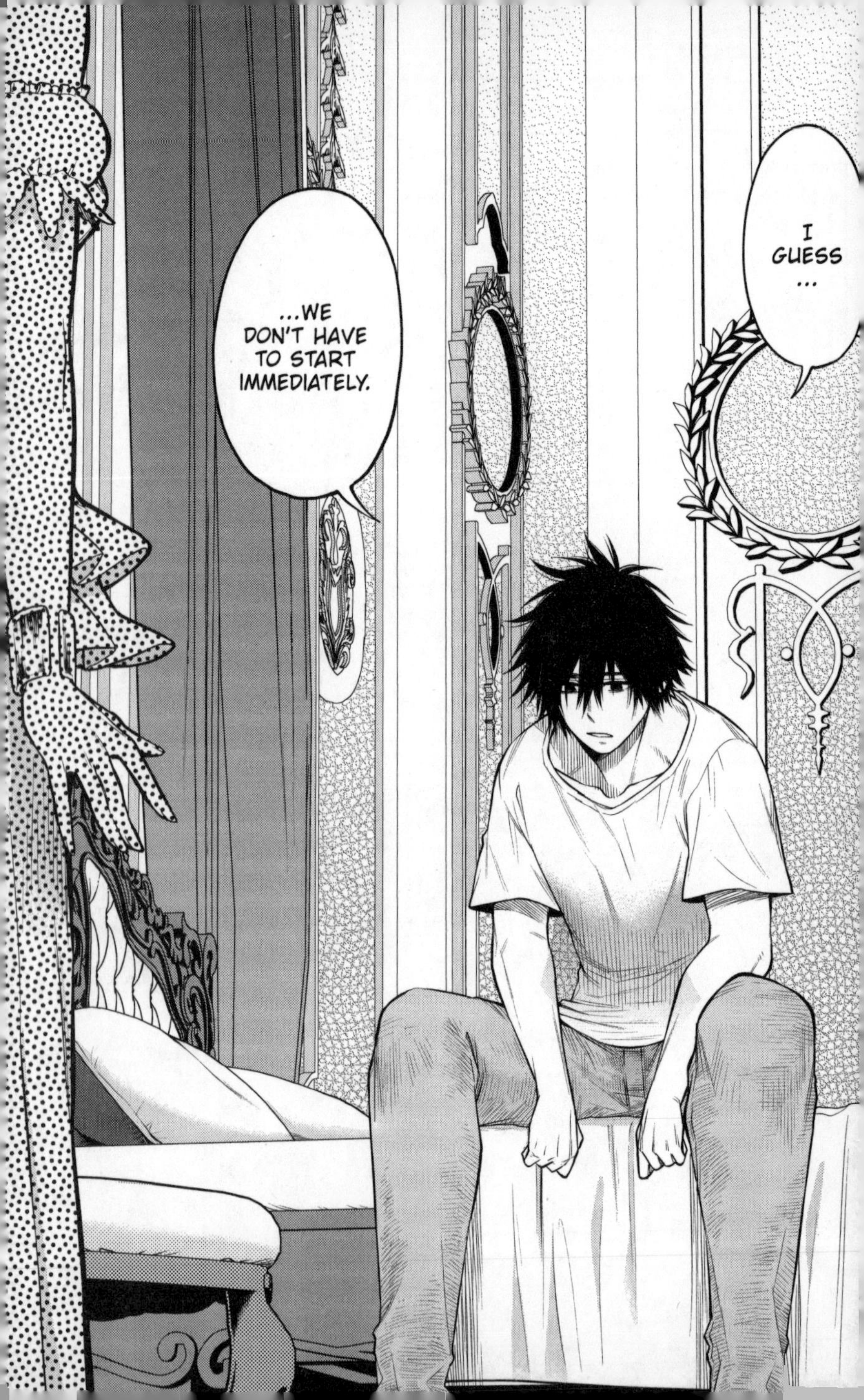
I GUESS ...
...WE DON'T HAVE TO START IMMEDIATELY.

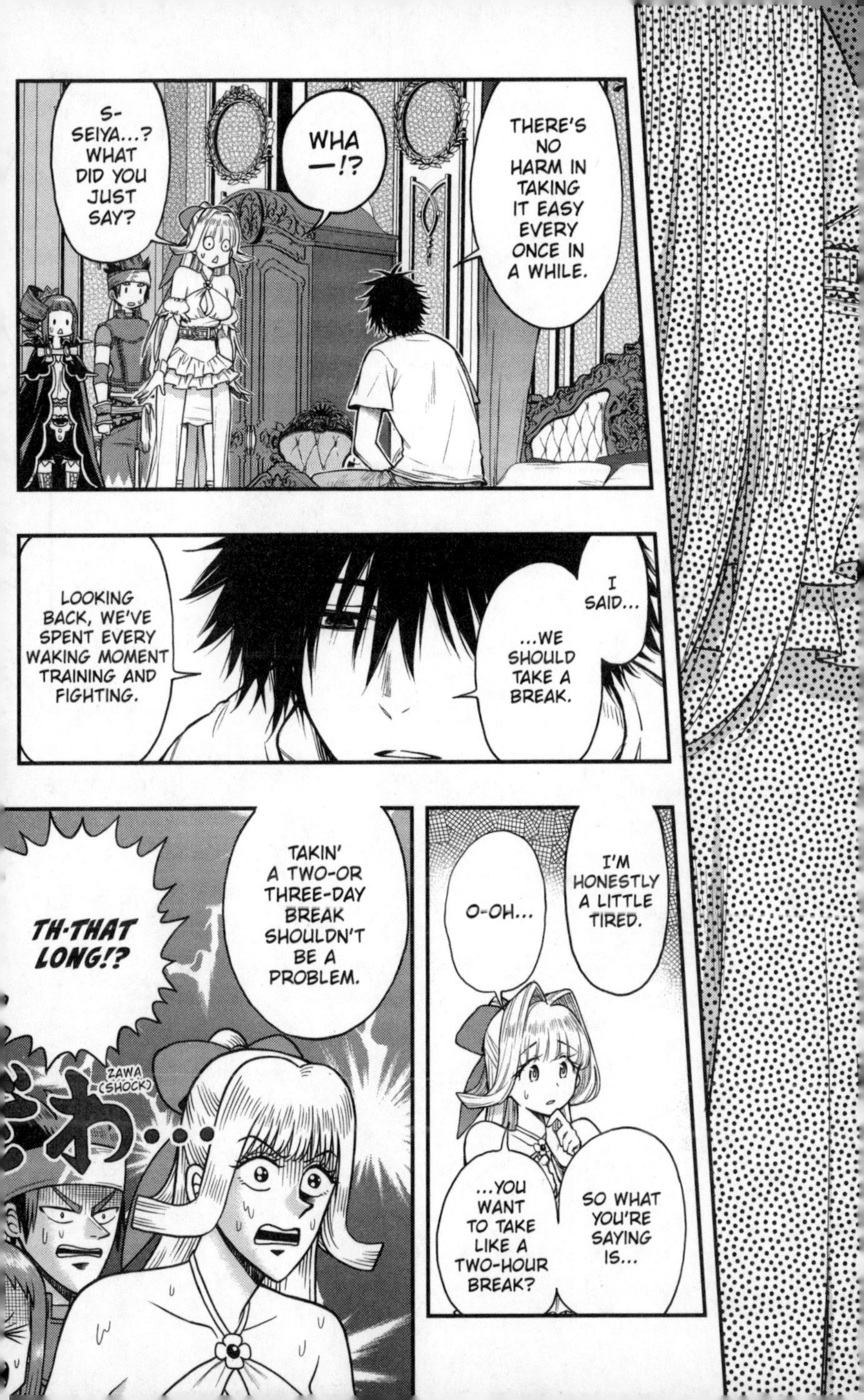
THERE'S NO HARM IN TAKING IT EASY EVERY ONCE IN A WHILE.
WHA—!?
S-SEIYA...? WHAT DID YOU JUST SAY?
I SAID...
...WE SHOULD TAKE A BREAK.
LOOKING BACK, WE'VE SPENT EVERY WAKING MOMENT TRAINING AND FIGHTING.
I'M HONESTLY A LITTLE TIRED.
O-OH...
SO WHAT YOU'RE SAYING IS...
...YOU WANT TO TAKE LIKE A TWO-HOUR BREAK?
TAKIN' A TWO-OR THREE-DAY BREAK SHOULDN'T BE A PROBLEM.
TH-THAT LONG!?
ZAWA (SHOCK)

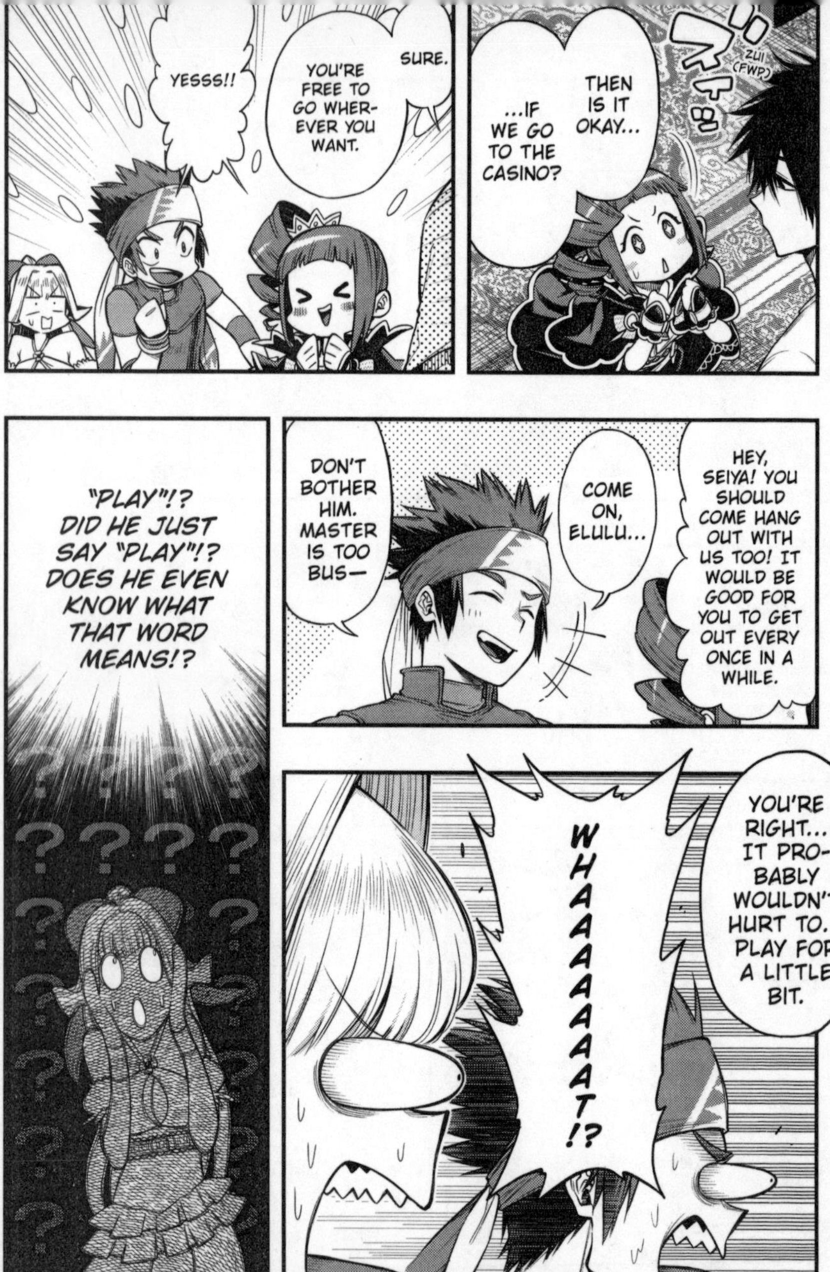
ZUI (FWP)
THEN IS IT OKAY...
...IF WE GO TO THE CASINO?
SURE.
YOU'RE FREE TO GO WHER-EVER YOU WANT.
YESSS!!
HEY, SEIYA! YOU SHOULD COME HANG OUT WITH US TOO! IT WOULD BE GOOD FOR YOU TO GET OUT EVERY ONCE IN A WHILE.
COME ON, ELULU...
DON'T BOTHER HIM. MASTER IS TOO BUS—
YOU'RE RIGHT... IT PRO-BABLY WOULDN'T HURT TO... PLAY FOR A LITTLE BIT.
WHAAAAAAAT!?
"PLAY"!? DID HE JUST SAY "PLAY"!? DOES HE EVEN KNOW WHAT THAT WORD MEANS!?

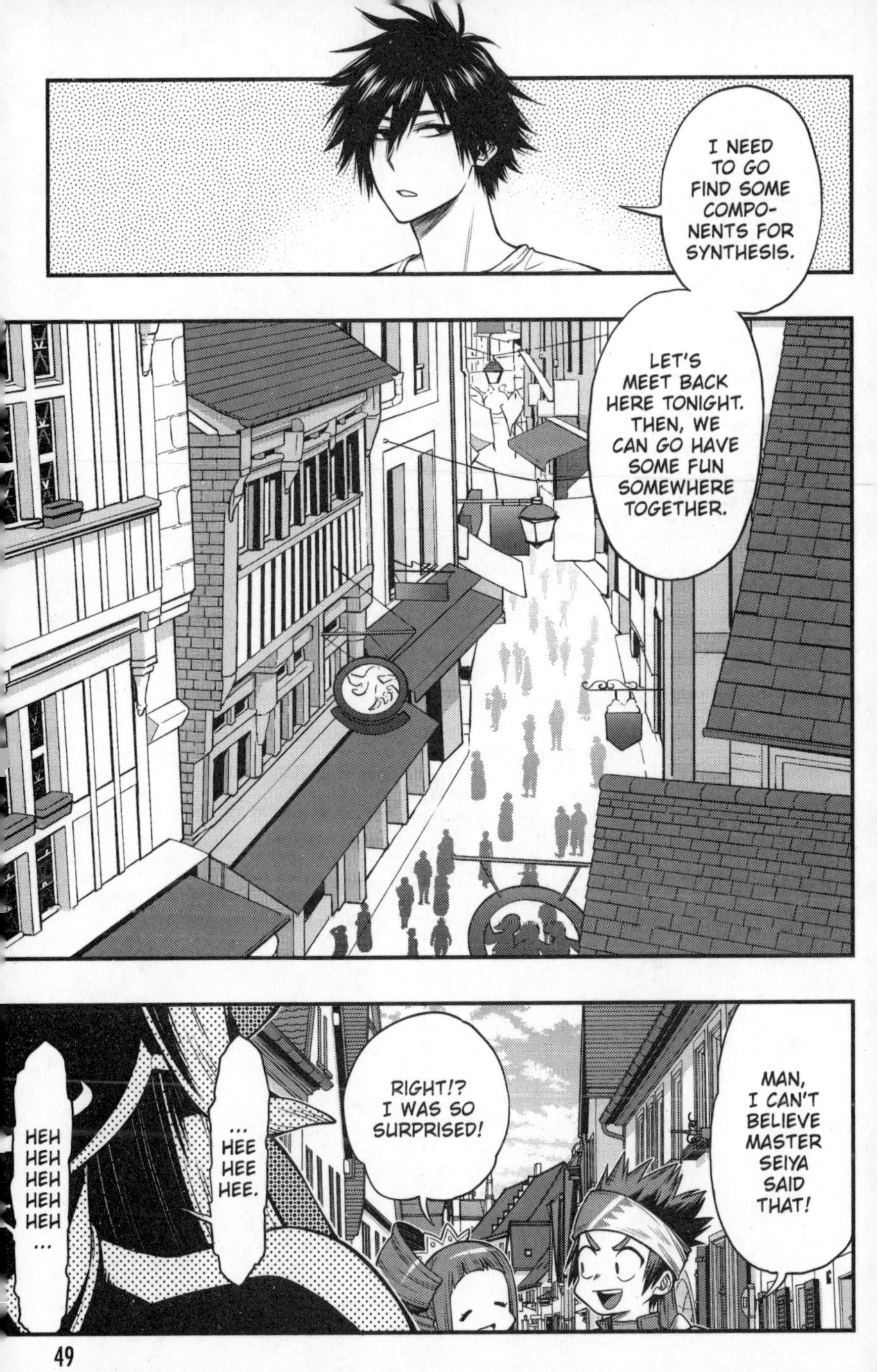
I NEED TO GO FIND SOME COMPO- NENTS FOR SYNTHESIS.
LET'S MEET BACK HERE TONIGHT. THEN, WE CAN GO HAVE SOME FUN SOMEWHERE TOGETHER.
MAN, I CAN'T BELIEVE MASTER SEIYA SAID THAT!
RIGHT!? I WAS SO SURPRISED!
... HEE HEE HEE.
HEH HEH HEH HEH HEH ...

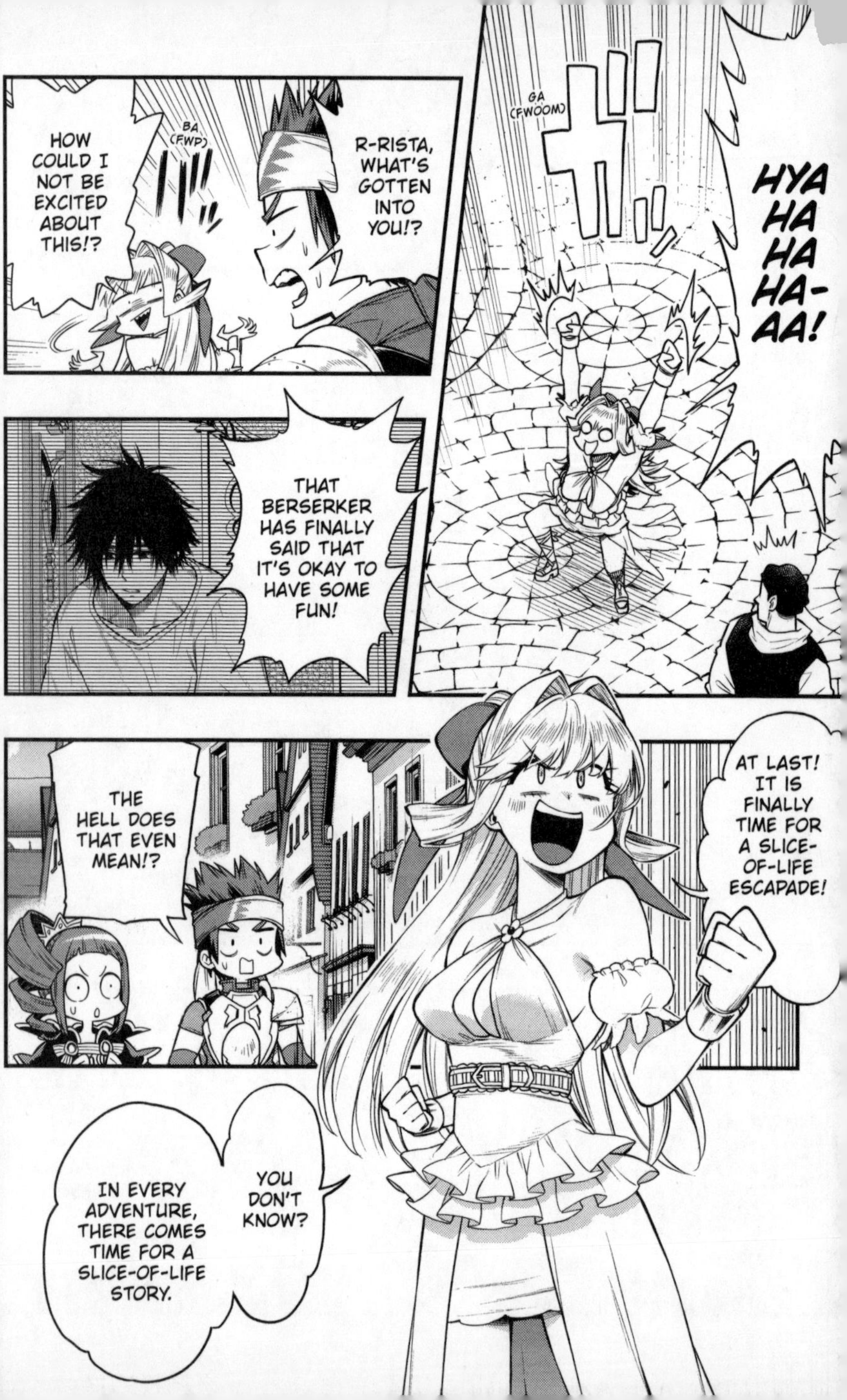
GA (FWOOM)
HYA HA HA HA-AA!
R-RISTA, WHAT'S GOTTEN INTO YOU!?
BA (FWP)
HOW COULD I NOT BE EXCITED ABOUT THIS!?
THAT BERSERKER HAS FINALLY SAID THAT IT'S OKAY TO HAVE SOME FUN!
AT LAST! IT IS FINALLY TIME FOR A SLICE-OF-LIFE ESCAPADE!
THE HELL DOES THAT EVEN MEAN!?
YOU DON'T KNOW?
IN EVERY ADVENTURE, THERE COMES TIME FOR A SLICE-OF-LIFE STORY.

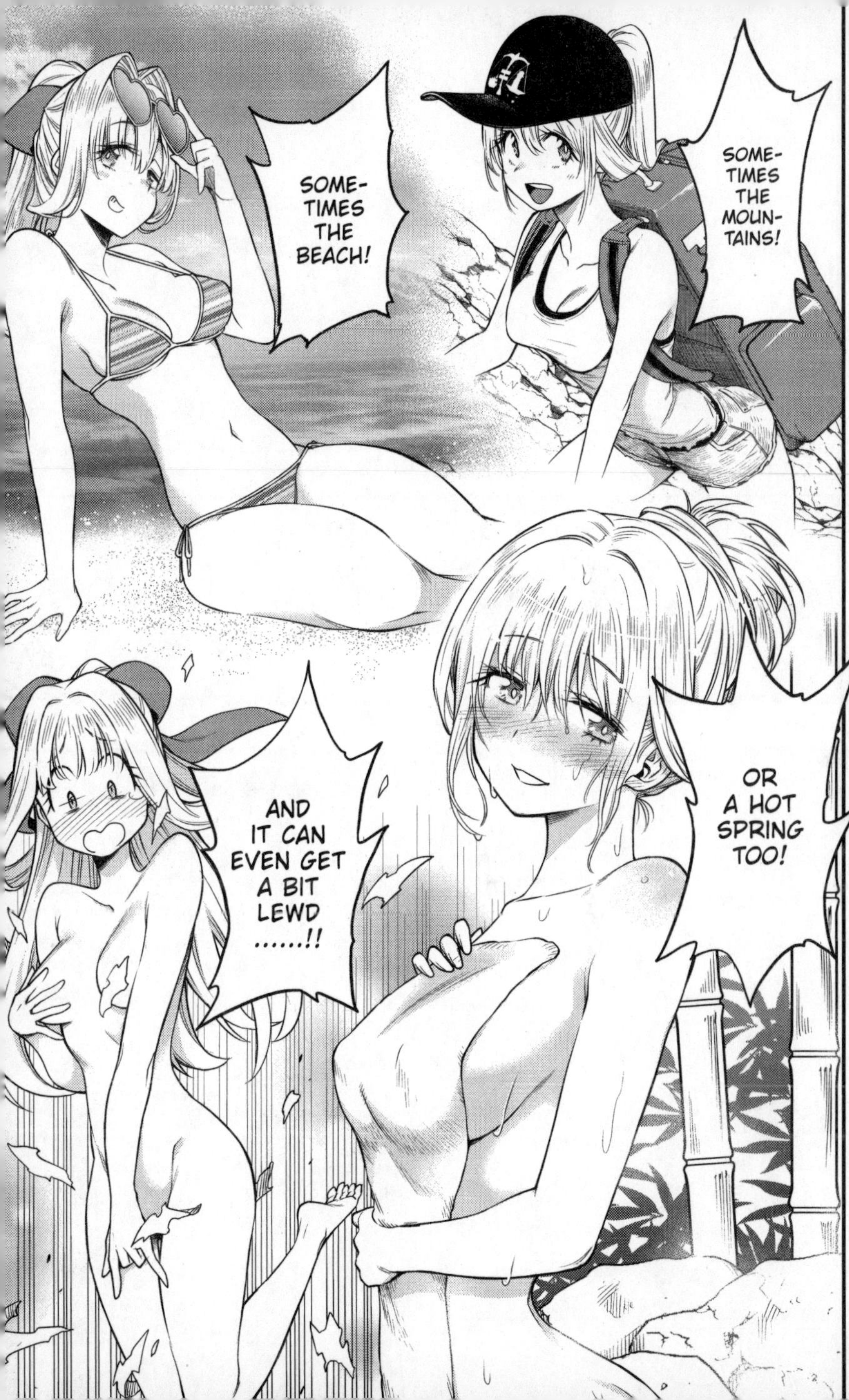
SOME-TIMES THE MOUN-TAINS!
SOME-TIMES THE BEACH!
OR A HOT SPRING TOO!
AND IT CAN EVEN GET A BIT LEWD ......!!

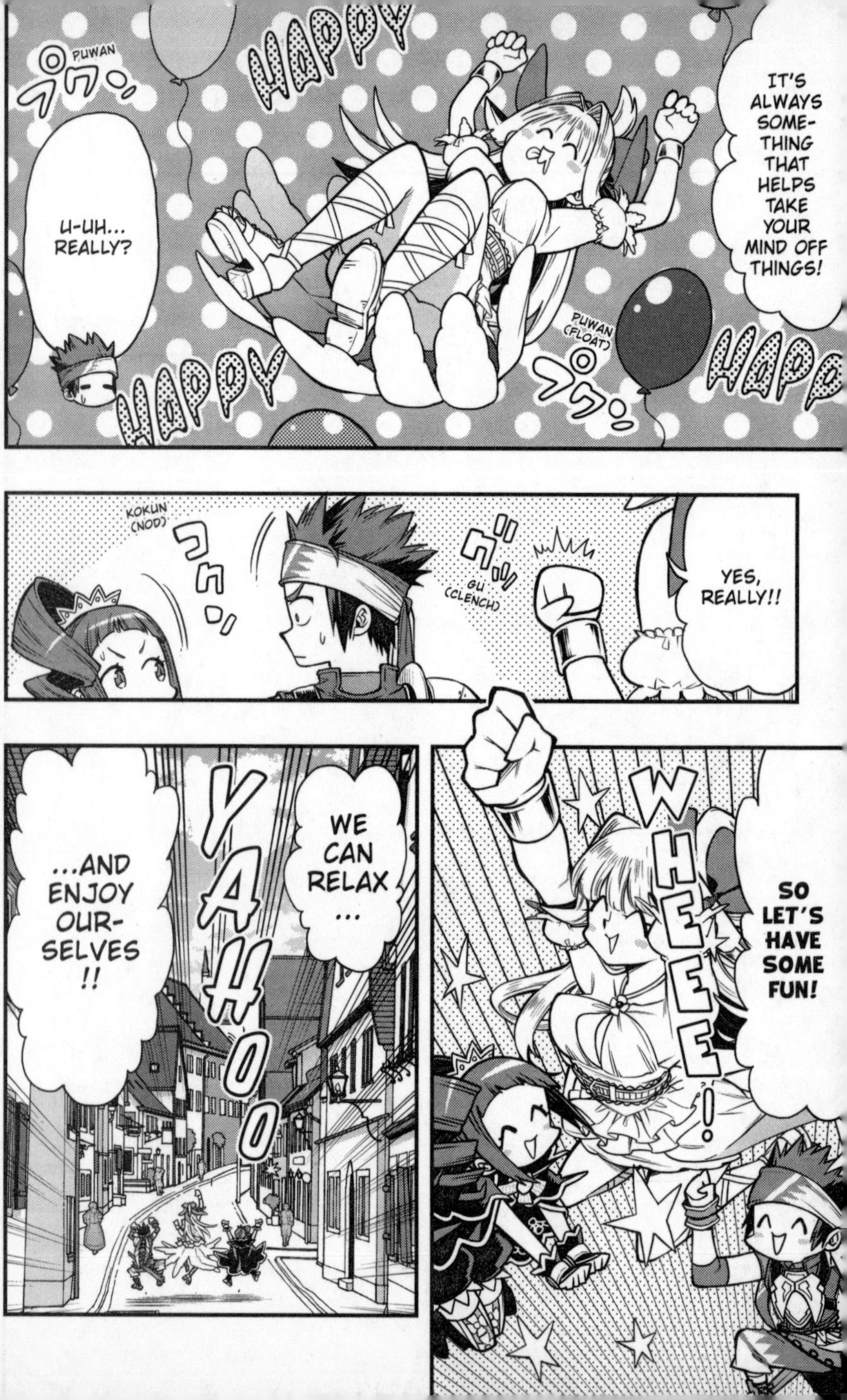
IT'S ALWAYS SOME-THING THAT HELPS TAKE YOUR MIND OFF THINGS!
HAPP
PUWAN (FLOAT)
HAPPY
PUWAN
U-UH... REALLY?
HAPPY
YES, REALLY!!
GU (CLENCH)
KOKUN (NOD)
SO LET'S HAVE SOME FUN!
WHEEE!
WE CAN RELAX...
YAHOO
...AND ENJOY OUR-SELVES!!

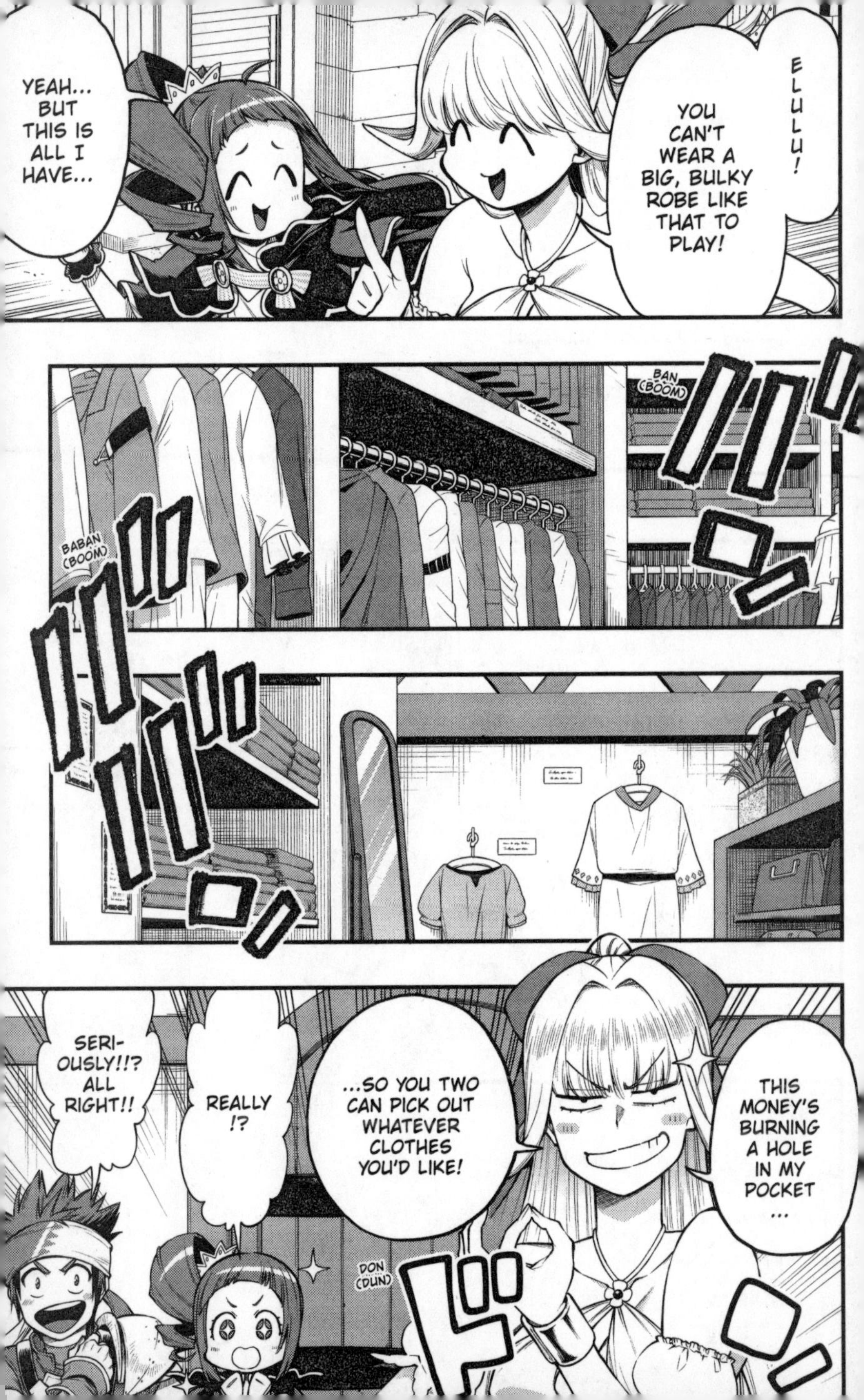
ELULU!
YOU CAN'T WEAR A BIG, BULKY ROBE LIKE THAT TO PLAY!
YEAH... BUT THIS IS ALL I HAVE...
BAN (BOOM)
BABAN (BOOM)
THIS MONEY'S BURNING A HOLE IN MY POCKET ...
...SO YOU TWO CAN PICK OUT WHATEVER CLOTHES YOU'D LIKE!
DON (DUN)
REALLY!?
SERIOUSLY!!? ALL RIGHT!!

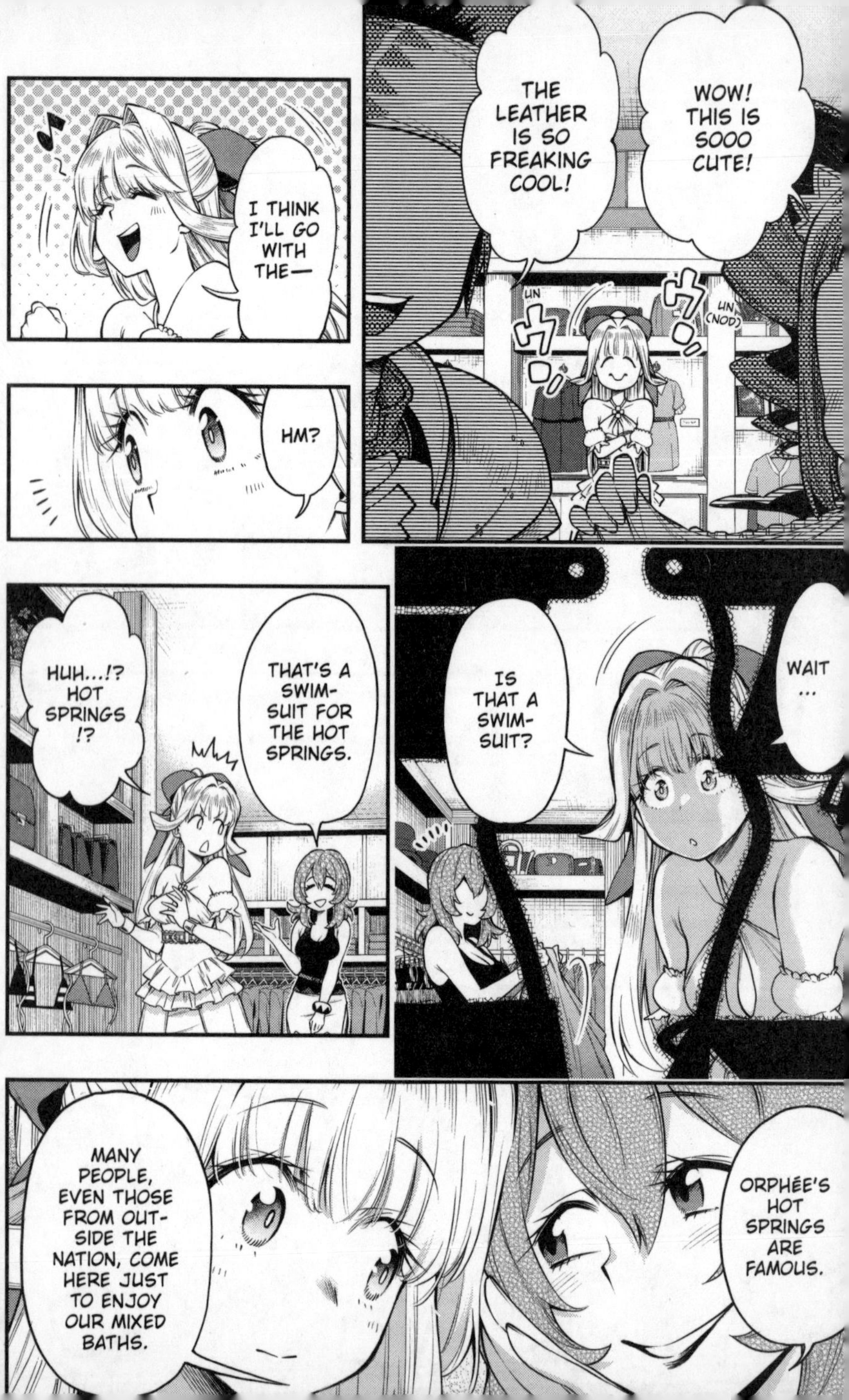
WOW! THIS IS SOOO CUTE!
THE LEATHER IS SO FREAKING COOL!
UN
UN (NOD)
I THINK I'LL GO WITH THE—
HM?
WAIT ...
IS THAT A SWIMSUIT?
THAT'S A SWIMSUIT FOR THE HOT SPRINGS.
HUH...!? HOT SPRINGS !?
ORPHÉE'S HOT SPRINGS ARE FAMOUS.
MANY PEOPLE, EVEN THOSE FROM OUTSIDE THE NATION, COME HERE JUST TO ENJOY OUR MIXED BATHS.

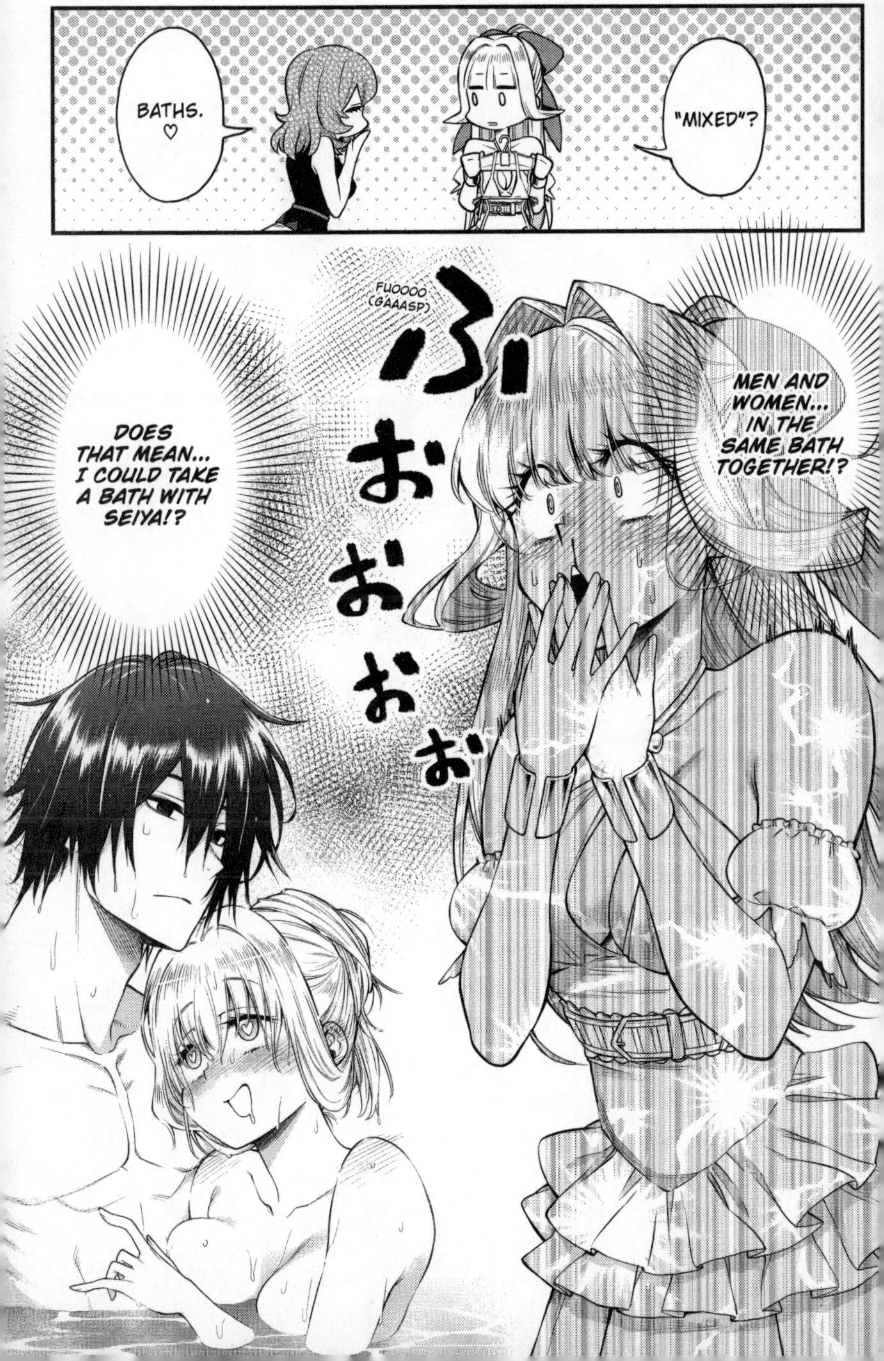
"MIXED"?
BATHS. ♡
MEN AND WOMEN... IN THE SAME BATH TOGETHER!?
ふおおおぉ
FUOOOO (GAAASP)
DOES THAT MEAN... I COULD TAKE A BATH WITH SEIYA!?

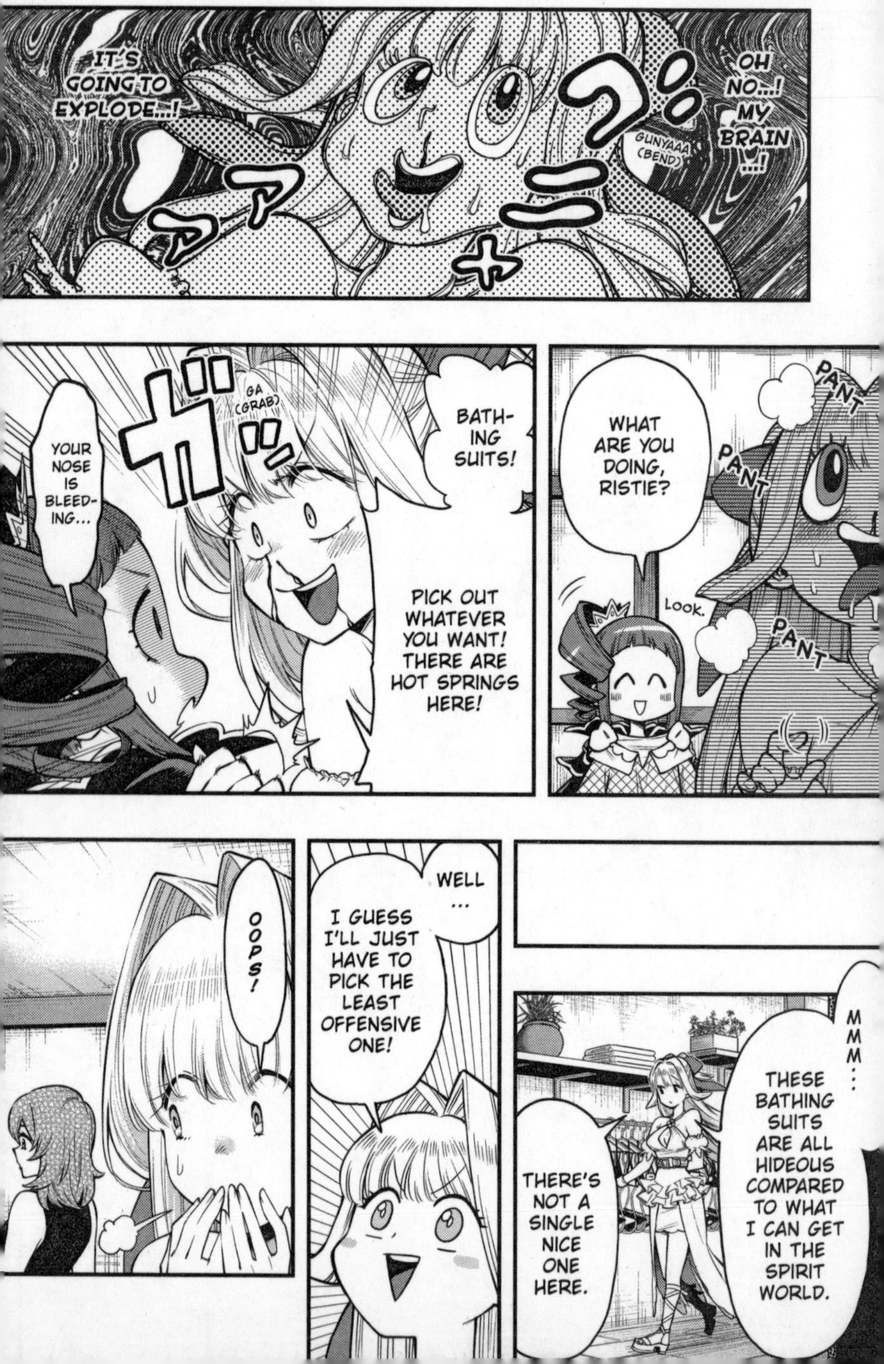
OH NO...! MY BRAIN...!
GUNYAAA (BEND)
IT'S GOING TO EXPLODE...!
PANT
WHAT ARE YOU DOING, RISTIE?
PANT
LOOK.
PANT
BATH-ING SUITS!
GA (GRAB)
YOUR NOSE IS BLEED-ING...
PICK OUT WHATEVER YOU WANT! THERE ARE HOT SPRINGS HERE!
MMM...
THESE BATHING SUITS ARE ALL HIDEOUS COMPARED TO WHAT I CAN GET IN THE SPIRIT WORLD.
THERE'S NOT A SINGLE NICE ONE HERE.
WELL...
I GUESS I'LL JUST HAVE TO PICK THE LEAST OFFENSIVE ONE!
OOPS!

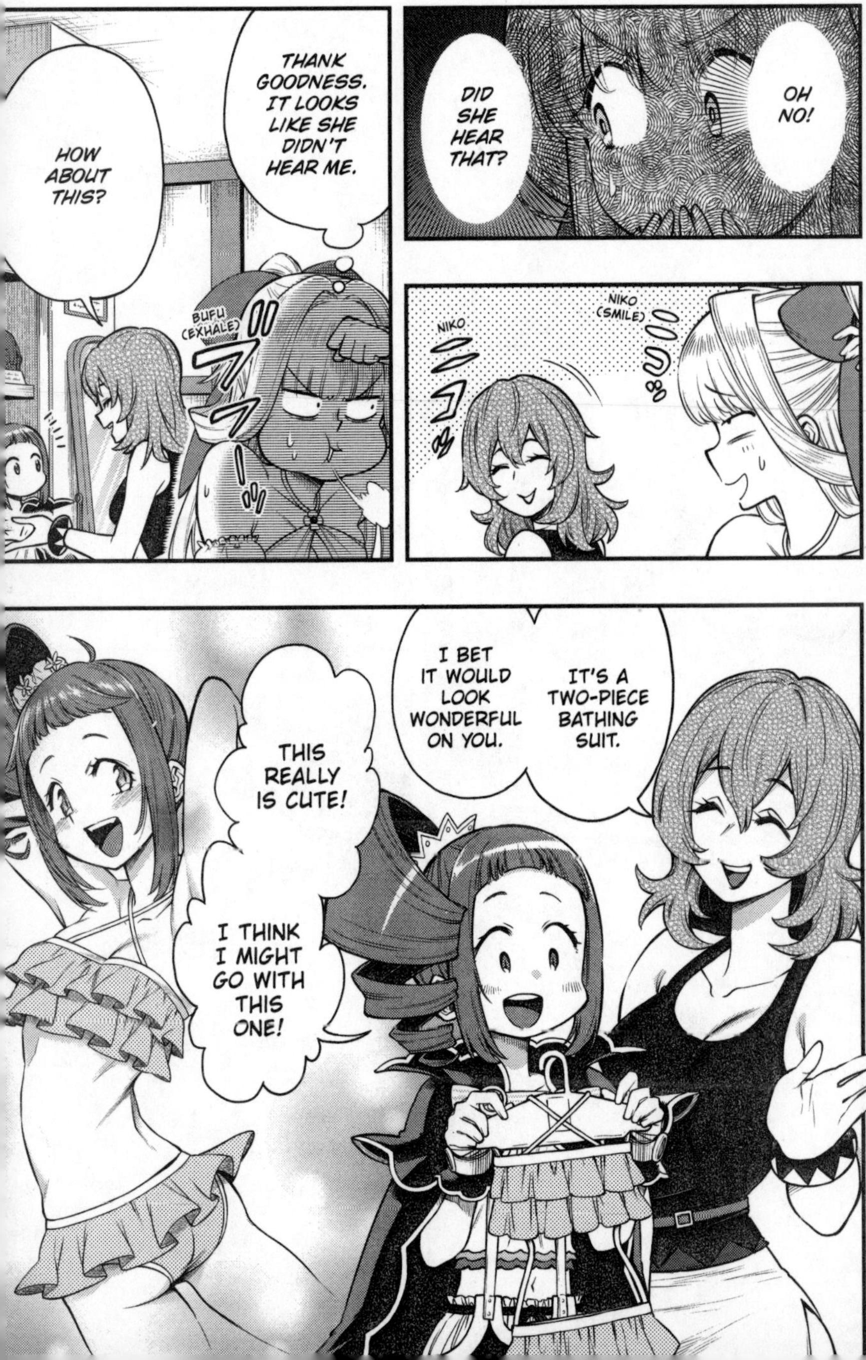
OH NO!
DID SHE HEAR THAT?
NIKO (SMILE)
NIKO
THANK GOODNESS. IT LOOKS LIKE SHE DIDN'T HEAR ME.
BUFU (EXHALE)
HOW ABOUT THIS?
IT'S A TWO-PIECE BATHING SUIT.
I BET IT WOULD LOOK WONDERFUL ON YOU.
THIS REALLY IS CUTE!
I THINK I MIGHT GO WITH THIS ONE!

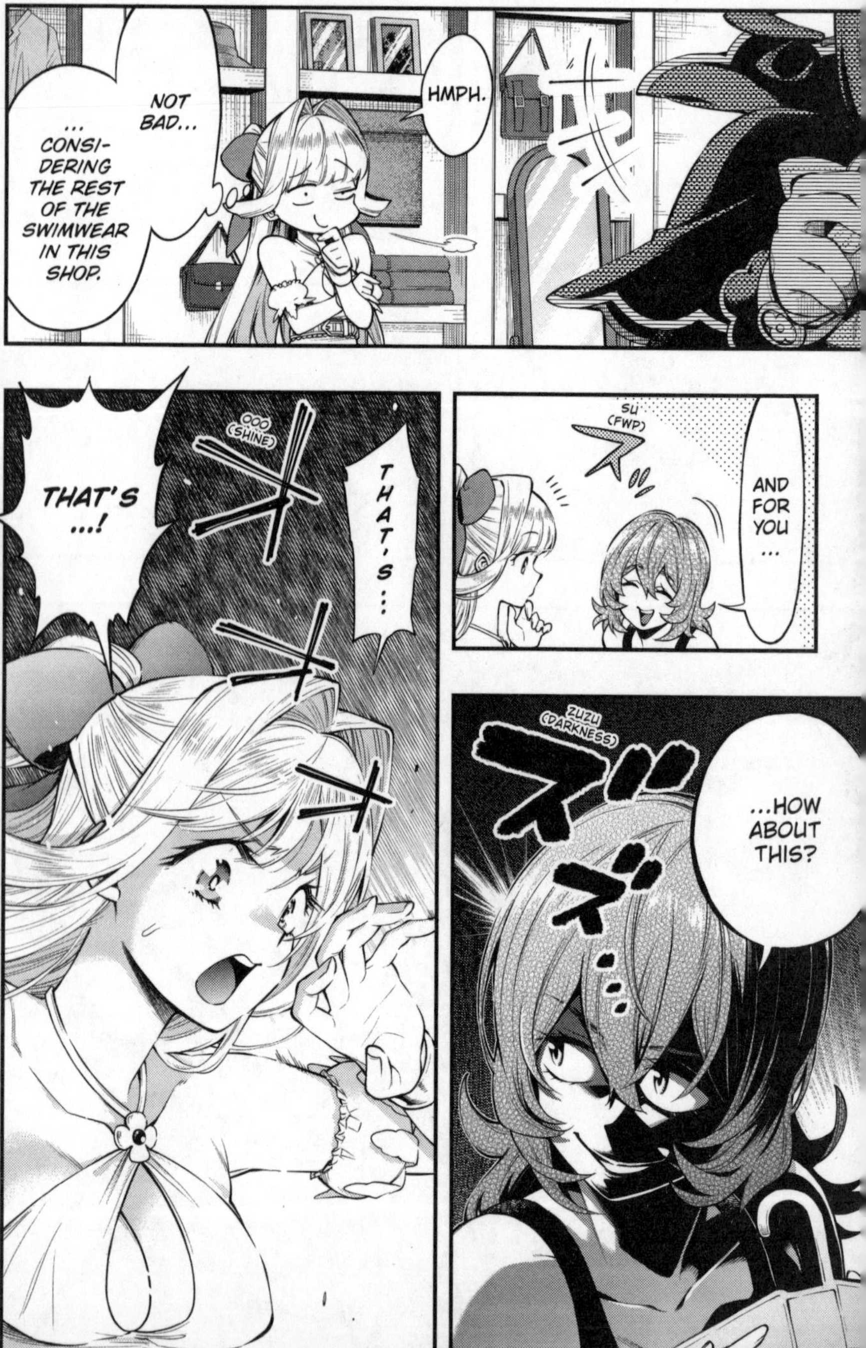
HMPH.
NOT BAD... ...CONSI-DERING THE REST OF THE SWIMWEAR IN THIS SHOP.
AND FOR YOU...
SU (FWP)
...HOW ABOUT THIS?
ZUZU (DARKNESS)
THAT'S...
OOO (SHINE)
THAT'S...!

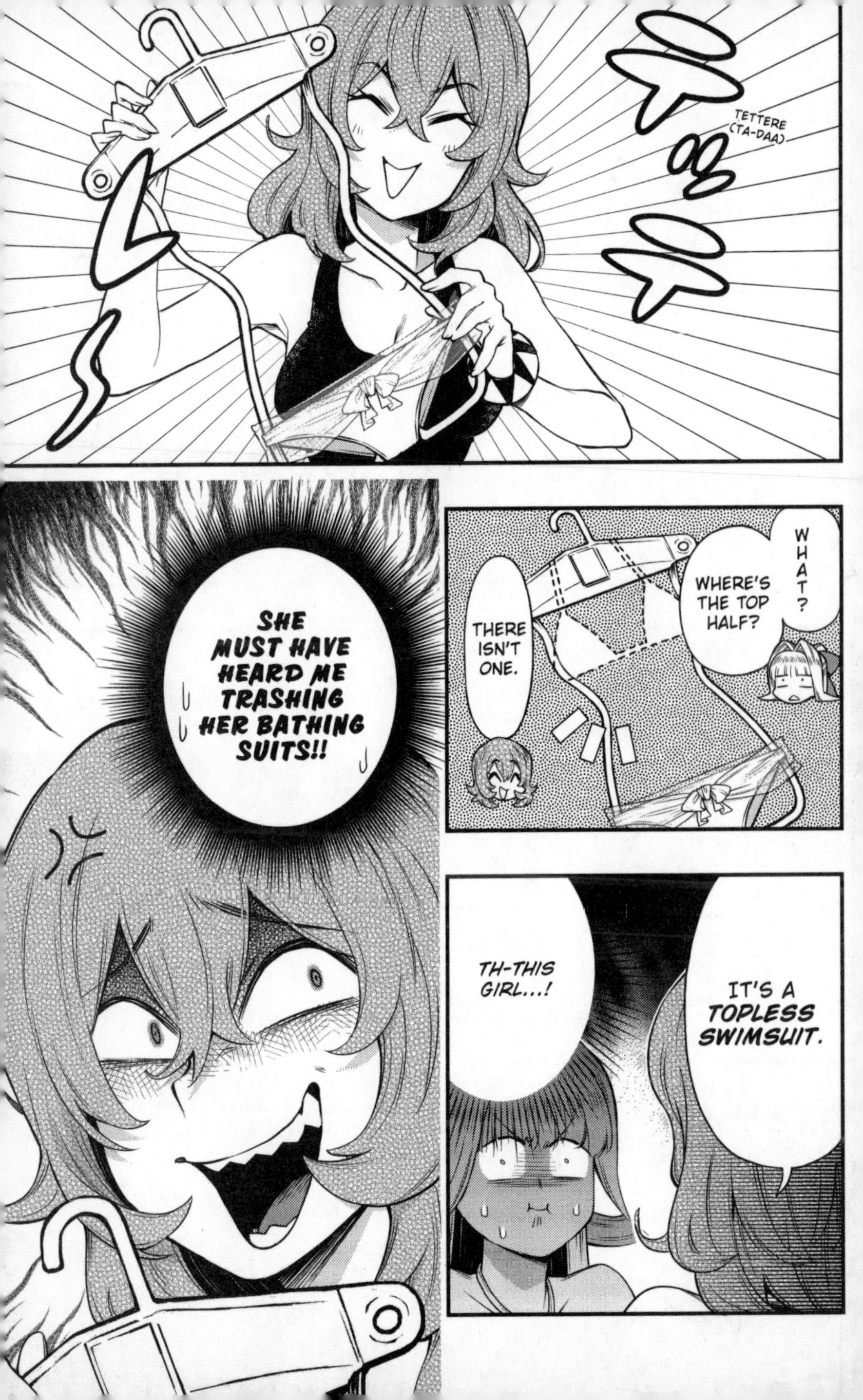
TETTERE (TA-DAA)
WHAT?
WHERE'S THE TOP HALF?
THERE ISN'T ONE.
IT'S A *TOPLESS* SWIMSUIT.
TH-THIS GIRL...!
SHE MUST HAVE HEARD ME TRASHING HER BATHING SUITS!!

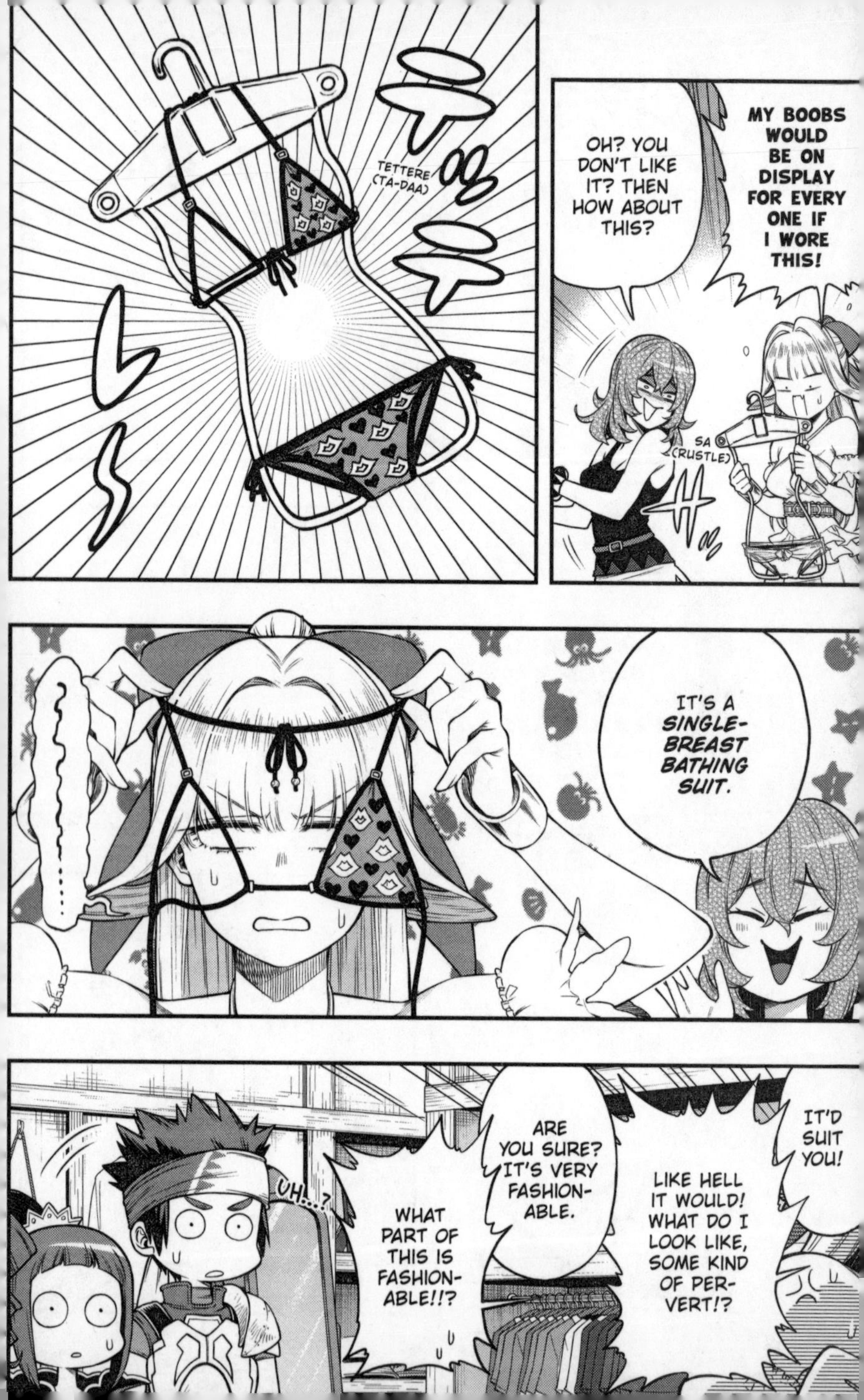
MY BOOBS WOULD BE ON DISPLAY FOR EVERY ONE IF I WORE THIS!
OH? YOU DON'T LIKE IT? THEN HOW ABOUT THIS?
SA (RUSTLE)
TETTERE (TA-DAA)
IT'S A *SINGLE-BREAST BATHING SUIT.*
IT'D SUIT YOU!
LIKE HELL IT WOULD! WHAT DO I LOOK LIKE, SOME KIND OF PER-VERT!?
ARE YOU SURE? IT'S VERY FASHION-ABLE.
WHAT PART OF THIS IS FASHION-ABLE!!?
UH...?

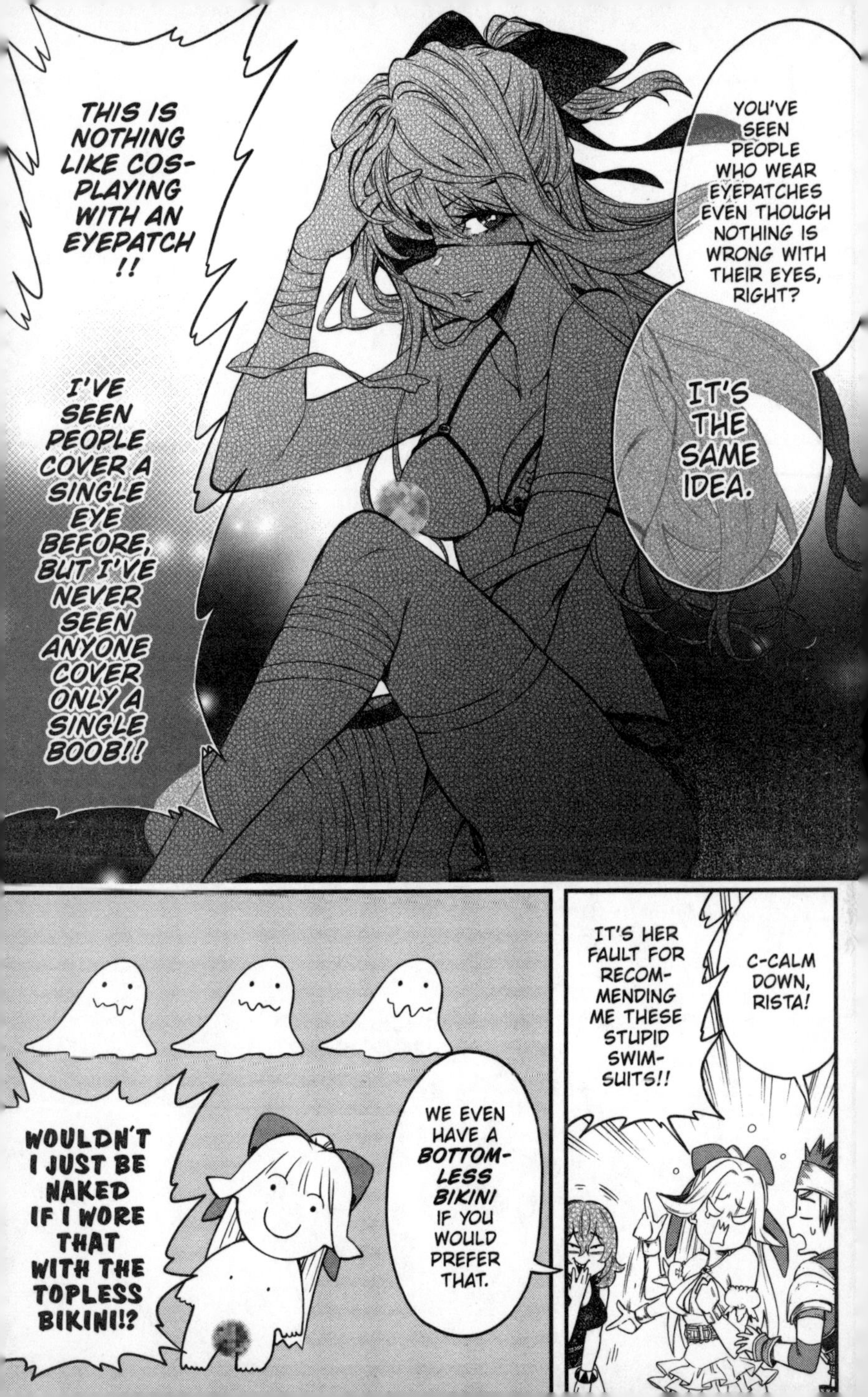
YOU'VE SEEN PEOPLE WHO WEAR EYEPATCHES EVEN THOUGH NOTHING IS WRONG WITH THEIR EYES, RIGHT?
IT'S THE SAME IDEA.
THIS IS NOTHING LIKE COS-PLAYING WITH AN EYEPATCH!!
I'VE SEEN PEOPLE COVER A SINGLE EYE BEFORE, BUT I'VE NEVER SEEN ANYONE COVER ONLY A SINGLE BOOB!!
C-CALM DOWN, RISTA!
IT'S HER FAULT FOR RECOM-MENDING ME THESE STUPID SWIM-SUITS!!
WE EVEN HAVE A *BOTTOM-LESS BIKINI* IF YOU WOULD PREFER THAT.
WOULDN'T I JUST BE NAKED IF I WORE THAT WITH THE TOPLESS BIKINI!?

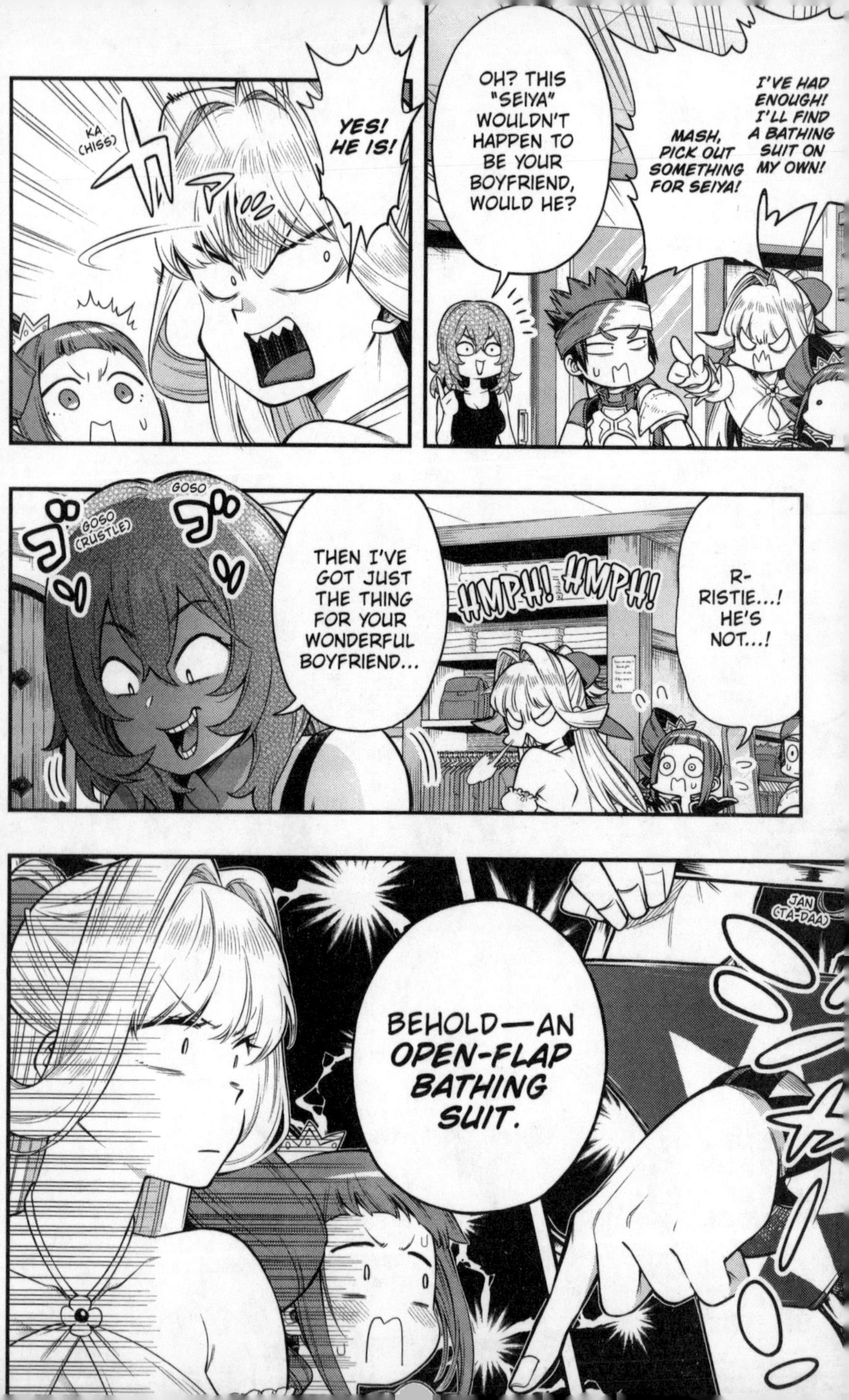
I'VE HAD ENOUGH! I'LL FIND A BATHING SUIT ON MY OWN!
MASH, PICK OUT SOMETHING FOR SEIYA!
OH? THIS "SEIYA" WOULDN'T HAPPEN TO BE YOUR BOYFRIEND, WOULD HE?
YES! HE IS!
KA (HISS)
R-RISTIE...! HE'S NOT...!
HMPH! HMPH!
THEN I'VE GOT JUST THE THING FOR YOUR WONDERFUL BOYFRIEND...
GOSO
GOSO (RUSTLE)
JAN (TA-DAA)
BEHOLD—AN *OPEN-FLAP BATHING SUIT*.

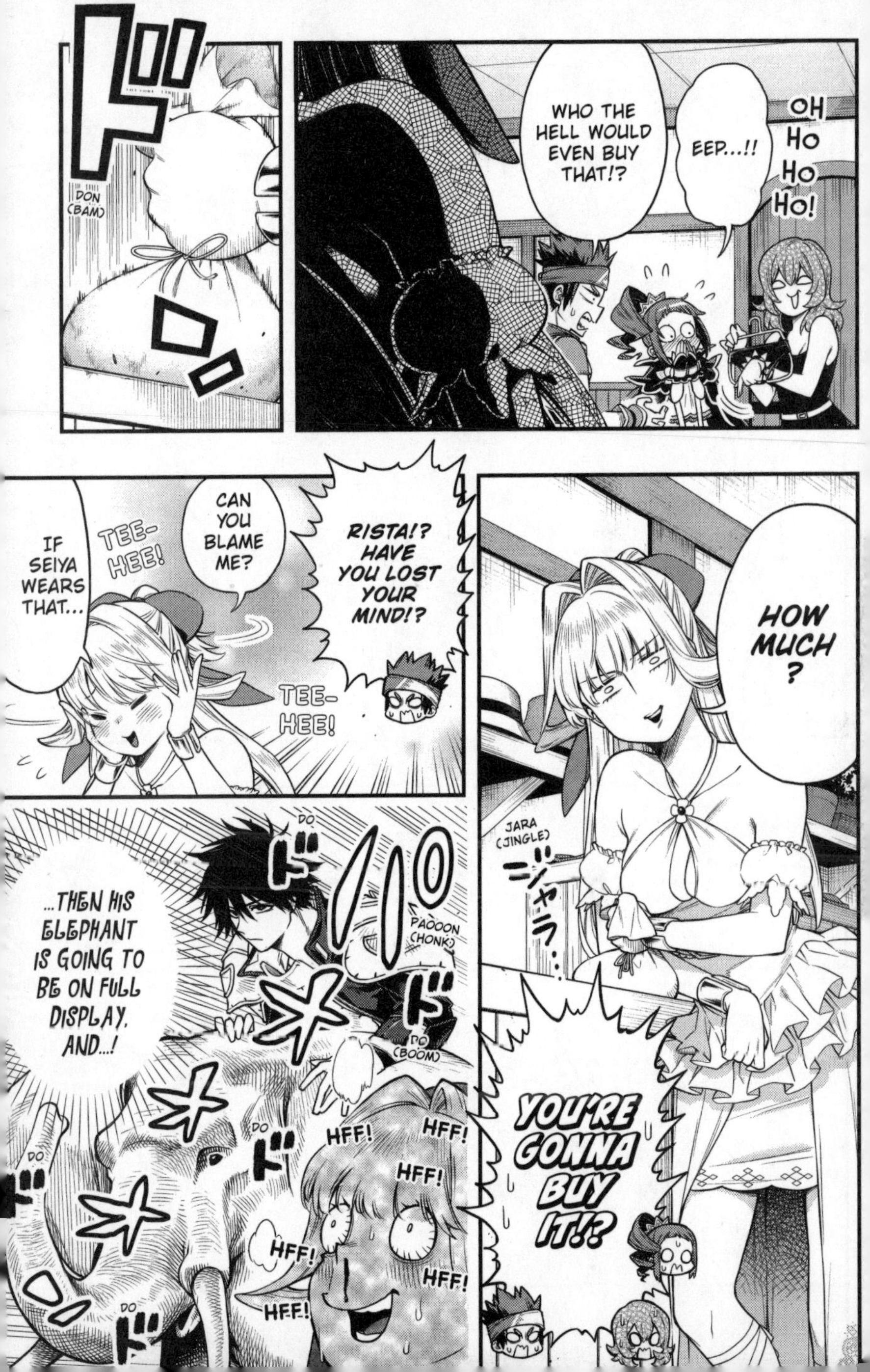
OH HO HO HO!
EEP...!!
WHO THE HELL WOULD EVEN BUY THAT!?
DON (BAM)
HOW MUCH?
JARA (JINGLE)
YOU'RE GONNA BUY IT!?
RISTA!? HAVE YOU LOST YOUR MIND!?
CAN YOU BLAME ME?
TEE-HEE!
IF SEIYA WEARS THAT...
TEE-HEE!
DO
PAOOON (HONK)
DO (BOOM)
...THEN HIS ELEPHANT IS GOING TO BE ON FULL DISPLAY, AND...!
HFF!
HFF!
HFF!
HFF!
HFF!
HFF!
DO
DO
DO

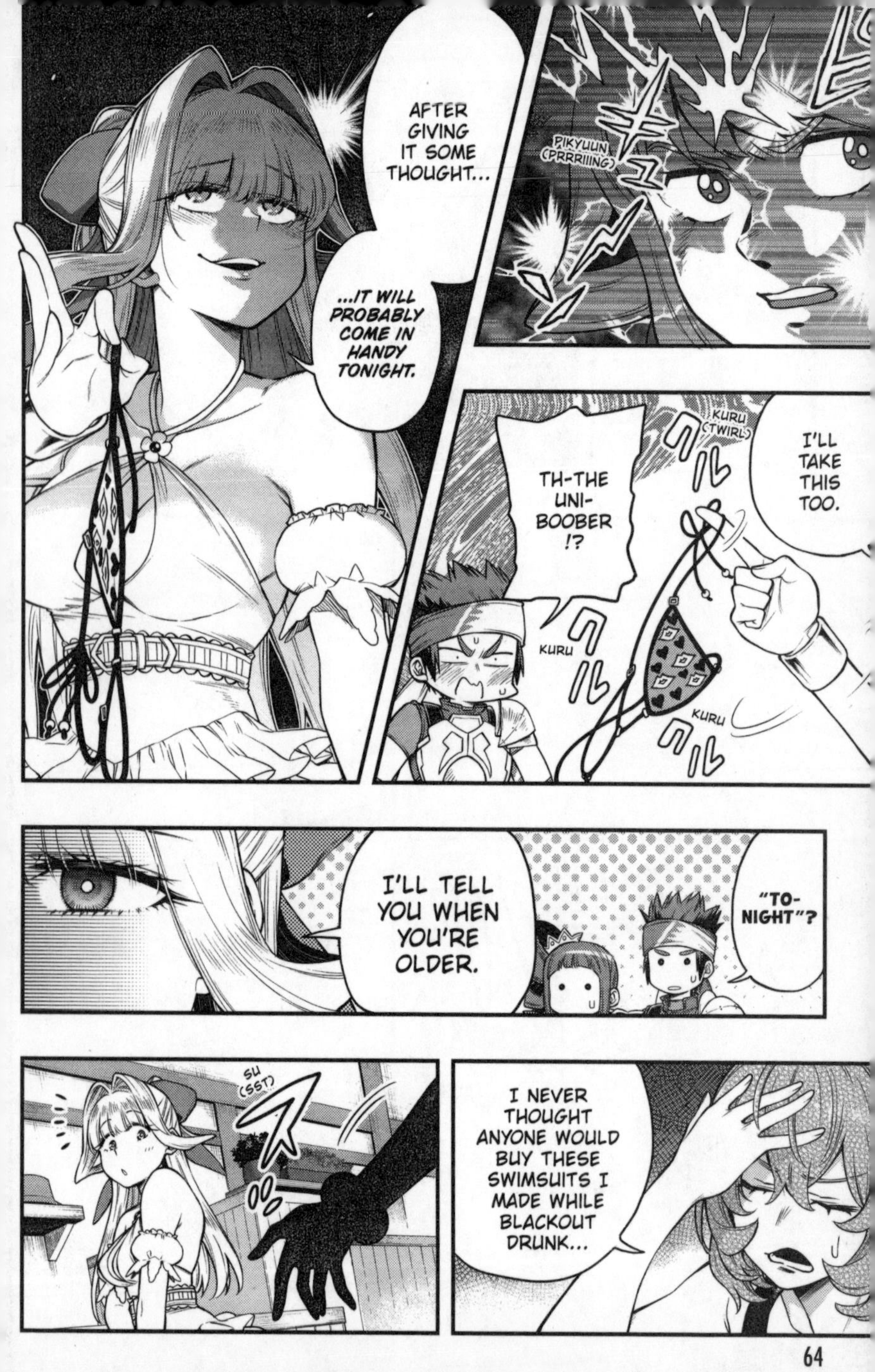
PIKYUUN (PRRRIIING)
I'LL TAKE THIS TOO.
KURU (TWIRL)
TH-THE UNI-BOOBER!?
KURU
KURU
AFTER GIVING IT SOME THOUGHT...
...IT WILL PROBABLY COME IN HANDY TONIGHT.
"TO-NIGHT"?
I'LL TELL YOU WHEN YOU'RE OLDER.
I NEVER THOUGHT ANYONE WOULD BUY THESE SWIMSUITS I MADE WHILE BLACKOUT DRUNK...
SU (SST)

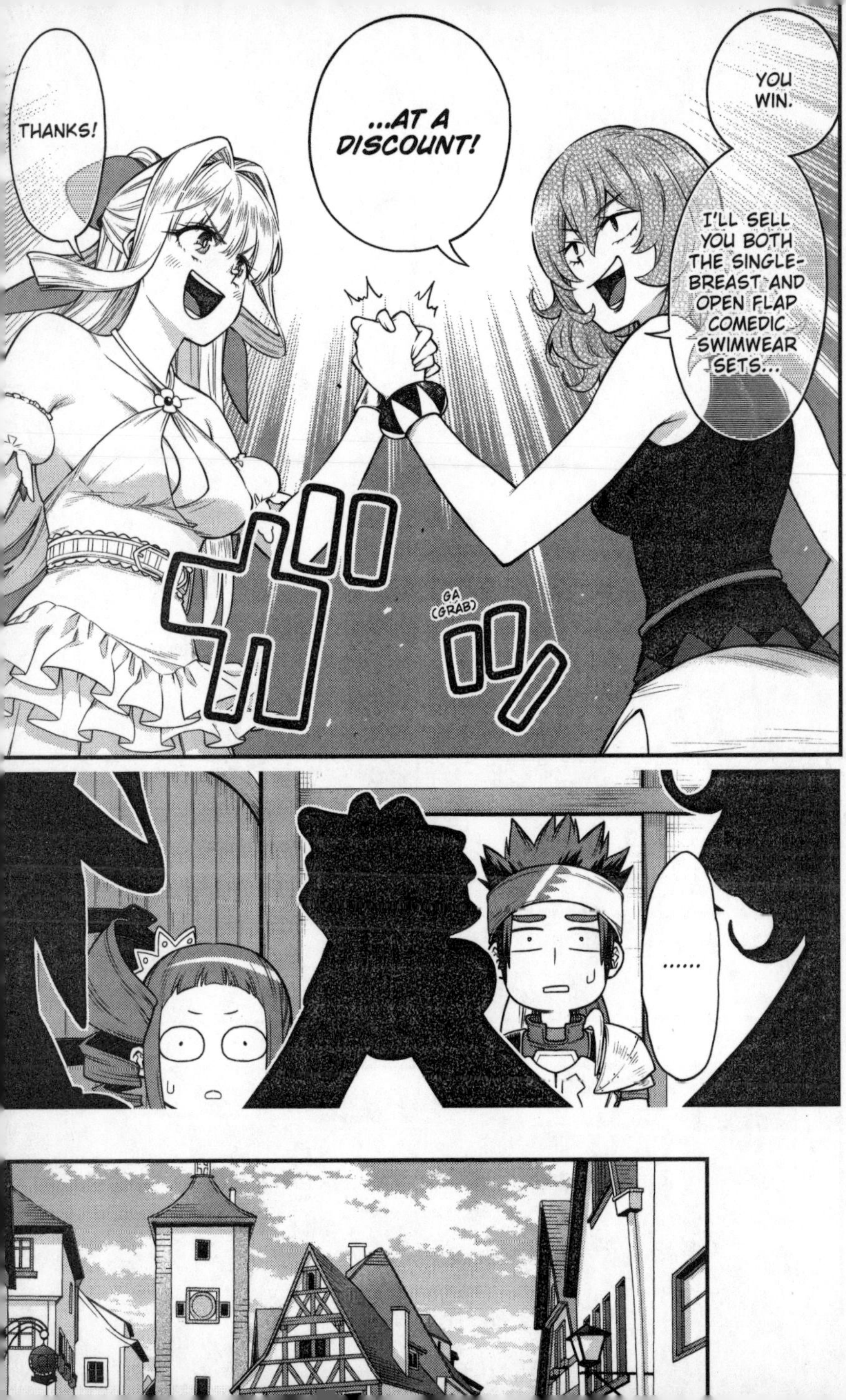
YOU WIN.
I'LL SELL YOU BOTH THE SINGLE-BREAST AND OPEN FLAP COMEDIC SWIMWEAR SETS...
...AT A DISCOUNT!
THANKS!
GA (GRAB)
......

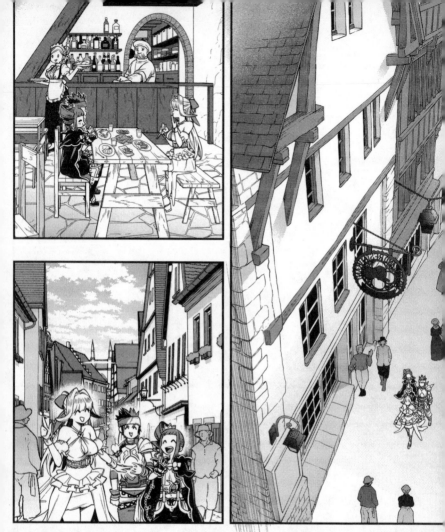

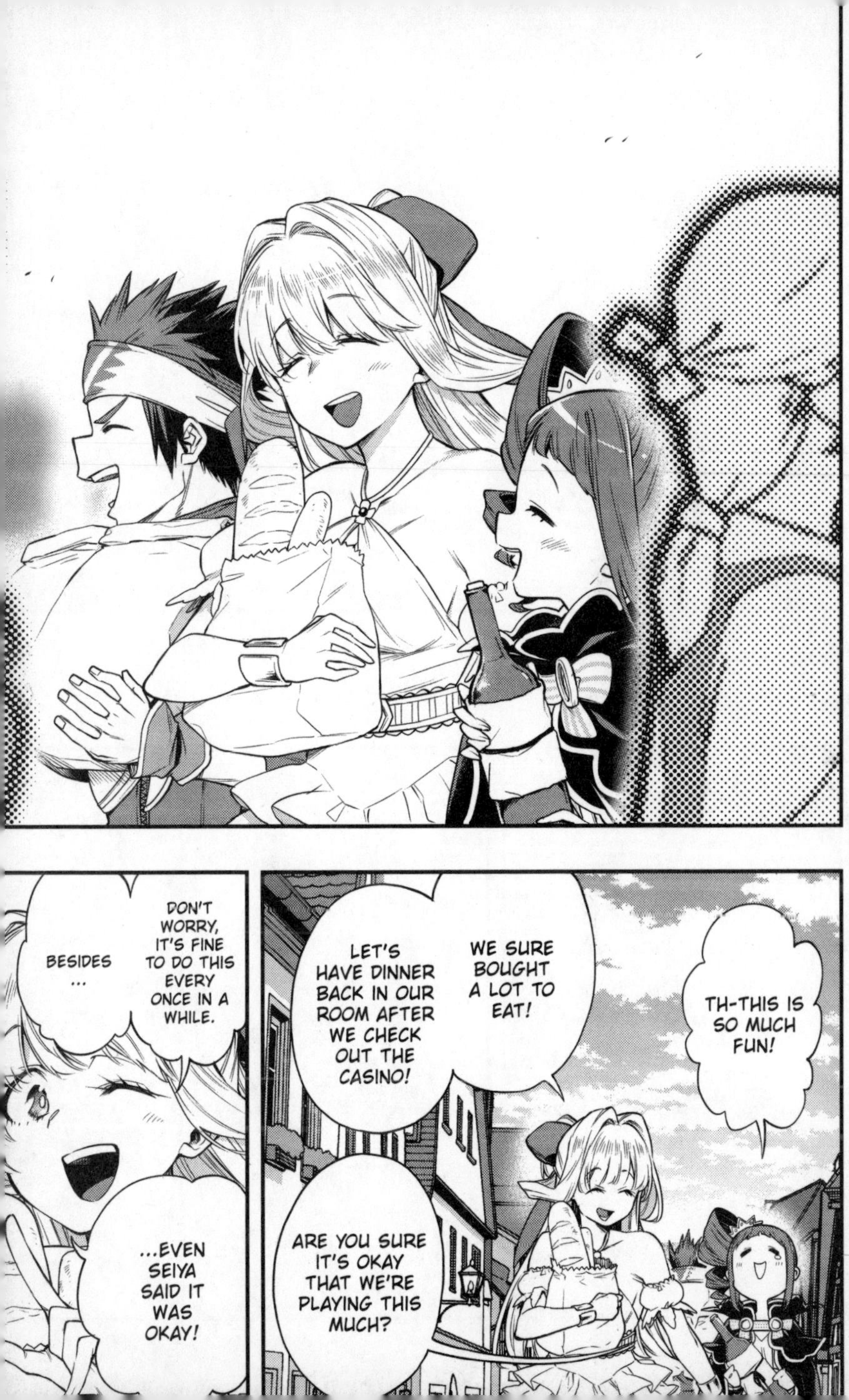
TH-THIS IS SO MUCH FUN!
WE SURE BOUGHT A LOT TO EAT!
LET'S HAVE DINNER BACK IN OUR ROOM AFTER WE CHECK OUT THE CASINO!
ARE YOU SURE IT'S OKAY THAT WE'RE PLAYING THIS MUCH?
DON'T WORRY, IT'S FINE TO DO THIS EVERY ONCE IN A WHILE.
BESIDES ...
...EVEN SEIYA SAID IT WAS OKAY!

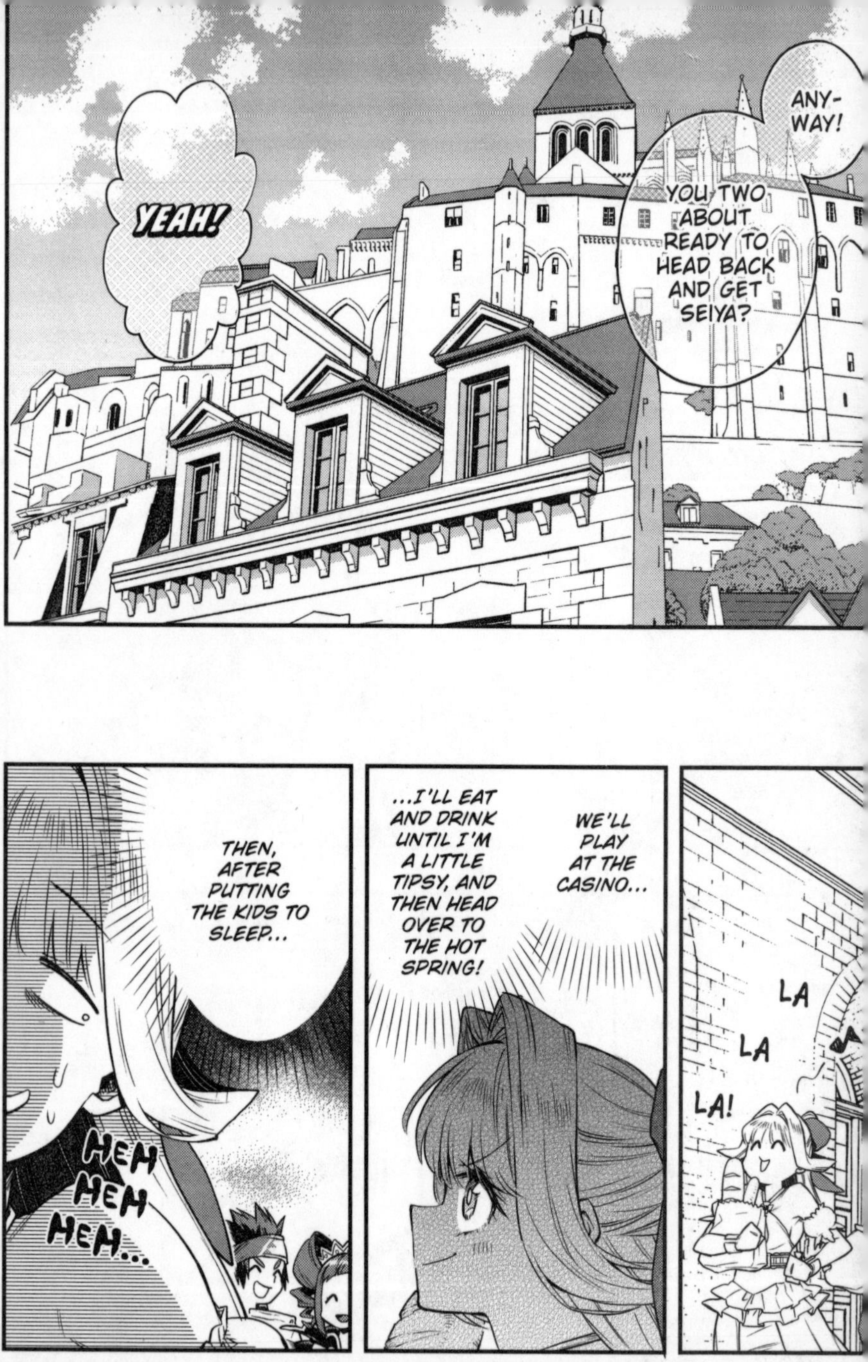
ANY-WAY!
YOU TWO ABOUT READY TO HEAD BACK AND GET SEIYA?
YEAH!
LA LA LA!
WE'LL PLAY AT THE CASINO...
...I'LL EAT AND DRINK UNTIL I'M A LITTLE TIPSY, AND THEN HEAD OVER TO THE HOT SPRING!
THEN, AFTER PUTTING THE KIDS TO SLEEP...
HEH HEH HEH...

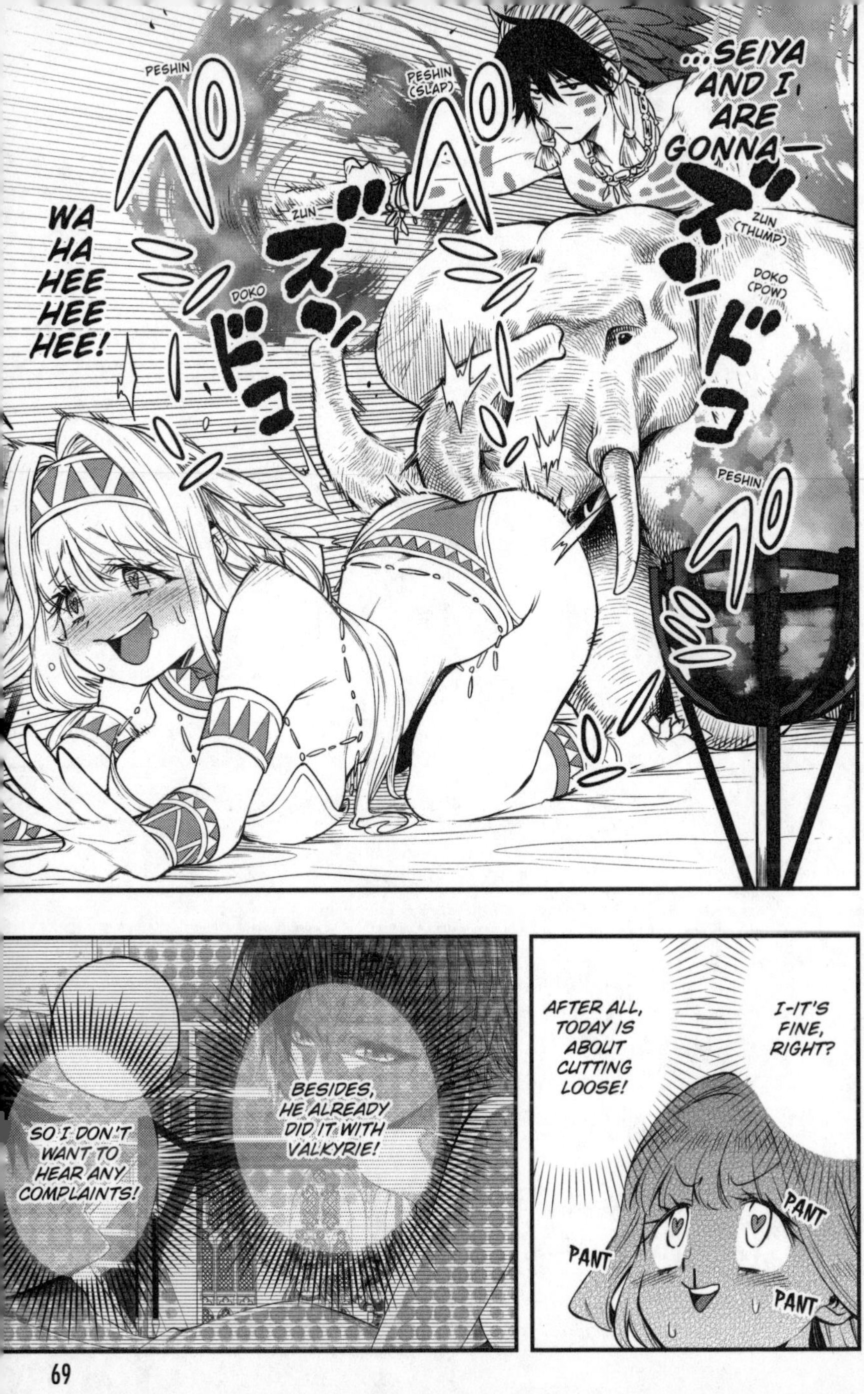
...SEIYA AND I ARE GONNA—
PESHIN (SLAP)
PESHIN
ZUN (THUMP)
DOKO (POW)
ZUN
DOKO
WA HA HEE HEE HEE!
PESHIN
I-IT'S FINE, RIGHT?
AFTER ALL, TODAY IS ABOUT CUTTING LOOSE!
PANT
PANT
PANT
BESIDES, HE ALREADY DID IT WITH VALKYRIE!
SO I DON'T WANT TO HEAR ANY COMPLAINTS!

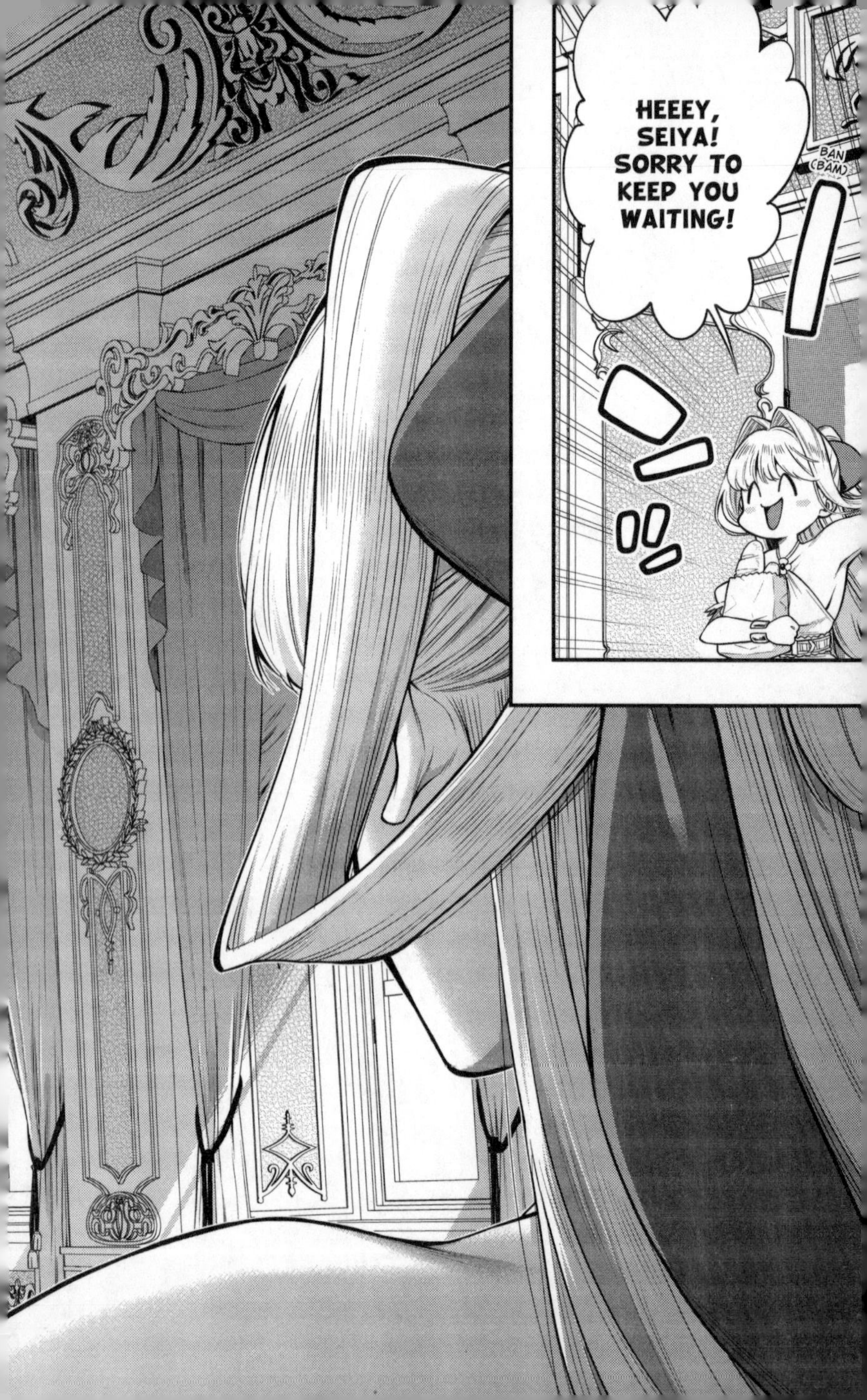
HEEEY, SEIYA! SORRY TO KEEP YOU WAITING!
BAN (BAM)

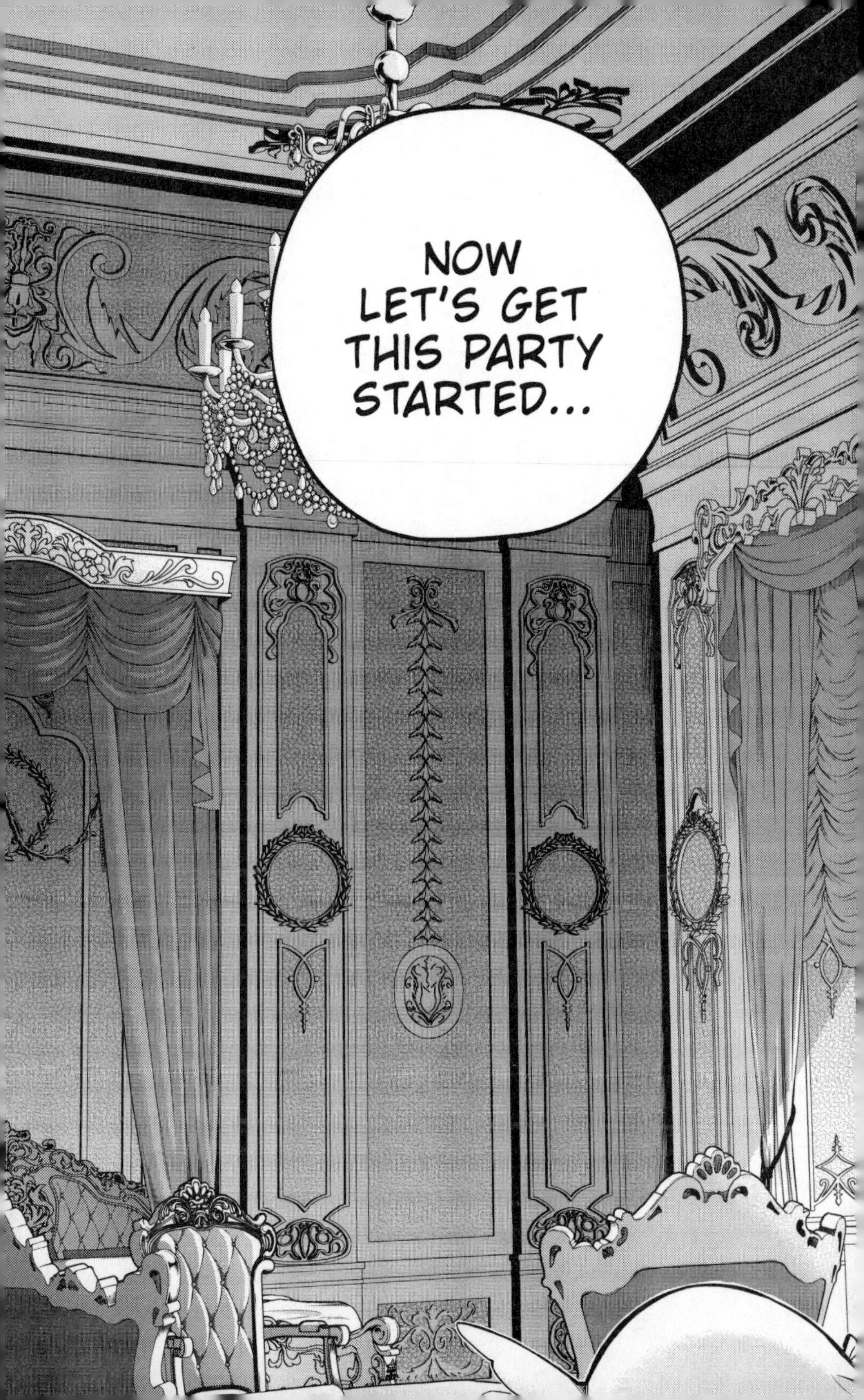
NOW LET'S GET THIS PARTY STARTED...

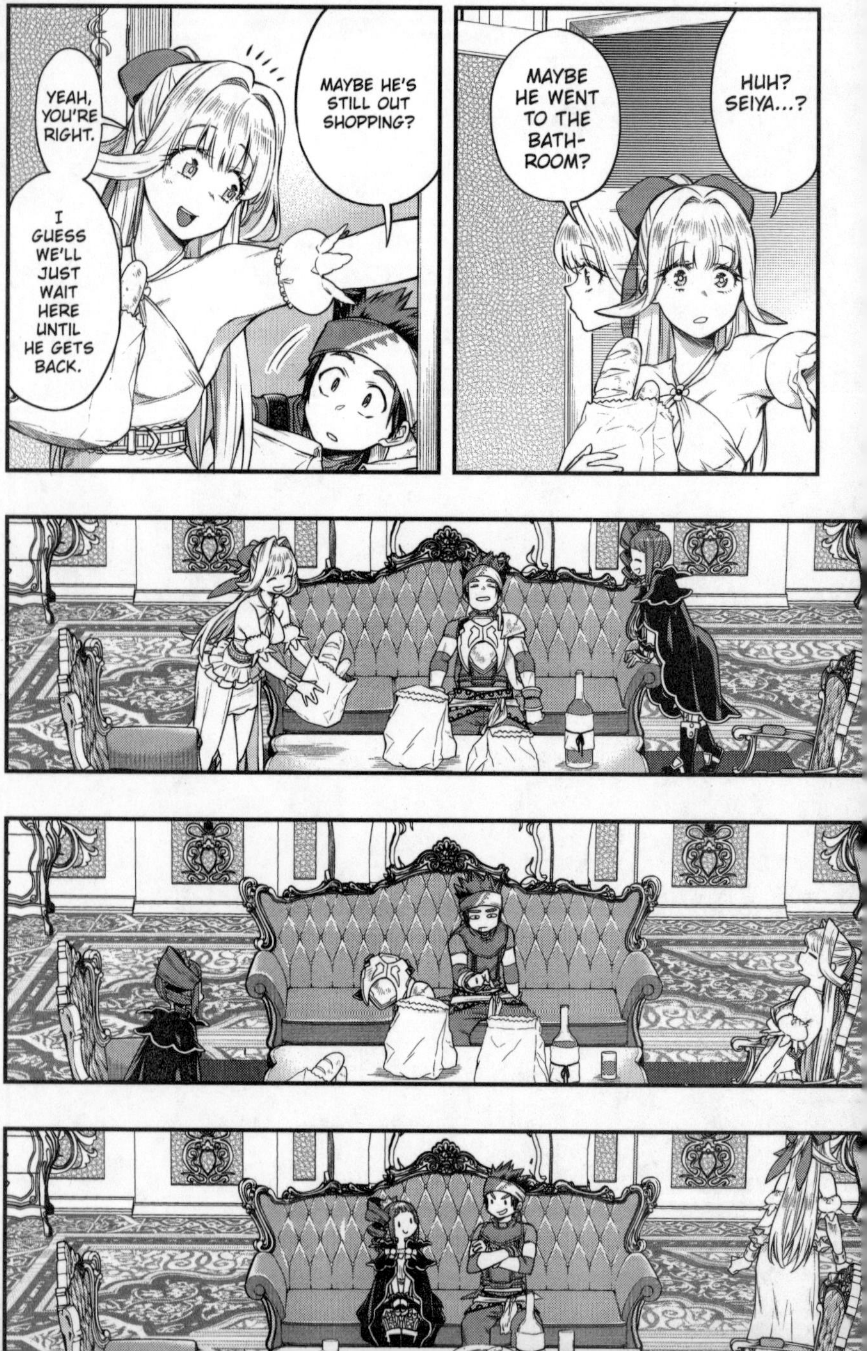
HUH? SEIYA...?
MAYBE HE WENT TO THE BATH-ROOM?
MAYBE HE'S STILL OUT SHOPPING?
YEAH, YOU'RE RIGHT.
I GUESS WE'LL JUST WAIT HERE UNTIL HE GETS BACK.

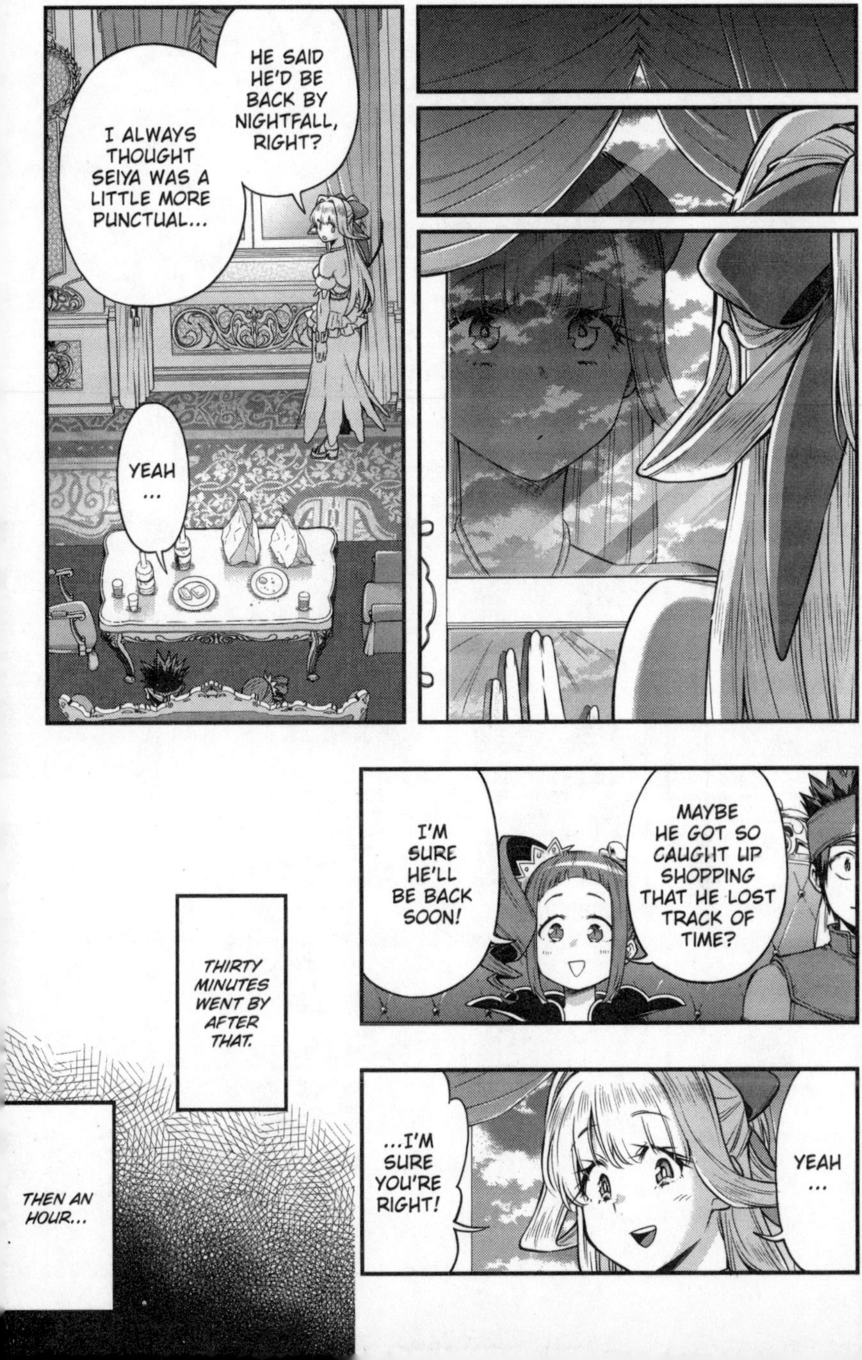
HE SAID HE'D BE BACK BY NIGHTFALL, RIGHT?
I ALWAYS THOUGHT SEIYA WAS A LITTLE MORE PUNCTUAL...
YEAH...
MAYBE HE GOT SO CAUGHT UP SHOPPING THAT HE LOST TRACK OF TIME?
I'M SURE HE'LL BE BACK SOON!
YEAH...
...I'M SURE YOU'RE RIGHT!
THIRTY MINUTES WENT BY AFTER THAT.
THEN AN HOUR...

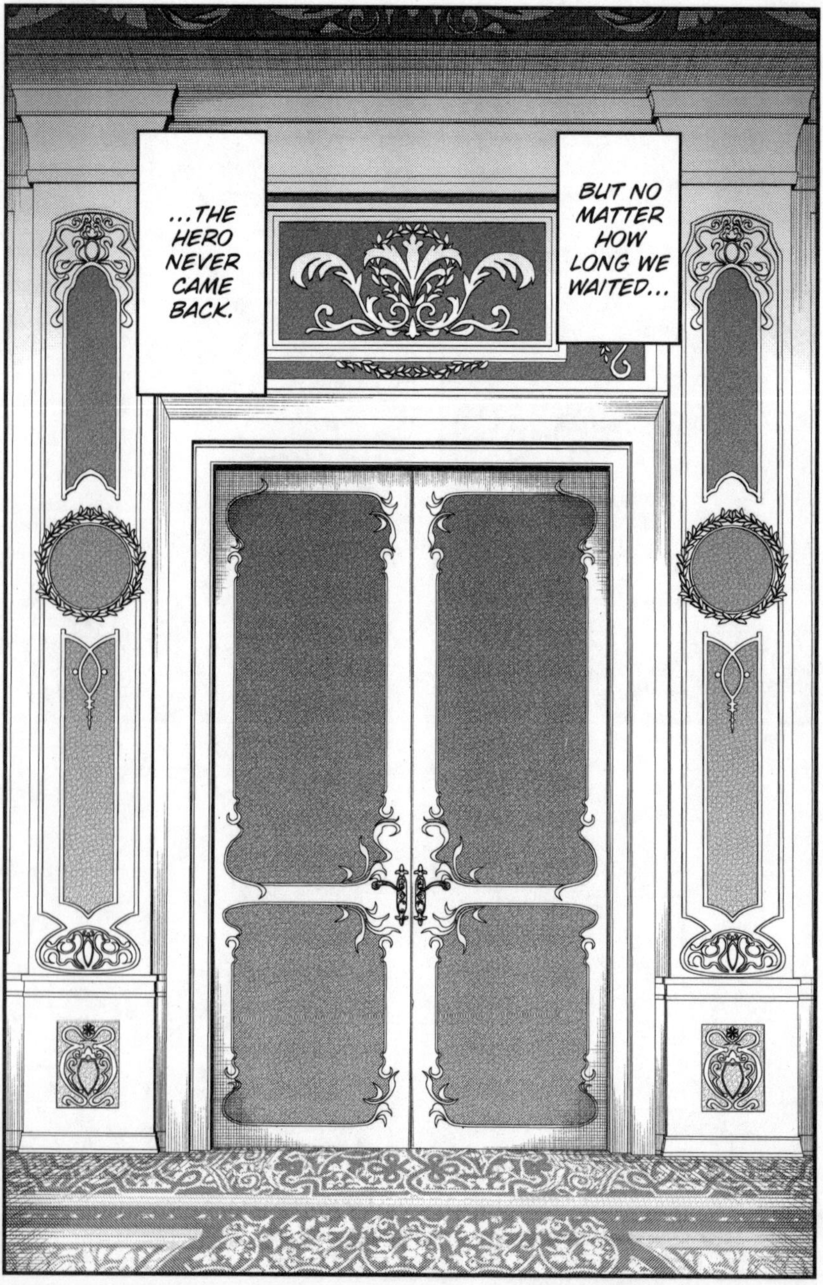
BUT NO MATTER HOW LONG WE WAITED...
...THE HERO NEVER CAME BACK.

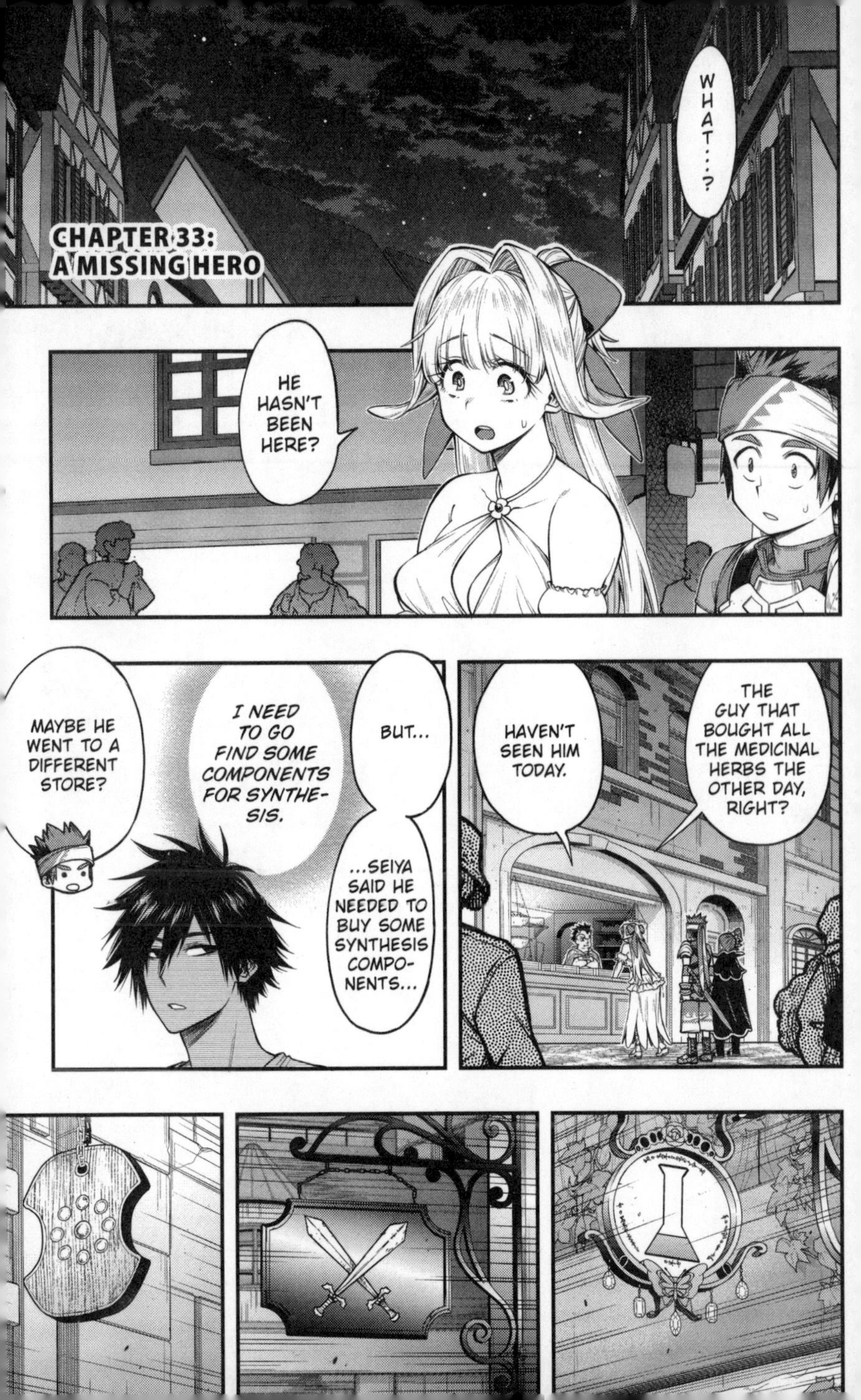
WHAT...?
CHAPTER 33: A MISSING HERO
HE HASN'T BEEN HERE?
THE GUY THAT BOUGHT ALL THE MEDICINAL HERBS THE OTHER DAY, RIGHT?
HAVEN'T SEEN HIM TODAY.
BUT...
...SEIYA SAID HE NEEDED TO BUY SOME SYNTHESIS COMPO-NENTS...
I NEED TO GO FIND SOME COMPONENTS FOR SYNTHE-SIS.
MAYBE HE WENT TO A DIFFERENT STORE?

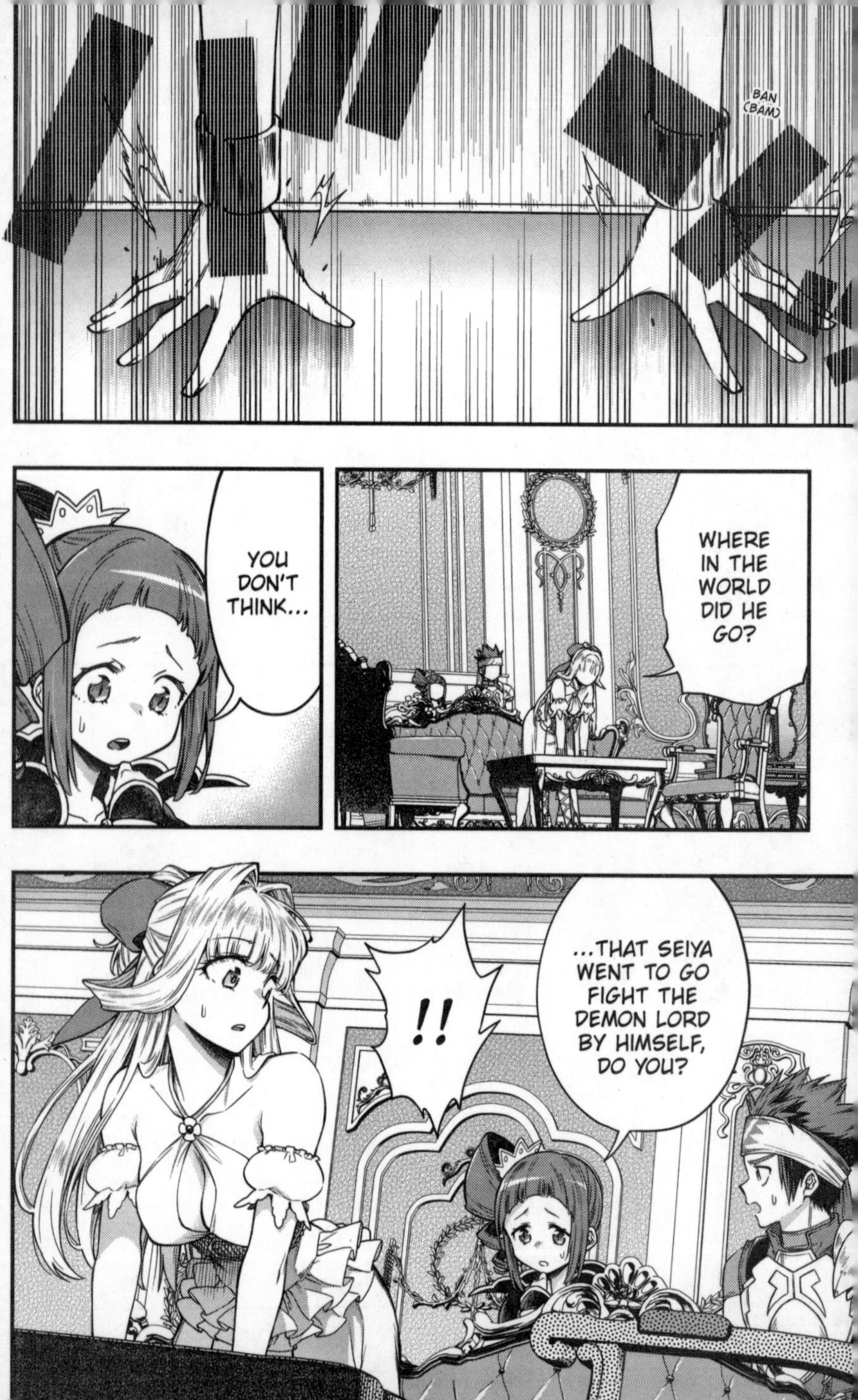
BAN (BAM)
WHERE IN THE WORLD DID HE GO?
YOU DON'T THINK...
...THAT SEIYA WENT TO GO FIGHT THE DEMON LORD BY HIMSELF, DO YOU?
!!

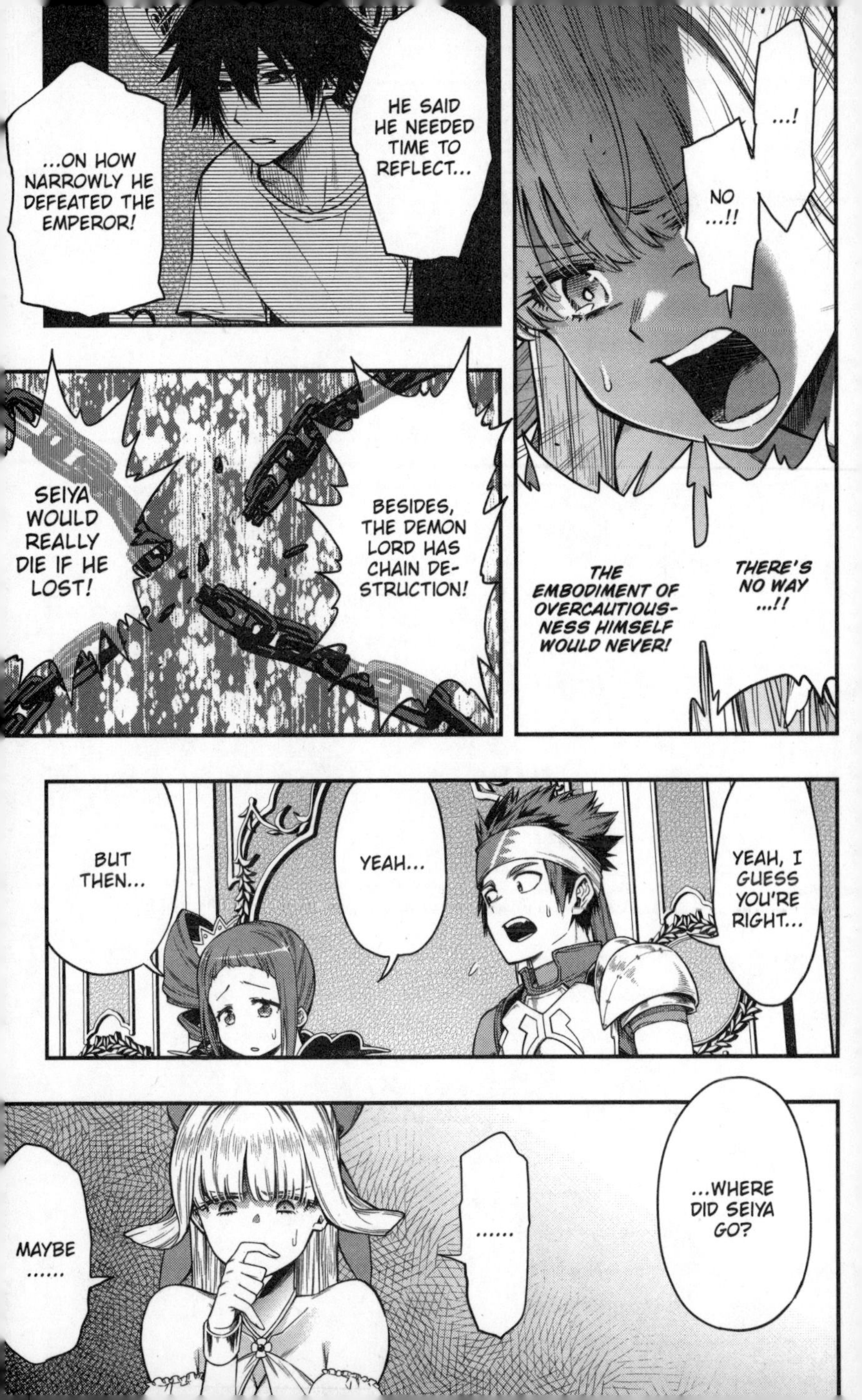
...!
NO ...!!
THERE'S NO WAY ...!!
THE EMBODIMENT OF OVERCAUTIOUSNESS HIMSELF WOULD NEVER!
HE SAID HE NEEDED TIME TO REFLECT...
...ON HOW NARROWLY HE DEFEATED THE EMPEROR!
BESIDES, THE DEMON LORD HAS CHAIN DESTRUCTION!
SEIYA WOULD REALLY DIE IF HE LOST!
YEAH, I GUESS YOU'RE RIGHT...
YEAH...
BUT THEN...
...WHERE DID SEIYA GO?
......
MAYBE ......

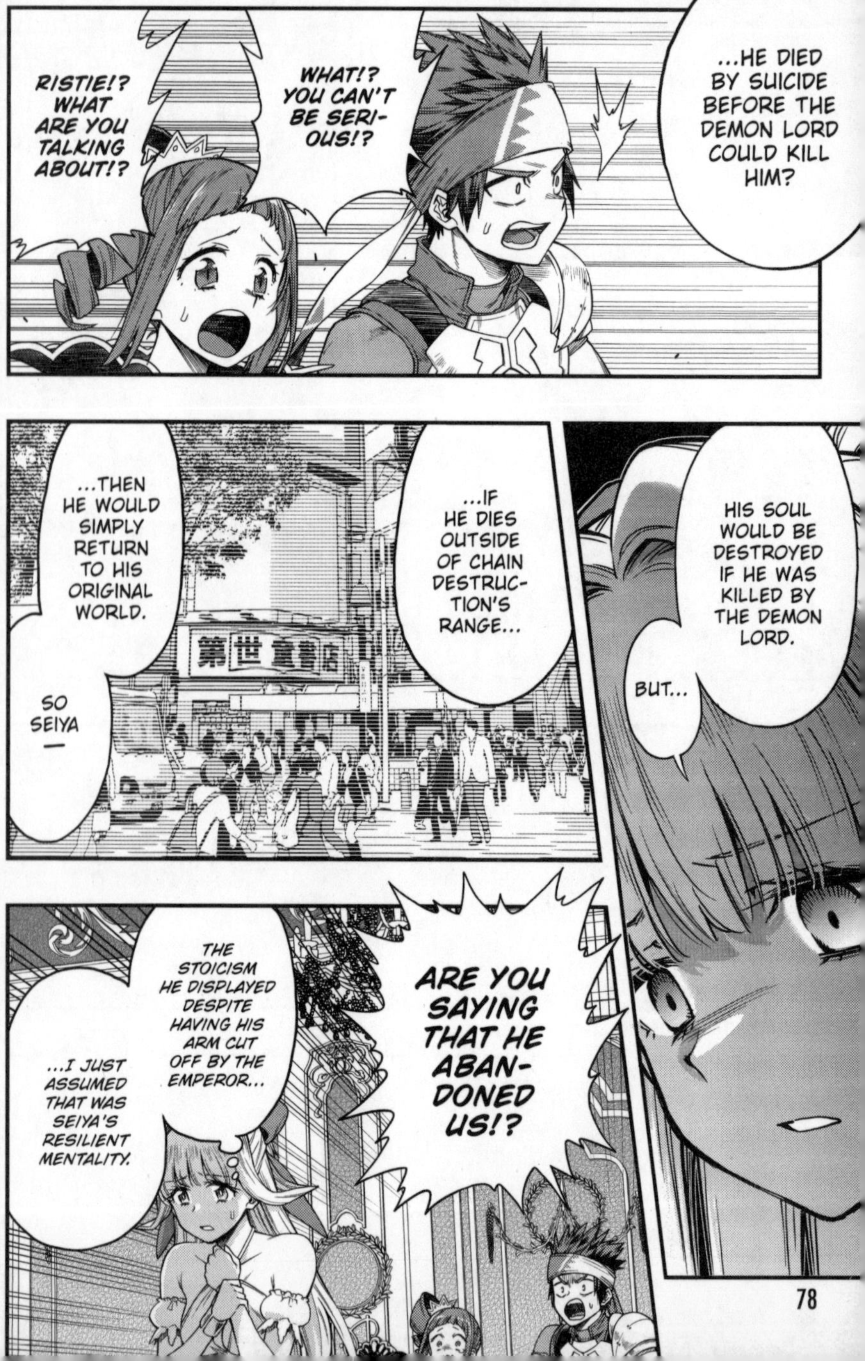
...HE DIED BY SUICIDE BEFORE THE DEMON LORD COULD KILL HIM?
WHAT!? YOU CAN'T BE SERI-OUS!?
RISTIE!? WHAT ARE YOU TALKING ABOUT!?
HIS SOUL WOULD BE DESTROYED IF HE WAS KILLED BY THE DEMON LORD.
BUT...
...IF HE DIES OUTSIDE OF CHAIN DESTRUC-TION'S RANGE...
...THEN HE WOULD SIMPLY RETURN TO HIS ORIGINAL WORLD.
SO SEIYA—
ARE YOU SAYING THAT HE ABAN-DONED US!?
THE STOICISM HE DISPLAYED DESPITE HAVING HIS ARM CUT OFF BY THE EMPEROR...
...I JUST ASSUMED THAT WAS SEIYA'S RESILIENT MENTALITY.

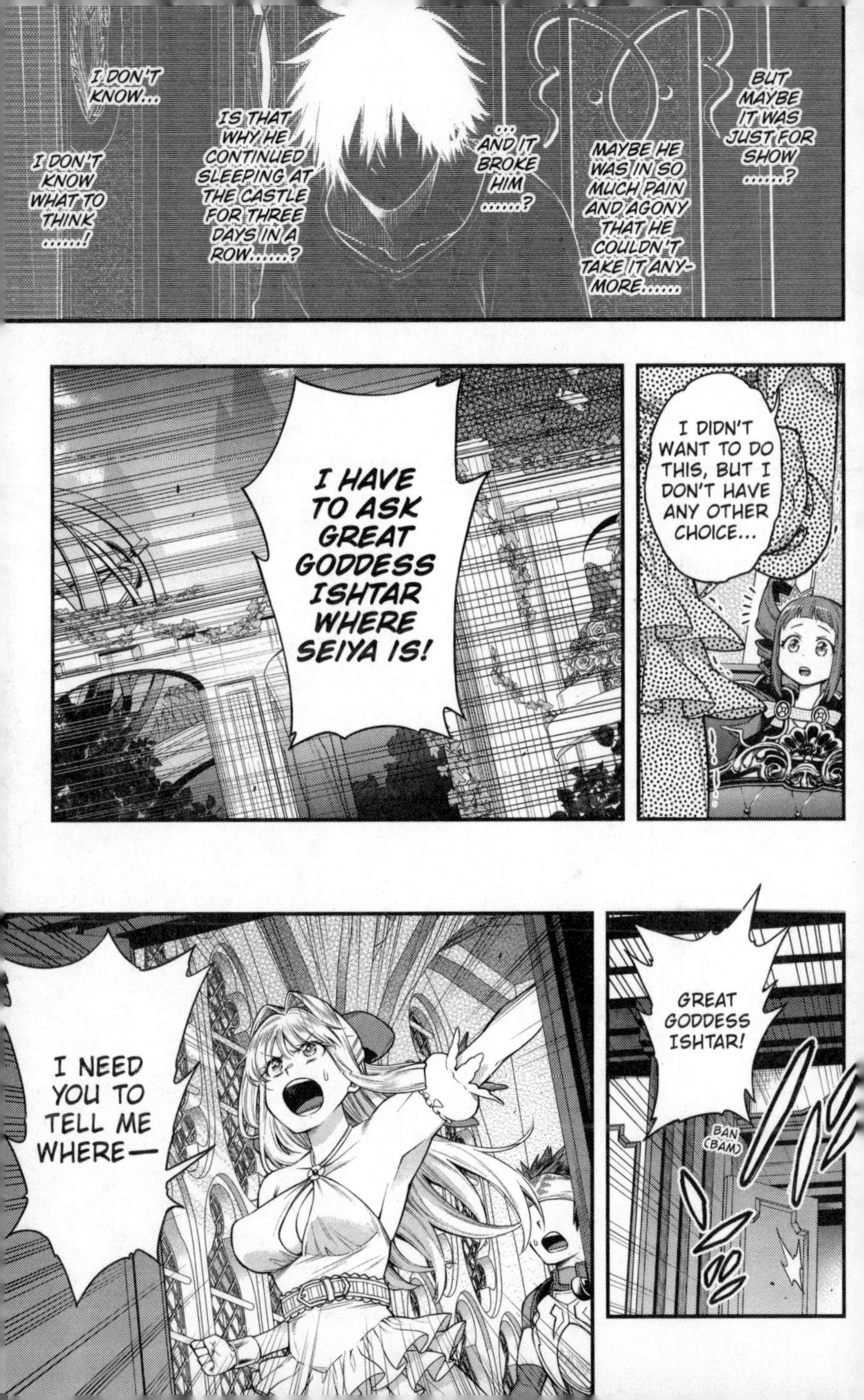
BUT MAYBE IT WAS JUST FOR SHOW ......?
MAYBE HE WAS IN SO MUCH PAIN AND AGONY THAT HE COULDN'T TAKE IT ANY-MORE......
...AND IT BROKE HIM ......?
IS THAT WHY HE CONTINUED SLEEPING AT THE CASTLE FOR THREE DAYS IN A ROW......?
I DON'T KNOW...
I DON'T KNOW WHAT TO THINK ......!
I DIDN'T WANT TO DO THIS, BUT I DON'T HAVE ANY OTHER CHOICE...
I HAVE TO ASK GREAT GODDESS ISHTAR WHERE SEIYA IS!
GREAT GODDESS ISHTAR!
BAN (BAM)
I NEED YOU TO TELL ME WHERE—

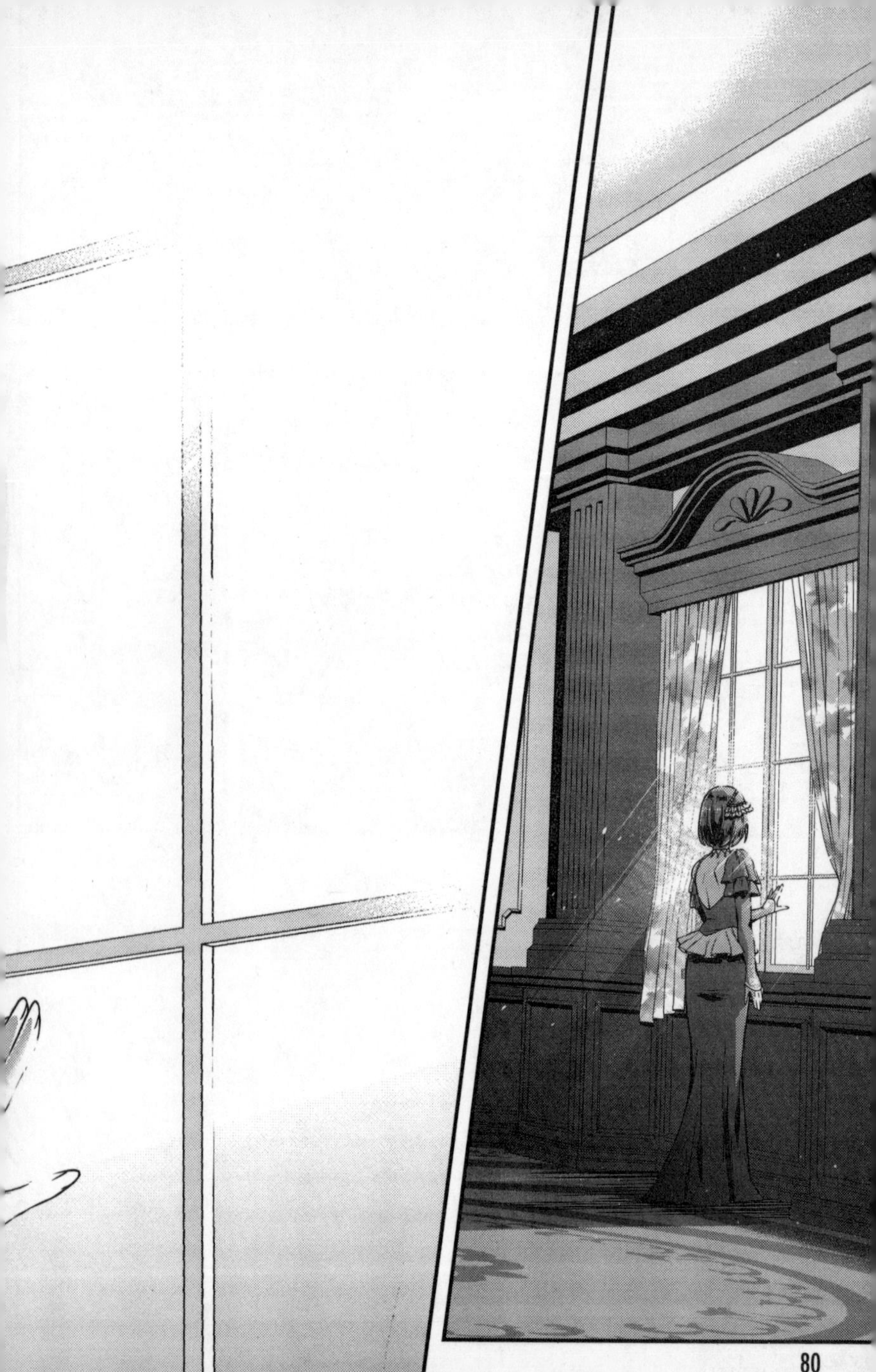

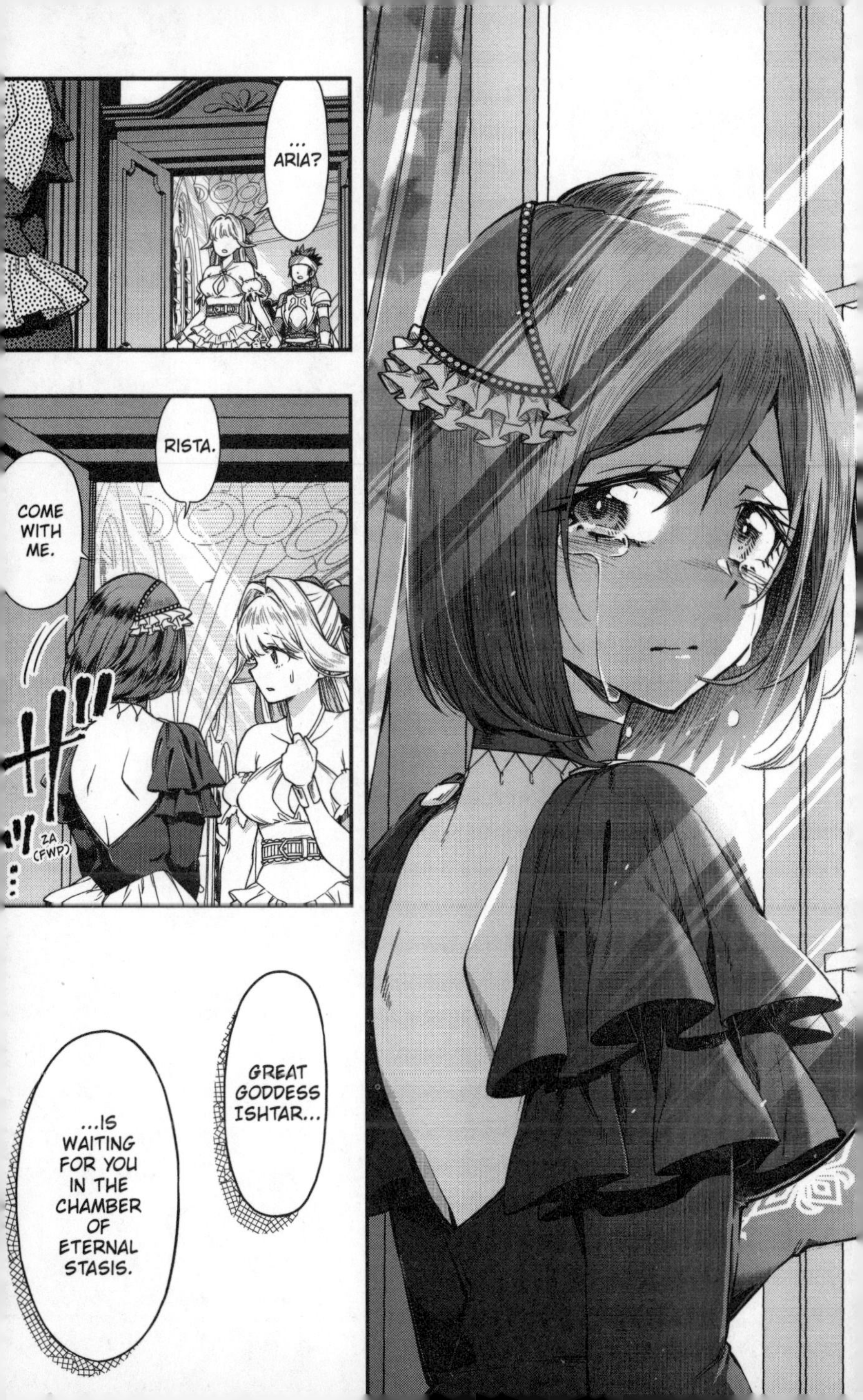
...ARIA?
RISTA.
COME WITH ME.
ZA (FWP)
...
GREAT GODDESS ISHTAR...
...IS WAITING FOR YOU IN THE CHAMBER OF ETERNAL STASIS.

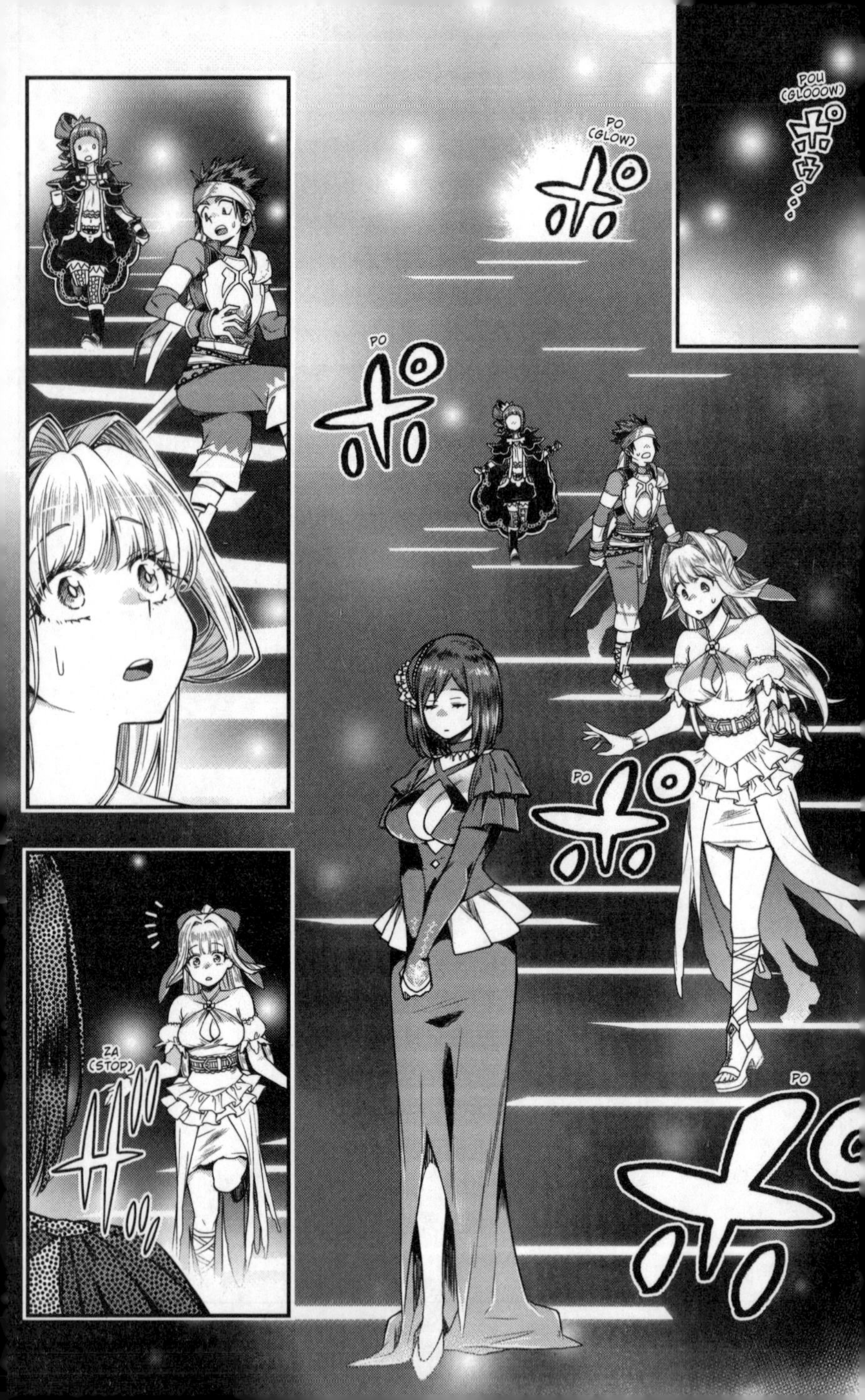
POU
(GLOOOW)
PO
(GLOW)
PO
PO
PO
ZA
(STOP)

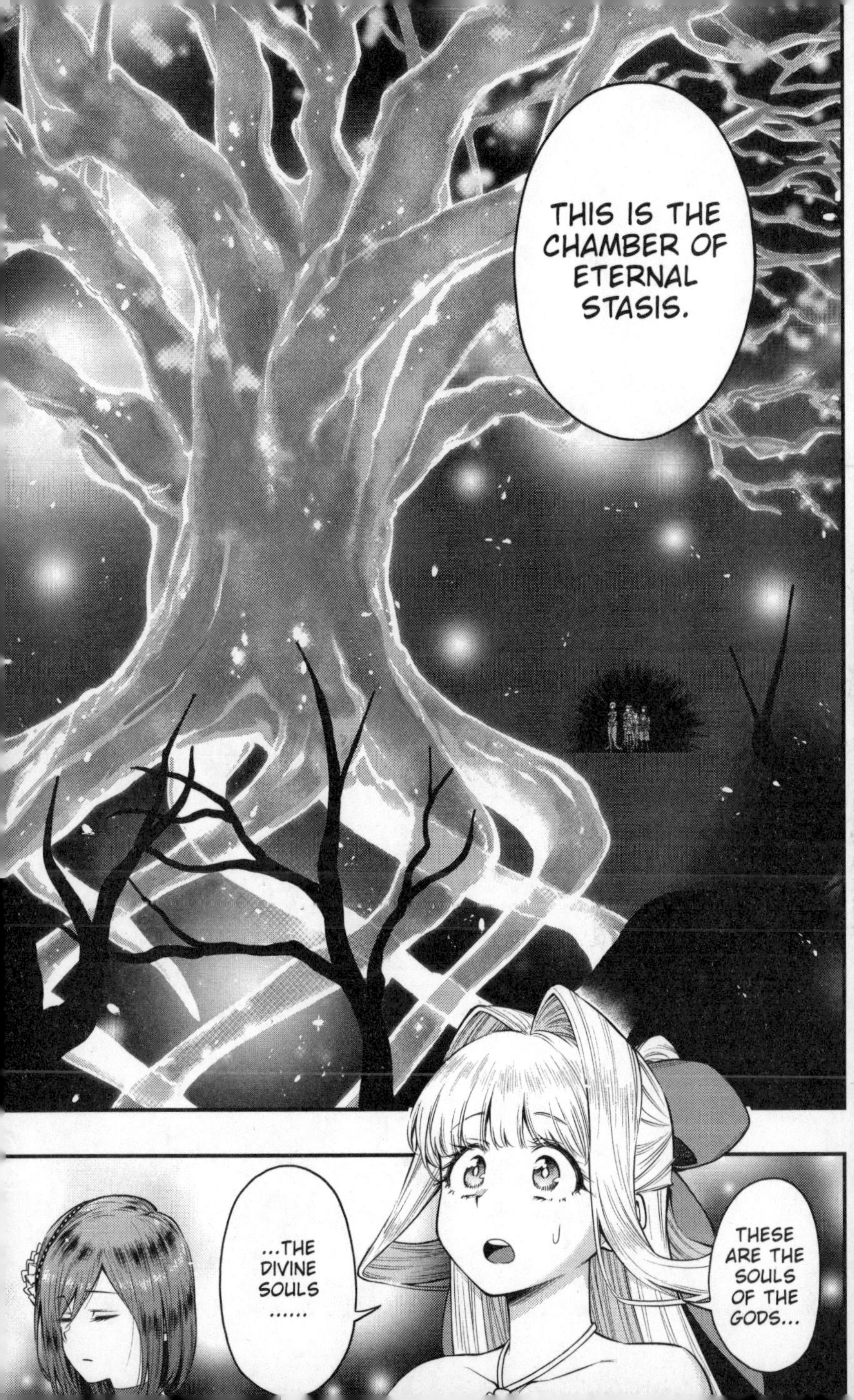
THIS IS THE CHAMBER OF ETERNAL STASIS.
THESE ARE THE SOULS OF THE GODS...
...THE DIVINE SOULS ......

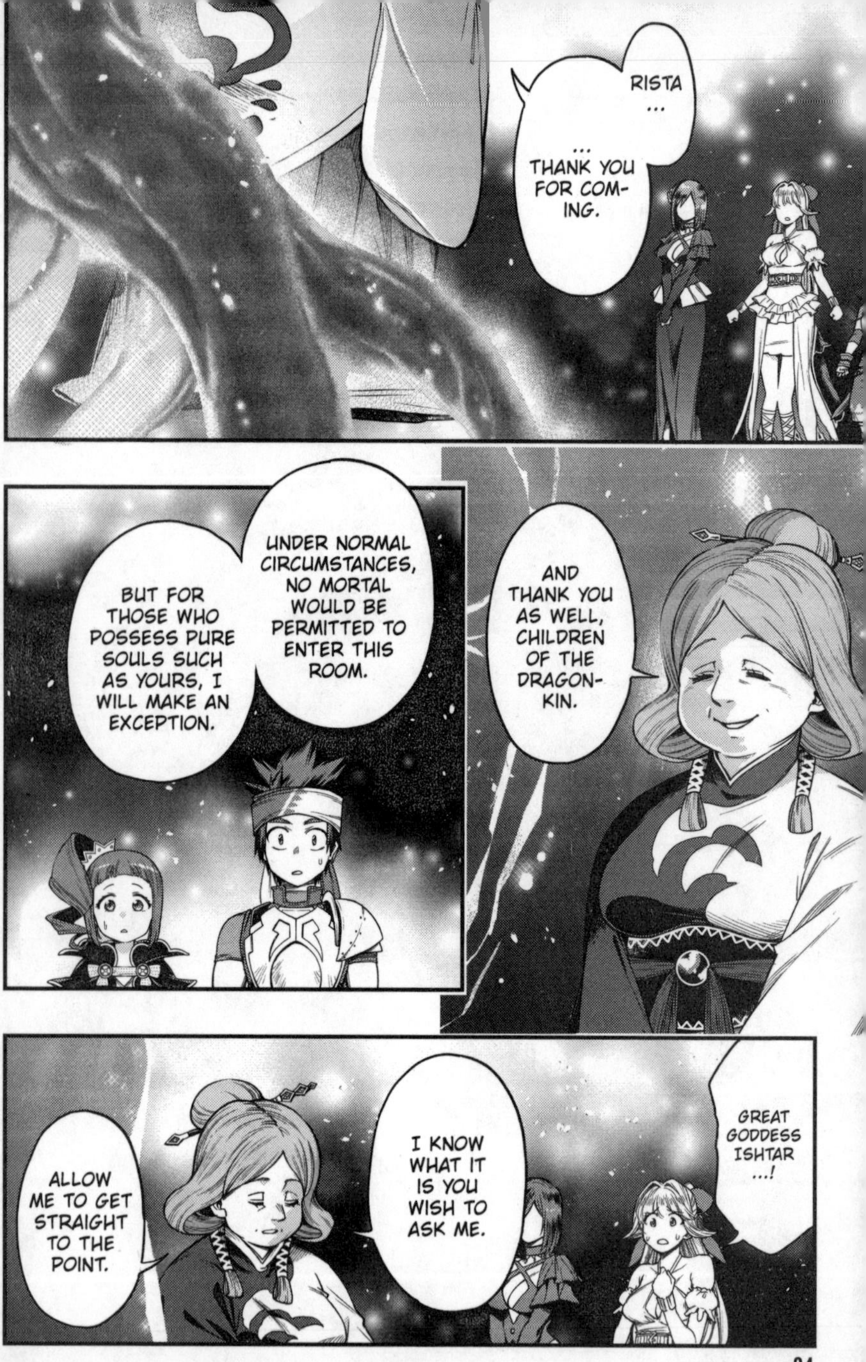
RISTA... ...THANK YOU FOR COMING.
AND THANK YOU AS WELL, CHILDREN OF THE DRAGONKIN.
UNDER NORMAL CIRCUMSTANCES, NO MORTAL WOULD BE PERMITTED TO ENTER THIS ROOM.
BUT FOR THOSE WHO POSSESS PURE SOULS SUCH AS YOURS, I WILL MAKE AN EXCEPTION.
GREAT GODDESS ISHTAR...!
I KNOW WHAT IT IS YOU WISH TO ASK ME.
ALLOW ME TO GET STRAIGHT TO THE POINT.

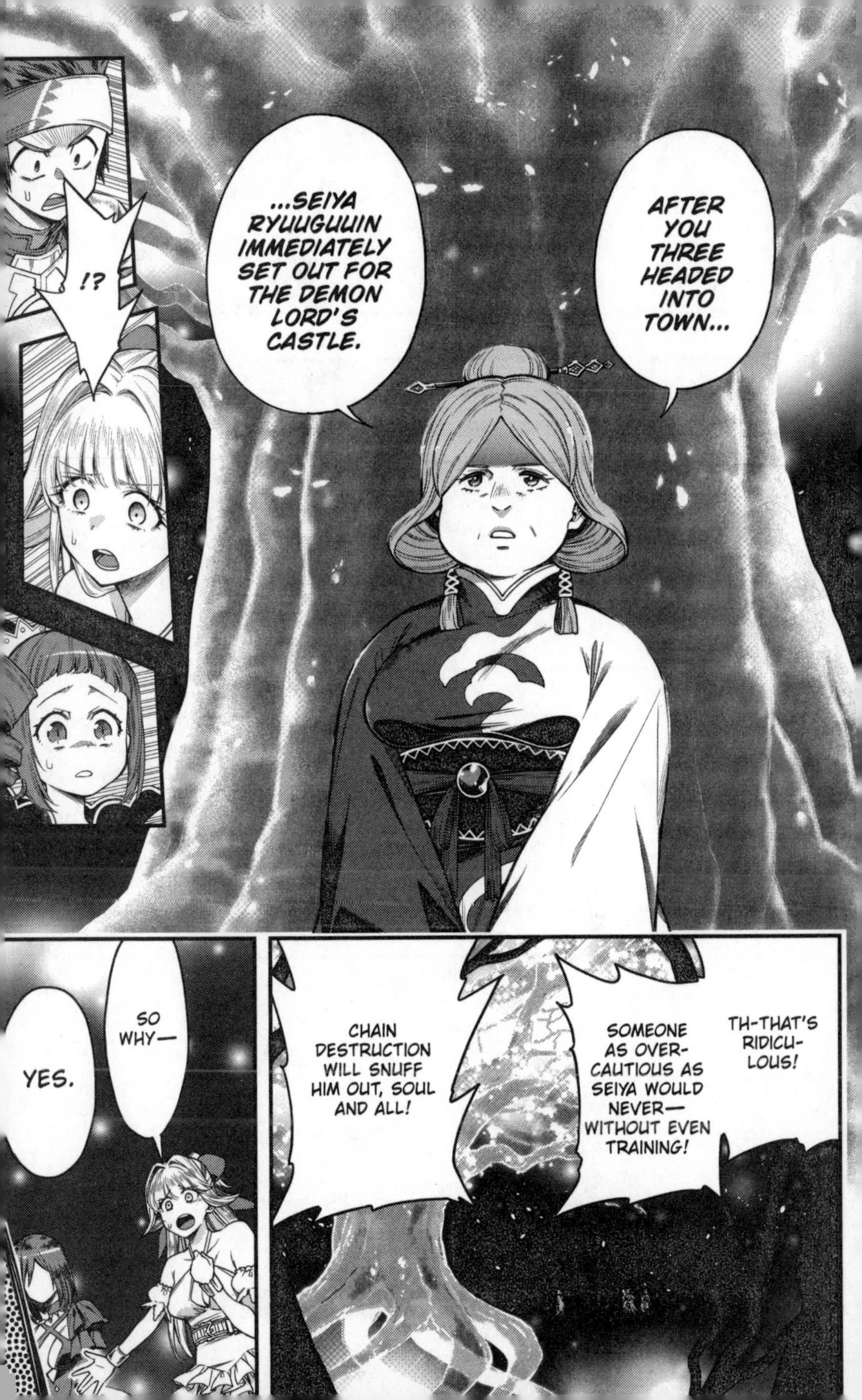
AFTER YOU THREE HEADED INTO TOWN...
...SEIYA RYUUGUUIN IMMEDIATELY SET OUT FOR THE DEMON LORD'S CASTLE.
!?
TH-THAT'S RIDICU-LOUS!
SOMEONE AS OVER-CAUTIOUS AS SEIYA WOULD NEVER— WITHOUT EVEN TRAINING!
CHAIN DESTRUCTION WILL SNUFF HIM OUT, SOUL AND ALL!
SO WHY—
YES.

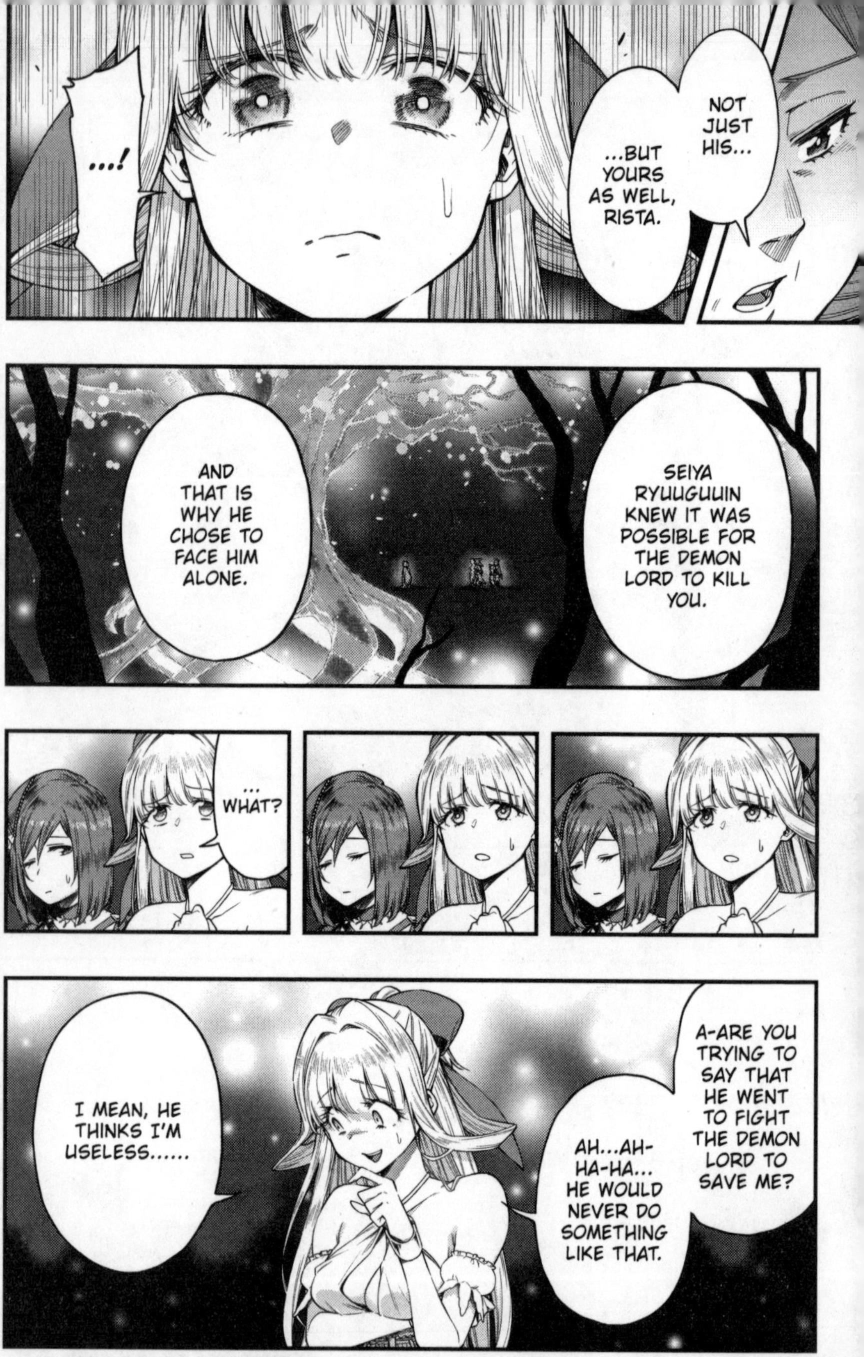
NOT JUST HIS...
...BUT YOURS AS WELL, RISTA.
...!
SEIYA RYUUGUUIN KNEW IT WAS POSSIBLE FOR THE DEMON LORD TO KILL YOU.
AND THAT IS WHY HE CHOSE TO FACE HIM ALONE.
... WHAT?
A-ARE YOU TRYING TO SAY THAT HE WENT TO FIGHT THE DEMON LORD TO SAVE ME?
AH...AH-HA-HA... HE WOULD NEVER DO SOMETHING LIKE THAT.
I MEAN, HE THINKS I'M USELESS......

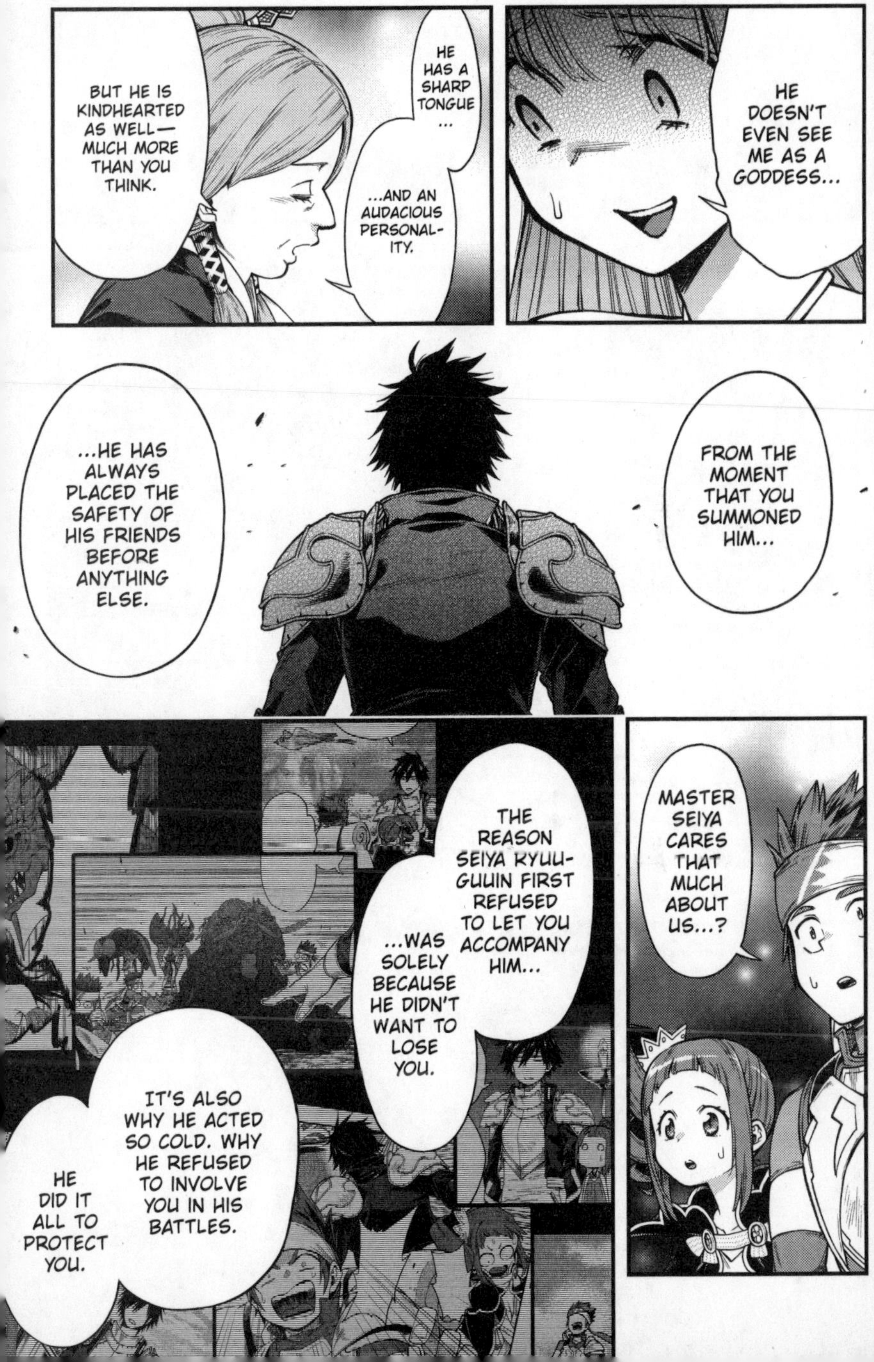
HE DOESN'T EVEN SEE ME AS A GODDESS...
HE HAS A SHARP TONGUE...
...AND AN AUDACIOUS PERSONAL-ITY.
BUT HE IS KINDHEARTED AS WELL—MUCH MORE THAN YOU THINK.
FROM THE MOMENT THAT YOU SUMMONED HIM...
...HE HAS ALWAYS PLACED THE SAFETY OF HIS FRIENDS BEFORE ANYTHING ELSE.
MASTER SEIYA CARES THAT MUCH ABOUT US...?
THE REASON SEIYA RYUU-GUUIN FIRST REFUSED TO LET YOU ACCOMPANY HIM...
...WAS SOLELY BECAUSE HE DIDN'T WANT TO LOSE YOU.
IT'S ALSO WHY HE ACTED SO COLD. WHY HE REFUSED TO INVOLVE YOU IN HIS BATTLES.
HE DID IT ALL TO PROTECT YOU.

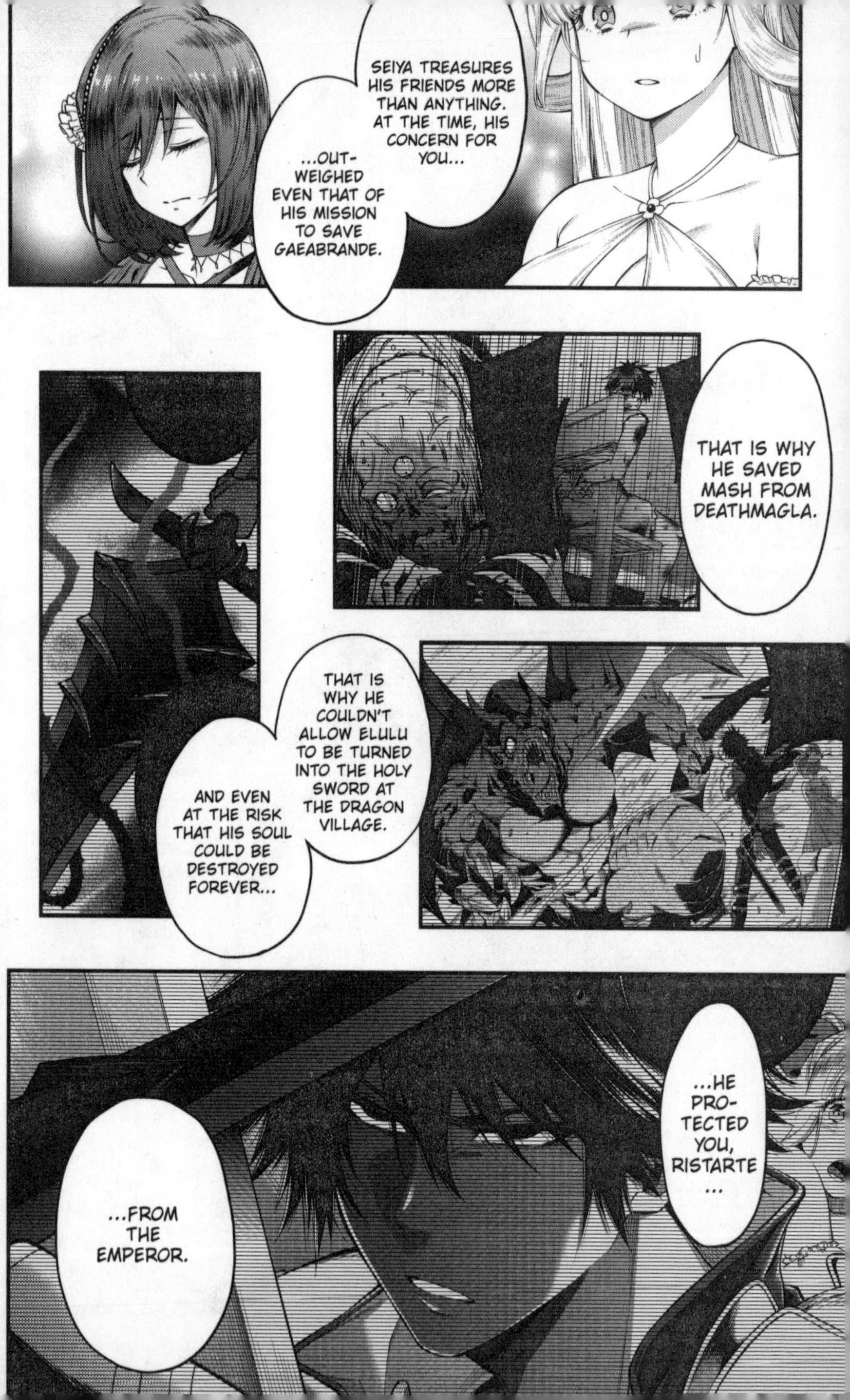
SEIYA TREASURES HIS FRIENDS MORE THAN ANYTHING. AT THE TIME, HIS CONCERN FOR YOU...
...OUT-WEIGHED EVEN THAT OF HIS MISSION TO SAVE GAEABRANDE.
THAT IS WHY HE SAVED MASH FROM DEATHMAGLA.
THAT IS WHY HE COULDN'T ALLOW ELULU TO BE TURNED INTO THE HOLY SWORD AT THE DRAGON VILLAGE.
AND EVEN AT THE RISK THAT HIS SOUL COULD BE DESTROYED FOREVER...
...HE PRO-TECTED YOU, RISTARTE...
...FROM THE EMPEROR.

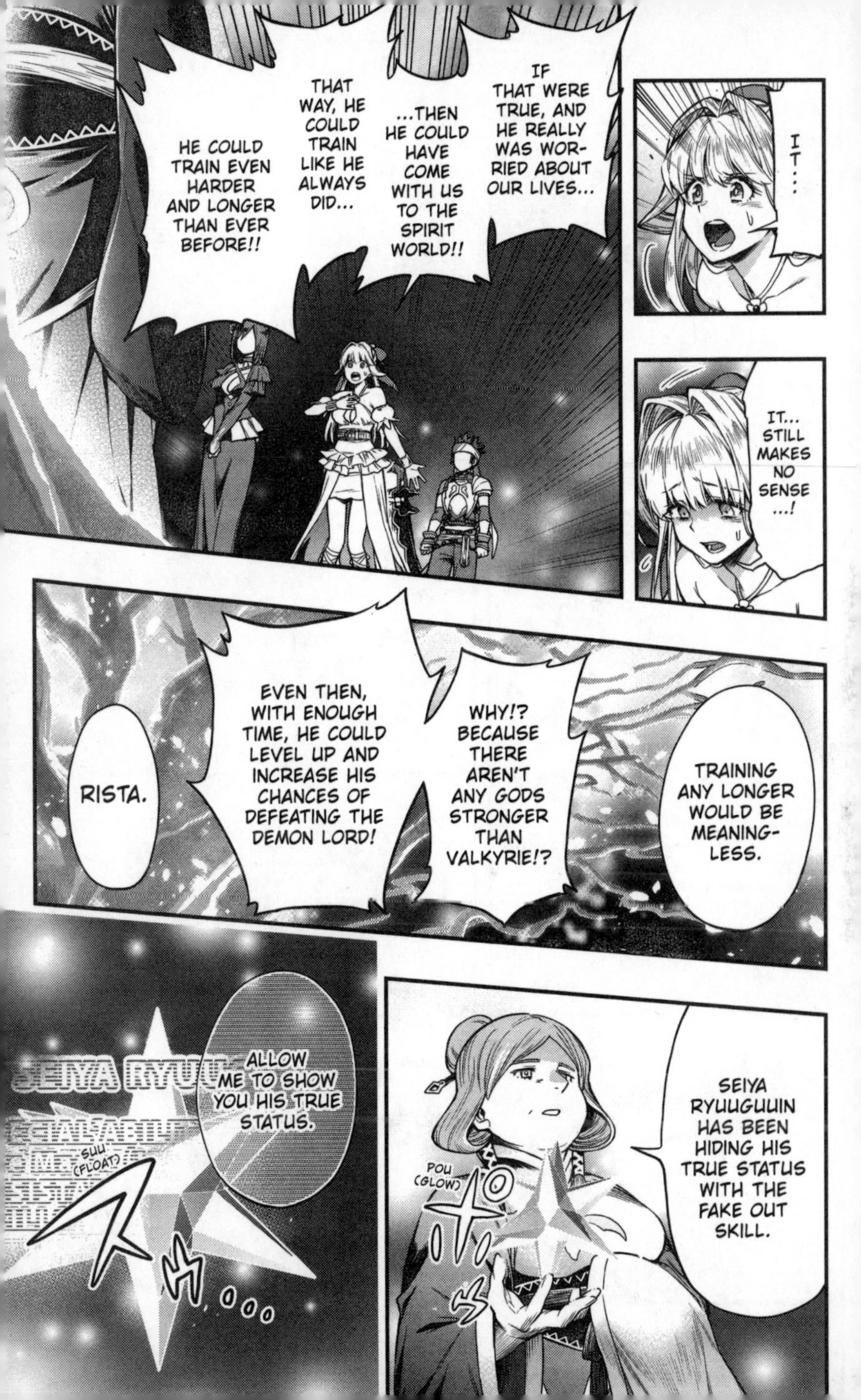
IT...
IT... STILL MAKES NO SENSE...!
IF THAT WERE TRUE, AND HE REALLY WAS WOR-RIED ABOUT OUR LIVES...
...THEN HE COULD HAVE COME WITH US TO THE SPIRIT WORLD!!
THAT WAY, HE COULD TRAIN LIKE HE ALWAYS DID...
HE COULD TRAIN EVEN HARDER AND LONGER THAN EVER BEFORE!!
TRAINING ANY LONGER WOULD BE MEANING-LESS.
WHY!? BECAUSE THERE AREN'T ANY GODS STRONGER THAN VALKYRIE!?
EVEN THEN, WITH ENOUGH TIME, HE COULD LEVEL UP AND INCREASE HIS CHANCES OF DEFEATING THE DEMON LORD!
RISTA.
SEIYA RYUUGUUIN HAS BEEN HIDING HIS TRUE STATUS WITH THE FAKE OUT SKILL.
POU (GLOW)
ALLOW ME TO SHOW YOU HIS TRUE STATUS.
SUU (FLOAT)

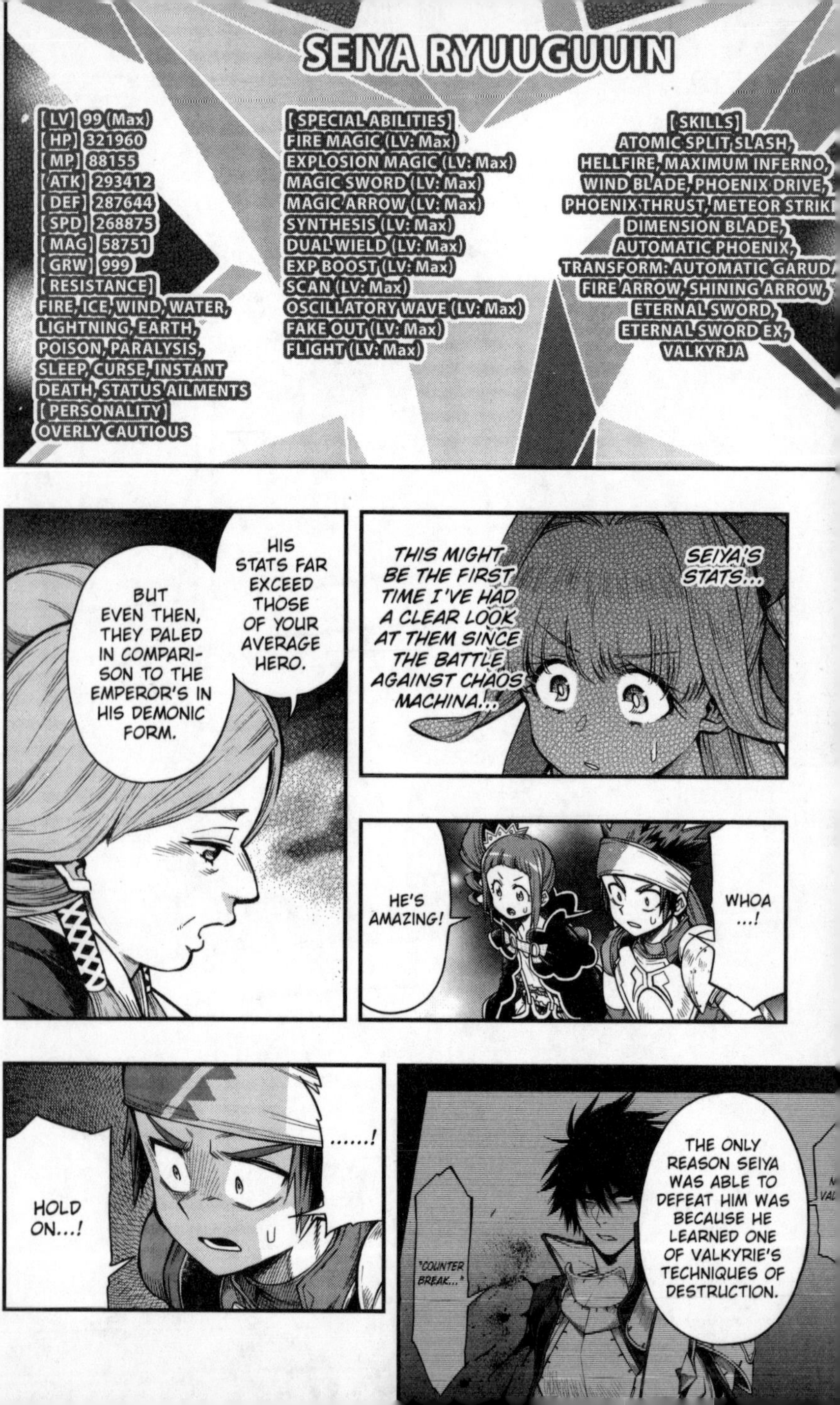
SEIYA RYUUGUUIN
[LV] 99 (Max)
[HP] 321960
[MP] 88155
[ATK] 293412
[DEF] 287644
[SPD] 268875
[MAG] 58751
[GRW] 999
[RESISTANCE]
FIRE, ICE, WIND, WATER, LIGHTNING, EARTH, POISON, PARALYSIS, SLEEP, CURSE, INSTANT DEATH, STATUS AILMENTS
[PERSONALITY]
OVERLY CAUTIOUS
[SPECIAL ABILITIES]
FIRE MAGIC (LV: Max)
EXPLOSION MAGIC (LV: Max)
MAGIC SWORD (LV: Max)
MAGIC ARROW (LV: Max)
SYNTHESIS (LV: Max)
DUAL WIELD (LV: Max)
EXP BOOST (LV: Max)
SCAN (LV: Max)
OSCILLATORY WAVE (LV: Max)
FAKE OUT (LV: Max)
FLIGHT (LV: Max)
[SKILLS]
ATOMIC SPLIT SLASH, HELLFIRE, MAXIMUM INFERNO, WIND BLADE, PHOENIX DRIVE, PHOENIX THRUST, METEOR STRIKE, DIMENSION BLADE, AUTOMATIC PHOENIX, TRANSFORM: AUTOMATIC GARUDA, FIRE ARROW, SHINING ARROW, ETERNAL SWORD, ETERNAL SWORD EX, VALKYRJA
SEIYA'S STATS...
THIS MIGHT BE THE FIRST TIME I'VE HAD A CLEAR LOOK AT THEM SINCE THE BATTLE AGAINST CHAOS MACHINA...
WHOA ...!
HE'S AMAZING!
HIS STATS FAR EXCEED THOSE OF YOUR AVERAGE HERO.
BUT EVEN THEN, THEY PALED IN COMPARISON TO THE EMPEROR'S IN HIS DEMONIC FORM.
THE ONLY REASON SEIYA WAS ABLE TO DEFEAT HIM WAS BECAUSE HE LEARNED ONE OF VALKYRIE'S TECHNIQUES OF DESTRUCTION.
"COUNTER BREAK..."
......!
HOLD ON...!

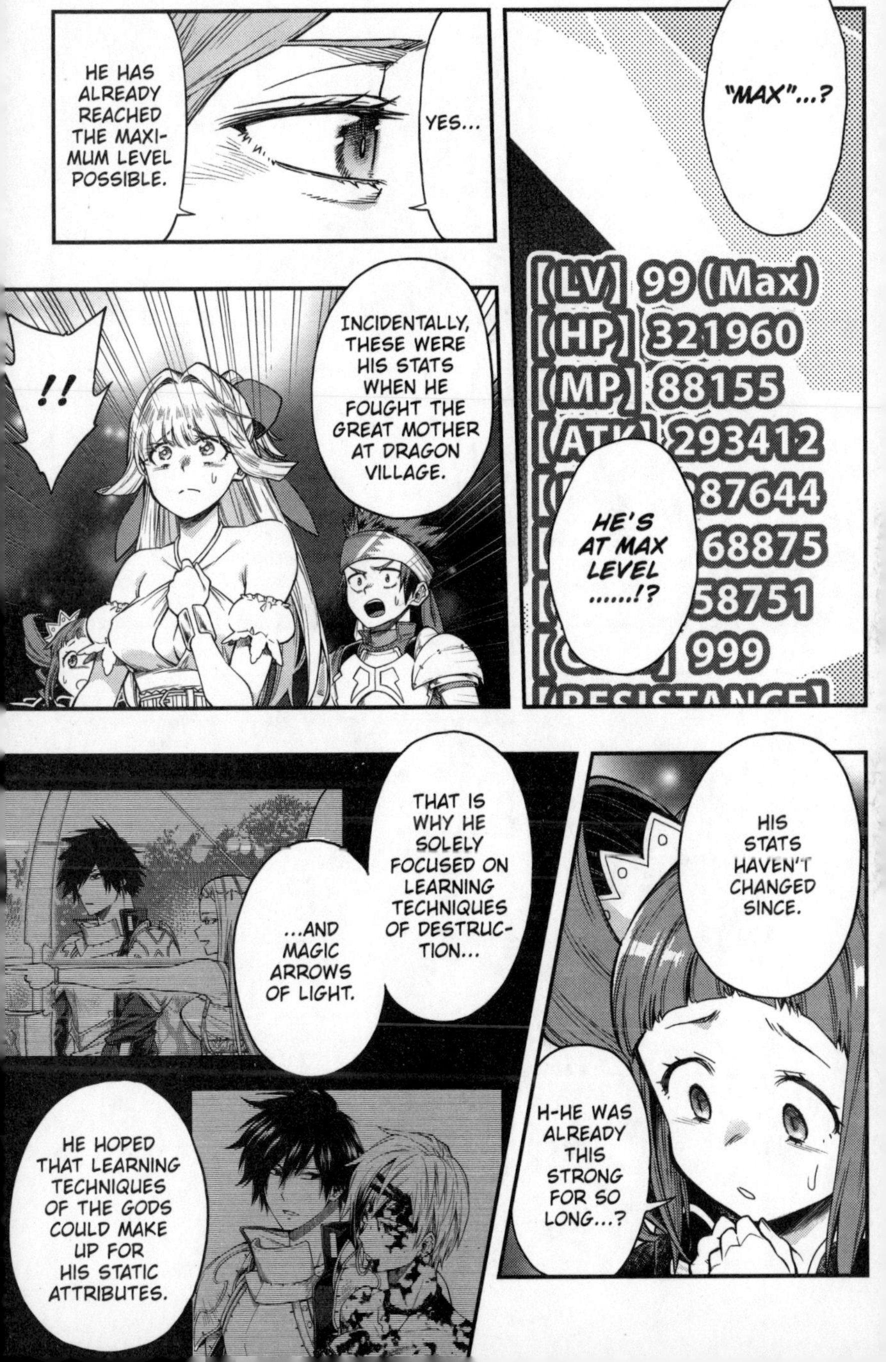
"MAX"...?
【LV】 99 (Max)
【HP】 321960
【MP】 88155
293412
87644
68875
58751
999
HE'S AT MAX LEVEL ......!?
YES...
HE HAS ALREADY REACHED THE MAXI-MUM LEVEL POSSIBLE.
INCIDENTALLY, THESE WERE HIS STATS WHEN HE FOUGHT THE GREAT MOTHER AT DRAGON VILLAGE.
!!
HIS STATS HAVEN'T CHANGED SINCE.
H-HE WAS ALREADY THIS STRONG FOR SO LONG...?
THAT IS WHY HE SOLELY FOCUSED ON LEARNING TECHNIQUES OF DESTRUC-TION...
...AND MAGIC ARROWS OF LIGHT.
HE HOPED THAT LEARNING TECHNIQUES OF THE GODS COULD MAKE UP FOR HIS STATIC ATTRIBUTES.

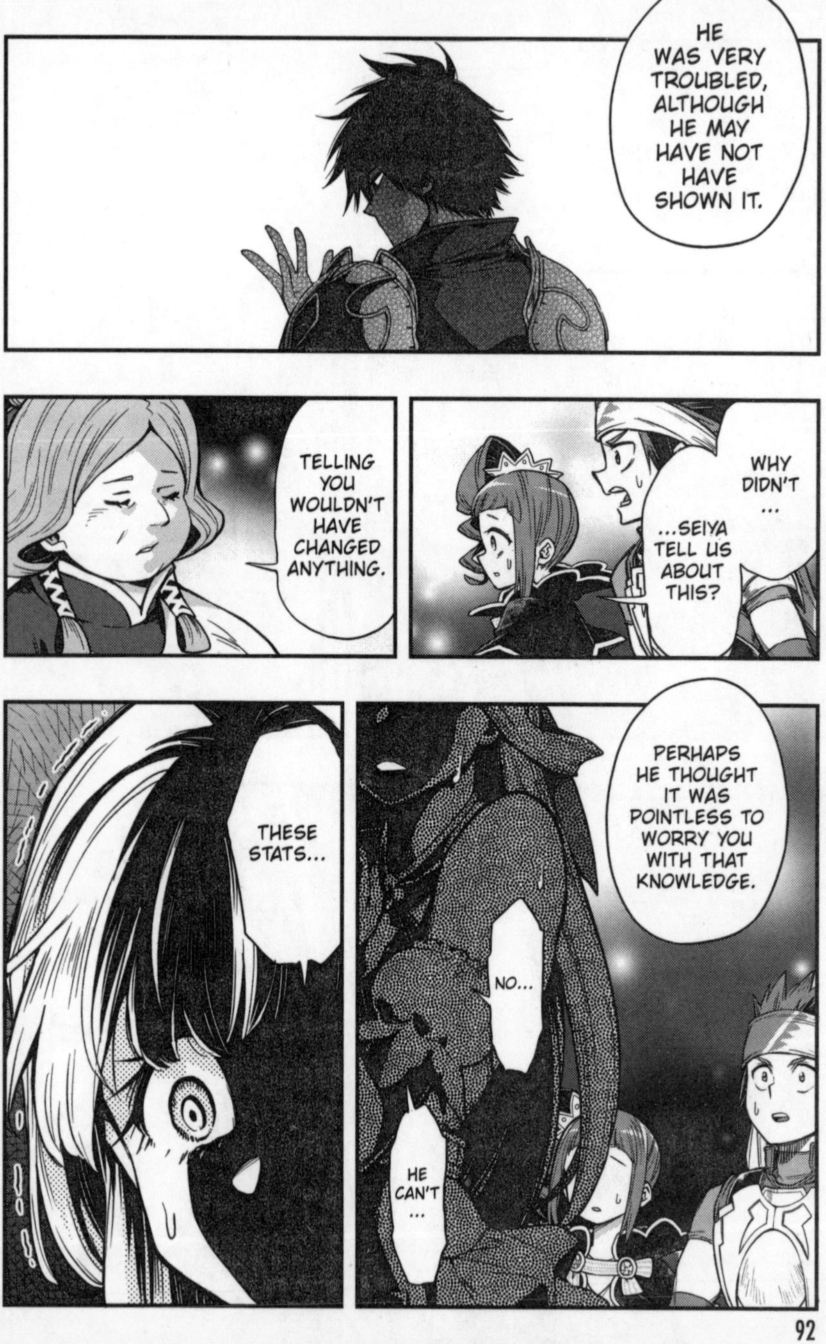
HE WAS VERY TROUBLED, ALTHOUGH HE MAY HAVE NOT HAVE SHOWN IT.
WHY DIDN'T ...
...SEIYA TELL US ABOUT THIS?
TELLING YOU WOULDN'T HAVE CHANGED ANYTHING.
PERHAPS HE THOUGHT IT WAS POINTLESS TO WORRY YOU WITH THAT KNOWLEDGE.
NO...
HE CAN'T ...
THESE STATS...

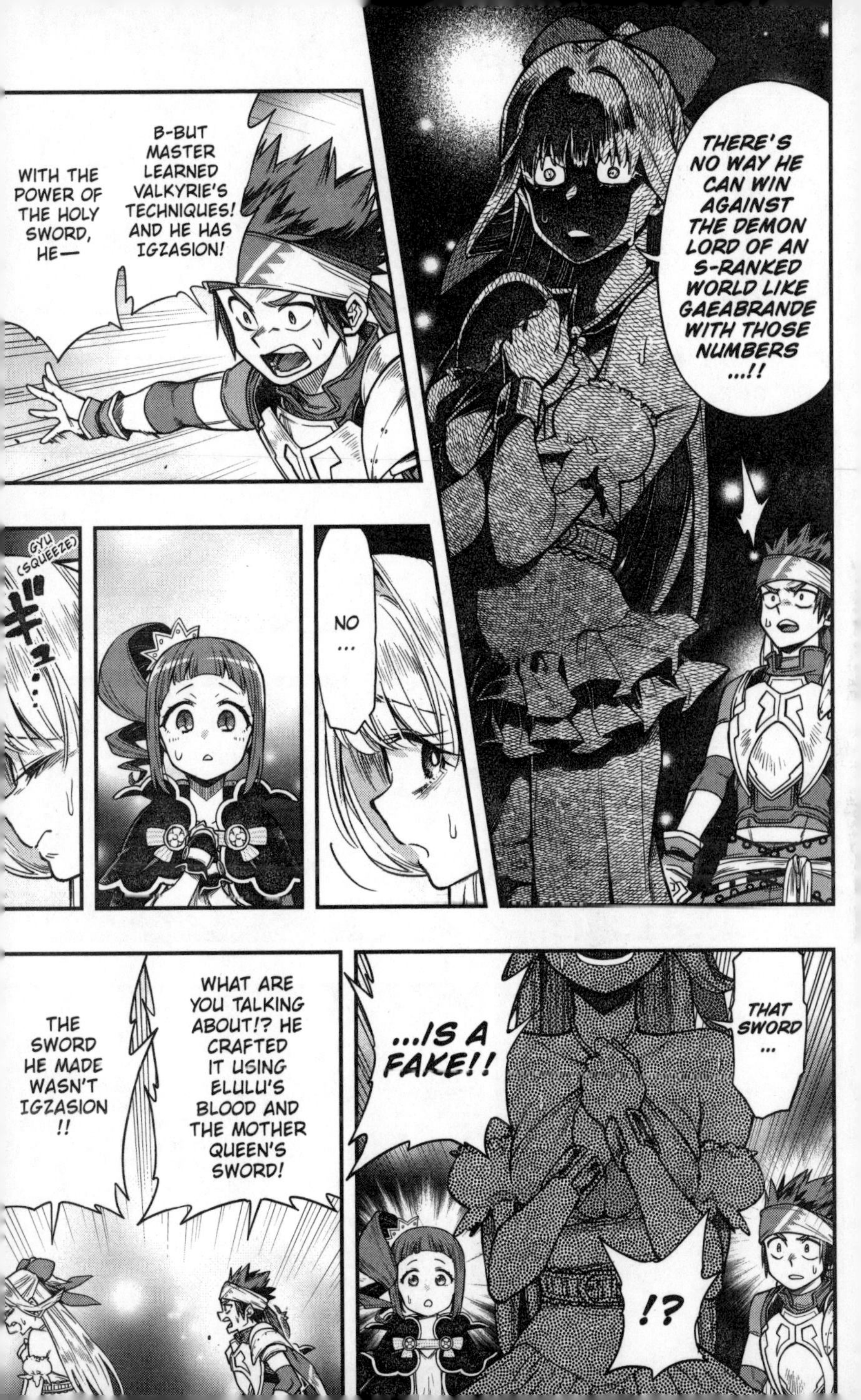
THERE'S NO WAY HE CAN WIN AGAINST THE DEMON LORD OF AN S-RANKED WORLD LIKE GAEABRANDE WITH THOSE NUMBERS ...!!
B-BUT MASTER LEARNED VALKYRIE'S TECHNIQUES! AND HE HAS IGZASION!
WITH THE POWER OF THE HOLY SWORD, HE—
NO ...
GYU (SQUEEZE)
ギュ…
THAT SWORD ...
...IS A FAKE!!
!?
WHAT ARE YOU TALKING ABOUT!? HE CRAFTED IT USING ELULU'S BLOOD AND THE MOTHER QUEEN'S SWORD!
THE SWORD HE MADE WASN'T IGZASION !!

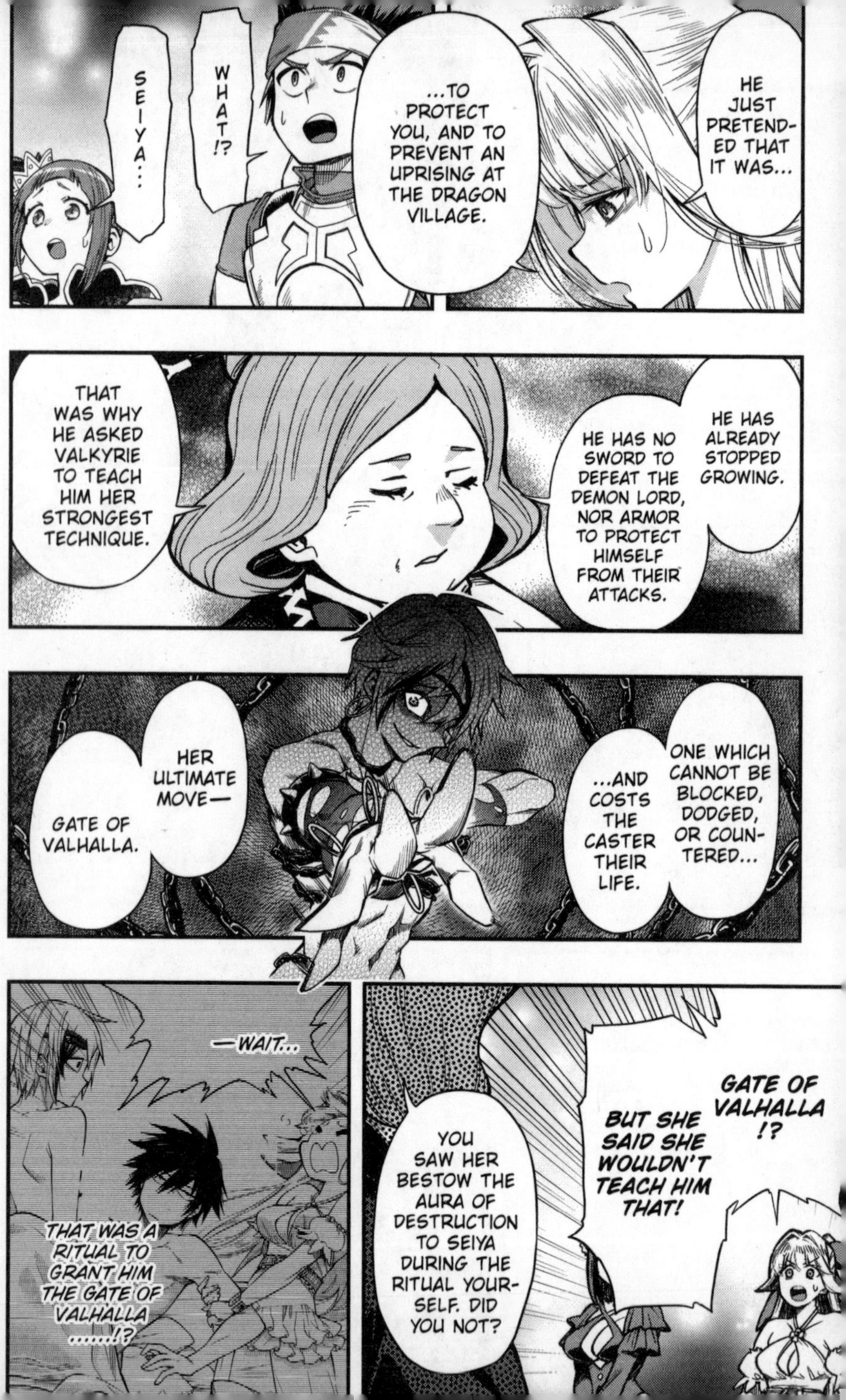
HE JUST PRETENDED THAT IT WAS...
...TO PROTECT YOU, AND TO PREVENT AN UPRISING AT THE DRAGON VILLAGE.
WHAT!?
SEIYA...
HE HAS ALREADY STOPPED GROWING.
HE HAS NO SWORD TO DEFEAT THE DEMON LORD, NOR ARMOR TO PROTECT HIMSELF FROM THEIR ATTACKS.
THAT WAS WHY HE ASKED VALKYRIE TO TEACH HIM HER STRONGEST TECHNIQUE.
ONE WHICH CANNOT BE BLOCKED, DODGED, OR COUNTERED...
...AND COSTS THE CASTER THEIR LIFE.
HER ULTIMATE MOVE—
GATE OF VALHALLA.
GATE OF VALHALLA!?
BUT SHE SAID SHE WOULDN'T TEACH HIM THAT!
YOU SAW HER BESTOW THE AURA OF DESTRUCTION TO SEIYA DURING THE RITUAL YOURSELF. DID YOU NOT?
—WAIT...
THAT WAS A RITUAL TO GRANT HIM THE GATE OF VALHALLA ......!?

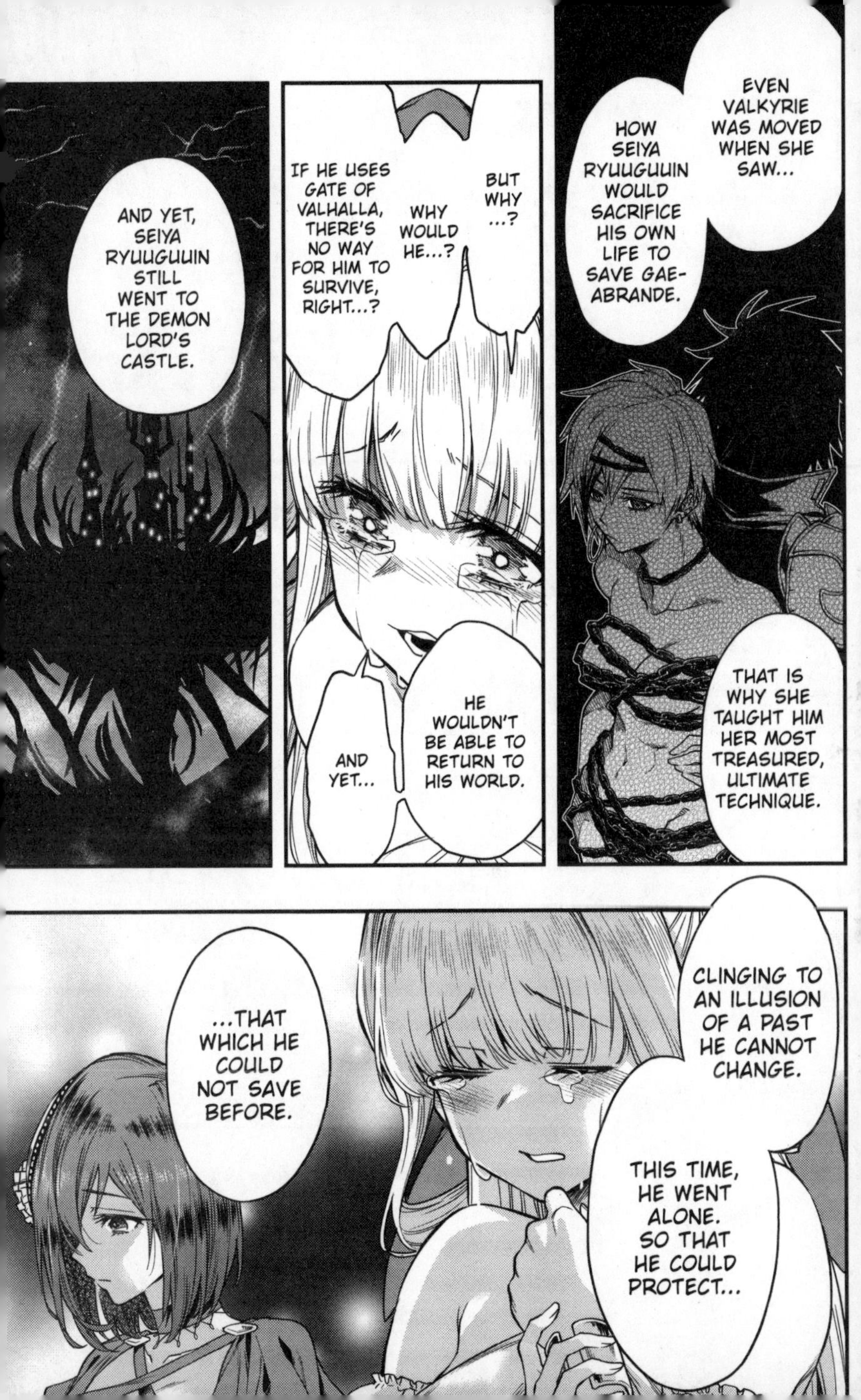
EVEN VALKYRIE WAS MOVED WHEN SHE SAW...
HOW SEIYA RYUUGUUIN WOULD SACRIFICE HIS OWN LIFE TO SAVE GAE-ABRANDE.
THAT IS WHY SHE TAUGHT HIM HER MOST TREASURED, ULTIMATE TECHNIQUE.
BUT WHY ...?
WHY WOULD HE...?
IF HE USES GATE OF VALHALLA, THERE'S NO WAY FOR HIM TO SURVIVE, RIGHT...?
HE WOULDN'T BE ABLE TO RETURN TO HIS WORLD.
AND YET...
AND YET, SEIYA RYUUGUUIN STILL WENT TO THE DEMON LORD'S CASTLE.
CLINGING TO AN ILLUSION OF A PAST HE CANNOT CHANGE.
THIS TIME, HE WENT ALONE. SO THAT HE COULD PROTECT...
...THAT WHICH HE COULD NOT SAVE BEFORE.

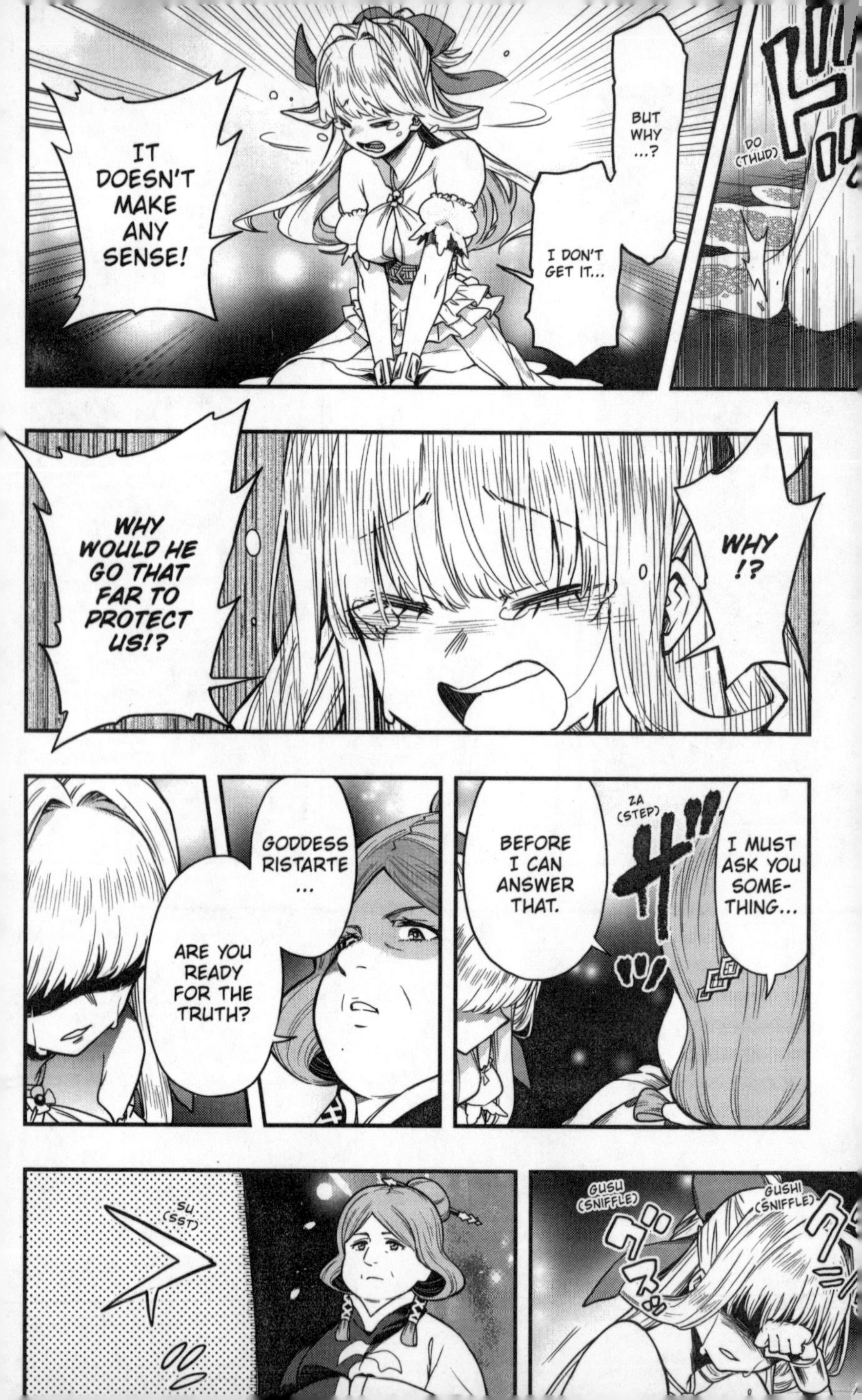
DO (THUD)
BUT WHY ...?
I DON'T GET IT...
IT DOESN'T MAKE ANY SENSE!
WHY !?
WHY WOULD HE GO THAT FAR TO PROTECT US!?
I MUST ASK YOU SOME-THING...
ZA (STEP)
BEFORE I CAN ANSWER THAT.
GODDESS RISTARTE ...
ARE YOU READY FOR THE TRUTH?
GUSHI (SNIFFLE)
GUSU (SNIFFLE)
SU (SST)

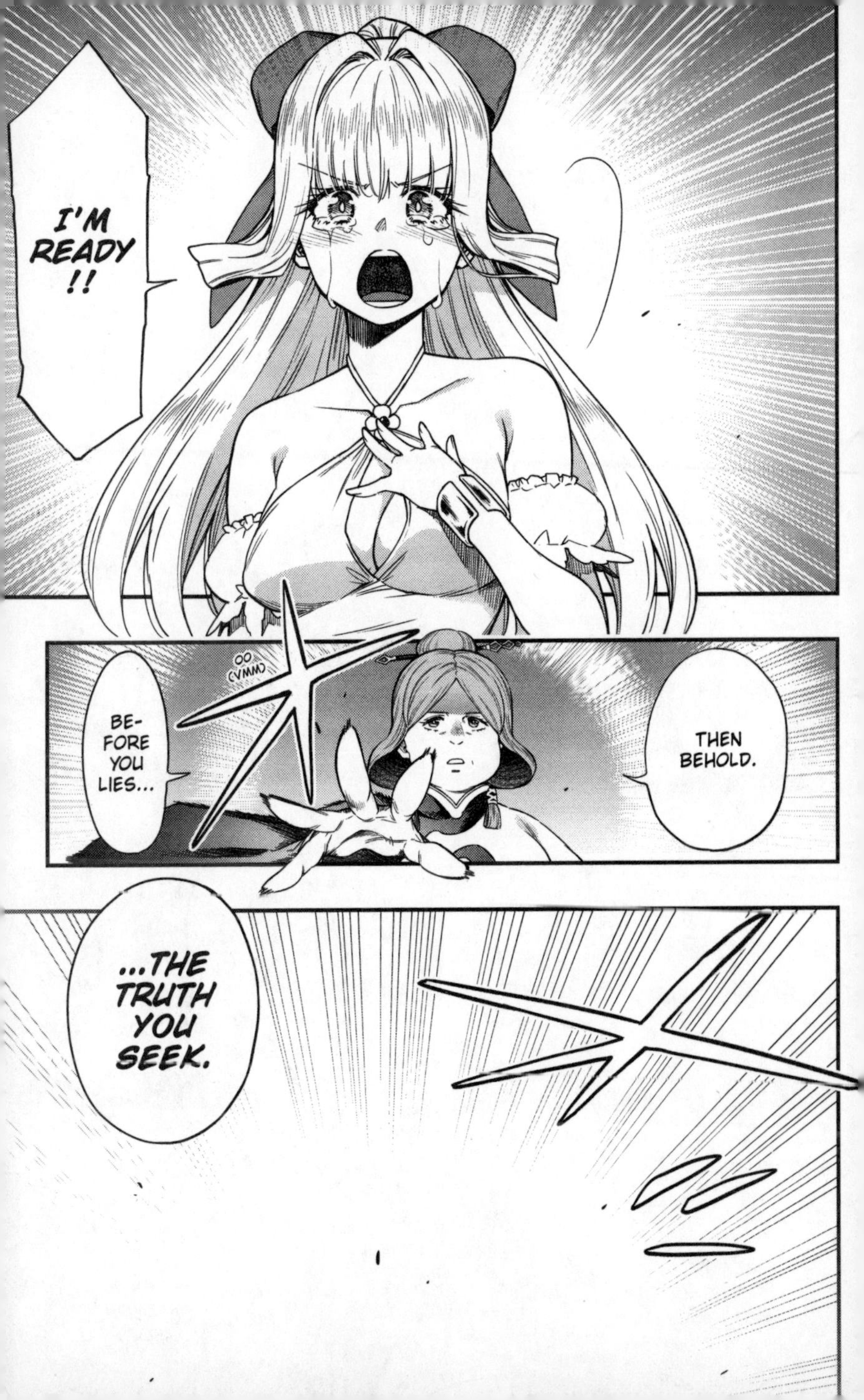
I'M READY!!
THEN BEHOLD.
OO (VMM)
BE-FORE YOU LIES...
...THE TRUTH YOU SEEK.

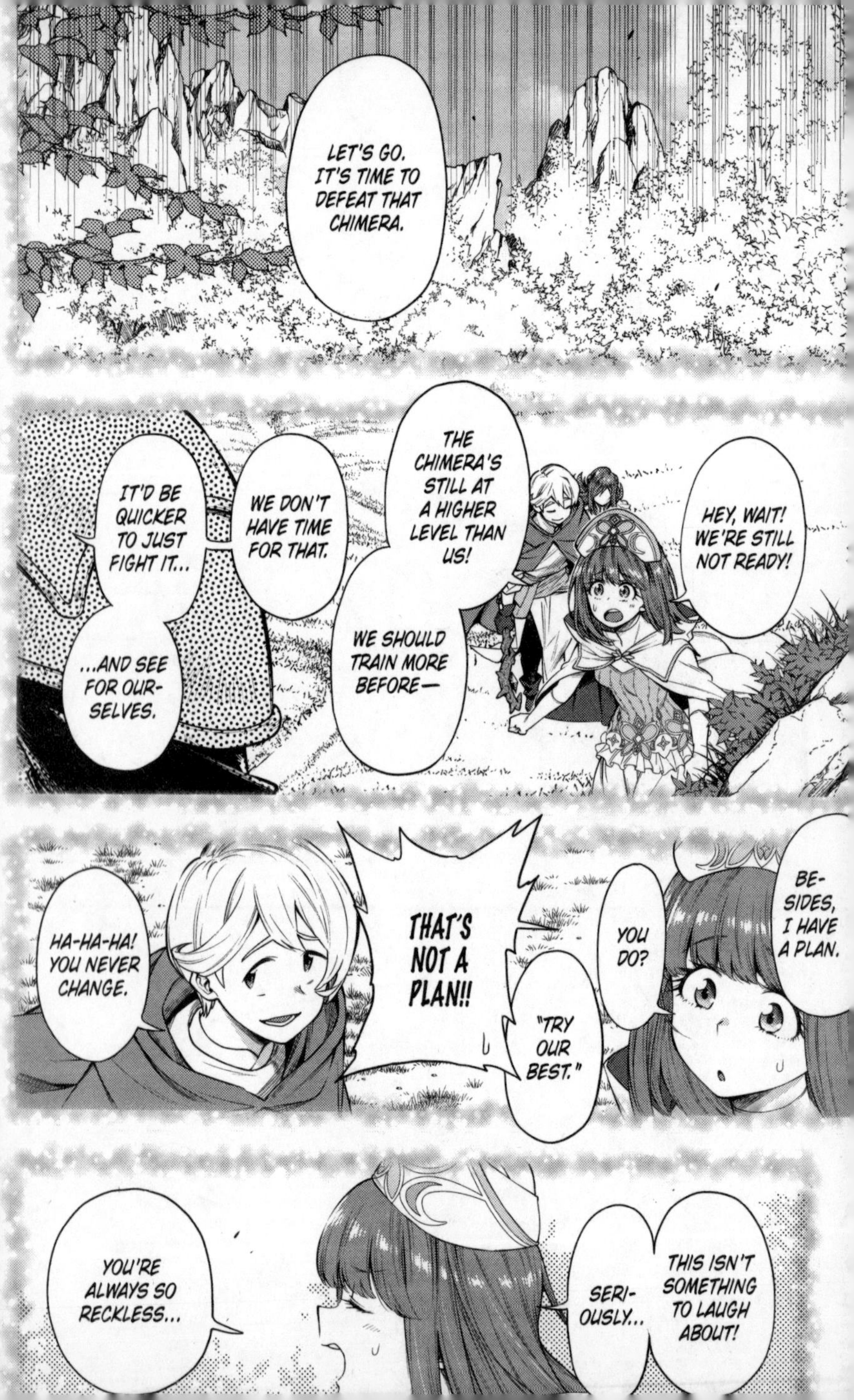
LET'S GO. IT'S TIME TO DEFEAT THAT CHIMERA.
HEY, WAIT! WE'RE STILL NOT READY!
THE CHIMERA'S STILL AT A HIGHER LEVEL THAN US!
WE SHOULD TRAIN MORE BEFORE—
WE DON'T HAVE TIME FOR THAT.
IT'D BE QUICKER TO JUST FIGHT IT...
...AND SEE FOR OURSELVES.
BESIDES, I HAVE A PLAN.
YOU DO?
"TRY OUR BEST."
THAT'S NOT A PLAN!!
HA-HA-HA! YOU NEVER CHANGE.
THIS ISN'T SOMETHING TO LAUGH ABOUT!
SERIOUSLY...
YOU'RE ALWAYS SO RECKLESS...

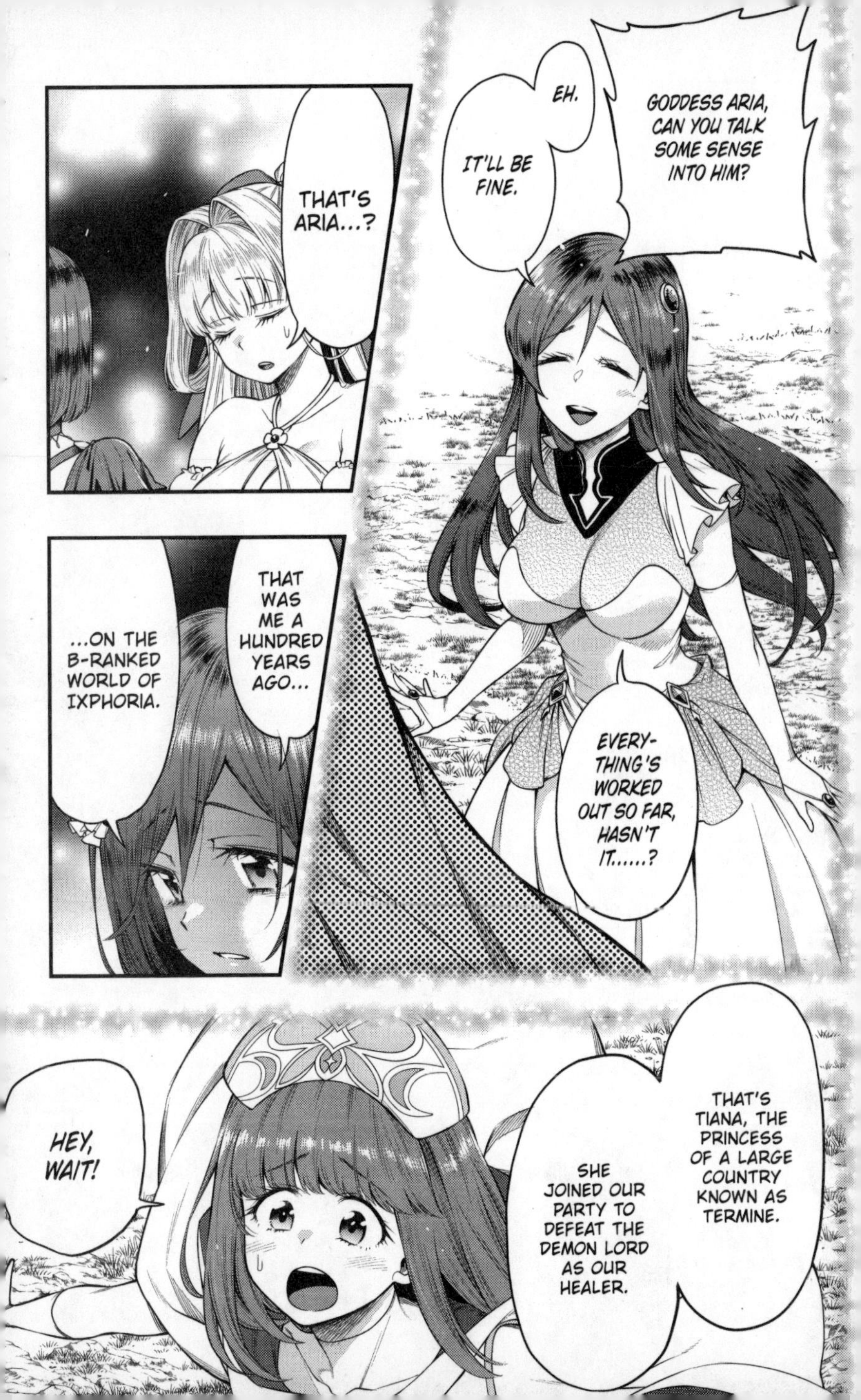
GODDESS ARIA, CAN YOU TALK SOME SENSE INTO HIM?
EH. IT'LL BE FINE.
EVERY-THING'S WORKED OUT SO FAR, HASN'T IT......?
THAT'S ARIA...?
THAT WAS ME A HUNDRED YEARS AGO...
...ON THE B-RANKED WORLD OF IXPHORIA.
THAT'S TIANA, THE PRINCESS OF A LARGE COUNTRY KNOWN AS TERMINE.
SHE JOINED OUR PARTY TO DEFEAT THE DEMON LORD AS OUR HEALER.
HEY, WAIT!

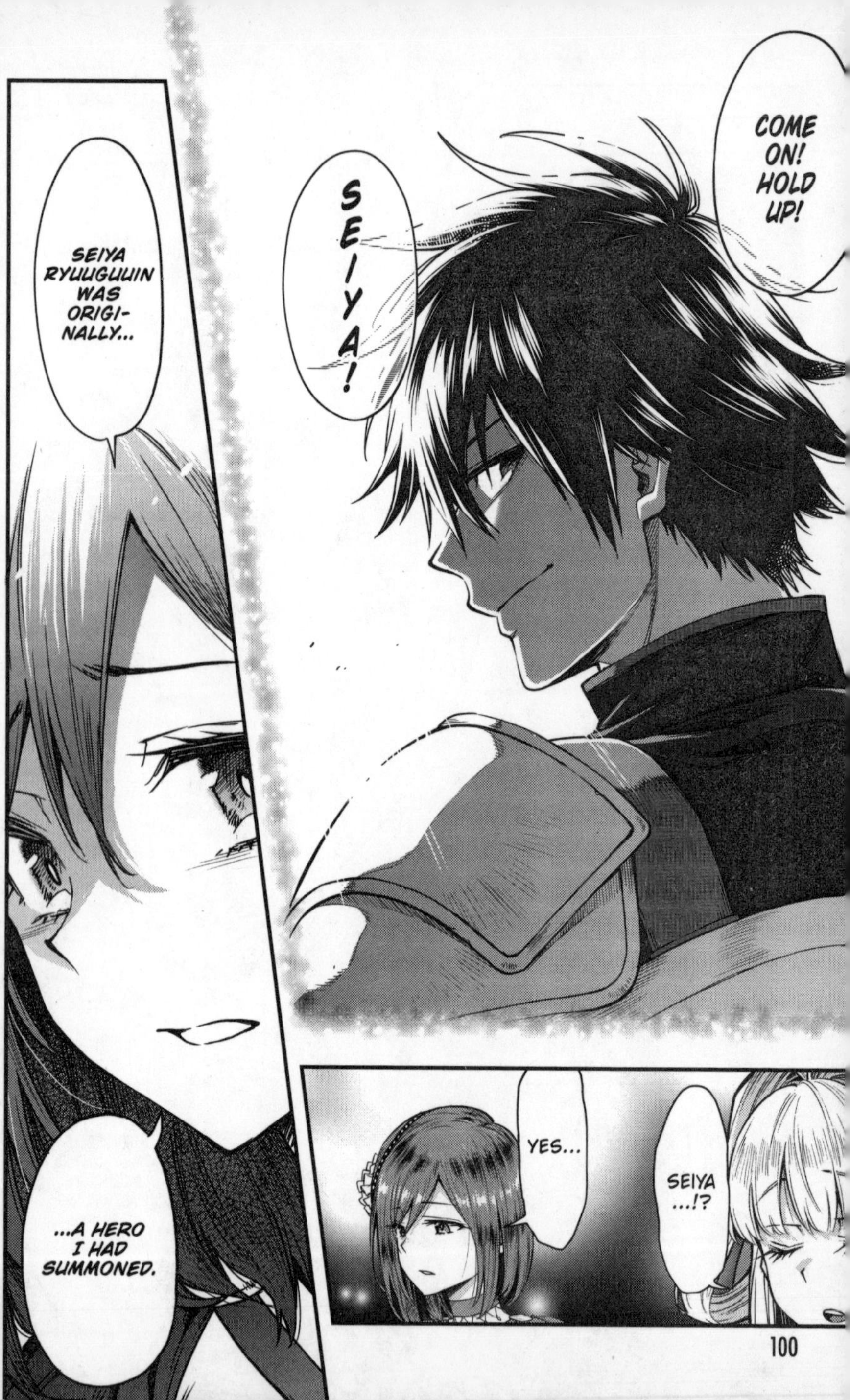
COME ON! HOLD UP!
SEIYA!
SEIYA ...!?
YES...
SEIYA RYUUGUUIN WAS ORIGI-NALLY...
...A HERO I HAD SUMMONED.

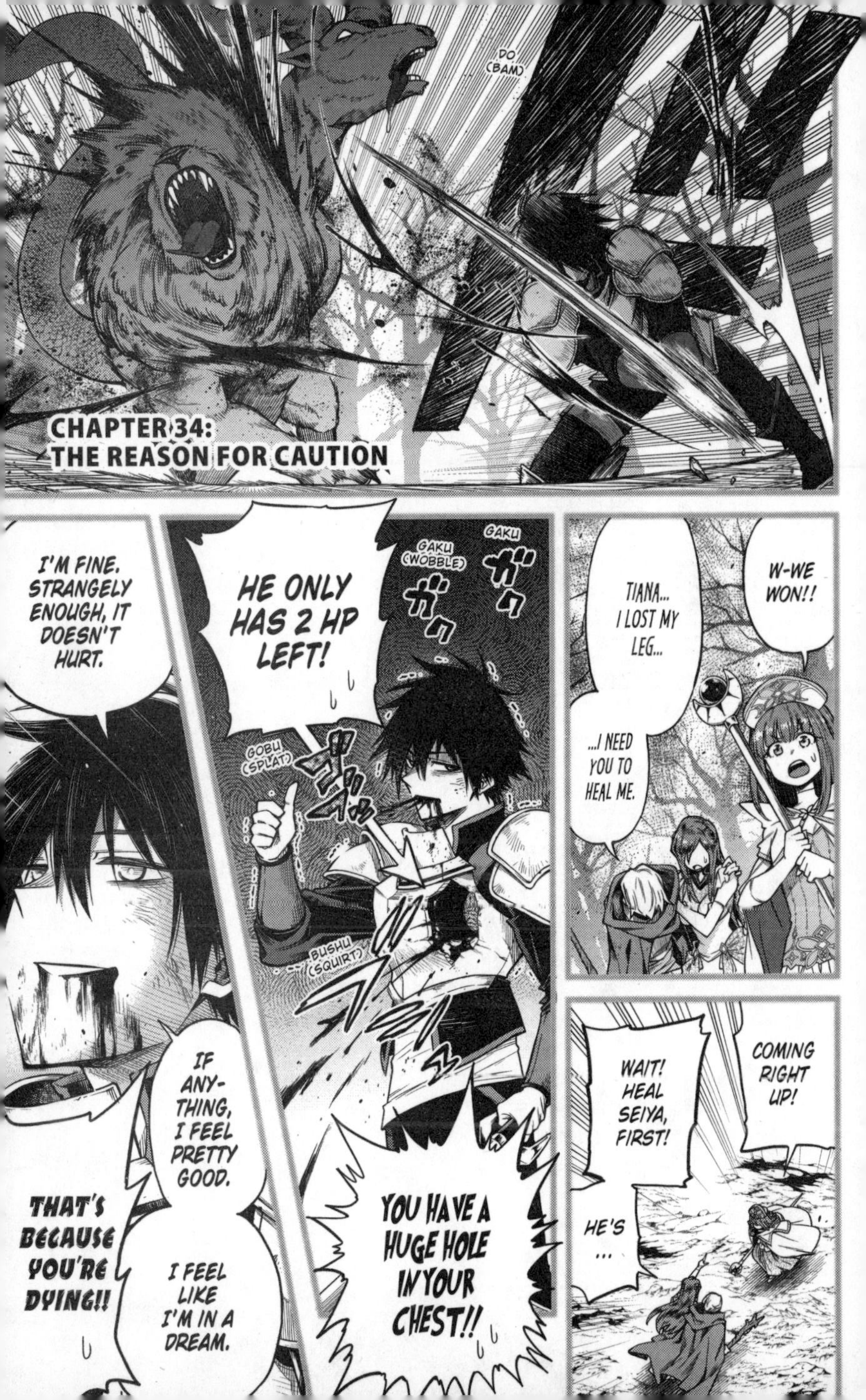
DO (BAM)
CHAPTER 34: THE REASON FOR CAUTION
W-WE WON!!
TIANA... I LOST MY LEG...
...I NEED YOU TO HEAL ME.
COMING RIGHT UP!
WAIT! HEAL SEIYA, FIRST!
HE'S ...
GAKU (WOBBLE)
GAKU
HE ONLY HAS 2 HP LEFT!
GOBU (SPLAT)
BUSHU (SQUIRT)
YOU HAVE A HUGE HOLE IN YOUR CHEST!!
I'M FINE. STRANGELY ENOUGH, IT DOESN'T HURT.
IF ANY-THING, I FEEL PRETTY GOOD.
THAT'S BECAUSE YOU'RE DYING!!
I FEEL LIKE I'M IN A DREAM.

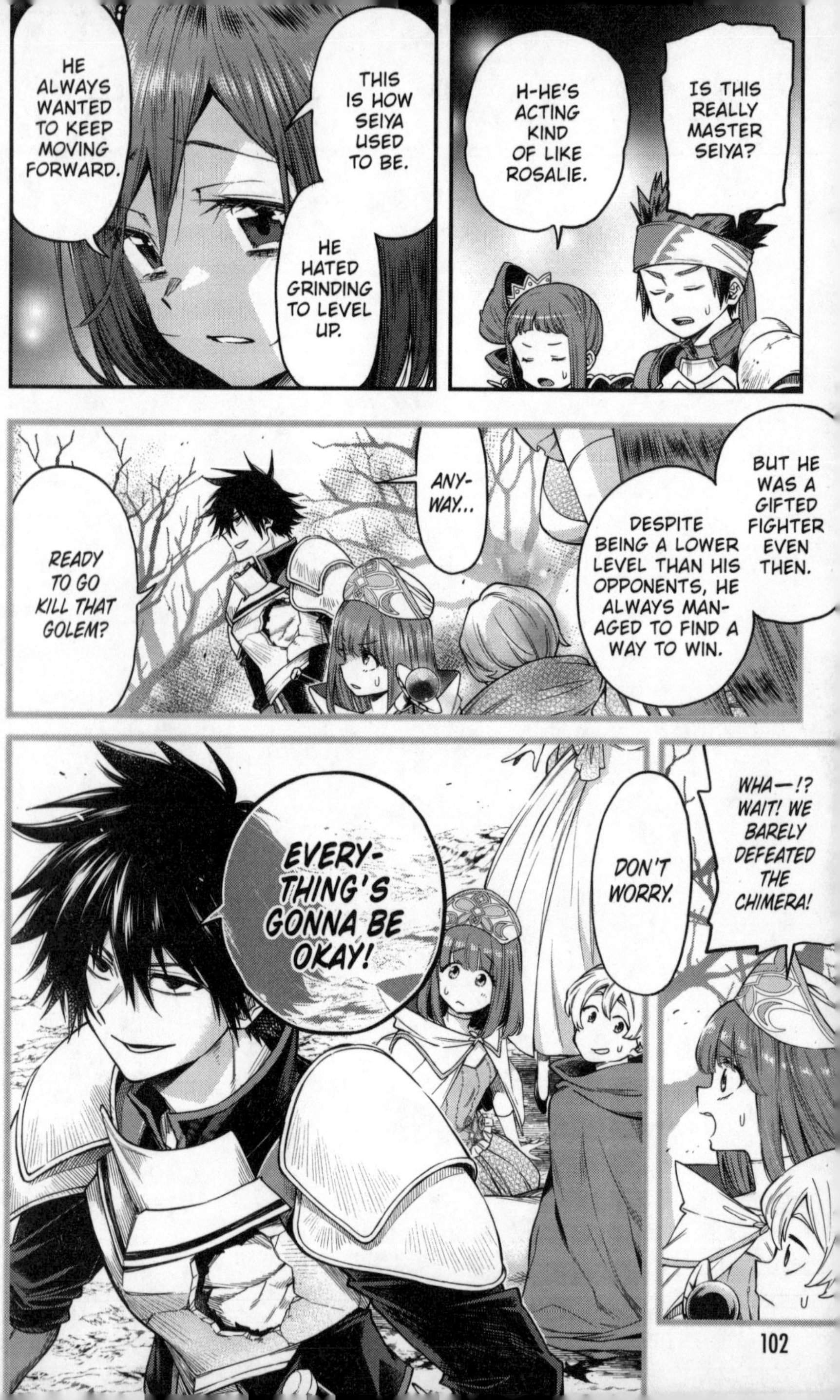

IS THIS REALLY MASTER SEIYA?
H-HE'S ACTING KIND OF LIKE ROSALIE.
THIS IS HOW SEIYA USED TO BE.
HE ALWAYS WANTED TO KEEP MOVING FORWARD.
HE HATED GRINDING TO LEVEL UP.
BUT HE WAS A GIFTED FIGHTER EVEN THEN.
DESPITE BEING A LOWER LEVEL THAN HIS OPPONENTS, HE ALWAYS MANAGED TO FIND A WAY TO WIN.
ANYWAY...
READY TO GO KILL THAT GOLEM?
WHA—!? WAIT! WE BARELY DEFEATED THE CHIMERA!
DON'T WORRY.
EVERYTHING'S GONNA BE OKAY!

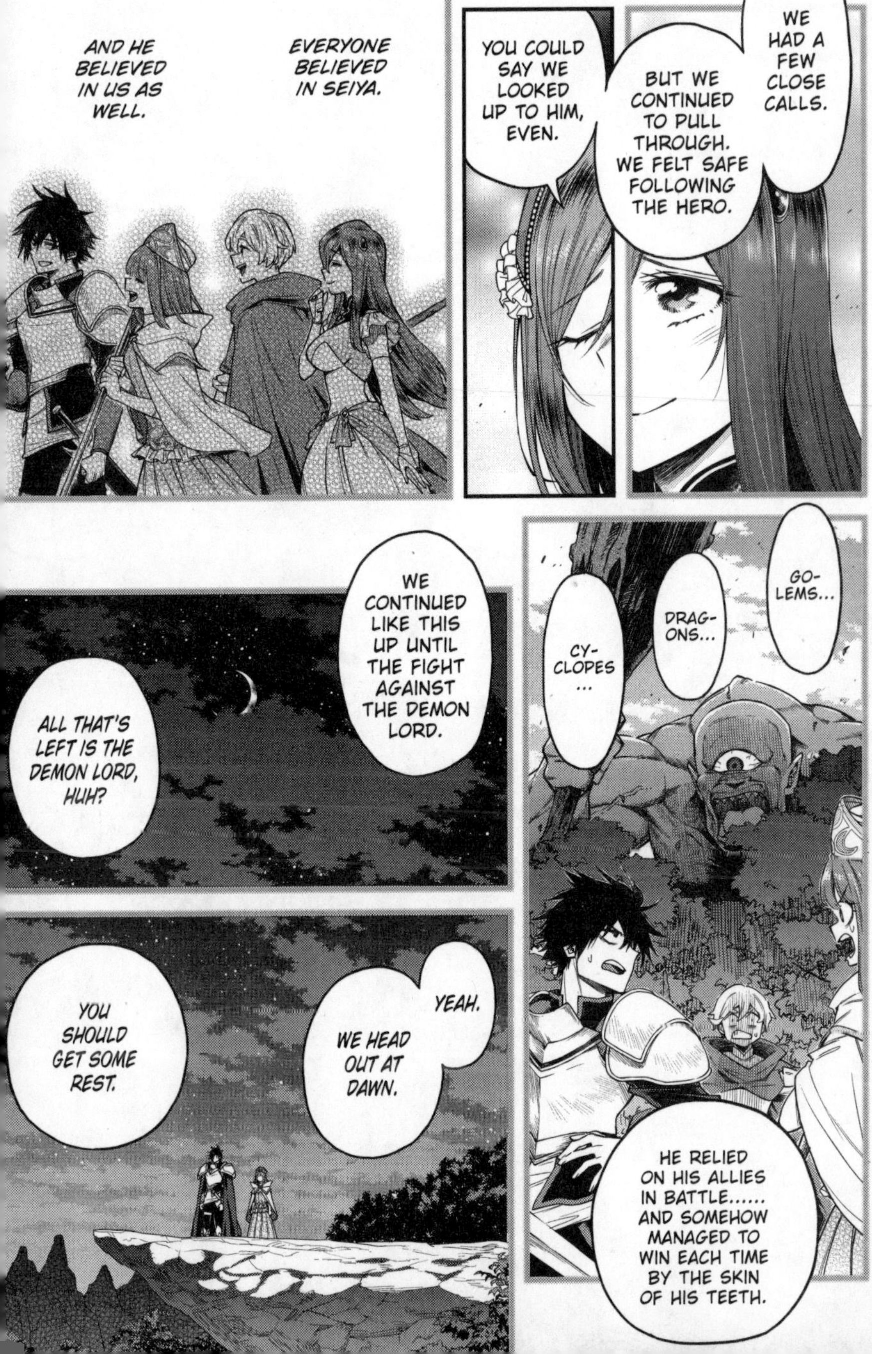
WE HAD A FEW CLOSE CALLS.
BUT WE CONTINUED TO PULL THROUGH. WE FELT SAFE FOLLOWING THE HERO.
YOU COULD SAY WE LOOKED UP TO HIM, EVEN.
EVERYONE BELIEVED IN SEIYA.
AND HE BELIEVED IN US AS WELL.
GO-LEMS...
DRAG-ONS...
CY-CLOPES...
HE RELIED ON HIS ALLIES IN BATTLE...... AND SOMEHOW MANAGED TO WIN EACH TIME BY THE SKIN OF HIS TEETH.
WE CONTINUED LIKE THIS UP UNTIL THE FIGHT AGAINST THE DEMON LORD.
ALL THAT'S LEFT IS THE DEMON LORD, HUH?
YEAH.
WE HEAD OUT AT DAWN.
YOU SHOULD GET SOME REST.

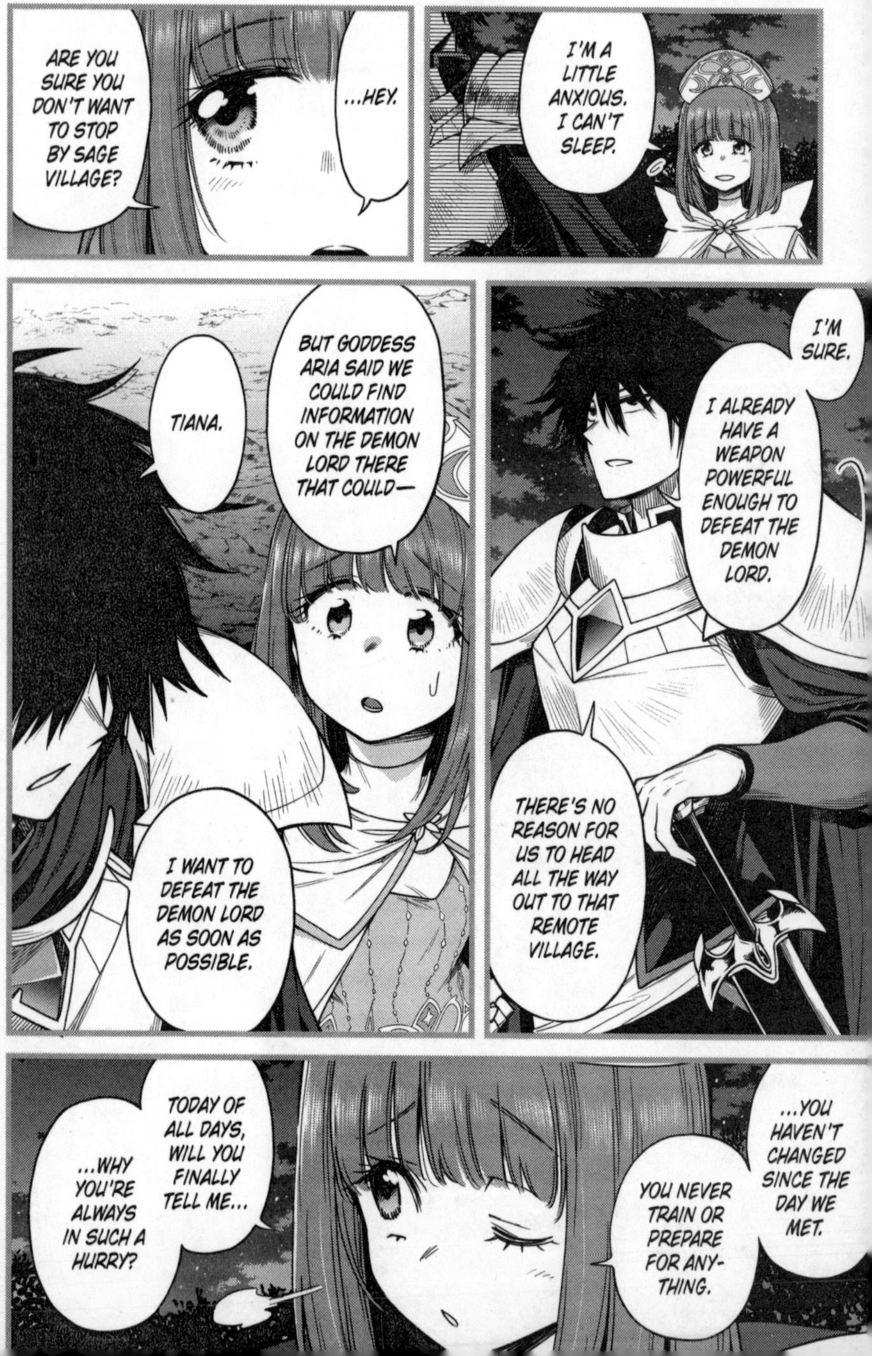
I'M A LITTLE ANXIOUS. I CAN'T SLEEP.
...HEY.
ARE YOU SURE YOU DON'T WANT TO STOP BY SAGE VILLAGE?
I'M SURE.
I ALREADY HAVE A WEAPON POWERFUL ENOUGH TO DEFEAT THE DEMON LORD.
THERE'S NO REASON FOR US TO HEAD ALL THE WAY OUT TO THAT REMOTE VILLAGE.
BUT GODDESS ARIA SAID WE COULD FIND INFORMATION ON THE DEMON LORD THERE THAT COULD—
TIANA.
I WANT TO DEFEAT THE DEMON LORD AS SOON AS POSSIBLE.
...YOU HAVEN'T CHANGED SINCE THE DAY WE MET.
YOU NEVER TRAIN OR PREPARE FOR ANY-THING.
TODAY OF ALL DAYS, WILL YOU FINALLY TELL ME...
...WHY YOU'RE ALWAYS IN SUCH A HURRY?

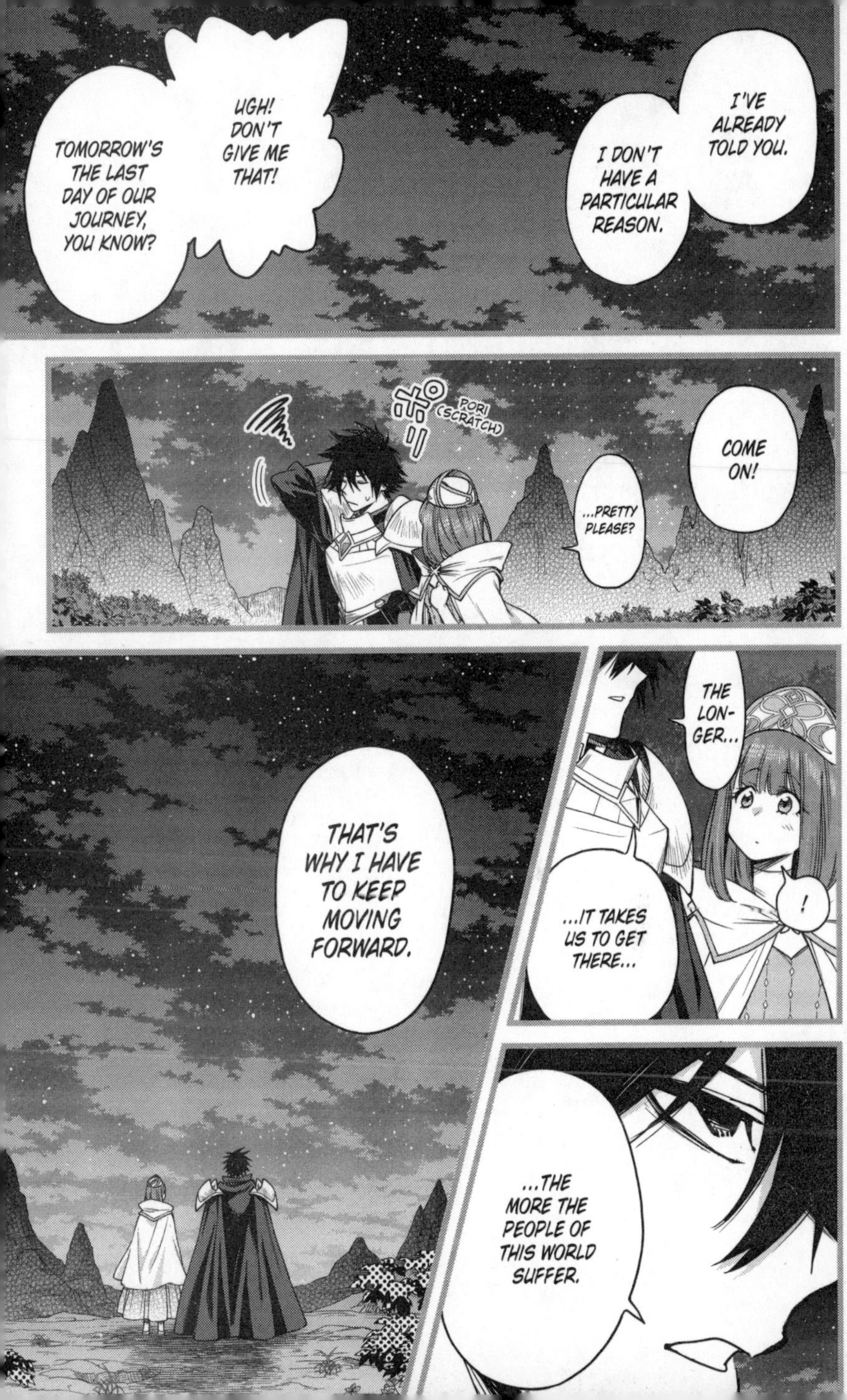
I'VE ALREADY TOLD YOU.
I DON'T HAVE A PARTICULAR REASON.
UGH! DON'T GIVE ME THAT!
TOMORROW'S THE LAST DAY OF OUR JOURNEY, YOU KNOW?
COME ON!
...PRETTY PLEASE?
PORI (SCRATCH)
THE LON-GER...
!
...IT TAKES US TO GET THERE...
...THE MORE THE PEOPLE OF THIS WORLD SUFFER.
THAT'S WHY I HAVE TO KEEP MOVING FORWARD.

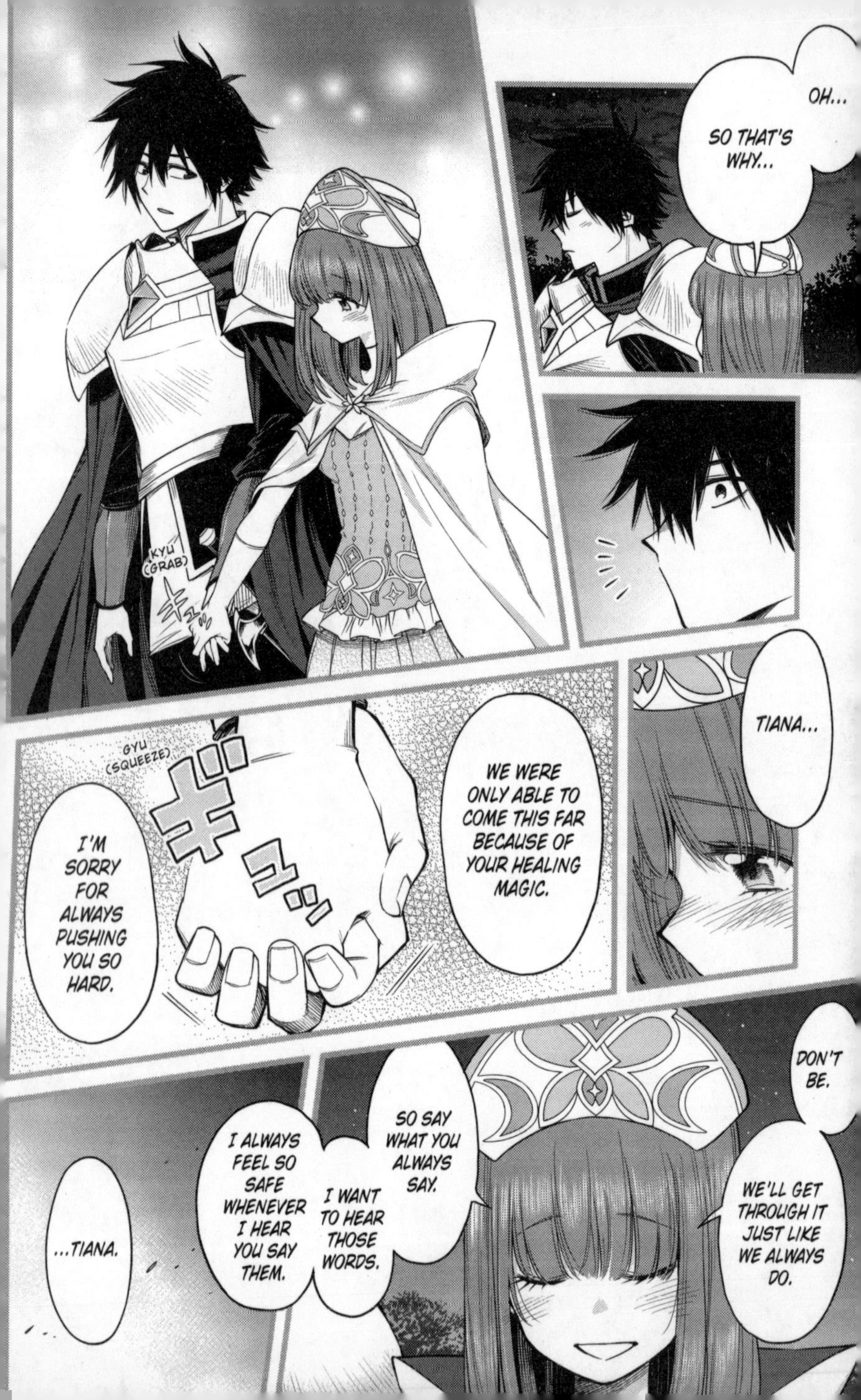
OH...
SO THAT'S WHY...
KYU (GRAB)
TIANA...
WE WERE ONLY ABLE TO COME THIS FAR BECAUSE OF YOUR HEALING MAGIC.
I'M SORRY FOR ALWAYS PUSHING YOU SO HARD.
GYU (SQUEEZE)
DON'T BE.
WE'LL GET THROUGH IT JUST LIKE WE ALWAYS DO.
SO SAY WHAT YOU ALWAYS SAY.
I WANT TO HEAR THOSE WORDS.
I ALWAYS FEEL SO SAFE WHENEVER I HEAR YOU SAY THEM.
...TIANA.

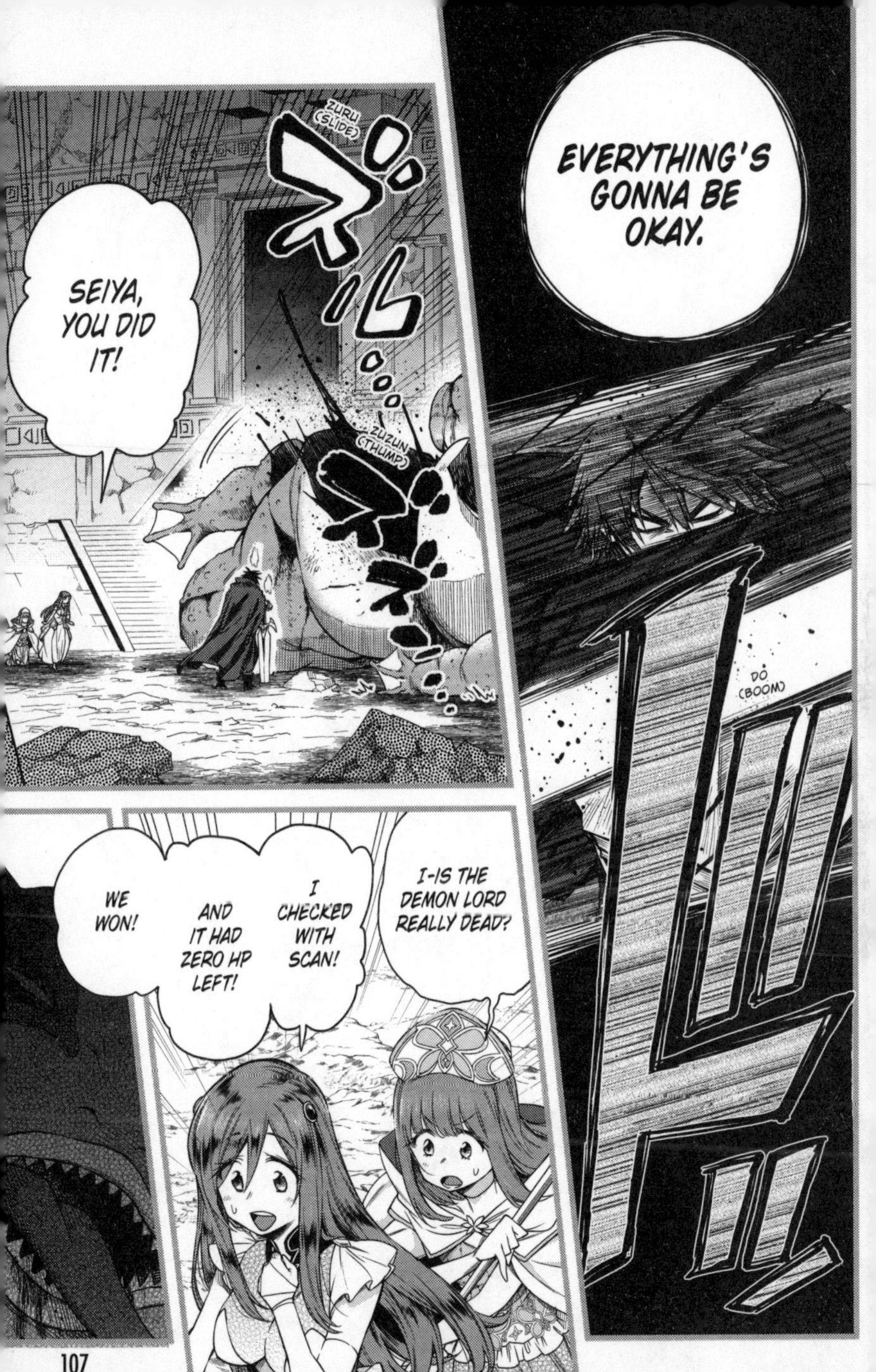
EVERYTHING'S GONNA BE OKAY.
DO (BOOM)
ZURU (SLIDE)
ZUZUN (THUMP)
SEIYA, YOU DID IT!
I-IS THE DEMON LORD REALLY DEAD?
I CHECKED WITH SCAN!
AND IT HAD ZERO HP LEFT!
WE WON!

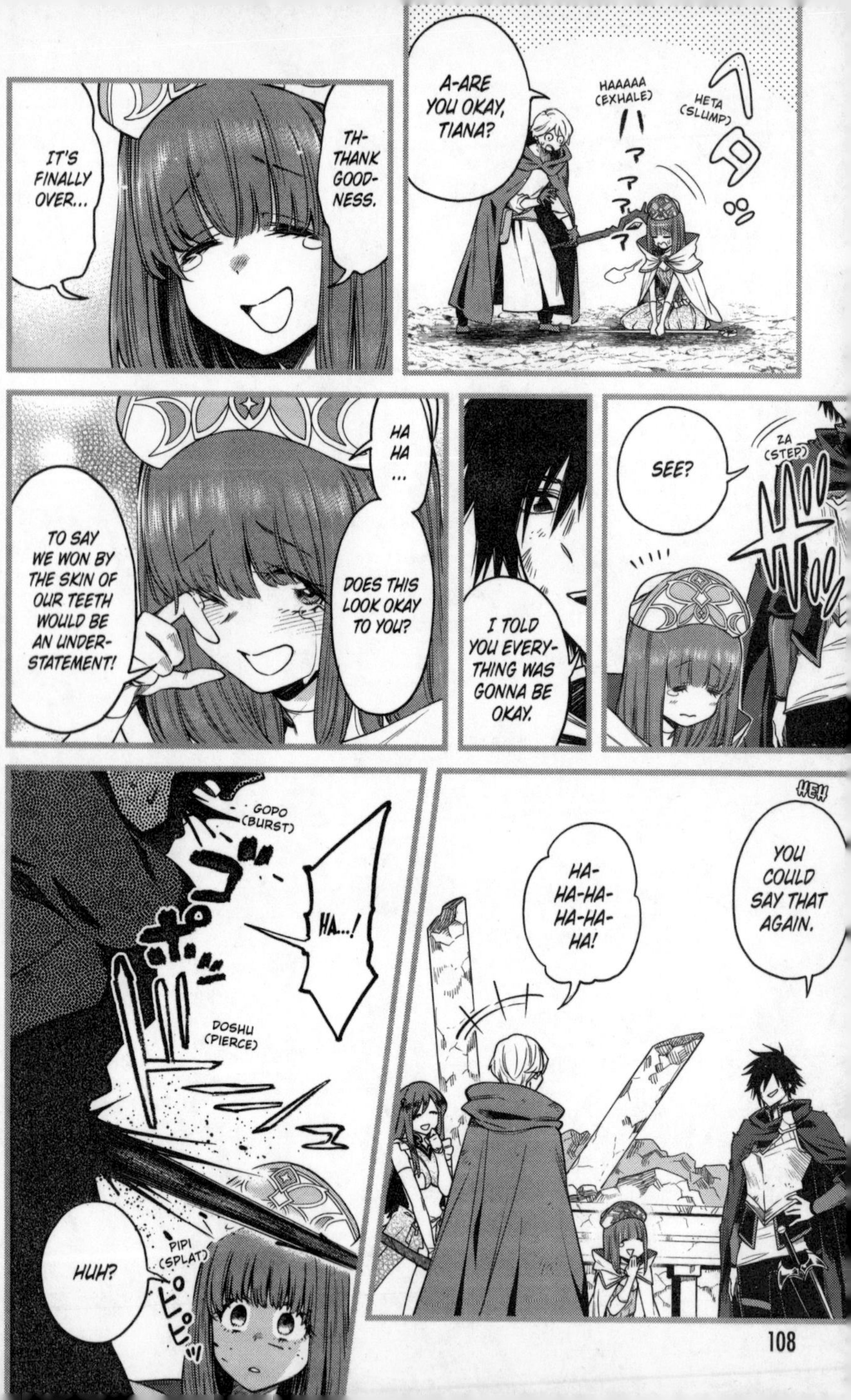
A-ARE YOU OKAY, TIANA?
HAAAAA (EXHALE)
HETA (SLUMP)
TH-THANK GOODNESS.
IT'S FINALLY OVER...
ZA (STEP)
SEE?
I TOLD YOU EVERYTHING WAS GONNA BE OKAY.
HA HA ...
DOES THIS LOOK OKAY TO YOU?
TO SAY WE WON BY THE SKIN OF OUR TEETH WOULD BE AN UNDERSTATEMENT!
HEH
YOU COULD SAY THAT AGAIN.
HA-HA-HA-HA-HA-HA!
GOPO (BURST)
HA...!
DOSHU (PIERCE)
PIPI (SPLAT)
HUH?

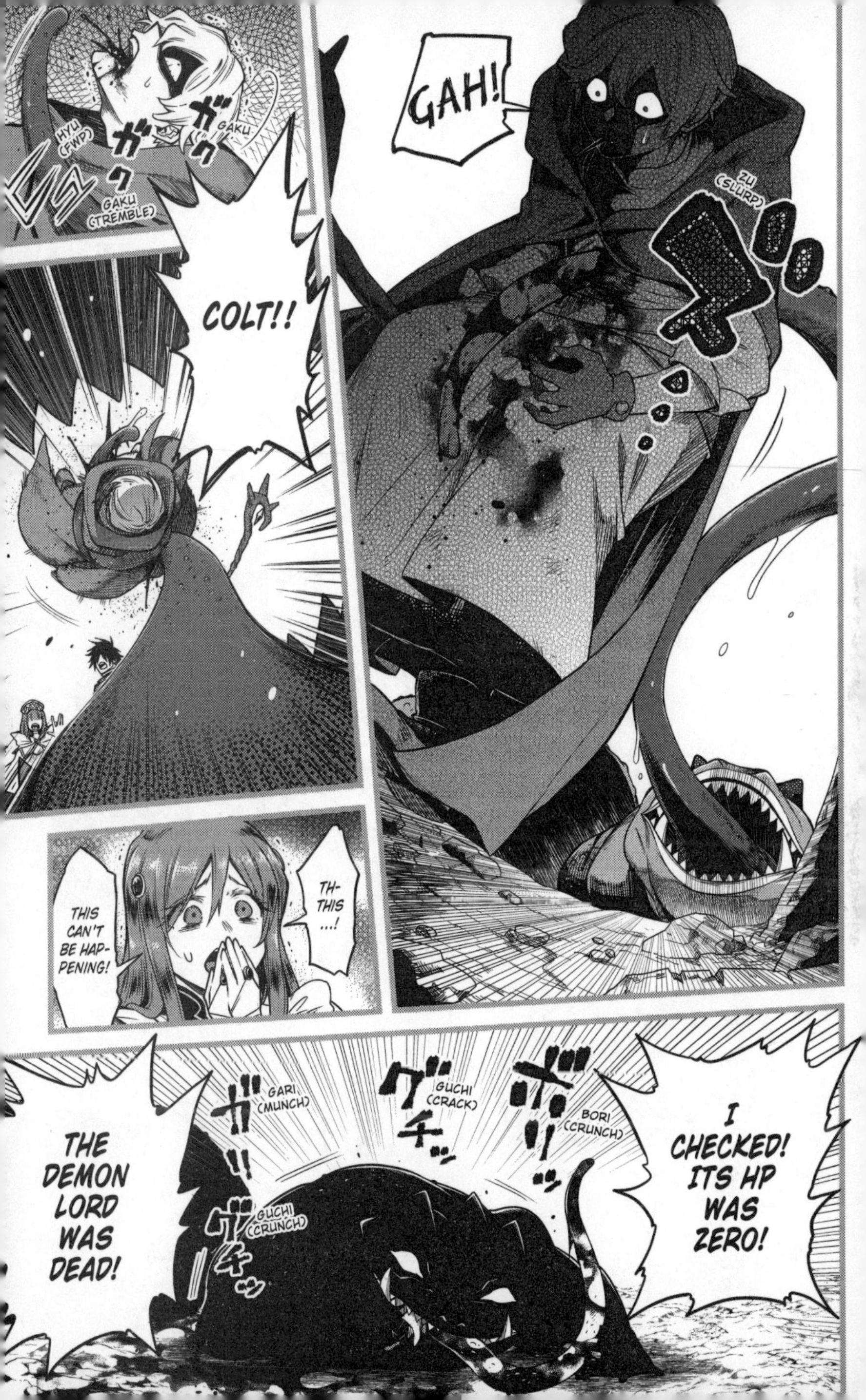
GAH!
ZU (SLURP)
GAKU
HYU (FWP)
GAKU (TREMBLE)
COLT!!
TH-THIS ...!
THIS CAN'T BE HAP-PENING!
I CHECKED! ITS HP WAS ZERO!
BORI (CRUNCH)
GUCHI (CRACK)
GARI (MUNCH)
GUCHI (CRUNCH)
THE DEMON LORD WAS DEAD!

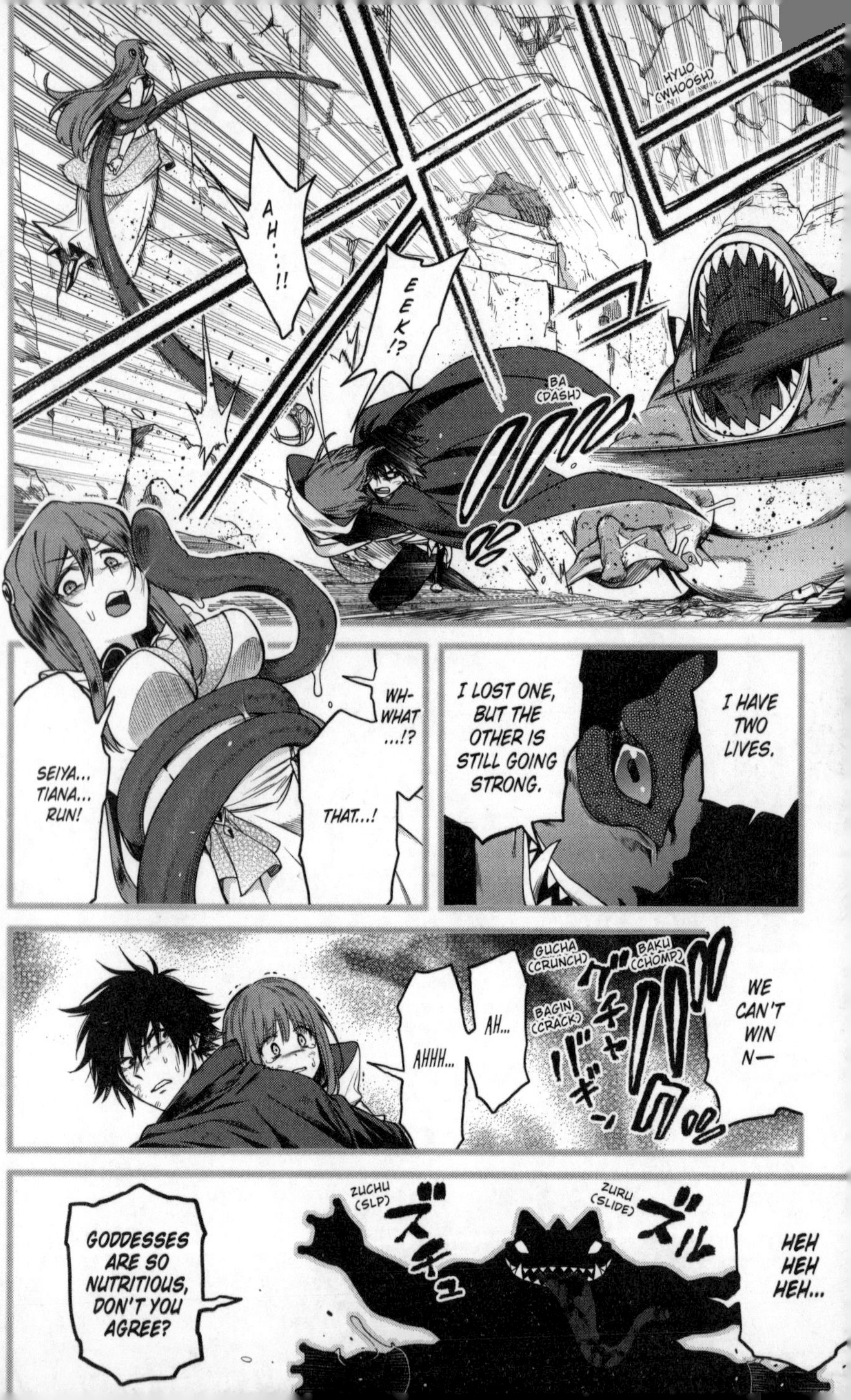
HYUO (WHOOSH)
EEK!?
AH...!!
BA (DASH)
I HAVE TWO LIVES.
I LOST ONE, BUT THE OTHER IS STILL GOING STRONG.
WH- WHAT ...!?
THAT...!
SEIYA... TIANA... RUN!
WE CAN'T WIN N—
BAKU (CHOMP)
GUCHA (CRUNCH)
BAGIN (CRACK)
AH...
AHHH...
HEH HEH HEH...
ZURU (SLIDE)
ZUCHU (SLP)
GODDESSES ARE SO NUTRITIOUS, DON'T YOU AGREE?

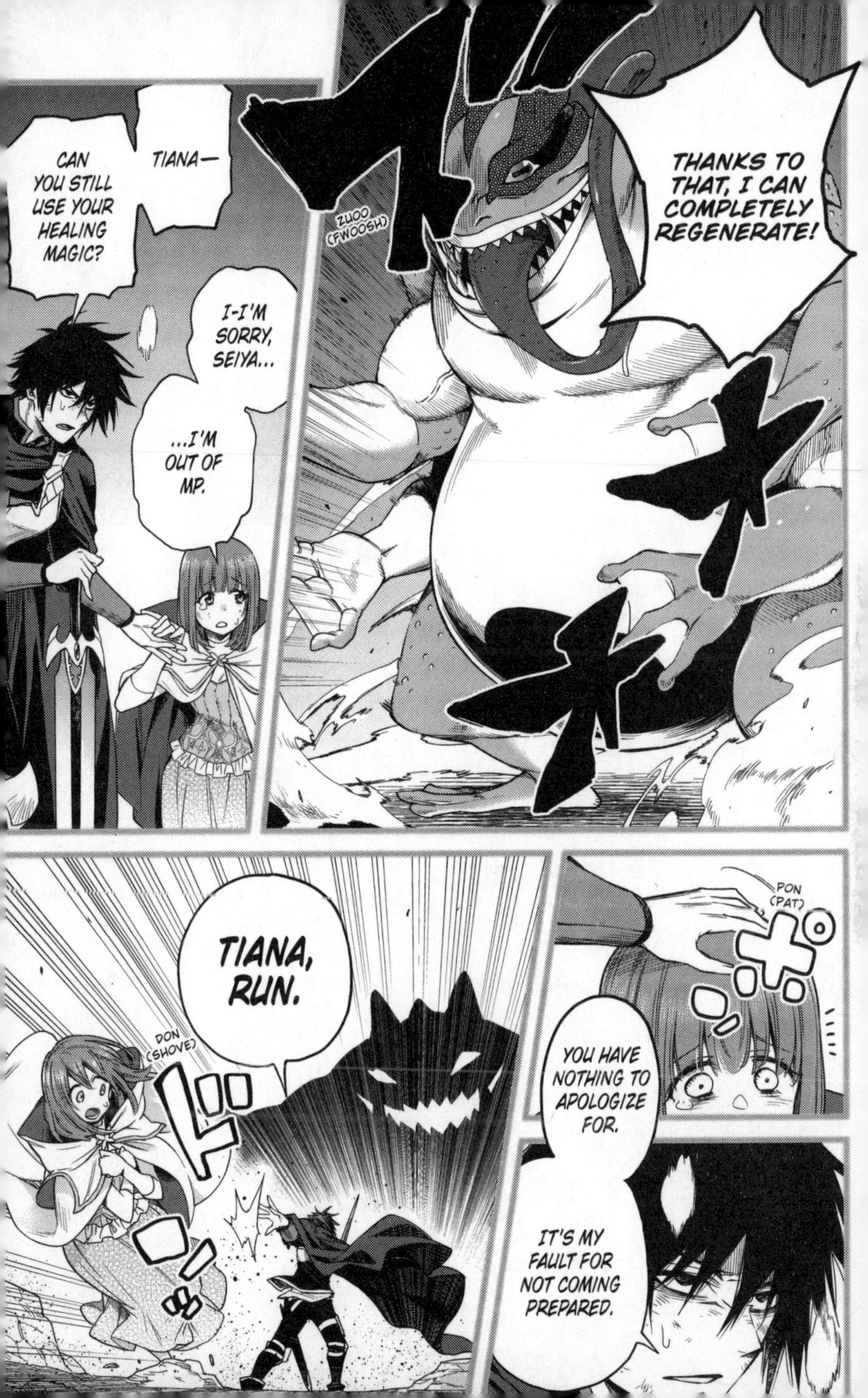
THANKS TO THAT, I CAN COMPLETELY REGENERATE!
ZUOO (FWOOSH)
TIANA—
CAN YOU STILL USE YOUR HEALING MAGIC?
I-I'M SORRY, SEIYA...
...I'M OUT OF MP.
PON (PAT)
YOU HAVE NOTHING TO APOLOGIZE FOR.
IT'S MY FAULT FOR NOT COMING PREPARED.
TIANA, RUN.
DON (SHOVE)

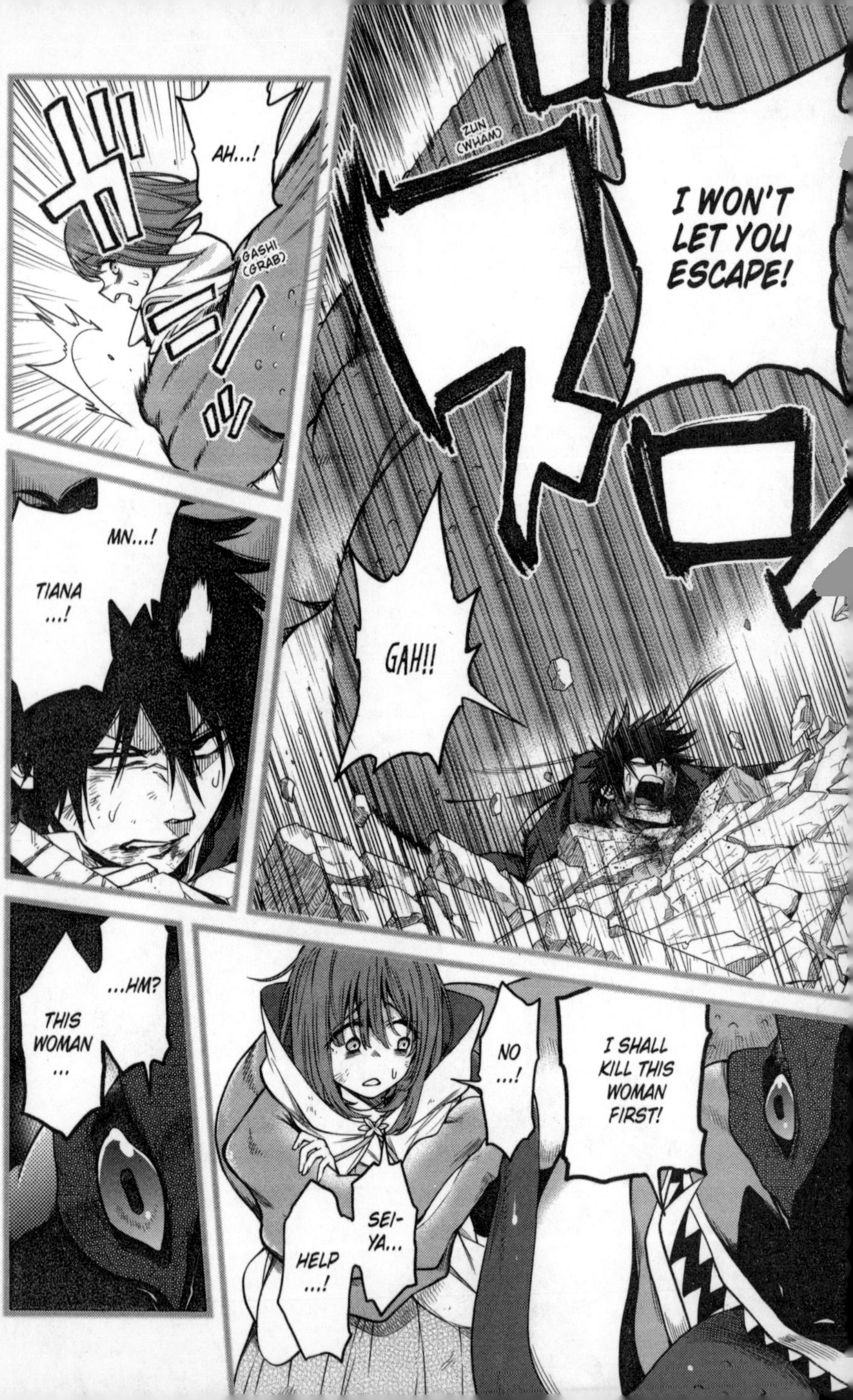
I WON'T LET YOU ESCAPE!
ZUN (WHAM)
GAH!!
AH...!
GASHI (GRAB)
MN...!
TIANA ...!
I SHALL KILL THIS WOMAN FIRST!
NO ...!
SEI-YA...
HELP ...!
...HM?
THIS WOMAN ...

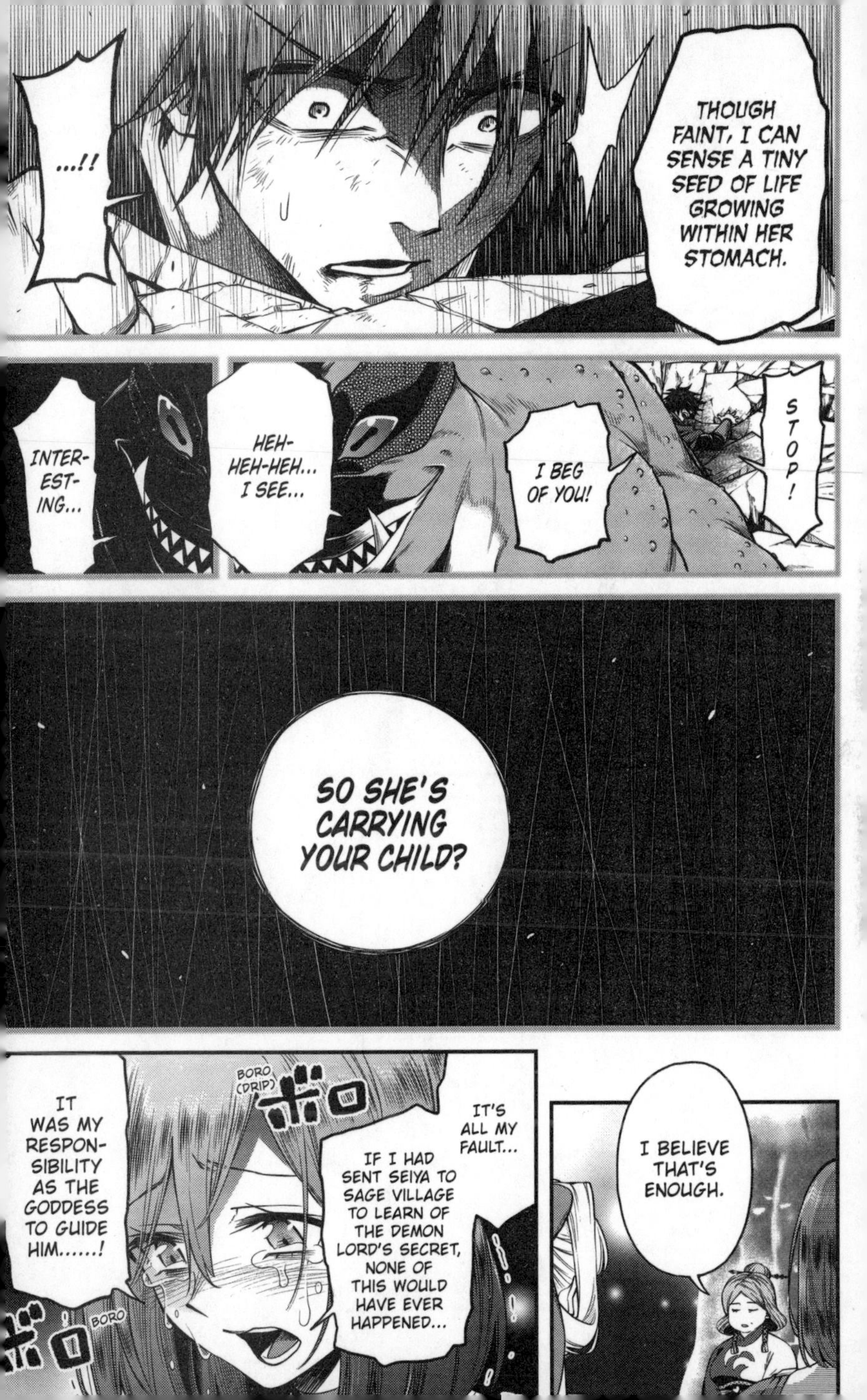
THOUGH FAINT, I CAN SENSE A TINY SEED OF LIFE GROWING WITHIN HER STOMACH.
...!!
STOP!
I BEG OF YOU!
HEH-HEH-HEH... I SEE...
INTER-EST-ING...
SO SHE'S CARRYING YOUR CHILD?
I BELIEVE THAT'S ENOUGH.
IT'S ALL MY FAULT...
IF I HAD SENT SEIYA TO SAGE VILLAGE TO LEARN OF THE DEMON LORD'S SECRET, NONE OF THIS WOULD HAVE EVER HAPPENED...
BORO (DRIP)
IT WAS MY RESPON-SIBILITY AS THE GODDESS TO GUIDE HIM......!
BORO

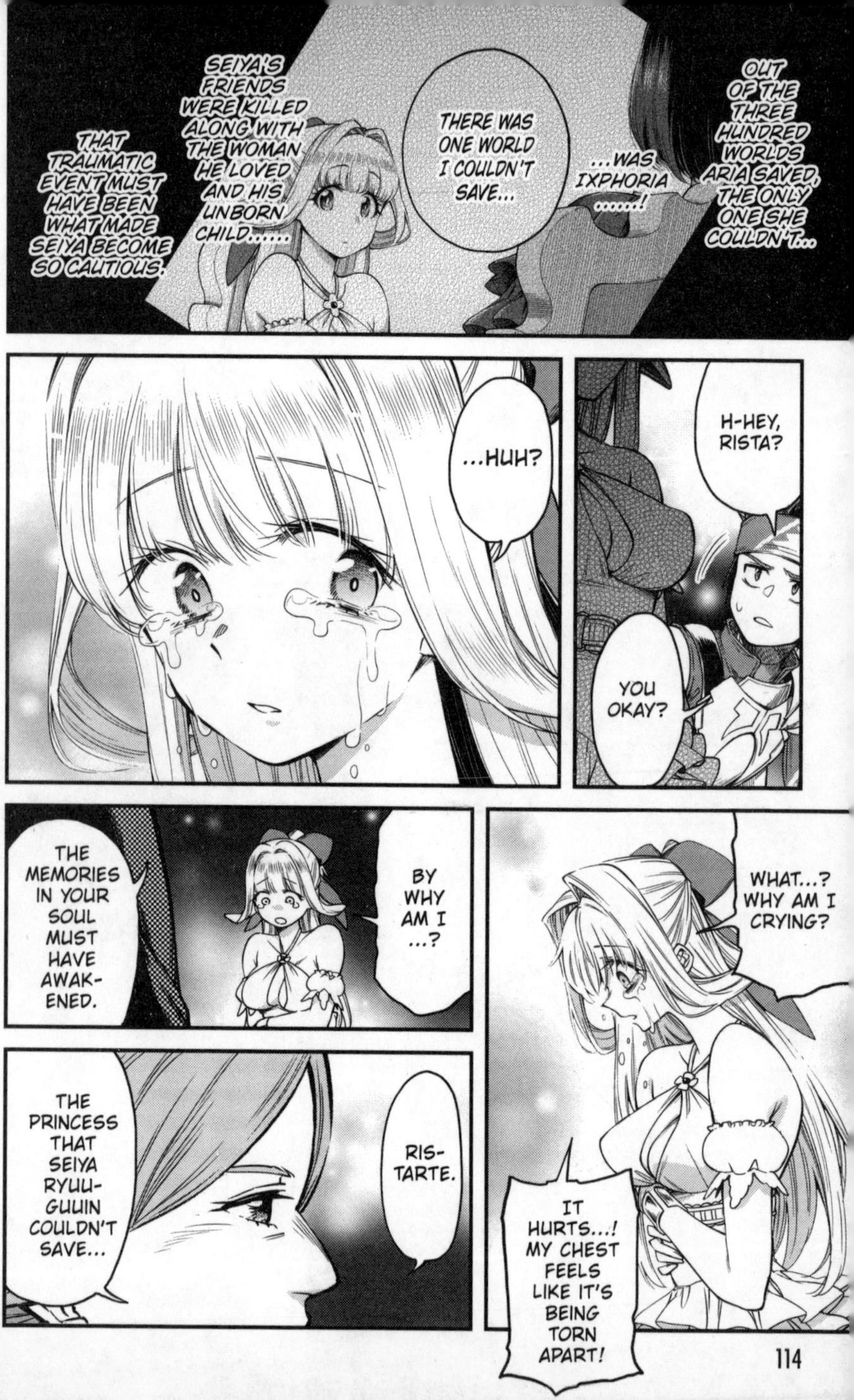
OUT OF THE THREE HUNDRED WORLDS ARIA SAVED, THE ONLY ONE SHE COULDN'T...
...WAS IXPHORIA ....!
THERE WAS ONE WORLD I COULDN'T SAVE...
SEIYA'S FRIENDS WERE KILLED ALONG WITH THE WOMAN HE LOVED AND HIS UNBORN CHILD......
THAT TRAUMATIC EVENT MUST HAVE BEEN WHAT MADE SEIYA BECOME SO CAUTIOUS.
H-HEY, RISTA?
YOU OKAY?
...HUH?
WHAT...? WHY AM I CRYING?
IT HURTS...! MY CHEST FEELS LIKE IT'S BEING TORN APART!
BY WHY AM I ...?
THE MEMORIES IN YOUR SOUL MUST HAVE AWAK-ENED.
RIS-TARTE.
THE PRINCESS THAT SEIYA RYUU-GUUIN COULDN'T SAVE...

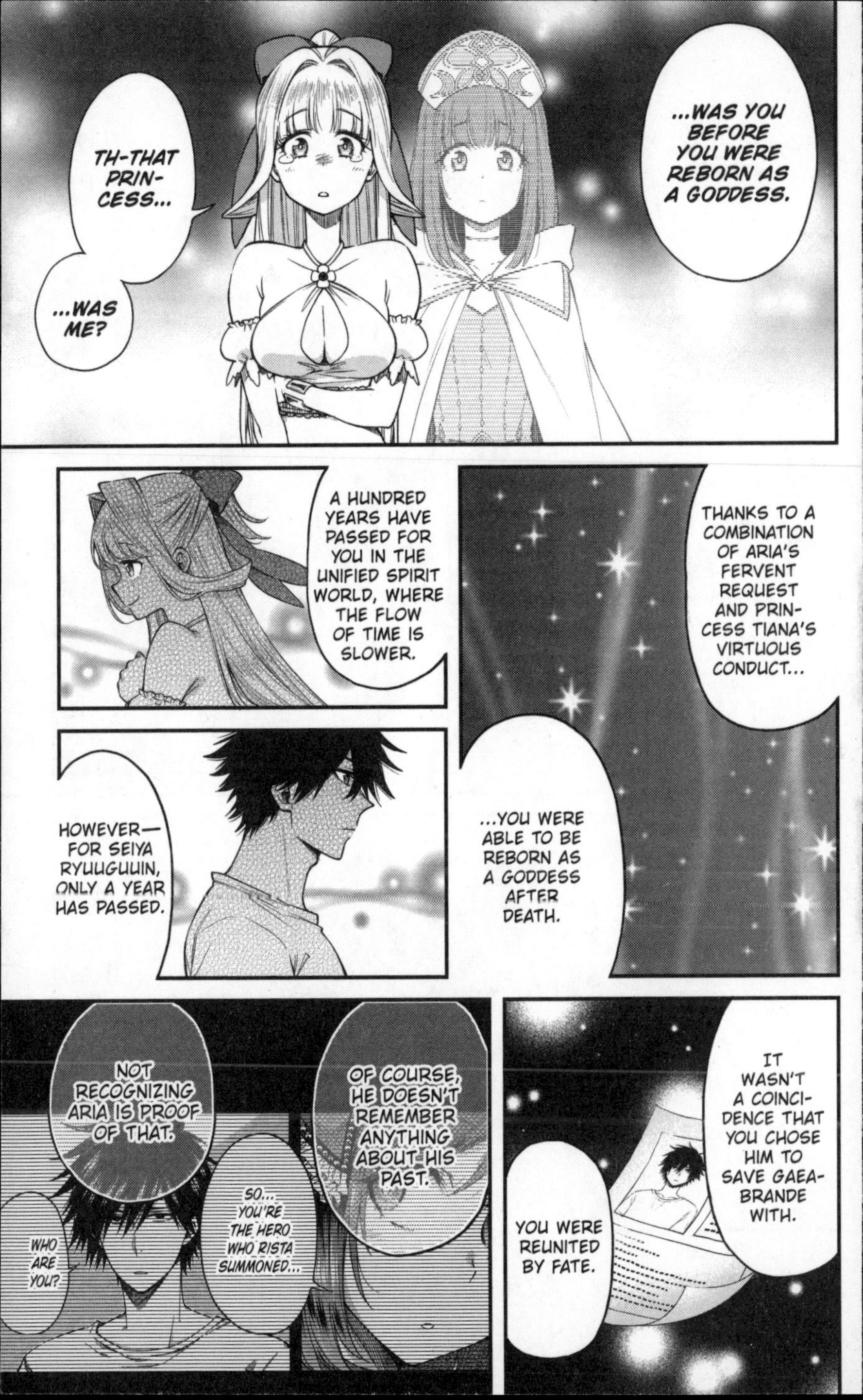
...WAS YOU BEFORE YOU WERE REBORN AS A GODDESS.
TH-THAT PRIN-CESS...
...WAS ME?
THANKS TO A COMBINATION OF ARIA'S FERVENT REQUEST AND PRIN-CESS TIANA'S VIRTUOUS CONDUCT...
...YOU WERE ABLE TO BE REBORN AS A GODDESS AFTER DEATH.
A HUNDRED YEARS HAVE PASSED FOR YOU IN THE UNIFIED SPIRIT WORLD, WHERE THE FLOW OF TIME IS SLOWER.
HOWEVER—FOR SEIYA RYUUGUUIN, ONLY A YEAR HAS PASSED.
IT WASN'T A COINCI-DENCE THAT YOU CHOSE HIM TO SAVE GAEA-BRANDE WITH.
YOU WERE REUNITED BY FATE.
OF COURSE, HE DOESN'T REMEMBER ANYTHING ABOUT HIS PAST.
NOT RECOGNIZING ARIA IS PROOF OF THAT.
SO... YOU'RE THE HERO WHO RISTA SUMMONED...
WHO ARE YOU?

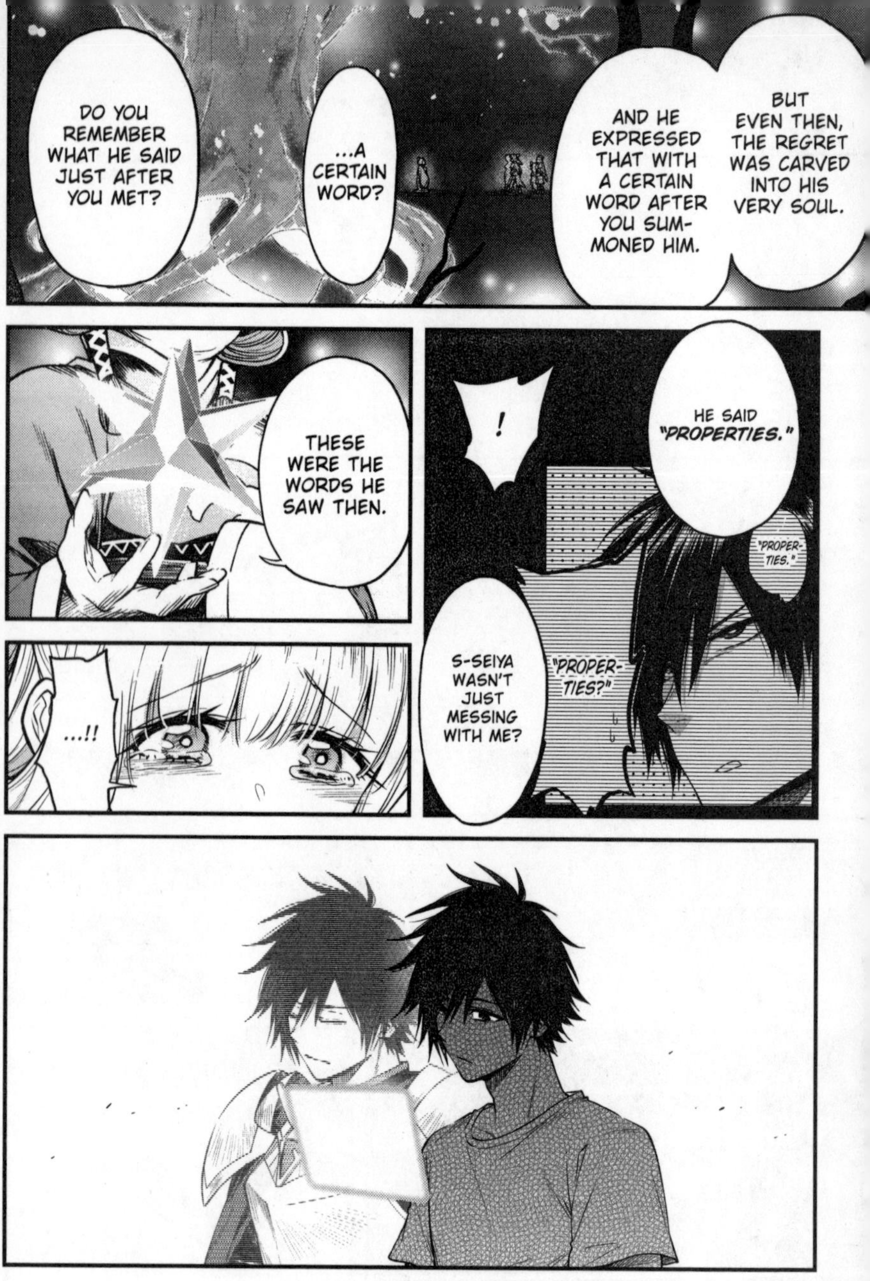
BUT EVEN THEN, THE REGRET WAS CARVED INTO HIS VERY SOUL.
AND HE EXPRESSED THAT WITH A CERTAIN WORD AFTER YOU SUM-MONED HIM.
...A CERTAIN WORD?
DO YOU REMEMBER WHAT HE SAID JUST AFTER YOU MET?
HE SAID "PROPERTIES."
!
"PROPER-TIES."
"PROPER-TIES?"
S-SEIYA WASN'T JUST MESSING WITH ME?
THESE WERE THE WORDS HE SAW THEN.
...!!

BE CAREFUL—

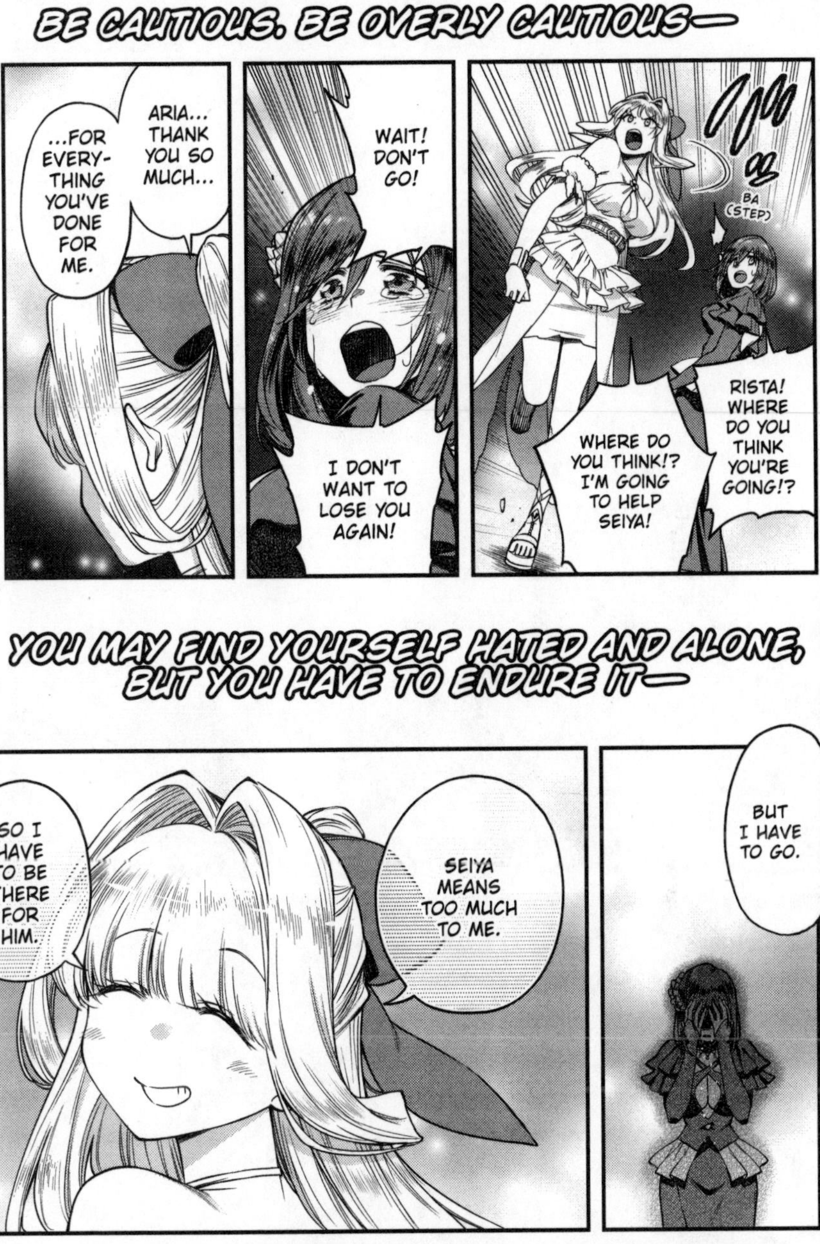
BE CAUTIOUS. BE OVERLY CAUTIOUS—
BA (STEP)
RISTA! WHERE DO YOU THINK YOU'RE GOING!?
WHERE DO YOU THINK!? I'M GOING TO HELP SEIYA!
WAIT! DON'T GO!
I DON'T WANT TO LOSE YOU AGAIN!
ARIA... THANK YOU SO MUCH...
...FOR EVERY-THING YOU'VE DONE FOR ME.
YOU MAY FIND YOURSELF HATED AND ALONE, BUT YOU HAVE TO ENDURE IT—
BUT I HAVE TO GO.
SEIYA MEANS TOO MUCH TO ME.
SO I HAVE TO BE THERE FOR HIM.
SO THAT THIS TIME, FOR SURE—

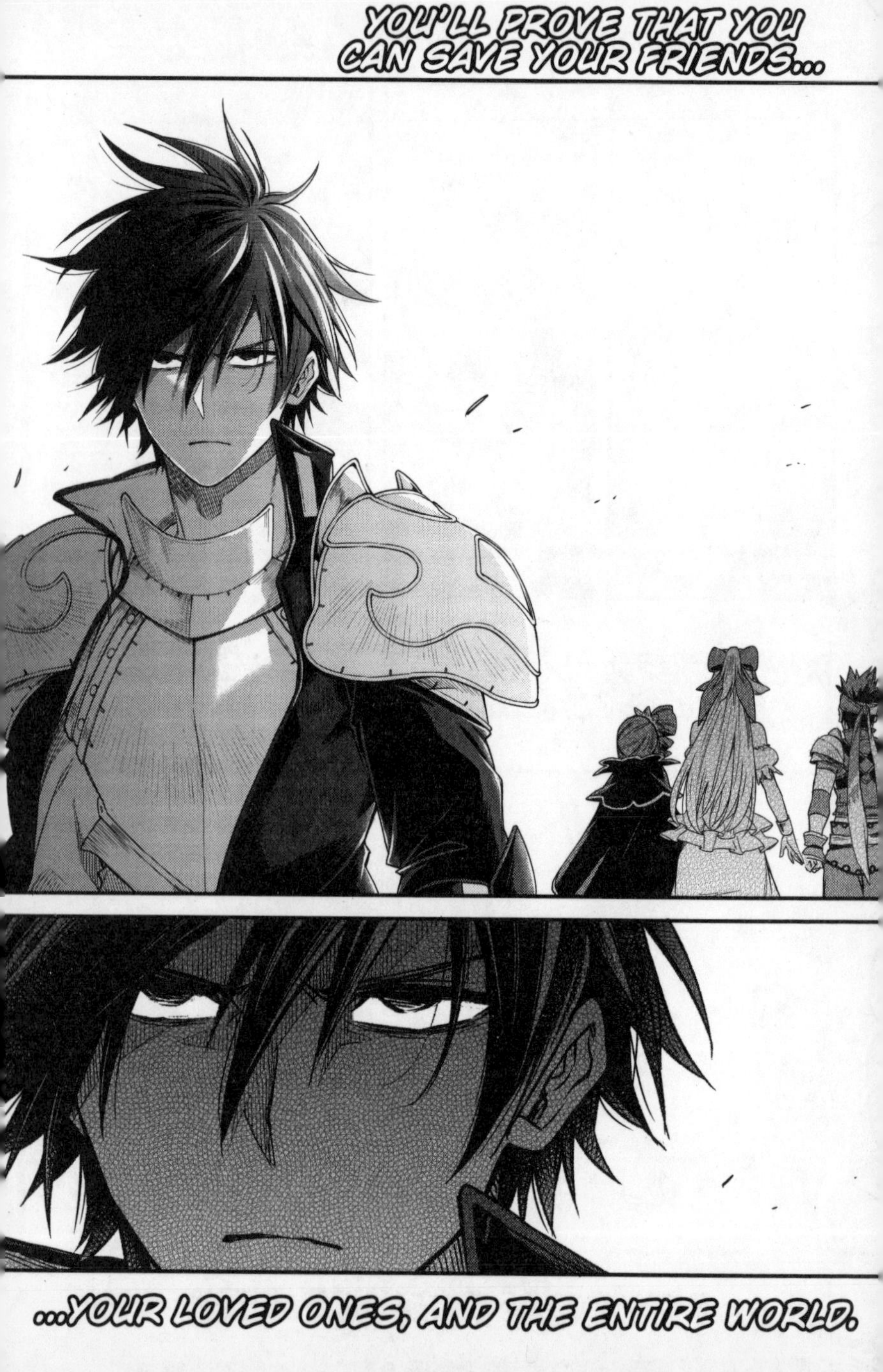
YOU'LL PROVE THAT YOU CAN SAVE YOUR FRIENDS...
...YOUR LOVED ONES, AND THE ENTIRE WORLD.

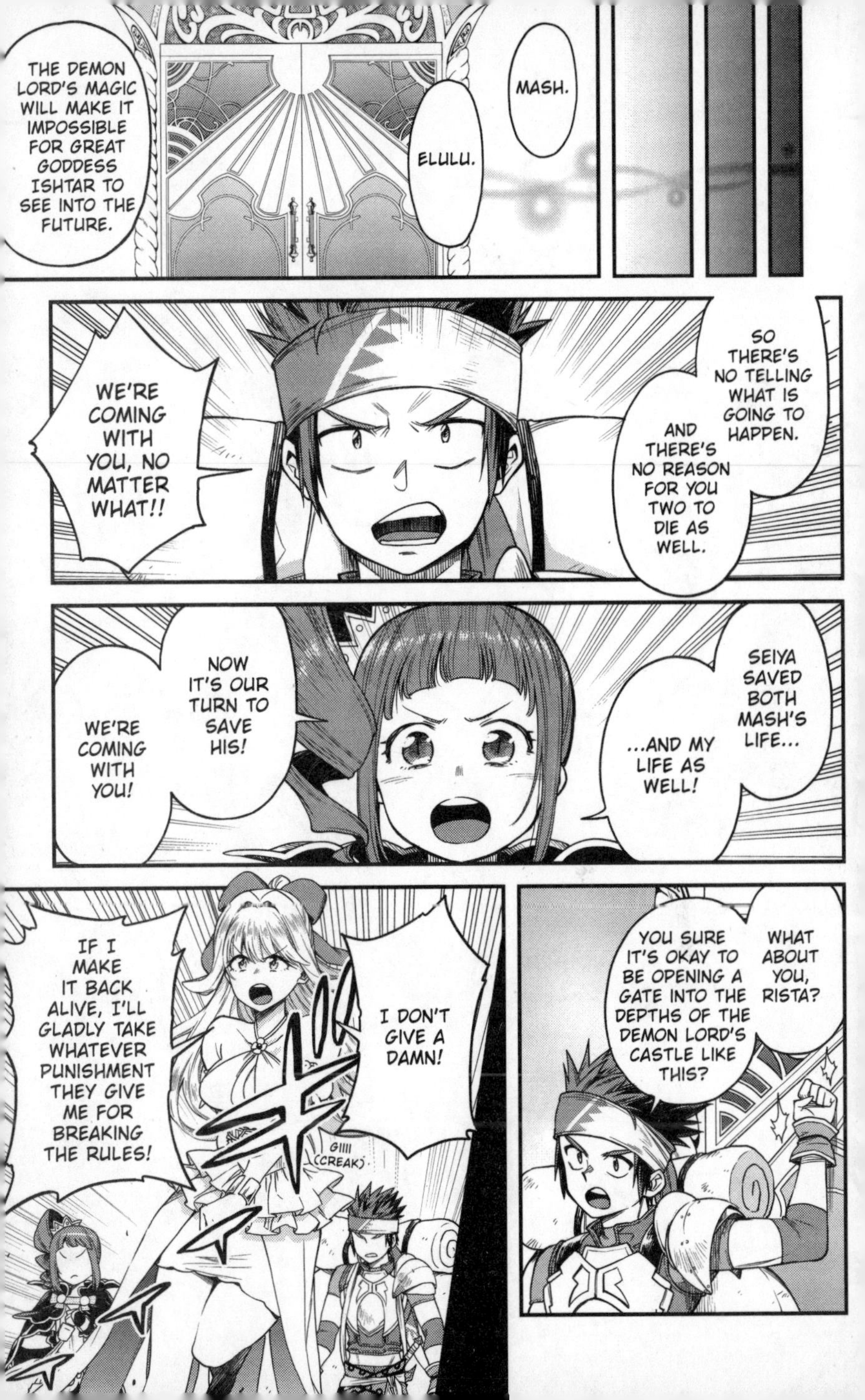
MASH.
ELULU.
THE DEMON LORD'S MAGIC WILL MAKE IT IMPOSSIBLE FOR GREAT GODDESS ISHTAR TO SEE INTO THE FUTURE.
SO THERE'S NO TELLING WHAT IS GOING TO HAPPEN.
AND THERE'S NO REASON FOR YOU TWO TO DIE AS WELL.
WE'RE COMING WITH YOU, NO MATTER WHAT!!
SEIYA SAVED BOTH MASH'S LIFE...
...AND MY LIFE AS WELL!
NOW IT'S OUR TURN TO SAVE HIS!
WE'RE COMING WITH YOU!
WHAT ABOUT YOU, RISTA?
YOU SURE IT'S OKAY TO BE OPENING A GATE INTO THE DEPTHS OF THE DEMON LORD'S CASTLE LIKE THIS?
I DON'T GIVE A DAMN!
IF I MAKE IT BACK ALIVE, I'LL GLADLY TAKE WHATEVER PUNISHMENT THEY GIVE ME FOR BREAKING THE RULES!
GIIII (CREAK)

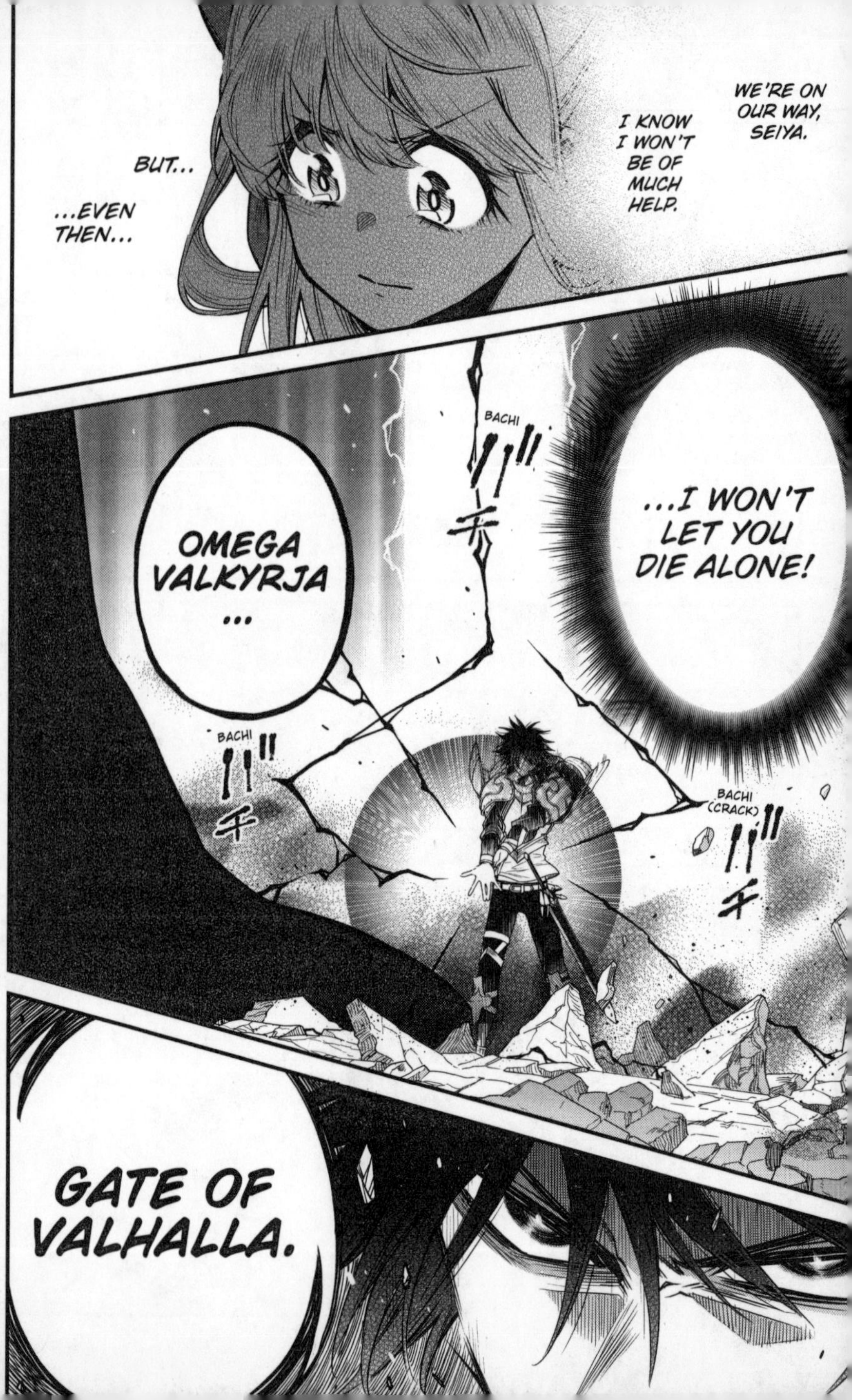
WE'RE ON OUR WAY, SEIYA.
I KNOW I WON'T BE OF MUCH HELP.
BUT...
...EVEN THEN...
...I WON'T LET YOU DIE ALONE!
BACHI
OMEGA VALKYRJA ...
BACHI (CRACK)
BACHI
GATE OF VALHALLA.

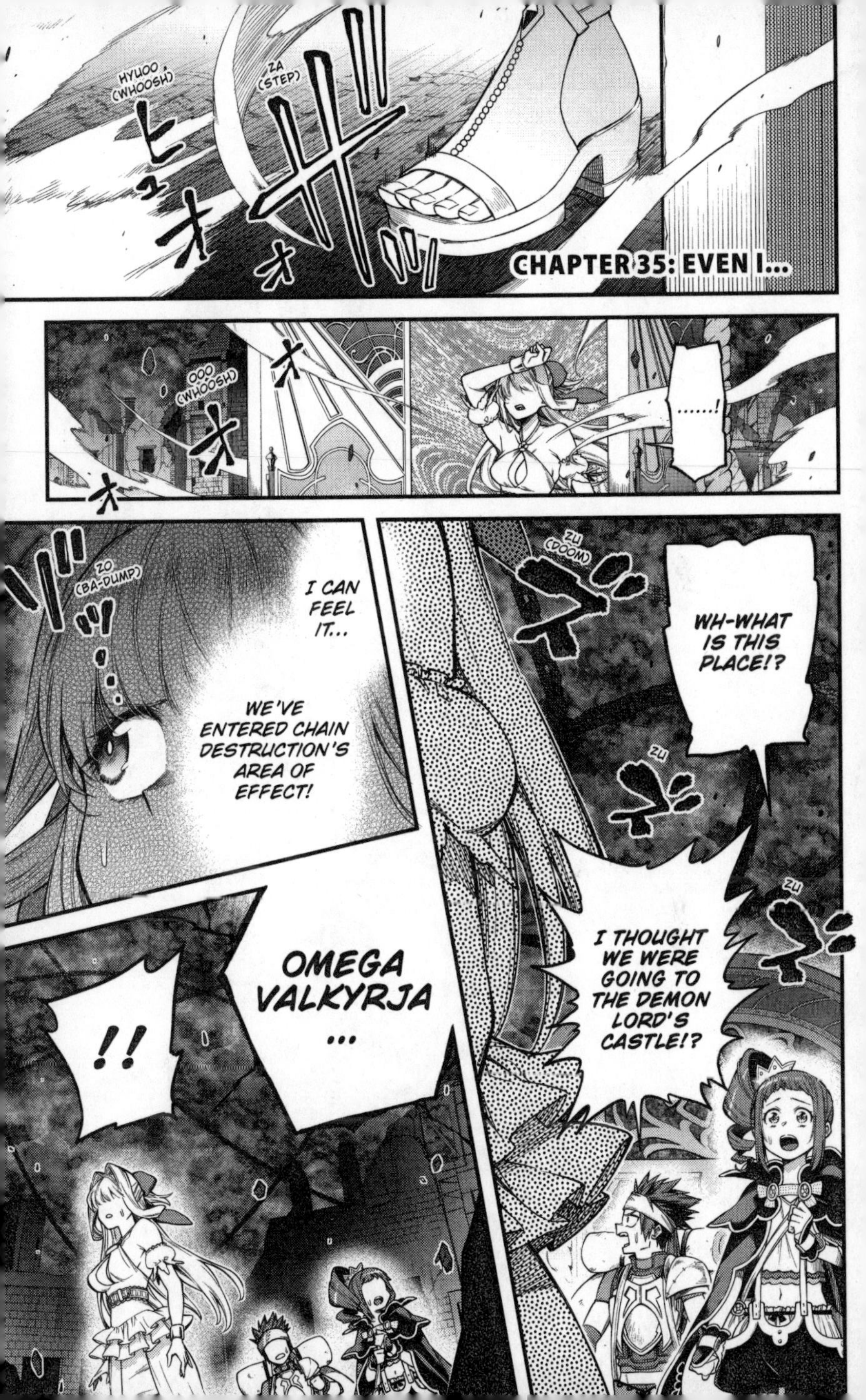
CHAPTER 35: EVEN I...
ZA (STEP)
HYUOO (WHOOSH)
......!
OOO (WHOOSH)
ZU (DOOM)
WH-WHAT IS THIS PLACE!?
ZU
ZU
I THOUGHT WE WERE GOING TO THE DEMON LORD'S CASTLE!?
ZO (BA-DUMP)
I CAN FEEL IT...
WE'VE ENTERED CHAIN DESTRUCTION'S AREA OF EFFECT!
OMEGA VALKYRJA ...
!!

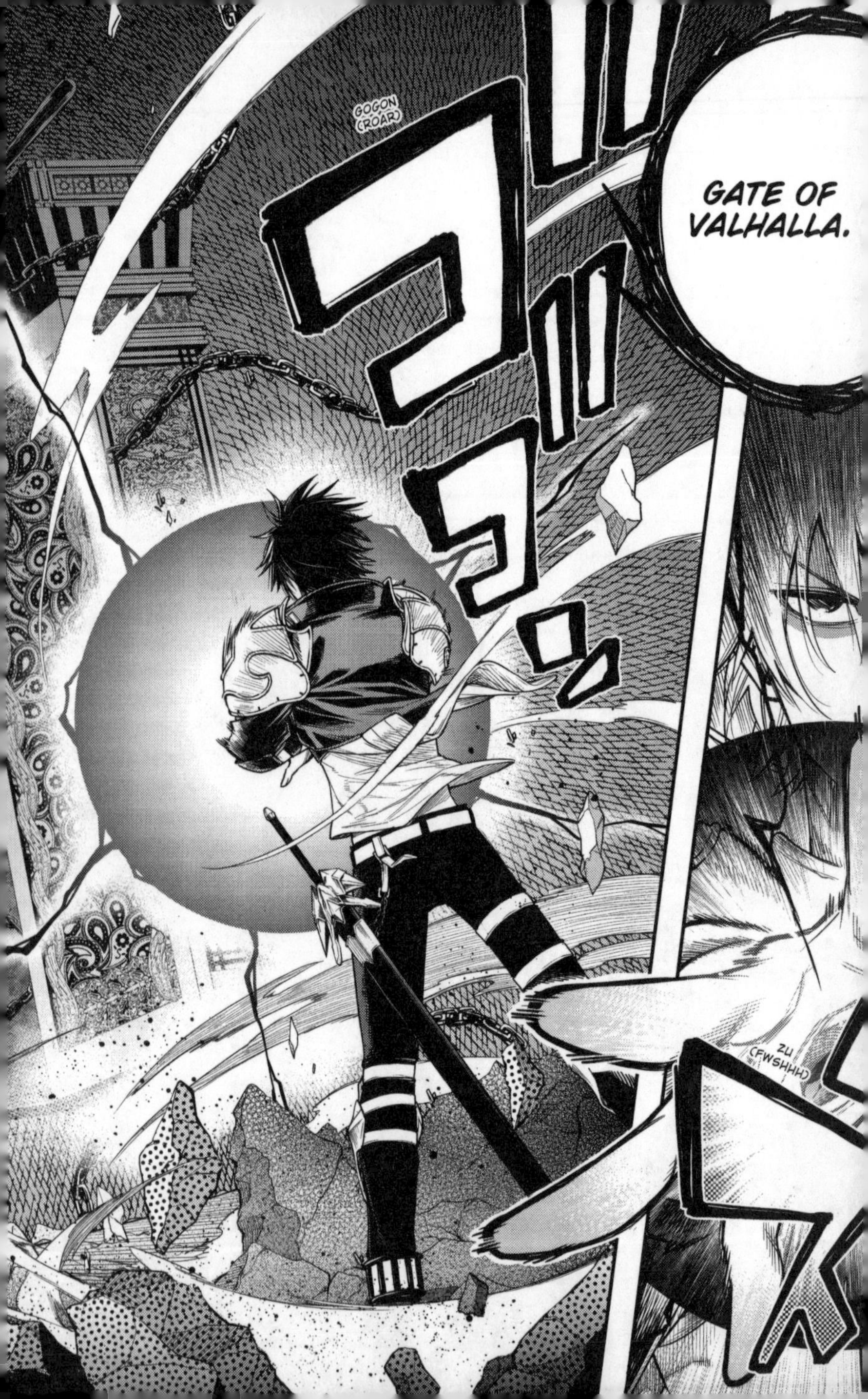
GATE OF VALHALLA.
GOGON (ROAR)
ZU (FWSHHH)

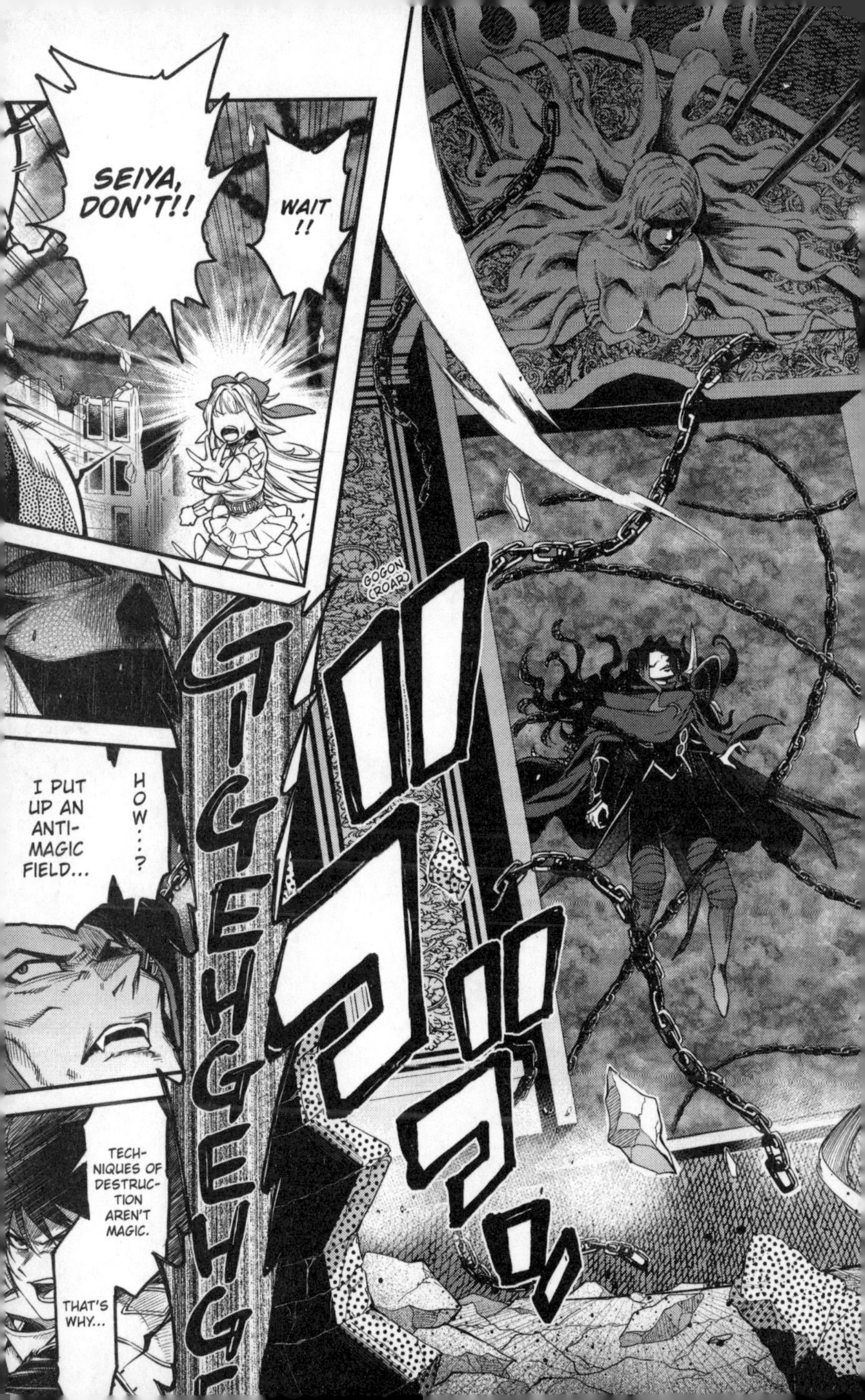
WAIT !!
SEIYA, DON'T!!
GOGON (ROAR)
HOW...?
I PUT UP AN ANTI-MAGIC FIELD...
TECHNIQUES OF DESTRUCTION AREN'T MAGIC.
THAT'S WHY...
GIGEHGEHG

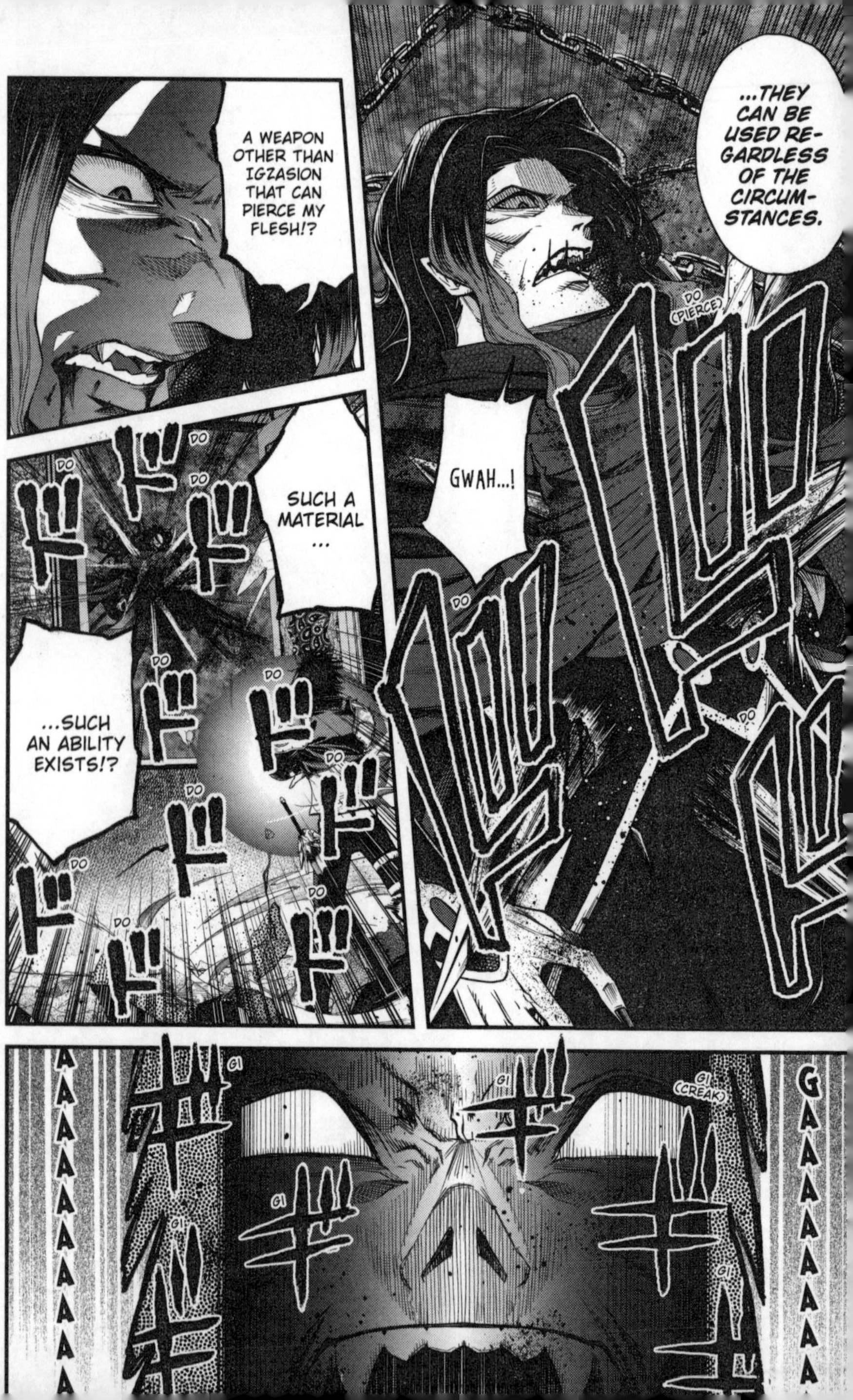
...THEY CAN BE USED RE-GARDLESS OF THE CIRCUM-STANCES.
DO (PIERCE)
GWAH...!
DO
DO
A WEAPON OTHER THAN IGZASION THAT CAN PIERCE MY FLESH!?
SUCH A MATERIAL ...
DO
DO
DO
...SUCH AN ABILITY EXISTS!?
DO
DO
DO
DO
DO
DO
GI (CREAK)
GI
GI
GI
GI
GI
GAAAAAAAAAAAA
AAAAAAAAAAAA

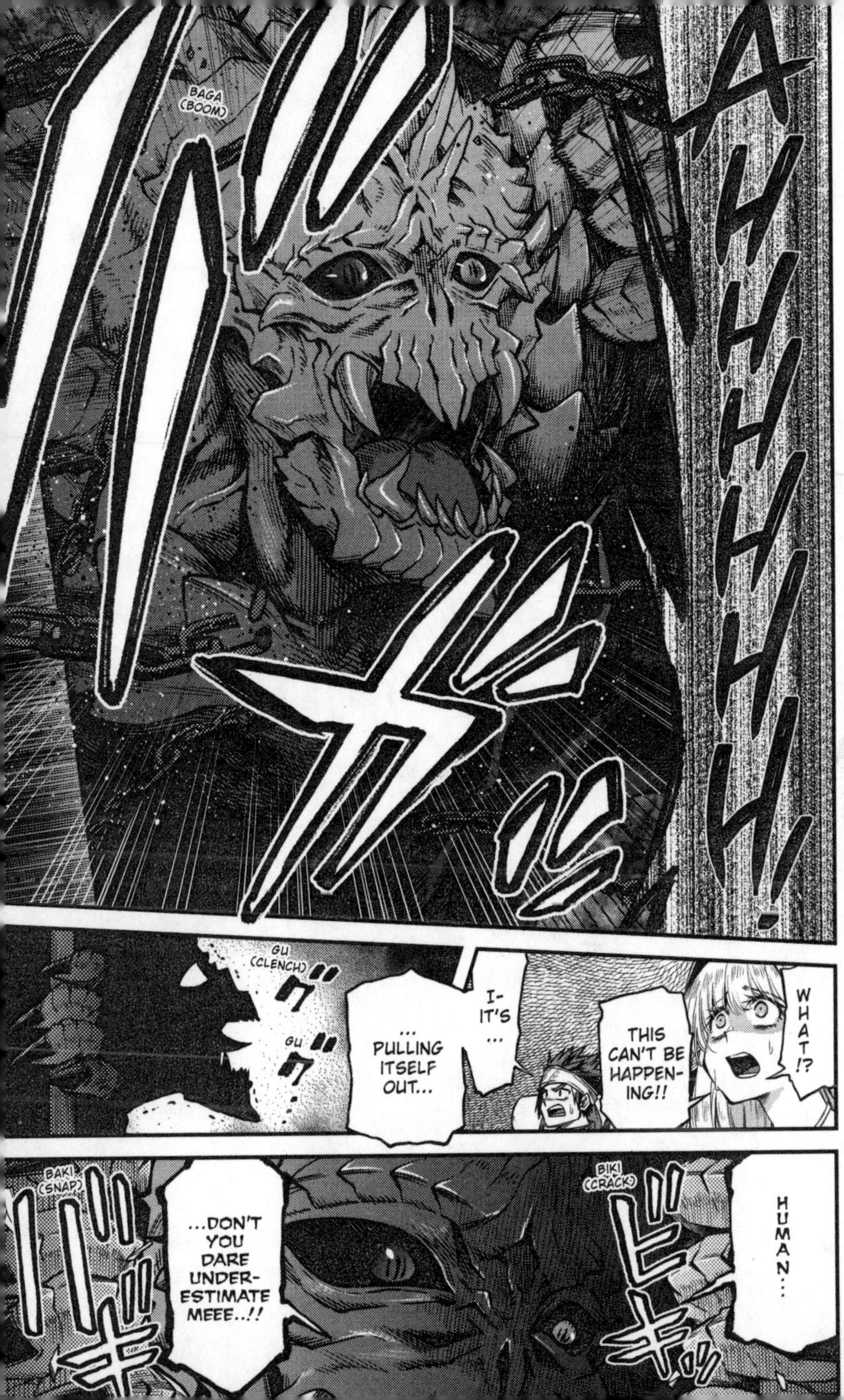
AHHHHHH!
BAGA (BOOM)
WHAT!?
THIS CAN'T BE HAPPENING!!
I-IT'S...
...PULLING ITSELF OUT...
GU (CLENCH)
GU
HUMAN...
BIKI (CRACK)
...DON'T YOU DARE UNDER-ESTIMATE MEEE..!!
BAKI (SNAP)

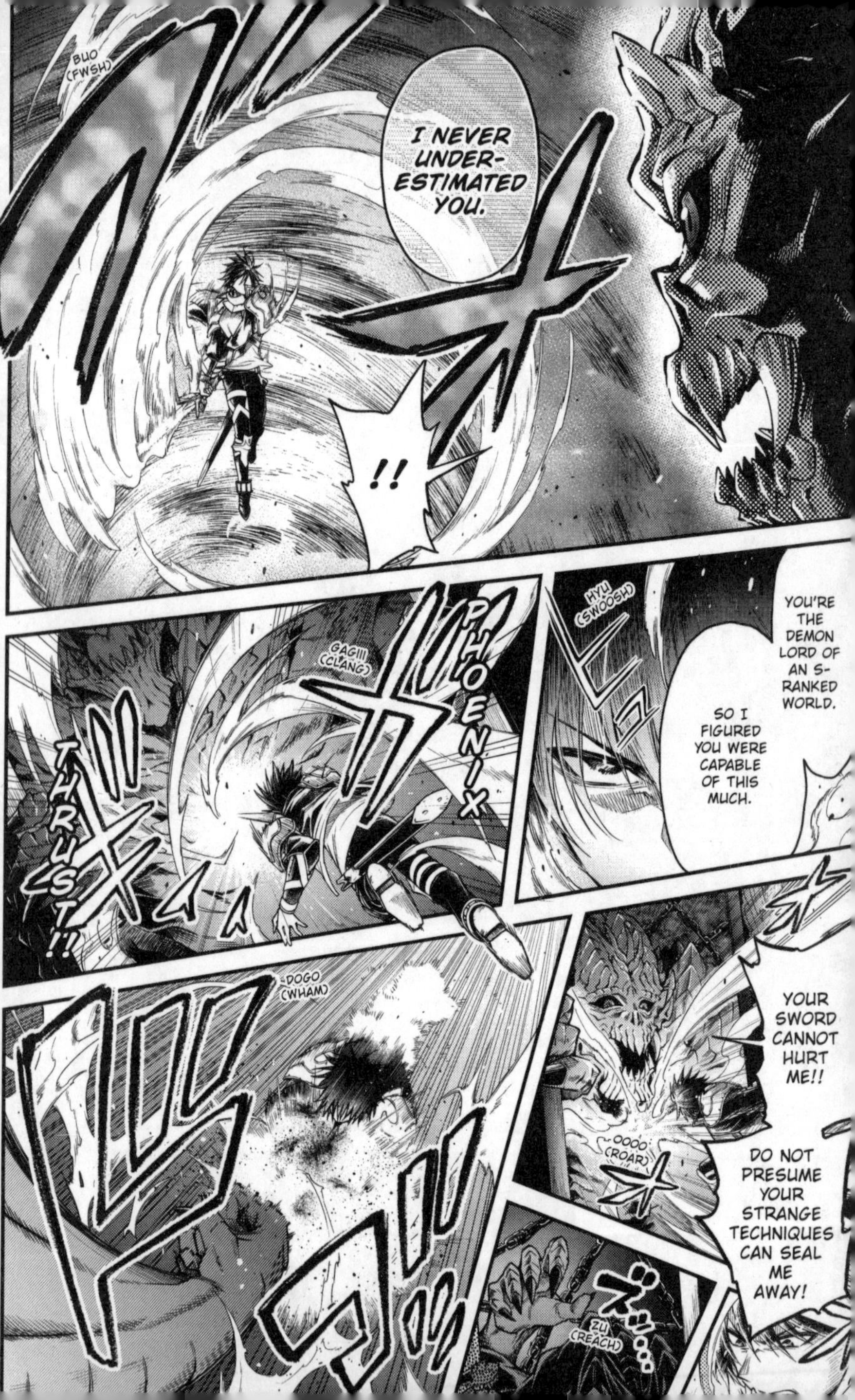
I NEVER UNDER-ESTIMATED YOU.
BUO (FWSH)
!!
YOU'RE THE DEMON LORD OF AN S-RANKED WORLD.
HYU (SWOOSH)
SO I FIGURED YOU WERE CAPABLE OF THIS MUCH.
PHOENIX
GAGIII (CLANG)
THRUST!!
YOUR SWORD CANNOT HURT ME!!
OOOO (ROAR)
DO NOT PRESUME YOUR STRANGE TECHNIQUES CAN SEAL ME AWAY!
ZU (REACH)
DOGO (WHAM)

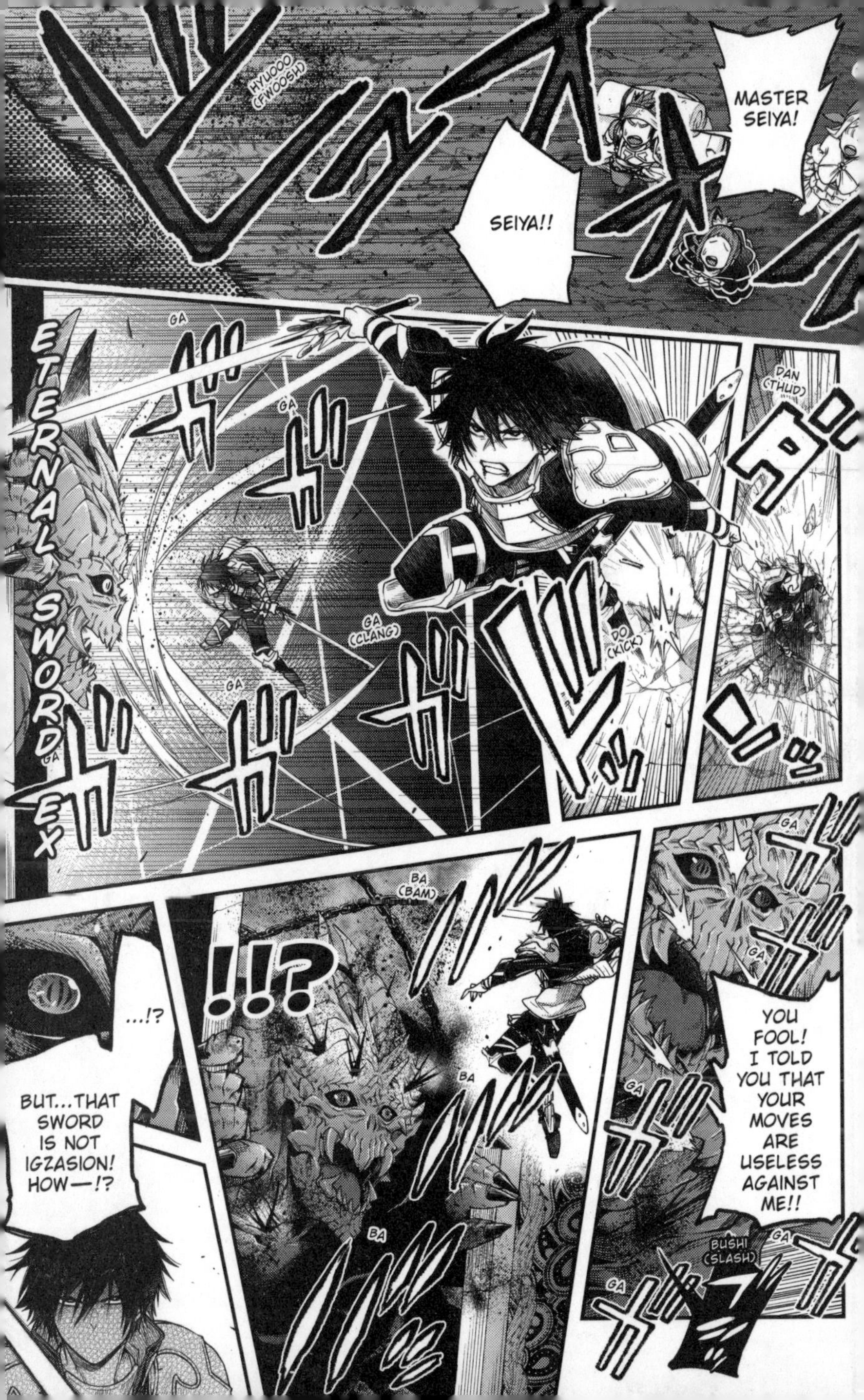
MASTER SEIYA!
SEIYA!!
HYUOOO (FWOOSH)
DAN (THUD)
DO (KICK)
GA
GA
GA (CLANG)
GA
GA
ETERNAL SWORD EX
GA
GA
YOU FOOL! I TOLD YOU THAT YOUR MOVES ARE USELESS AGAINST ME!!
GA
BUSHI (SLASH)
GA
BA (BAM)
!!?
BA
BA
...!?
BUT...THAT SWORD IS NOT IGZASION! HOW—!?

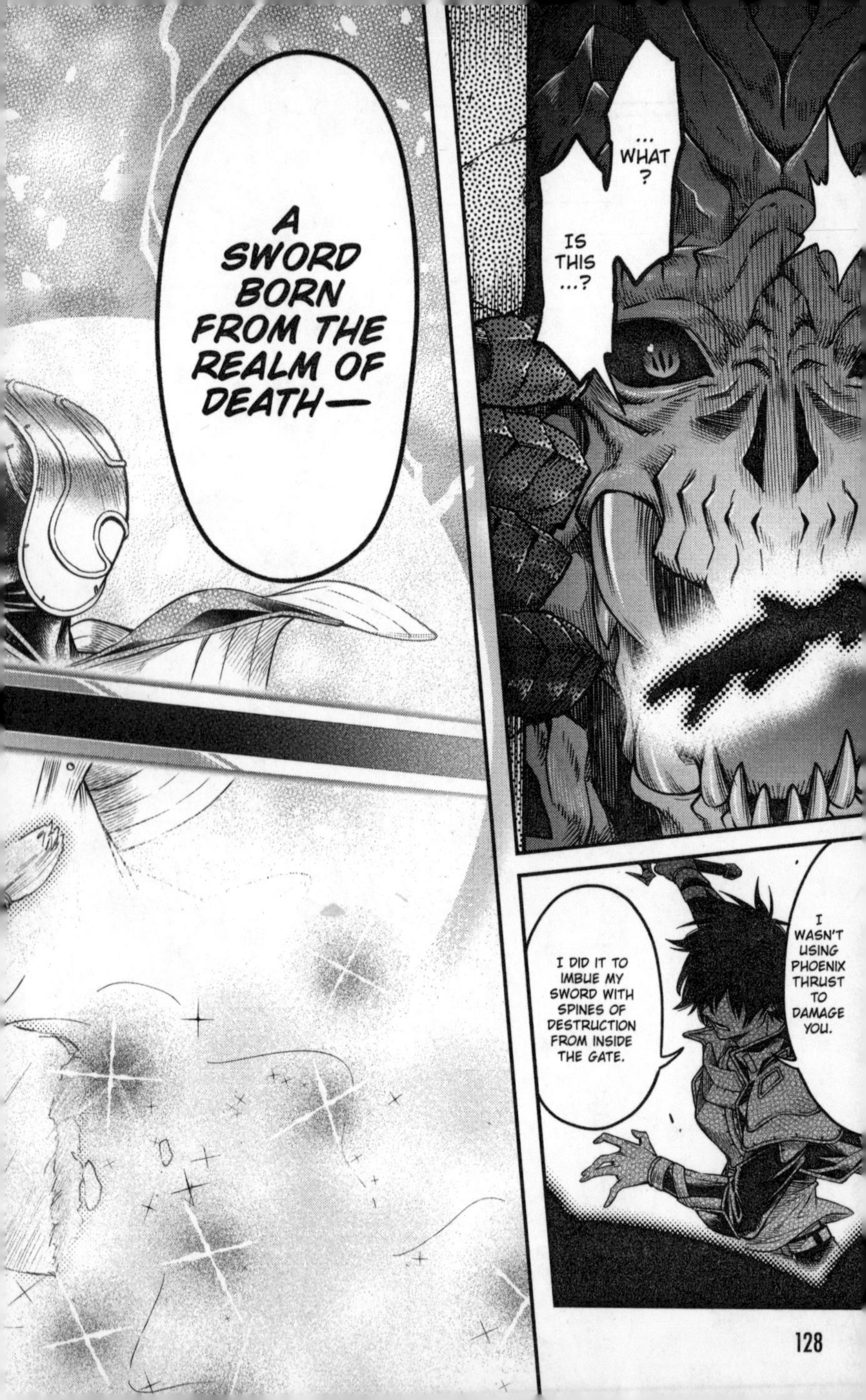
... WHAT ?
IS THIS ...?
I WASN'T USING PHOENIX THRUST TO DAMAGE YOU.
I DID IT TO IMBUE MY SWORD WITH SPINES OF DESTRUCTION FROM INSIDE THE GATE.
A SWORD BORN FROM THE REALM OF DEATH—

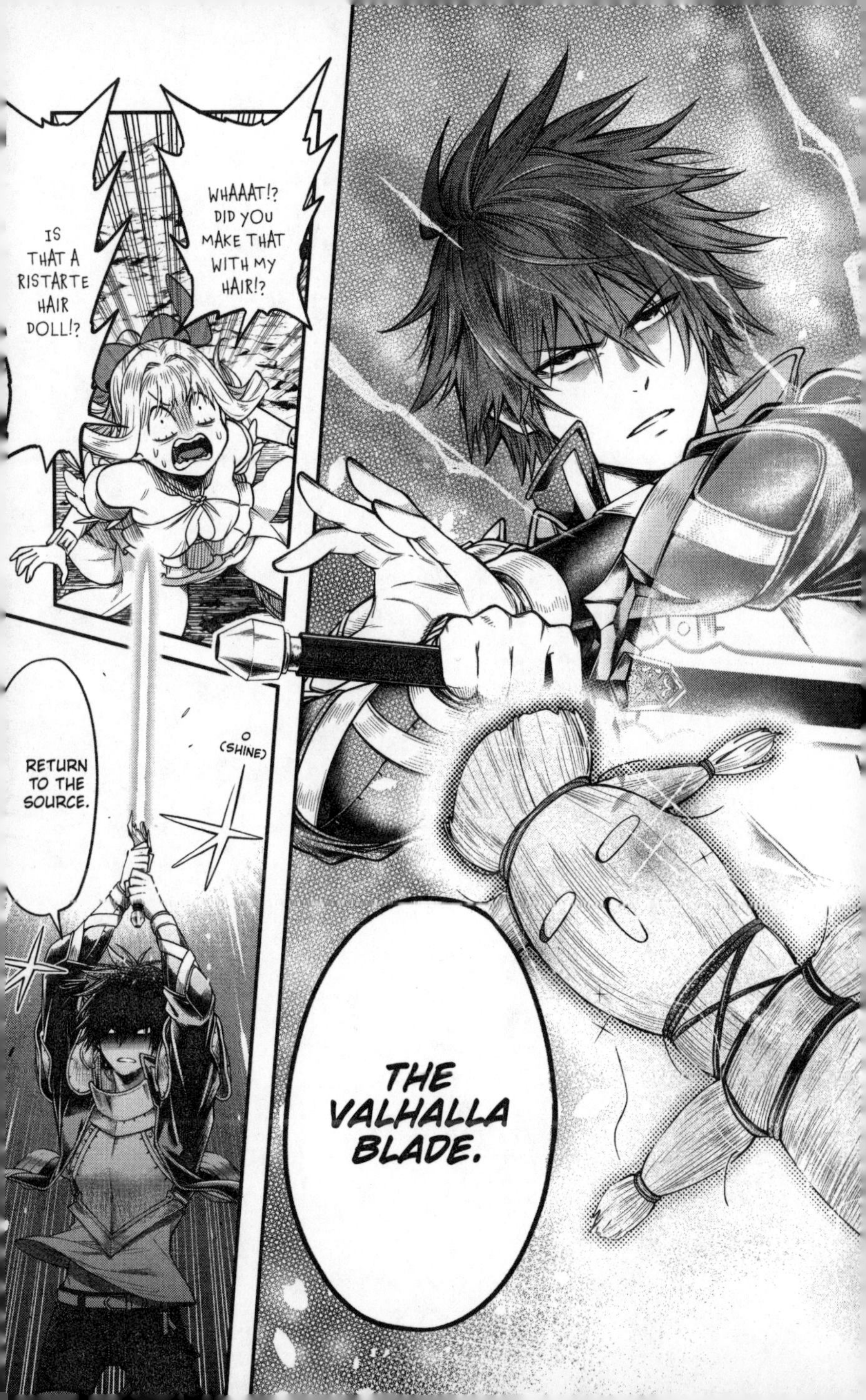
THE VALHALLA BLADE.
WHAAAT!? DID YOU MAKE THAT WITH MY HAIR!?
IS THAT A RISTARTE HAIR DOLL!?
(SHINE)
RETURN TO THE SOURCE.

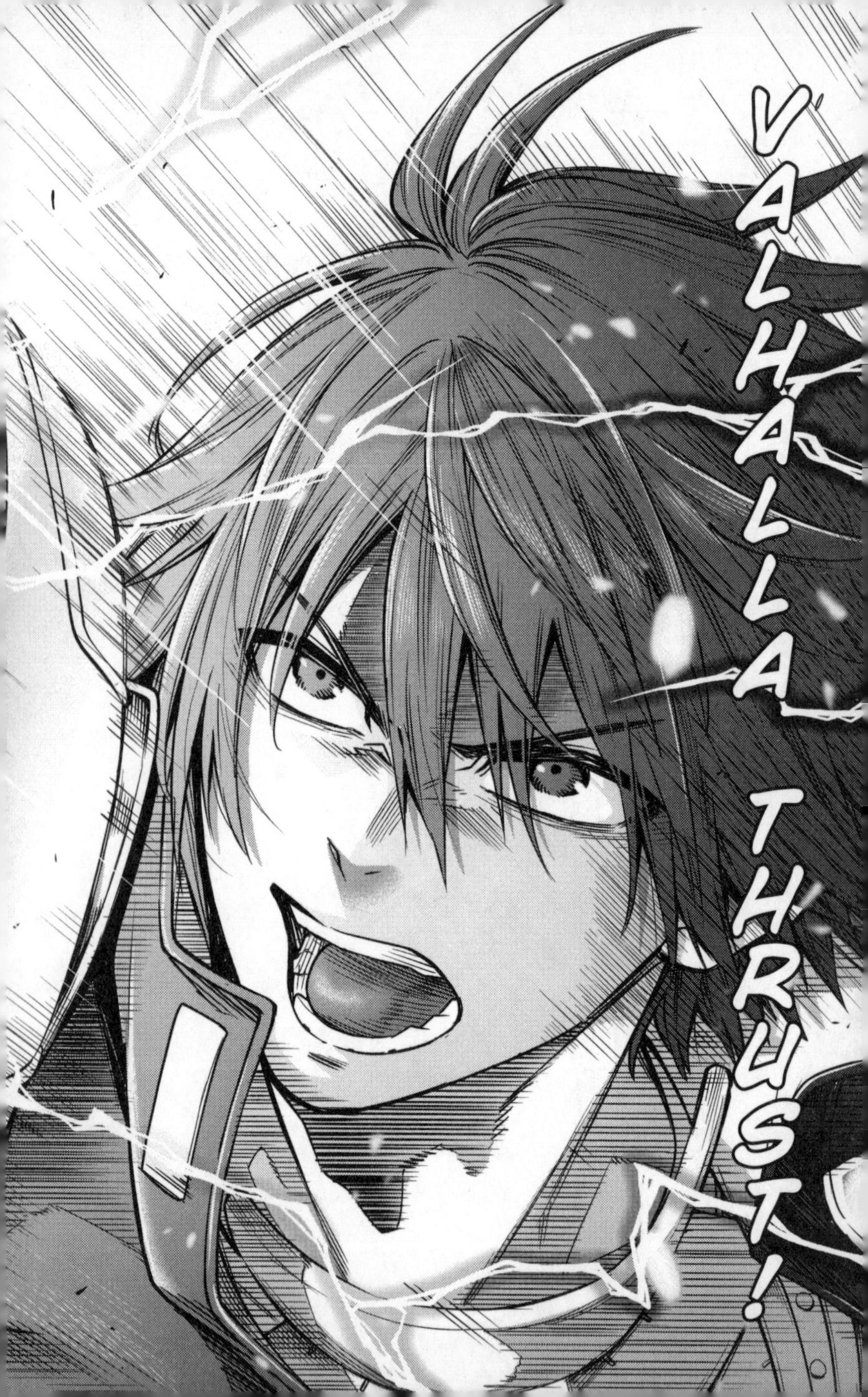
VALHALLA THRUST!

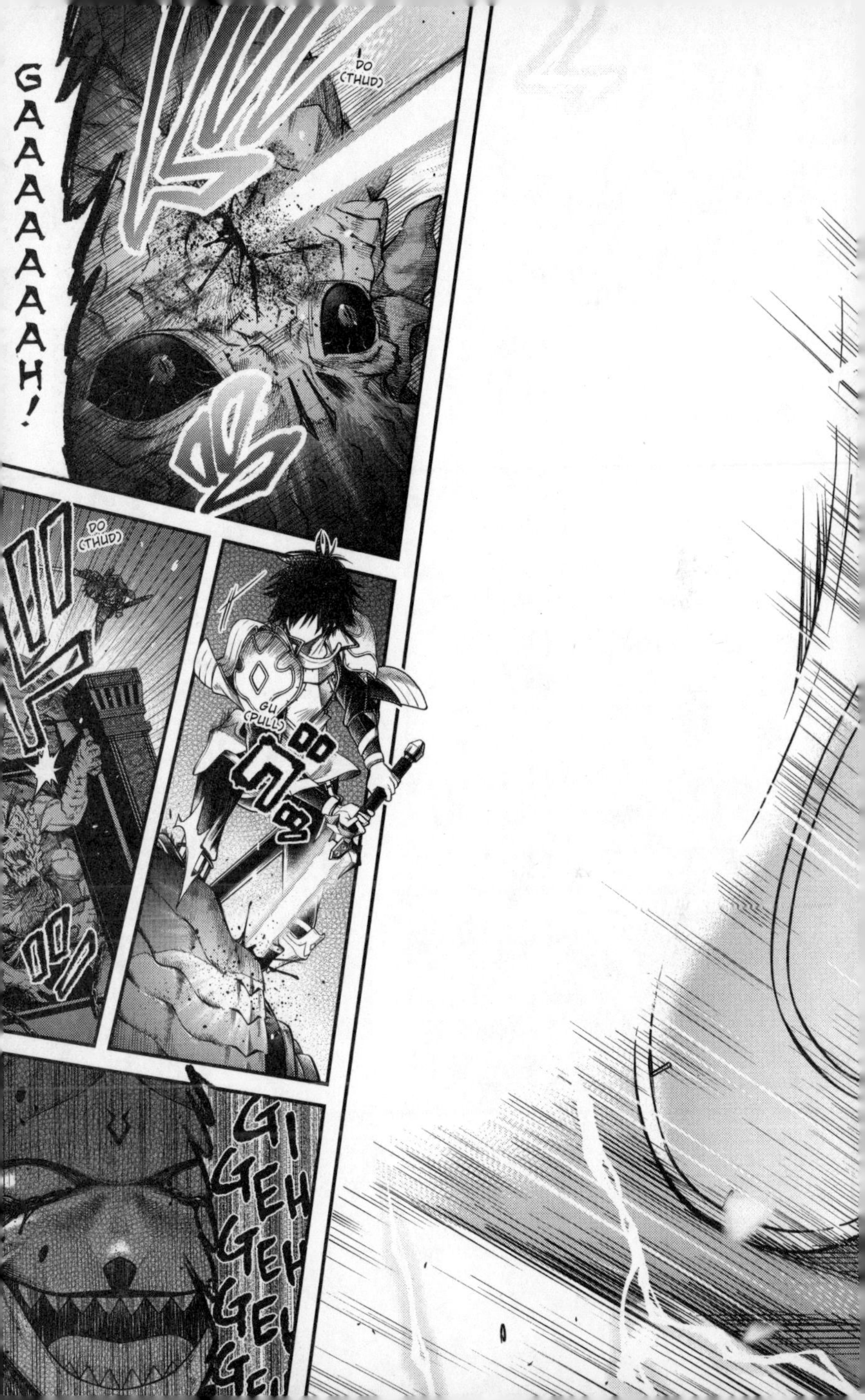

DO (THUD)
GAAAAAAAH!
GU (PULL)
DO (THUD)
GI GEH GEH GEH

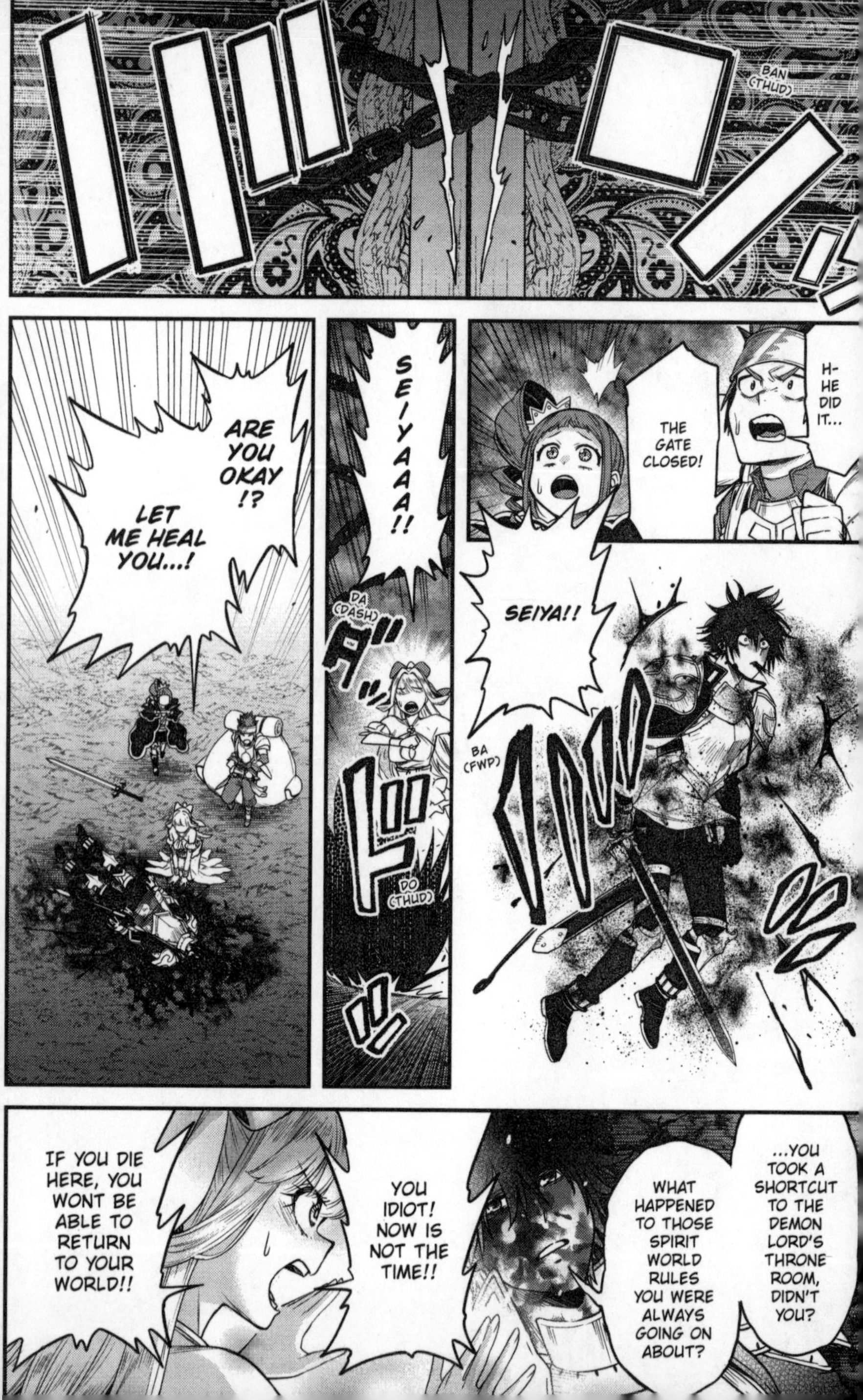
BAN
(THUD)
H-HE DID IT...
THE GATE CLOSED!
SEIYAAAA!!
DA
(DASH)
DO
(THUD)
ARE YOU OKAY!?
LET ME HEAL YOU...!
SEIYA!!
BA
(FWP)
...YOU TOOK A SHORTCUT TO THE DEMON LORD'S THRONE ROOM, DIDN'T YOU?
WHAT HAPPENED TO THOSE SPIRIT WORLD RULES YOU WERE ALWAYS GOING ON ABOUT?
YOU IDIOT! NOW IS NOT THE TIME!!
IF YOU DIE HERE, YOU WONT BE ABLE TO RETURN TO YOUR WORLD!!

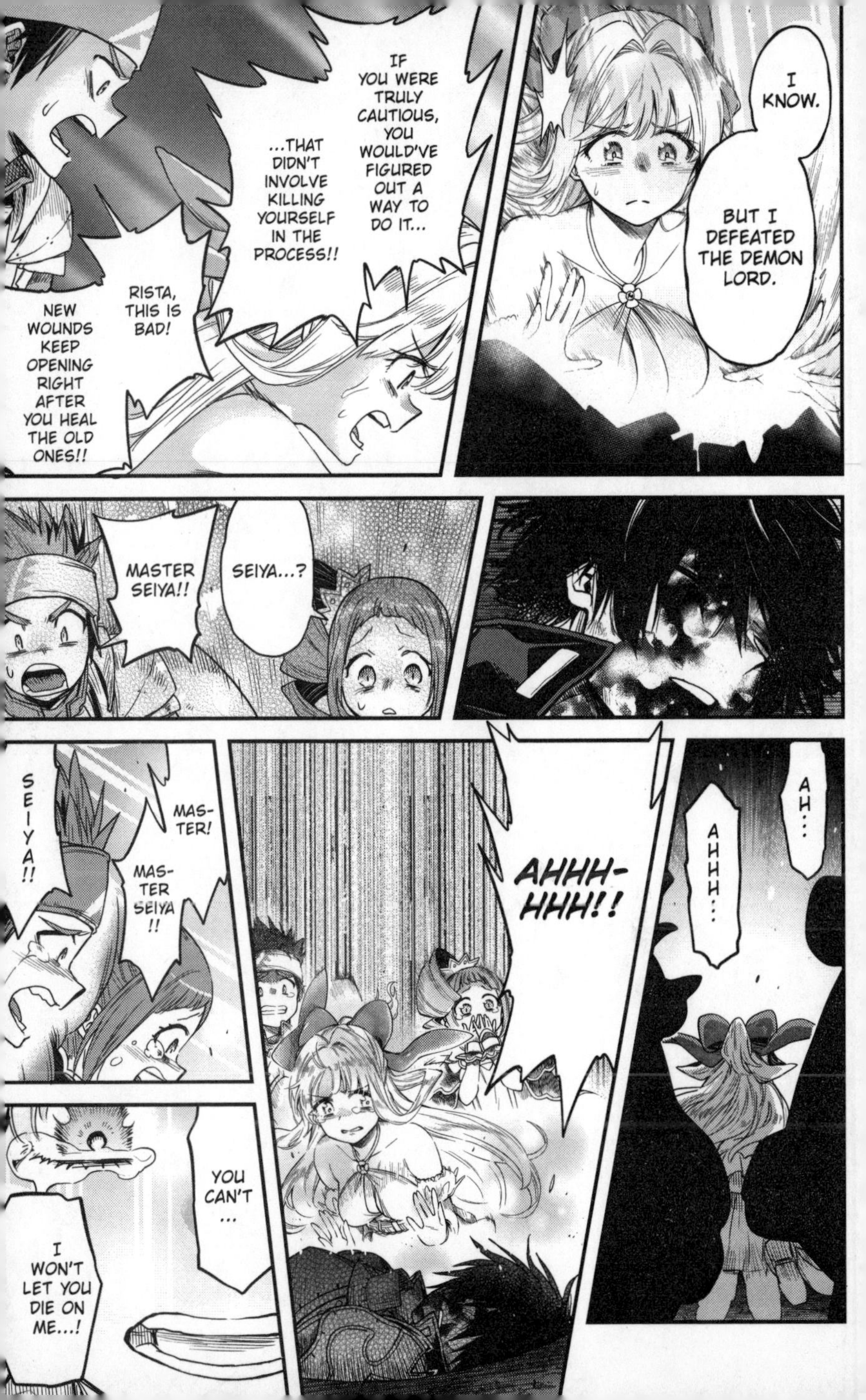
I KNOW.
BUT I DEFEATED THE DEMON LORD.
IF YOU WERE TRULY CAUTIOUS, YOU WOULD'VE FIGURED OUT A WAY TO DO IT...
...THAT DIDN'T INVOLVE KILLING YOURSELF IN THE PROCESS!!
RISTA, THIS IS BAD!
NEW WOUNDS KEEP OPENING RIGHT AFTER YOU HEAL THE OLD ONES!!
SEIYA...?
MASTER SEIYA!!
AH...
AHHH...
AHHH-HHH!!
MAS-TER!
MAS-TER SEIYA!!
SEIYA!!
YOU CAN'T...
I WON'T LET YOU DIE ON ME...!

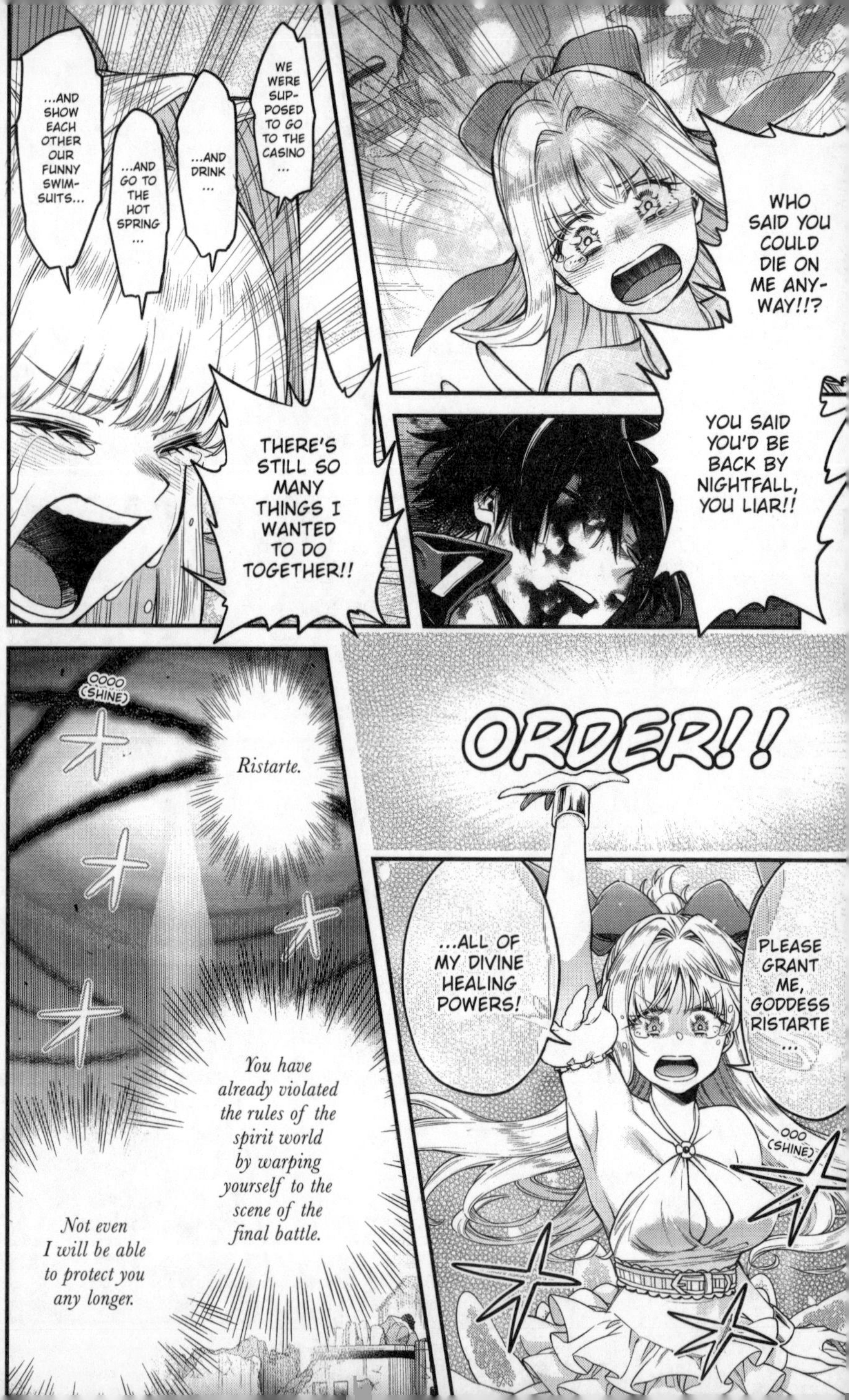
WHO SAID YOU COULD DIE ON ME ANYWAY!!?
YOU SAID YOU'D BE BACK BY NIGHTFALL, YOU LIAR!!
WE WERE SUPPOSED TO GO TO THE CASINO...
...AND DRINK...
...AND GO TO THE HOT SPRING...
...AND SHOW EACH OTHER OUR FUNNY SWIMSUITS...
THERE'S STILL SO MANY THINGS I WANTED TO DO TOGETHER!!
ORDER!!
PLEASE GRANT ME, GODDESS RISTARTE...
...ALL OF MY DIVINE HEALING POWERS!
OOO (SHINE)
OOOO (SHINE)
Ristarte.
You have already violated the rules of the spirit world by warping yourself to the scene of the final battle.
Not even I will be able to protect you any longer.

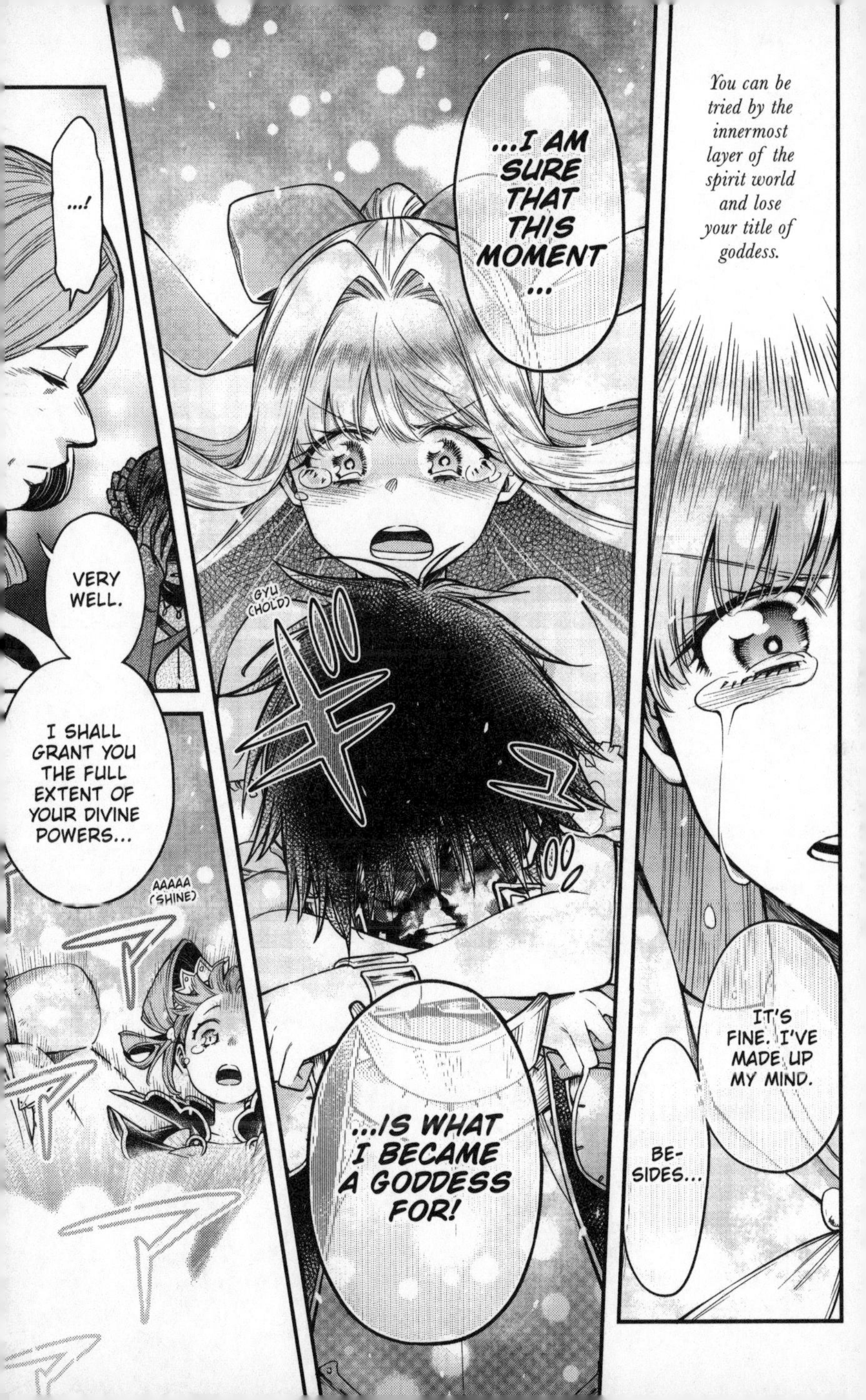
You can be tried by the innermost layer of the spirit world and lose your title of goddess.
IT'S FINE. I'VE MADE UP MY MIND.
BE-SIDES...
...I AM SURE THAT THIS MOMENT...
GYU (HOLD)
...IS WHAT I BECAME A GODDESS FOR!
...!
VERY WELL.
I SHALL GRANT YOU THE FULL EXTENT OF YOUR DIVINE POWERS...
AAAAA (SHINE)

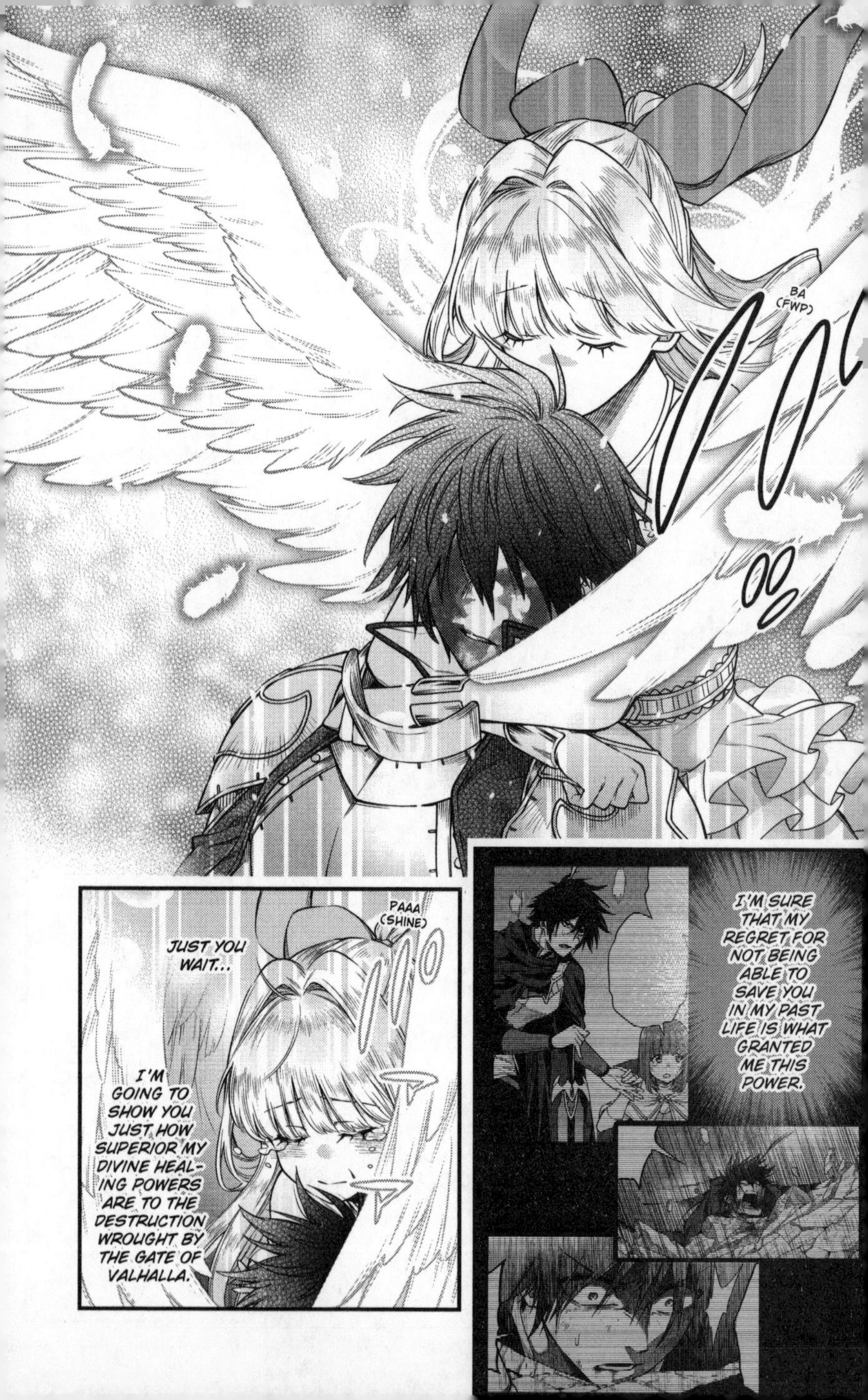
BA
(FWP)
I'M SURE THAT MY REGRET FOR NOT BEING ABLE TO SAVE YOU IN MY PAST LIFE IS WHAT GRANTED ME THIS POWER.
PAAA
(SHINE)
JUST YOU WAIT...
I'M GOING TO SHOW YOU JUST HOW SUPERIOR MY DIVINE HEAL-ING POWERS ARE TO THE DESTRUCTION WROUGHT BY THE GATE OF VALHALLA.

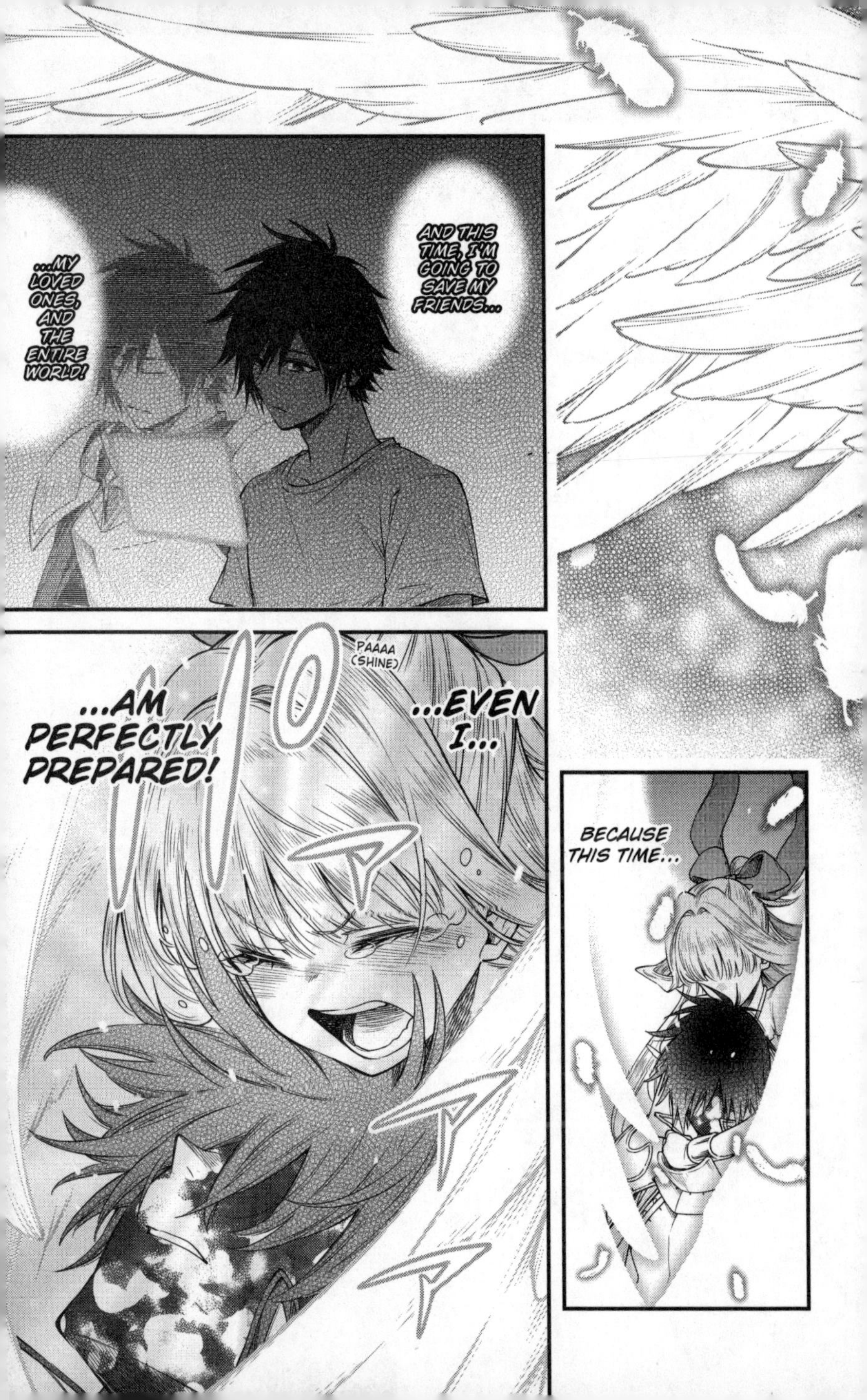
AND THIS TIME, I'M GOING TO SAVE MY FRIENDS...
...MY LOVED ONES, AND THE ENTIRE WORLD!
BECAUSE THIS TIME...
PAAAA (SHINE)
...EVEN I...
...AM PERFECTLY PREPARED!

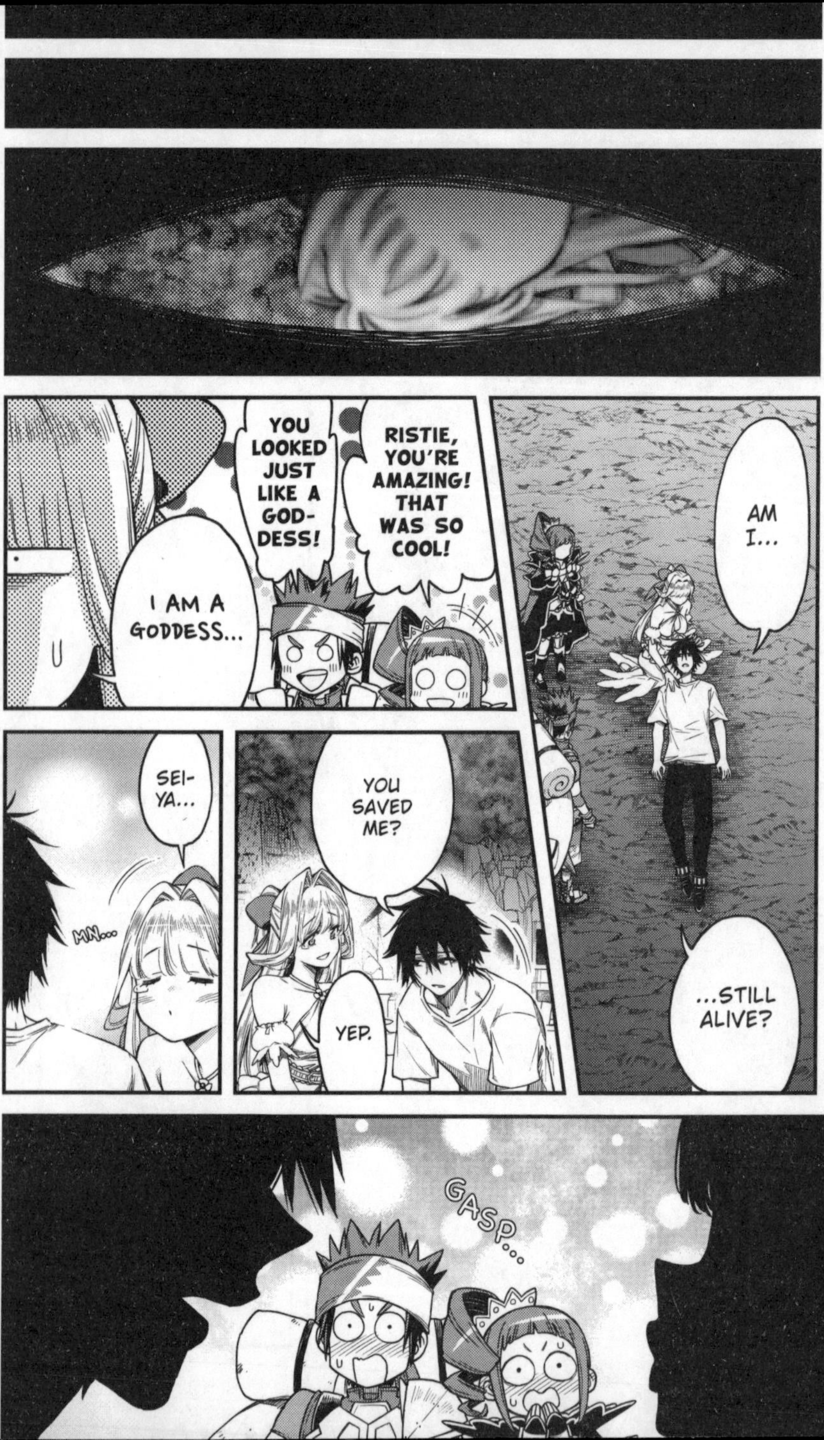
AM I...
...STILL ALIVE?
RISTIE, YOU'RE AMAZING! THAT WAS SO COOL!
YOU LOOKED JUST LIKE A GOD-DESS!
I AM A GODDESS...
YOU SAVED ME?
YEP.
SEI-YA...
MN...
GASP...

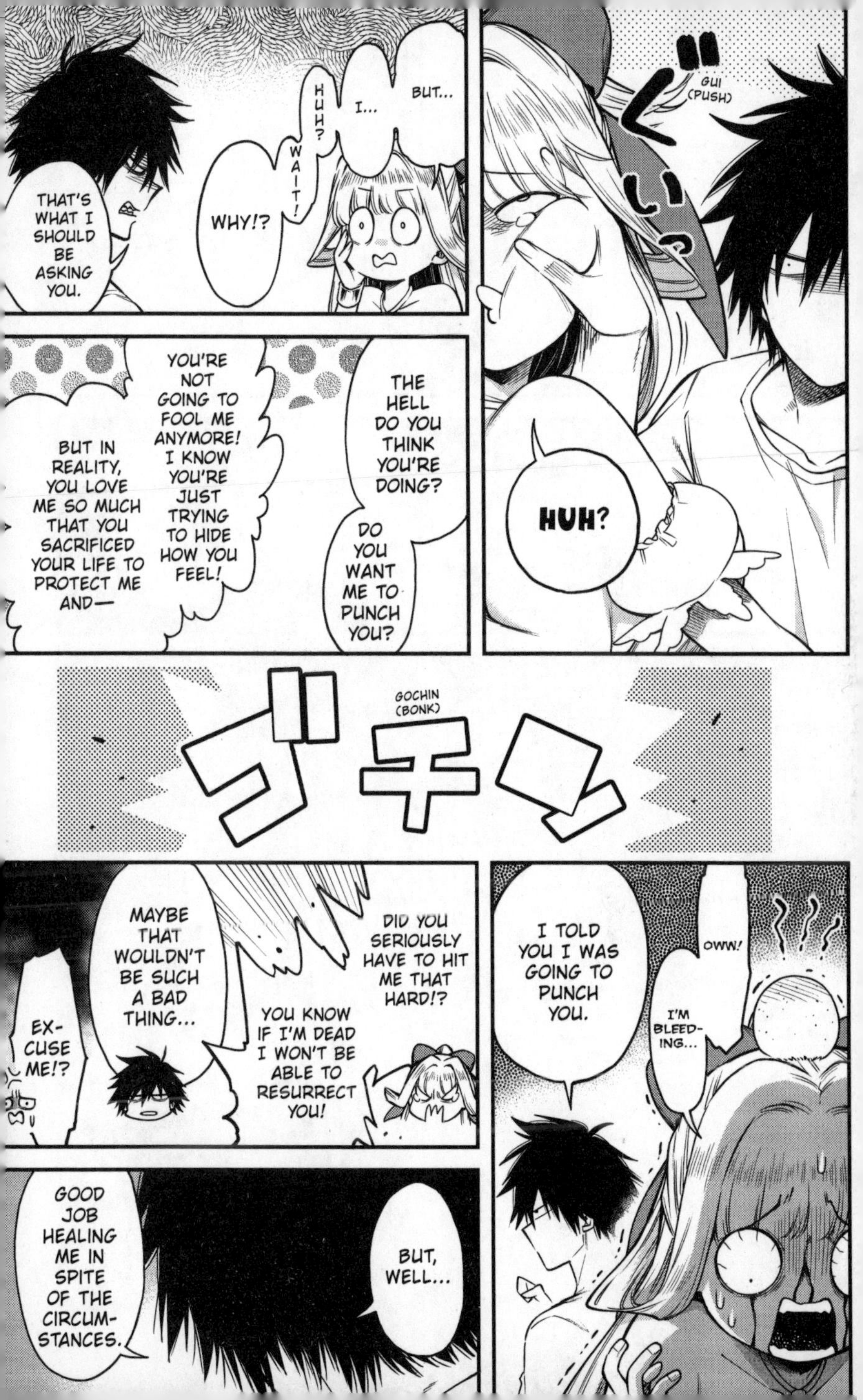
GUI (PUSH)
HUH?
BUT...
I...
HUH? WAIT!
WHY!?
THAT'S WHAT I SHOULD BE ASKING YOU.
THE HELL DO YOU THINK YOU'RE DOING?
DO YOU WANT ME TO PUNCH YOU?
YOU'RE NOT GOING TO FOOL ME ANYMORE! I KNOW YOU'RE JUST TRYING TO HIDE HOW YOU FEEL!
BUT IN REALITY, YOU LOVE ME SO MUCH THAT YOU SACRIFICED YOUR LIFE TO PROTECT ME AND—
GOCHIN (BONK)
OWW!
I'M BLEED-ING...
I TOLD YOU I WAS GOING TO PUNCH YOU.
DID YOU SERIOUSLY HAVE TO HIT ME THAT HARD!?
YOU KNOW IF I'M DEAD I WON'T BE ABLE TO RESURRECT YOU!
MAYBE THAT WOULDN'T BE SUCH A BAD THING...
EX-CUSE ME!?
BUT, WELL...
GOOD JOB HEALING ME IN SPITE OF THE CIRCUM-STANCES.

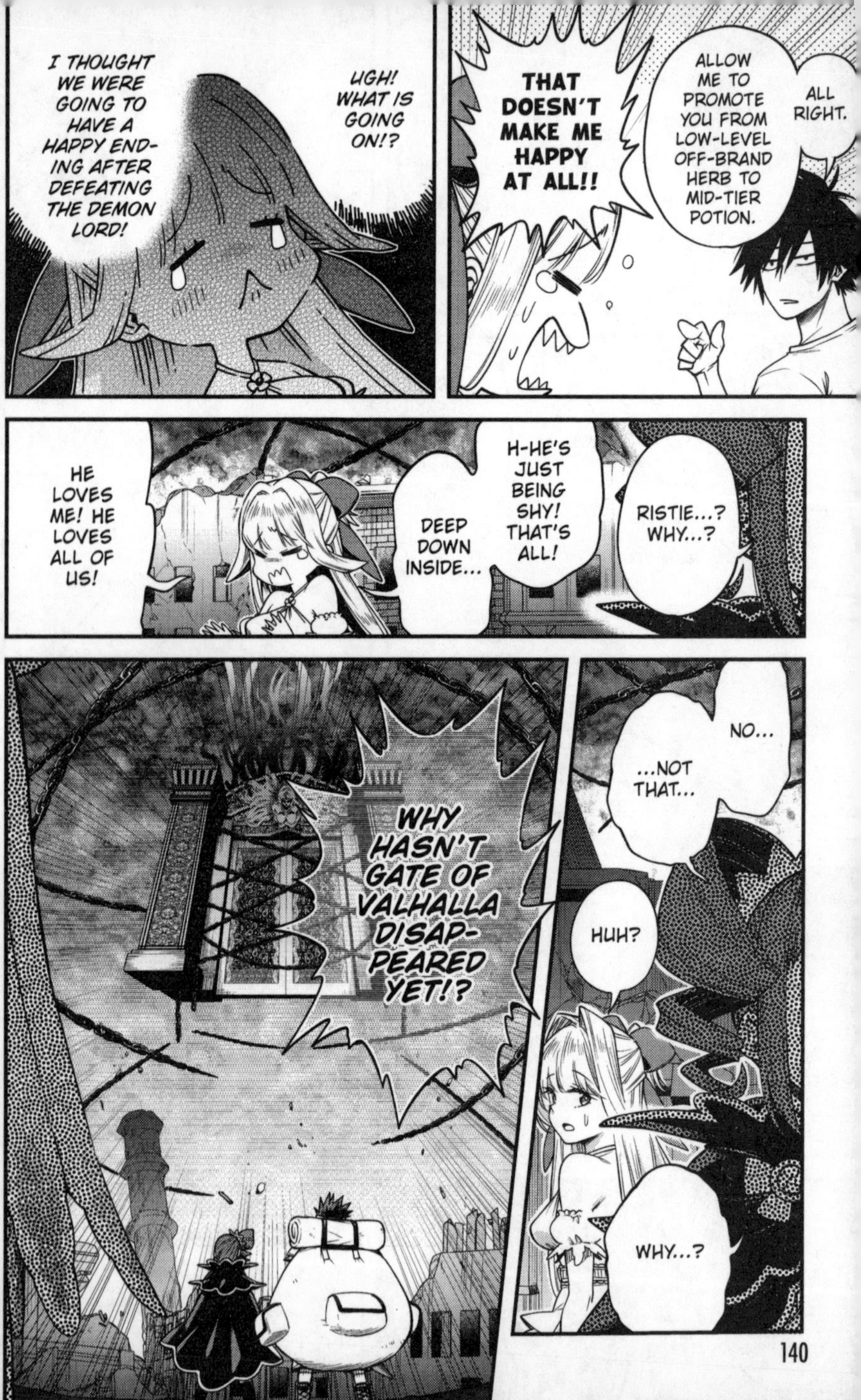
ALL RIGHT.
ALLOW ME TO PROMOTE YOU FROM LOW-LEVEL OFF-BRAND HERB TO MID-TIER POTION.
THAT DOESN'T MAKE ME HAPPY AT ALL!!
UGH! WHAT IS GOING ON!?
I THOUGHT WE WERE GOING TO HAVE A HAPPY END-ING AFTER DEFEATING THE DEMON LORD!
RISTIE...? WHY...?
H-HE'S JUST BEING SHY! THAT'S ALL!
DEEP DOWN INSIDE...
HE LOVES ME! HE LOVES ALL OF US!
NO...
...NOT THAT...
HUH?
WHY...?
WHY HASN'T GATE OF VALHALLA DISAP-PEARED YET!?

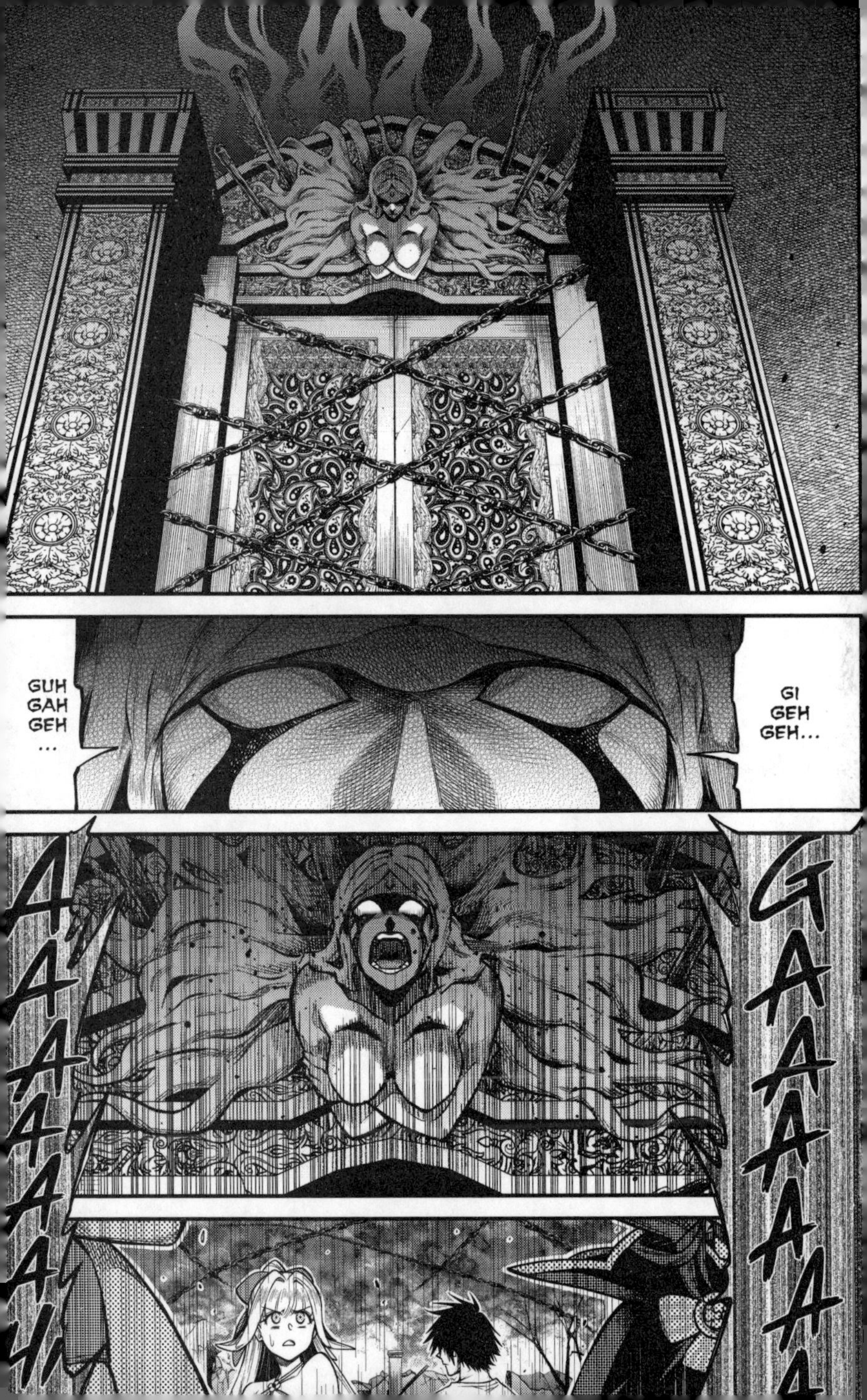
GI GEH GEH...
GUH GAH GEH ...
GAAAAAAAAA
AAAAAAAAAAH

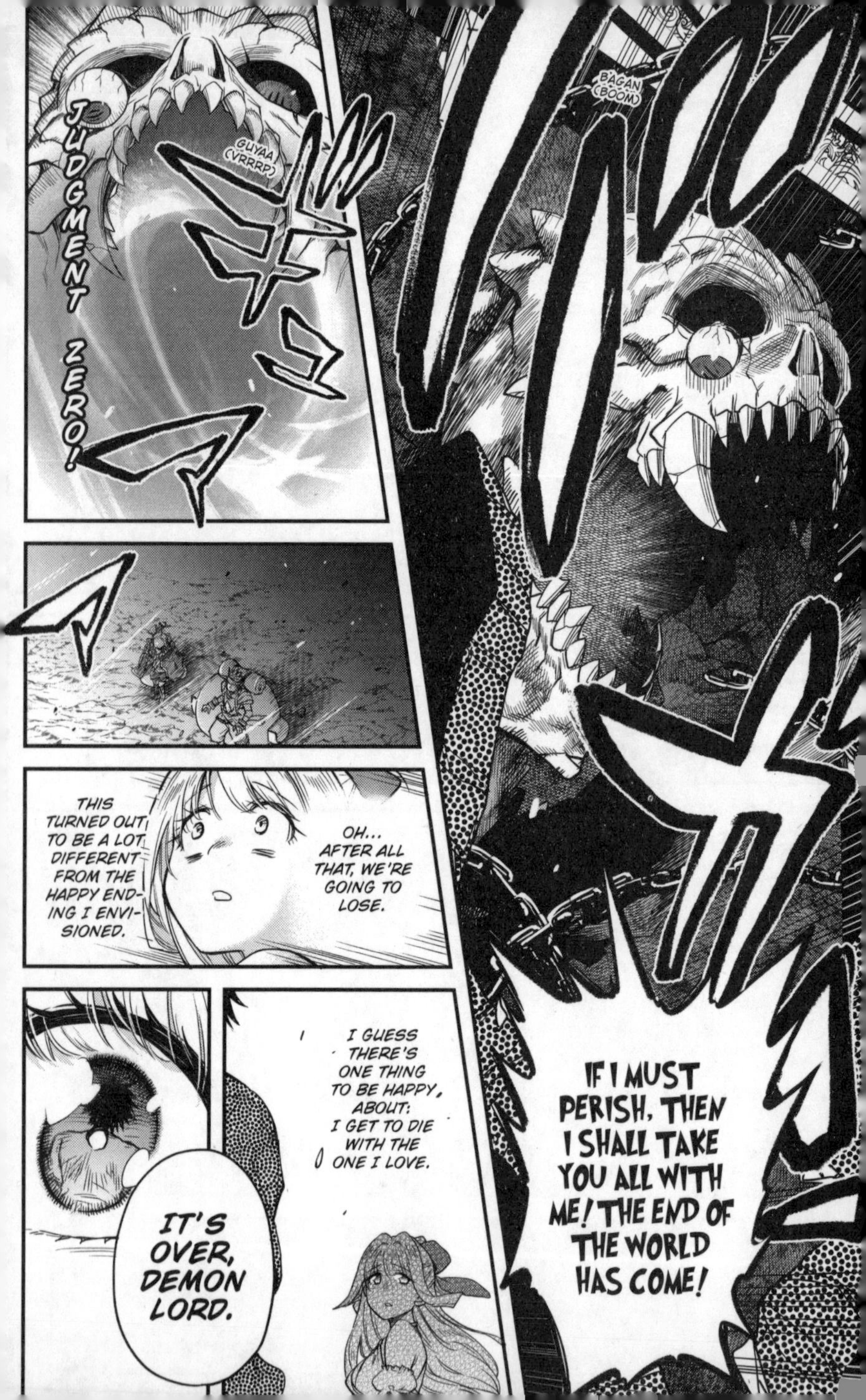
BAGAN (BOOM)
IF I MUST PERISH, THEN I SHALL TAKE YOU ALL WITH ME! THE END OF THE WORLD HAS COME!
GUYAA (VRRRP)
JUDGMENT ZERO!
OH... AFTER ALL THAT, WE'RE GOING TO LOSE.
THIS TURNED OUT TO BE A LOT DIFFERENT FROM THE HAPPY ENDING I ENVISIONED.
I GUESS THERE'S ONE THING TO BE HAPPY ABOUT: I GET TO DIE WITH THE ONE I LOVE.
IT'S OVER, DEMON LORD.

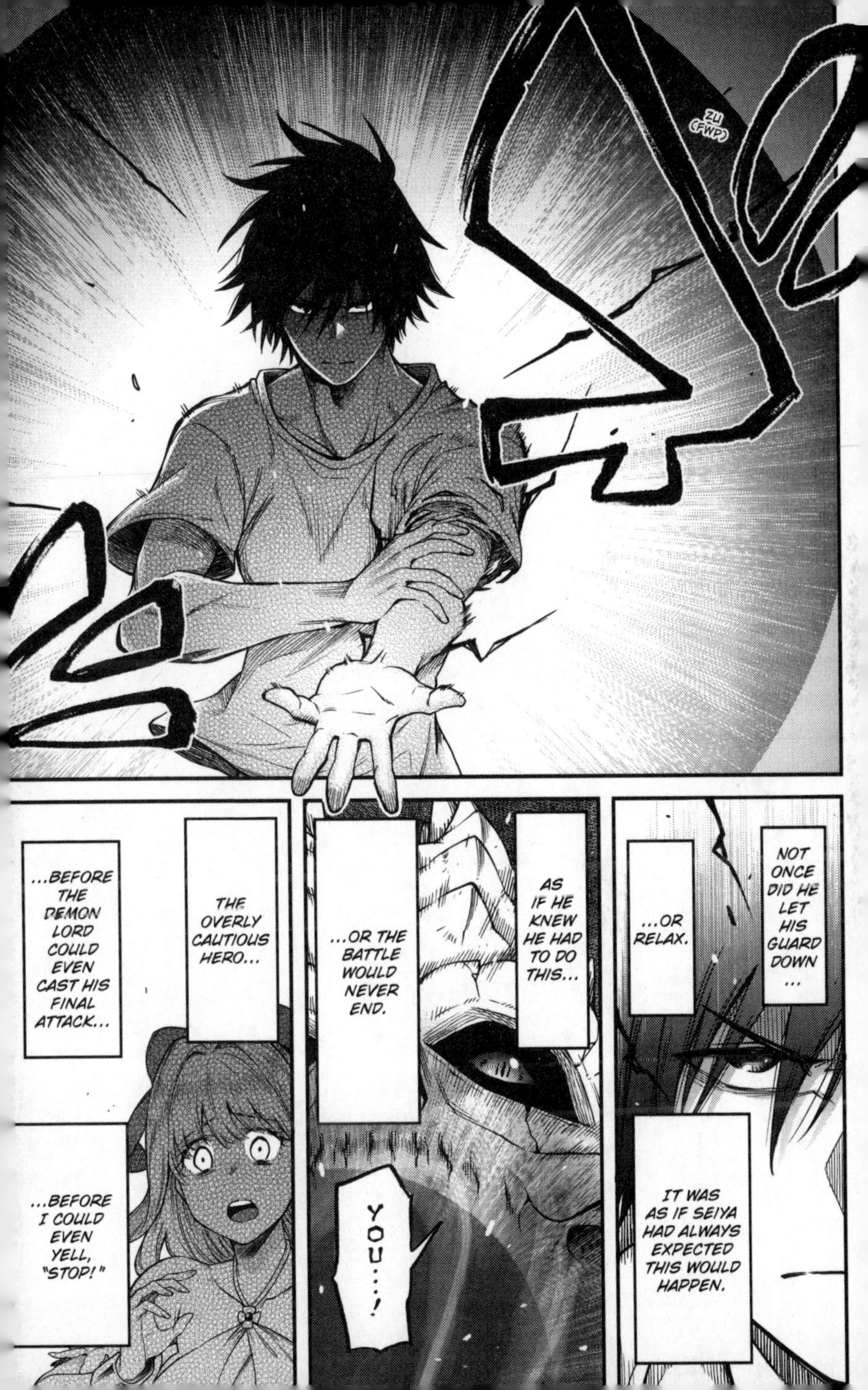
ZU (FWP)
NOT ONCE DID HE LET HIS GUARD DOWN...
...OR RELAX.
IT WAS AS IF SEIYA HAD ALWAYS EXPECTED THIS WOULD HAPPEN.
AS IF HE KNEW HE HAD TO DO THIS...
...OR THE BATTLE WOULD NEVER END.
YOU...!
THE OVERLY CAUTIOUS HERO...
...BEFORE THE DEMON LORD COULD EVEN CAST HIS FINAL ATTACK...
...BEFORE I COULD EVEN YELL, "STOP!"

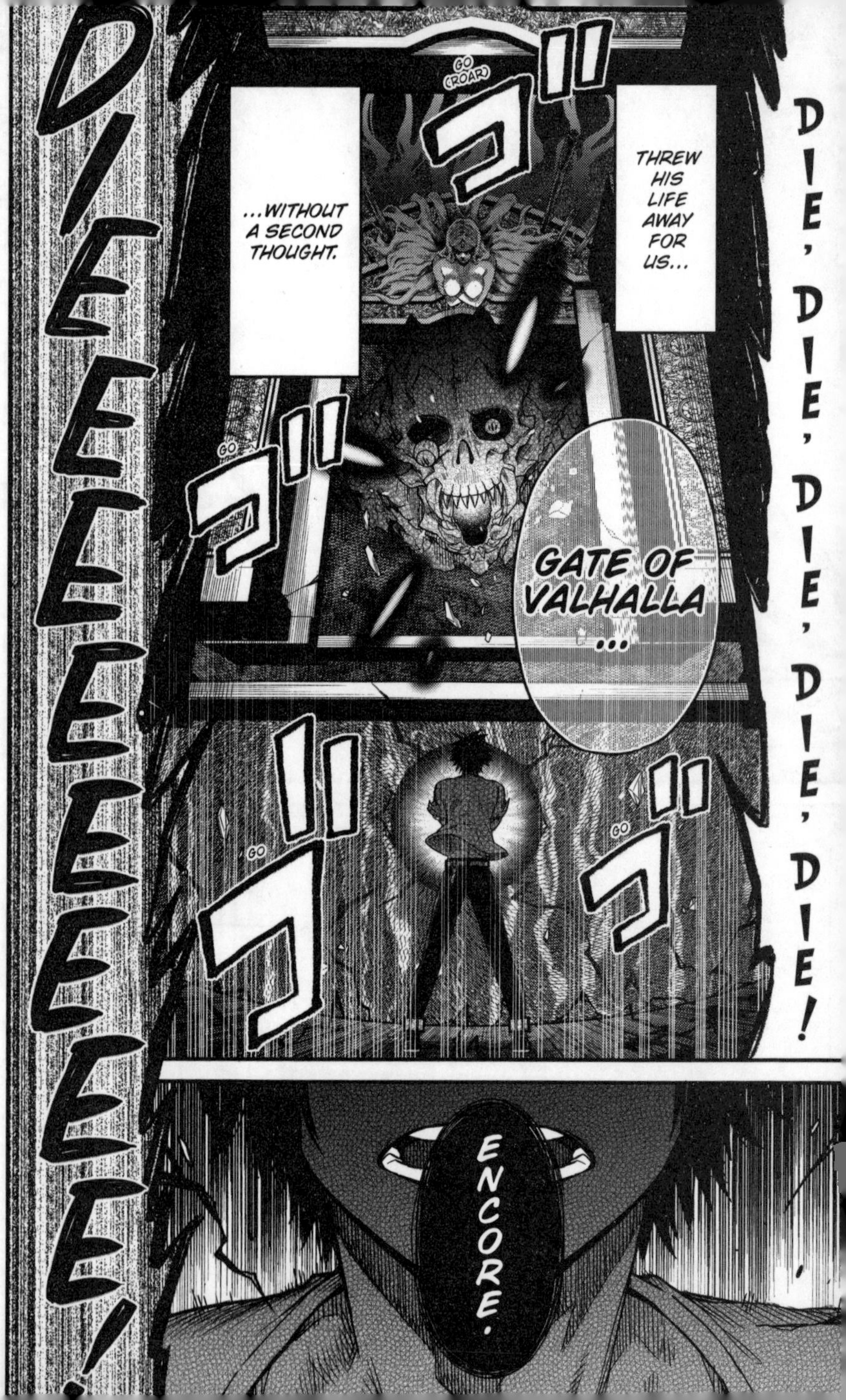
DIE, DIE, DIE, DIE, DIE, DIE!
THREW HIS LIFE AWAY FOR US...
...WITHOUT A SECOND THOUGHT.
GO (ROAR)
GATE OF VALHALLA...
GO
GO
GO
ENCORE.
DIEEEEEEEEEEEE!

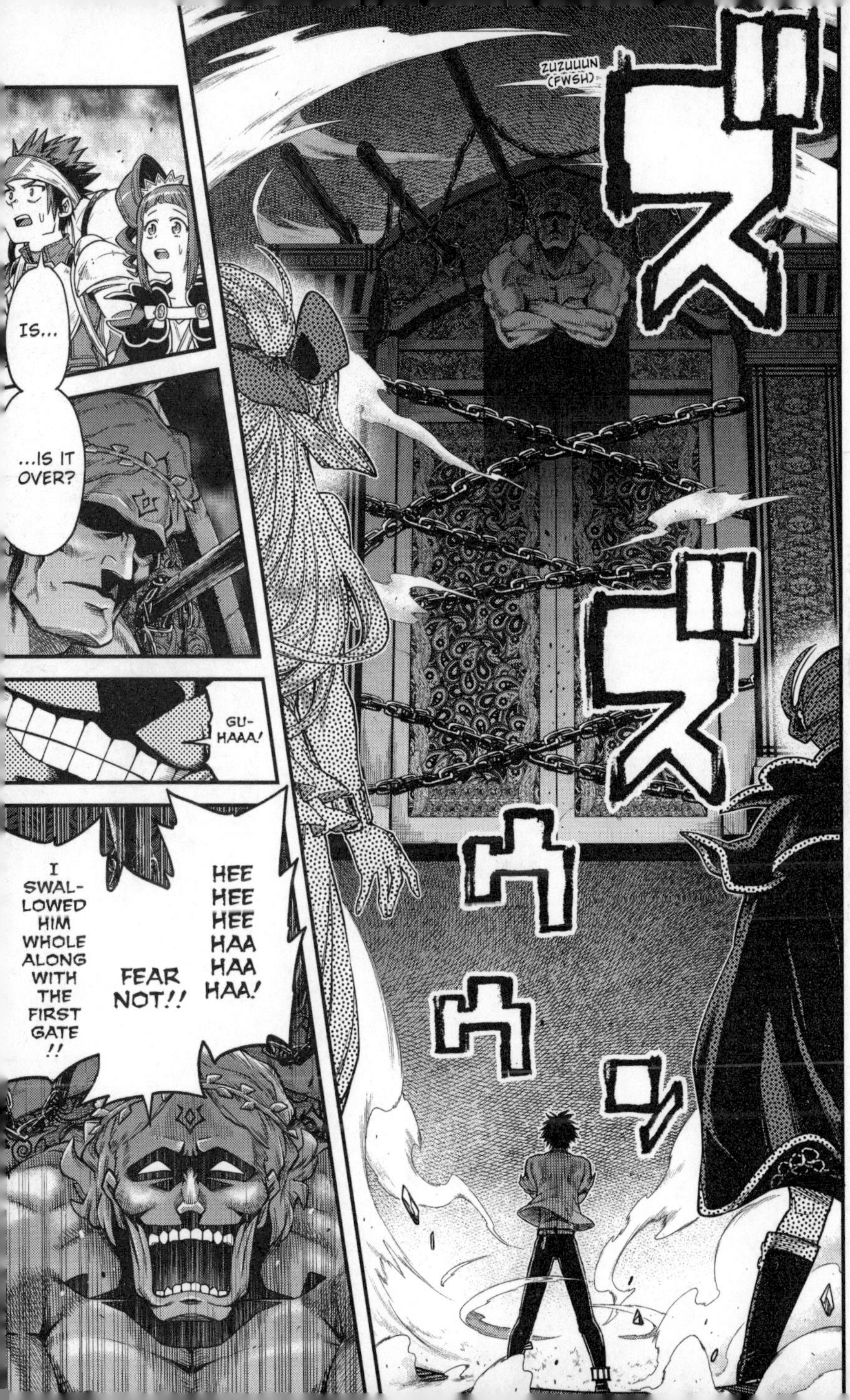
ズズウウッ
ZUZUUUN (FWSH)
IS...
...IS IT OVER?
GU-HAAA!
HEE HEE HEE HAA HAA HAA!
FEAR NOT!!
I SWALLOWED HIM WHOLE ALONG WITH THE FIRST GATE!!

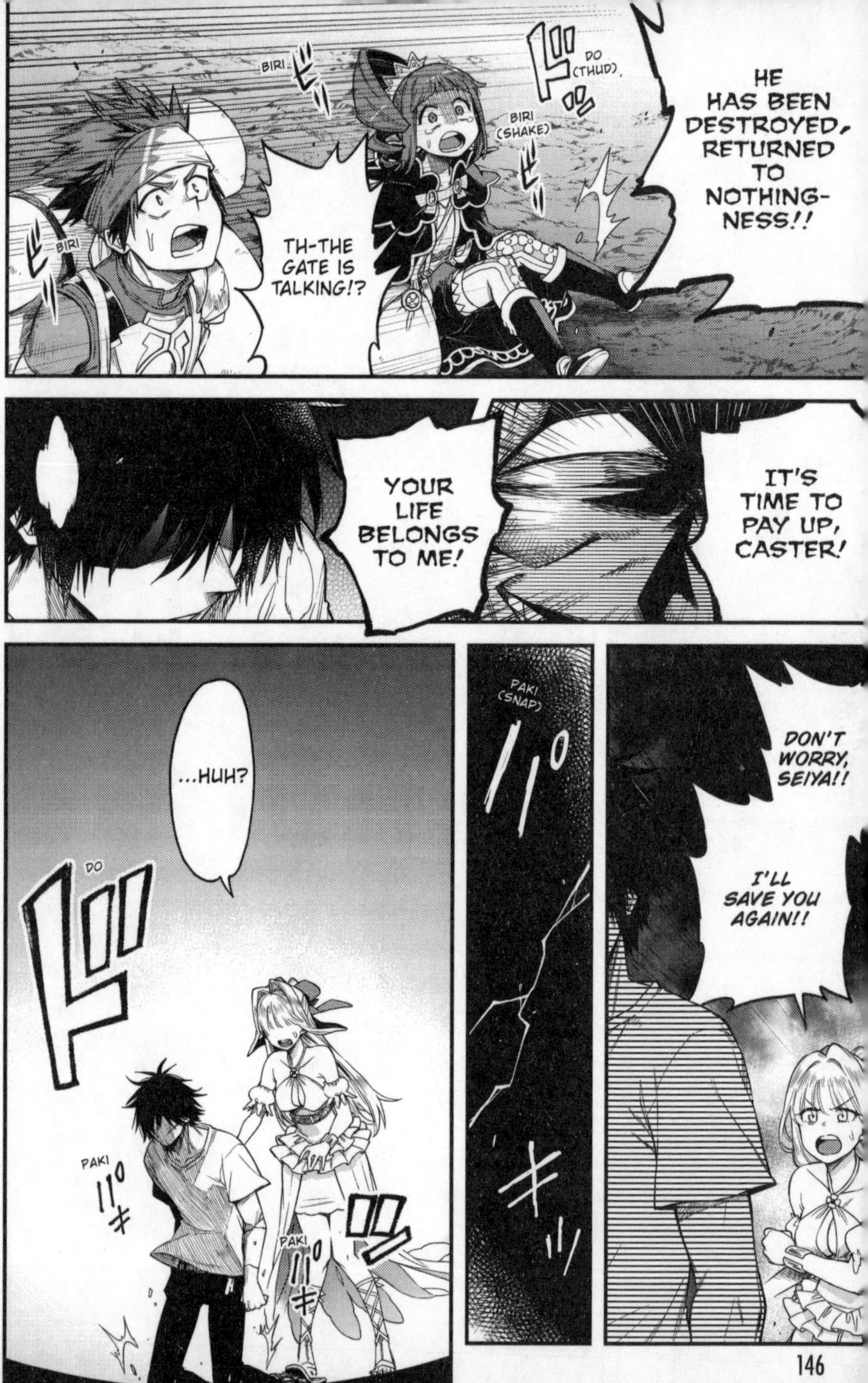
HE HAS BEEN DESTROYED, RETURNED TO NOTHING-NESS!!
DO (THUD)
BIRI (SHAKE)
BIRI
TH-THE GATE IS TALKING!?
BIRI
IT'S TIME TO PAY UP, CASTER!
YOUR LIFE BELONGS TO ME!
DON'T WORRY, SEIYA!!
I'LL SAVE YOU AGAIN!!
PAKI (SNAP)
...HUH?
DO
PAKI
PAKI

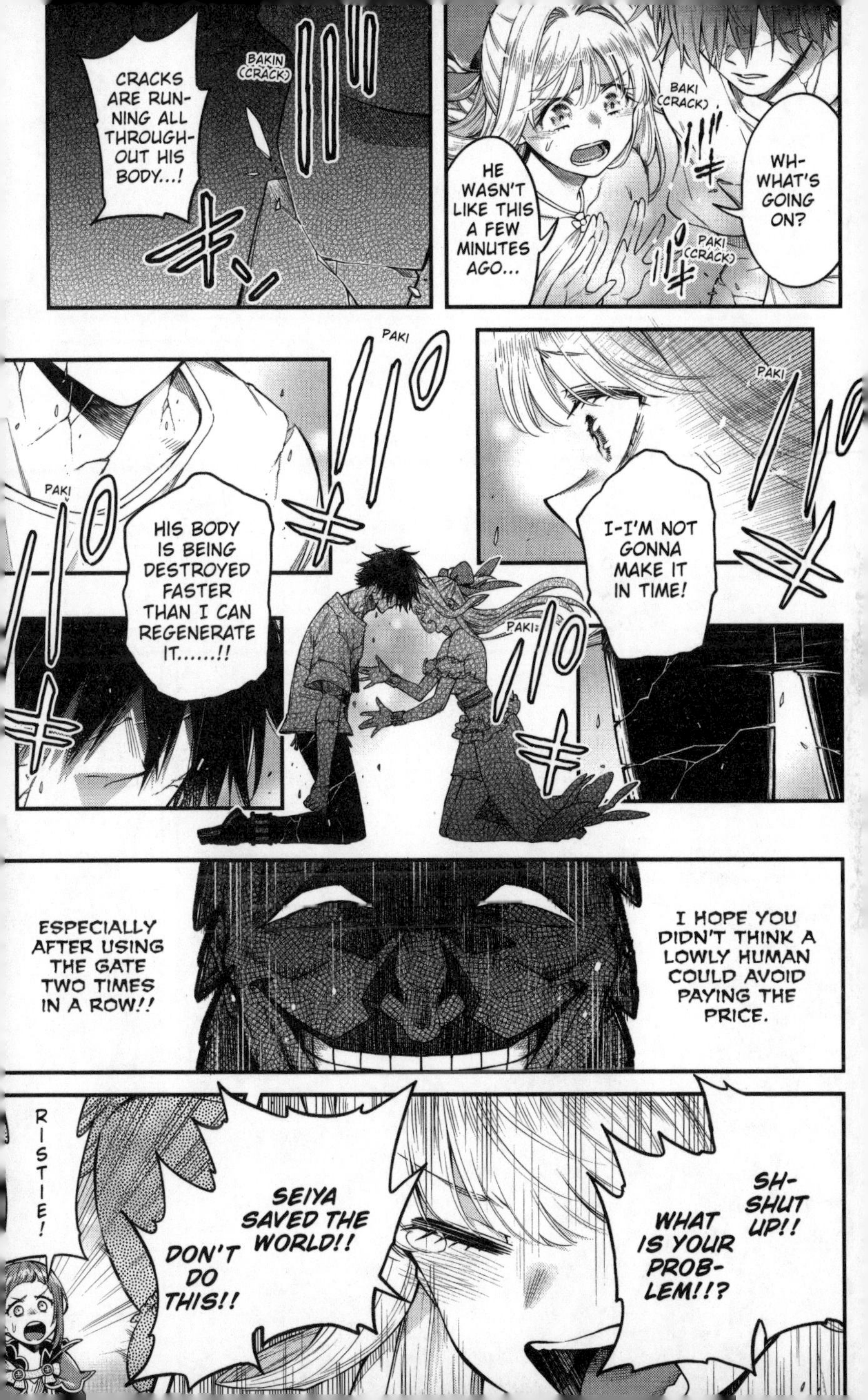
BAKI (CRACK)
WH-WHAT'S GOING ON?
PAKI (CRACK)
HE WASN'T LIKE THIS A FEW MINUTES AGO...
BAKIN (CRACK)
CRACKS ARE RUNNING ALL THROUGHOUT HIS BODY...!
PAKI
I-I'M NOT GONNA MAKE IT IN TIME!
PAKI
PAKI
HIS BODY IS BEING DESTROYED FASTER THAN I CAN REGENERATE IT......!!
PAKI
I HOPE YOU DIDN'T THINK A LOWLY HUMAN COULD AVOID PAYING THE PRICE.
ESPECIALLY AFTER USING THE GATE TWO TIMES IN A ROW!!
SH-SHUT UP!!
WHAT IS YOUR PROBLEM!!?
SEIYA SAVED THE WORLD!!
DON'T DO THIS!!
RISTIE!

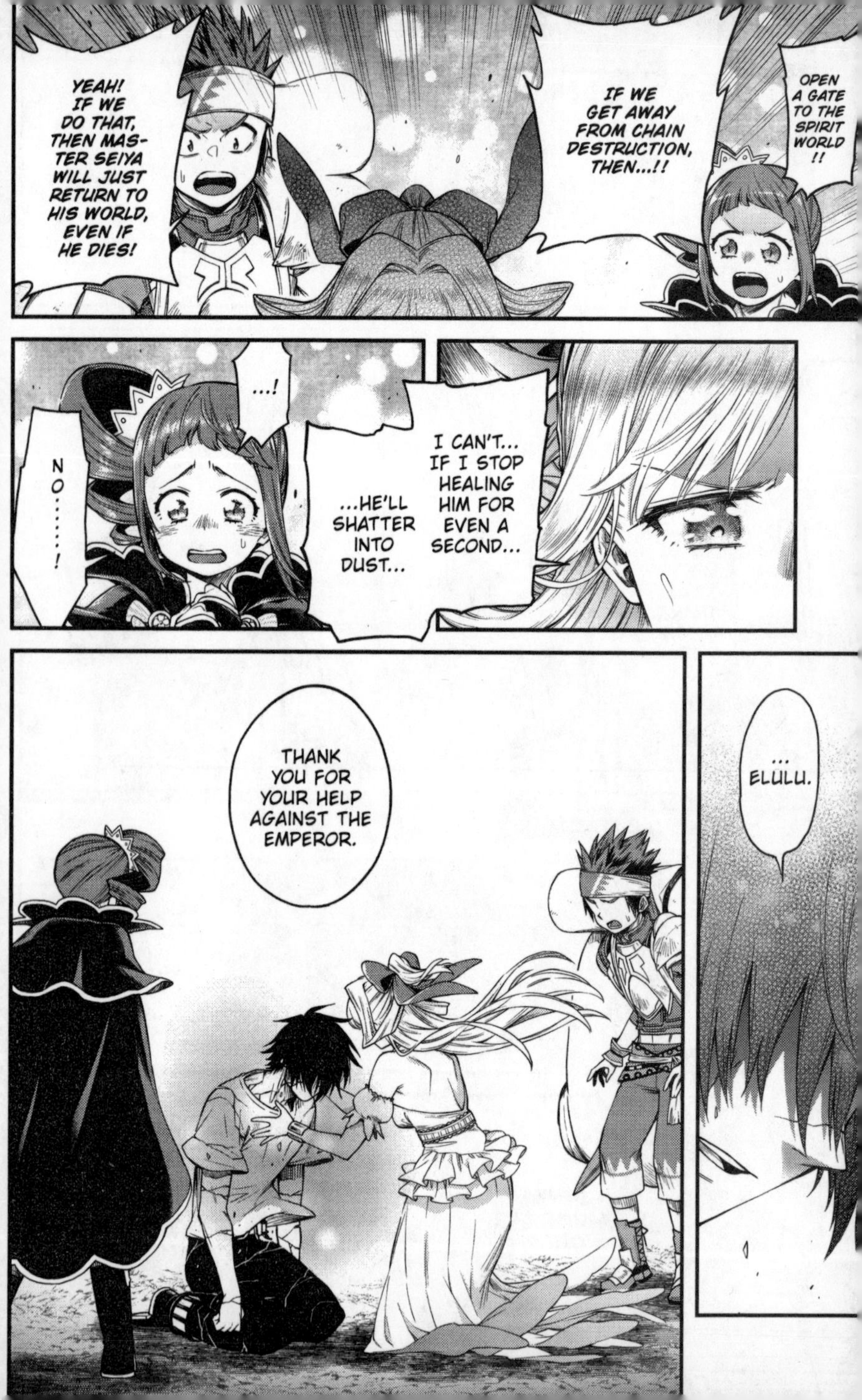
OPEN A GATE TO THE SPIRIT WORLD!!
IF WE GET AWAY FROM CHAIN DESTRUCTION, THEN...!!
YEAH! IF WE DO THAT, THEN MASTER SEIYA WILL JUST RETURN TO HIS WORLD, EVEN IF HE DIES!
I CAN'T... IF I STOP HEALING HIM FOR EVEN A SECOND...
...HE'LL SHATTER INTO DUST...
...!
NO......!
...ELULU.
THANK YOU FOR YOUR HELP AGAINST THE EMPEROR.

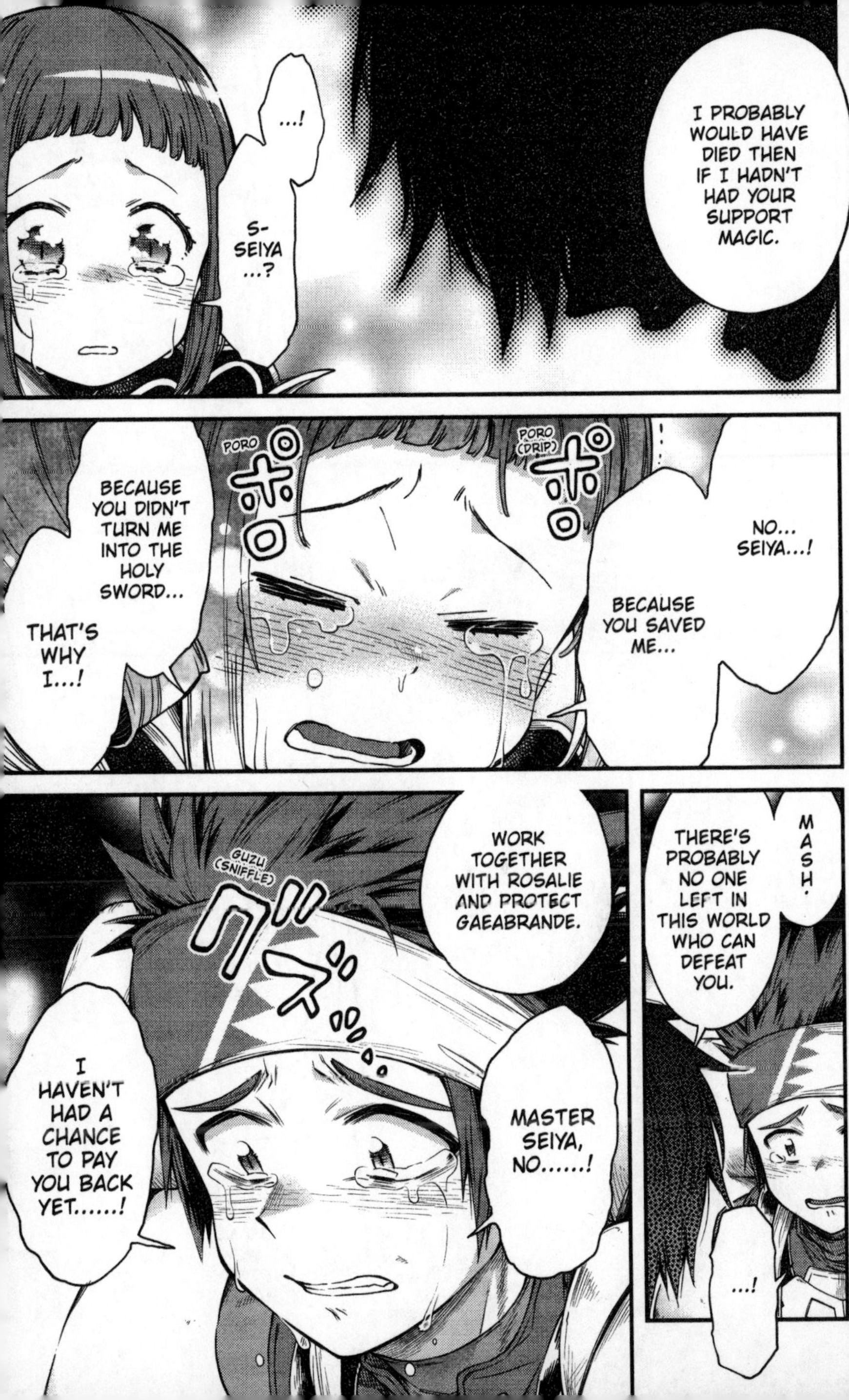

I PROBABLY WOULD HAVE DIED THEN IF I HADN'T HAD YOUR SUPPORT MAGIC.
...!
S-SEIYA...?
NO... SEIYA...!
BECAUSE YOU SAVED ME...
PORO (DRIP)
PORO
BECAUSE YOU DIDN'T TURN ME INTO THE HOLY SWORD...
THAT'S WHY I...!
MASH.
THERE'S PROBABLY NO ONE LEFT IN THIS WORLD WHO CAN DEFEAT YOU.
...!
WORK TOGETHER WITH ROSALIE AND PROTECT GAEABRANDE.
GUZU (SNIFFLE)
MASTER SEIYA, NO......!
I HAVEN'T HAD A CHANCE TO PAY YOU BACK YET......!

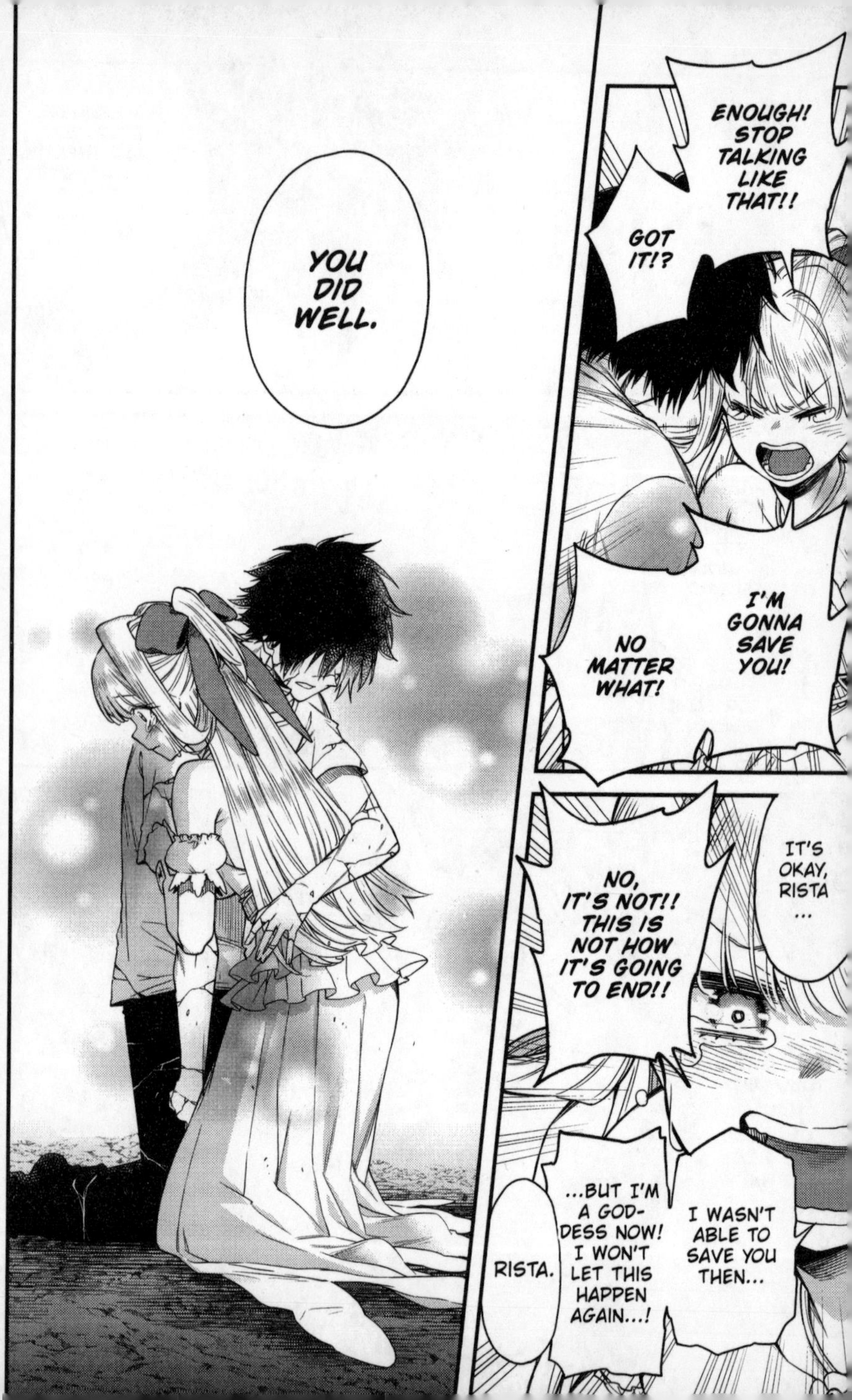
ENOUGH! STOP TALKING LIKE THAT!!
GOT IT!?
I'M GONNA SAVE YOU!
NO MATTER WHAT!
IT'S OKAY, RISTA ...
NO, IT'S NOT!! THIS IS NOT HOW IT'S GOING TO END!!
I WASN'T ABLE TO SAVE YOU THEN...
...BUT I'M A GOD-DESS NOW! I WON'T LET THIS HAPPEN AGAIN...!
RISTA.
YOU DID WELL.

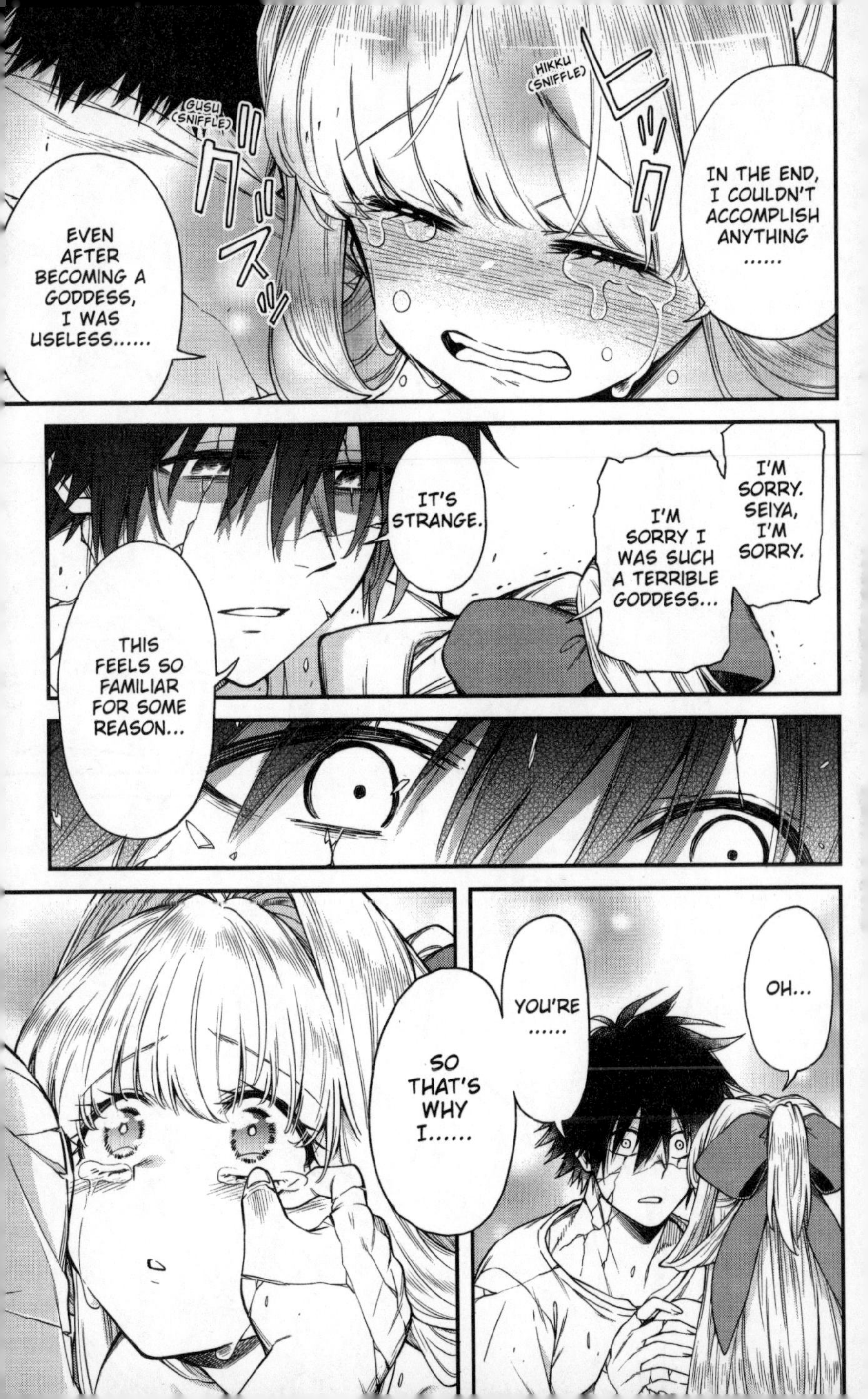
HIKKU (SNIFFLE)
IN THE END, I COULDN'T ACCOMPLISH ANYTHING ......
GUSU (SNIFFLE)
EVEN AFTER BECOMING A GODDESS, I WAS USELESS......
I'M SORRY. SEIYA, I'M SORRY.
I'M SORRY I WAS SUCH A TERRIBLE GODDESS...
IT'S STRANGE.
THIS FEELS SO FAMILIAR FOR SOME REASON...
OH...
YOU'RE ......
SO THAT'S WHY I......

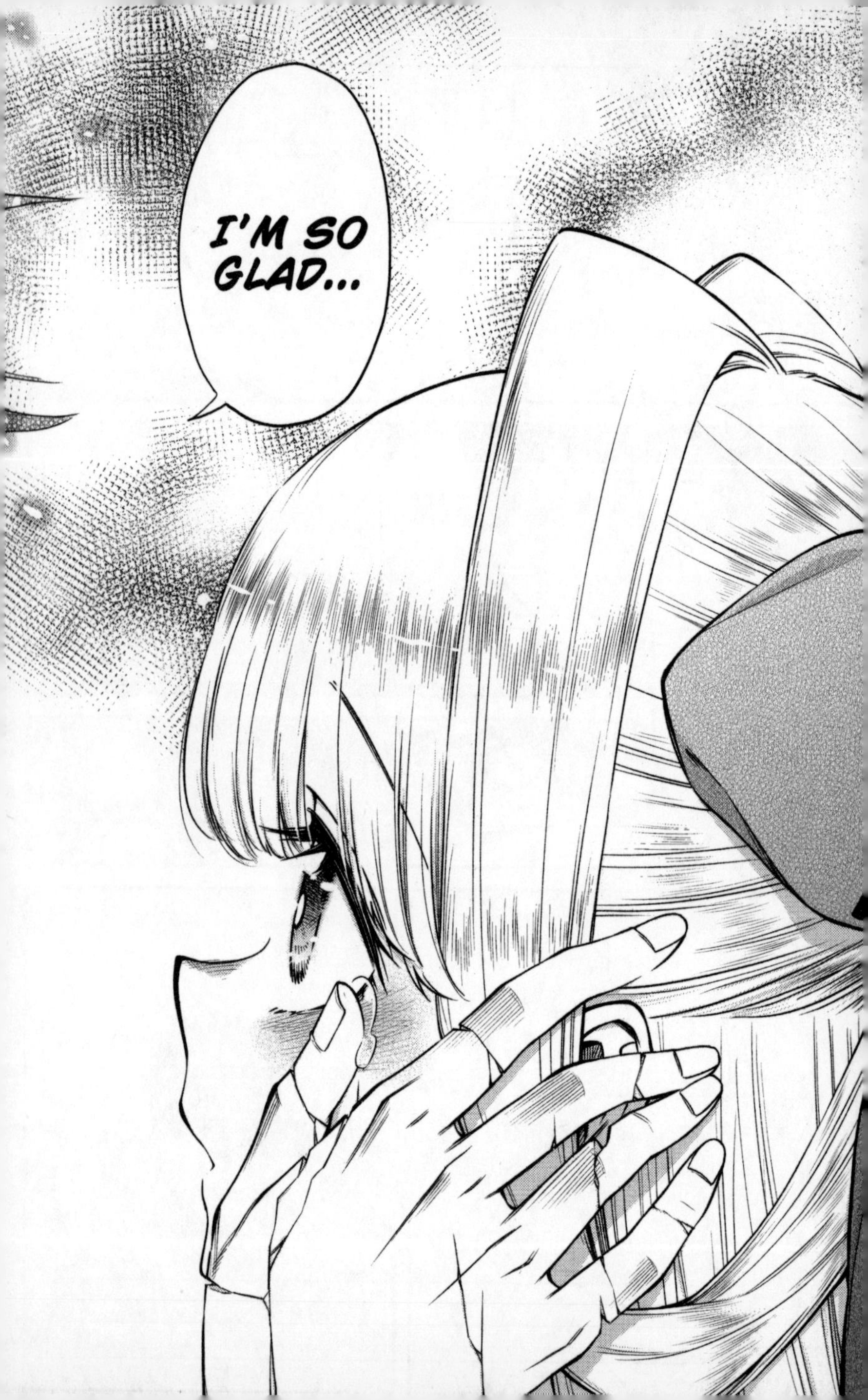
I'M SO GLAD...

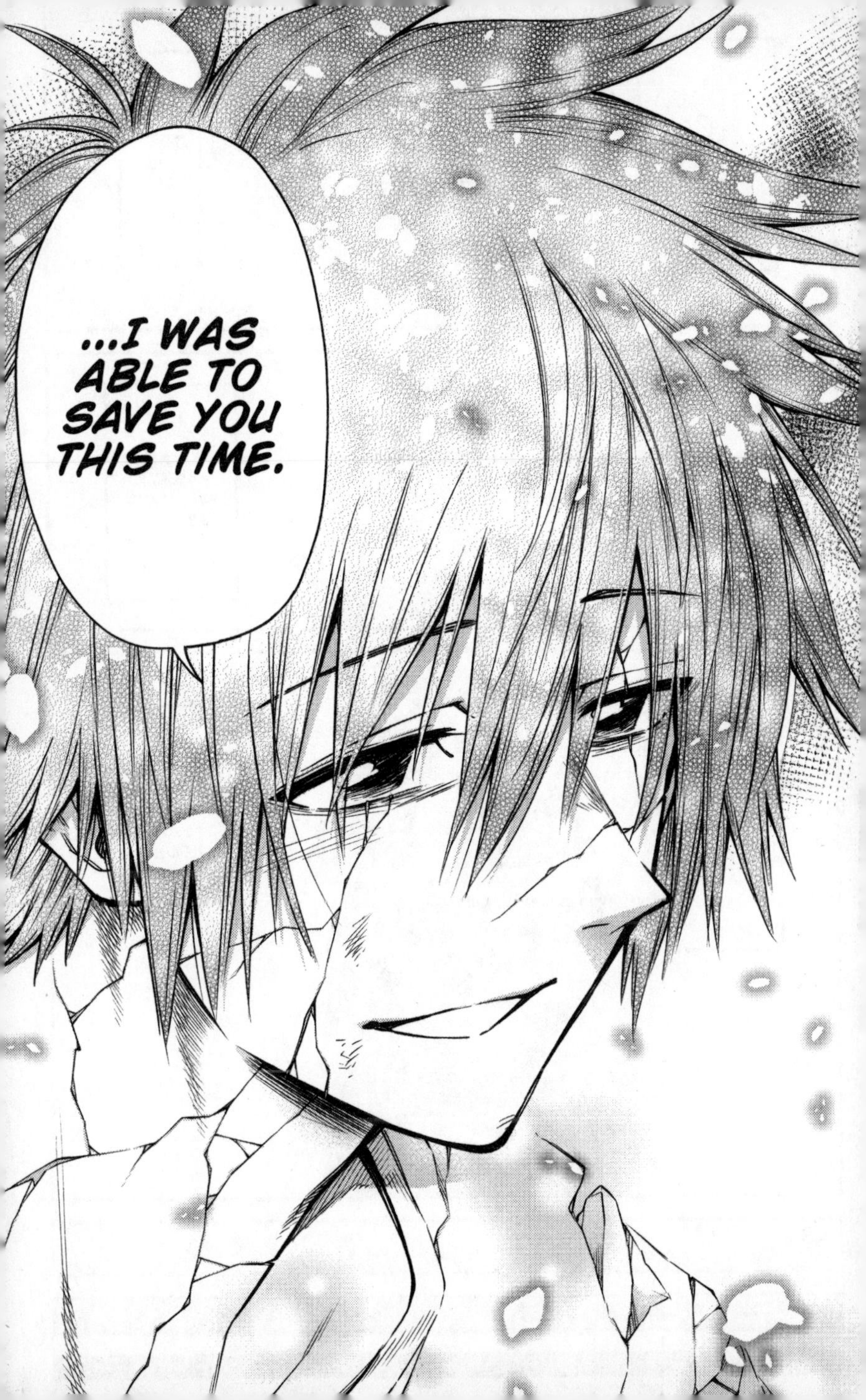
...I WAS ABLE TO SAVE YOU THIS TIME.

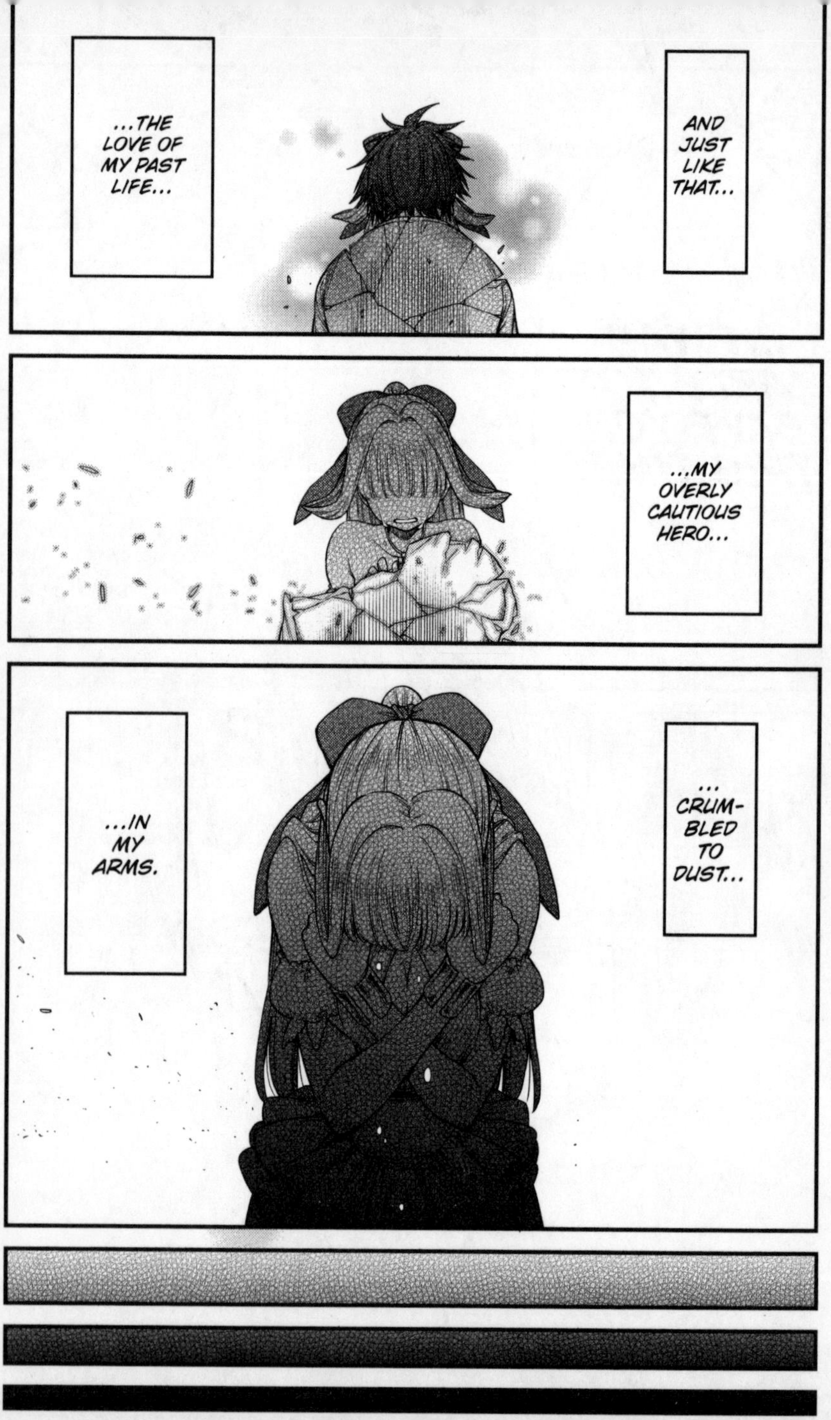
AND JUST LIKE THAT...
...THE LOVE OF MY PAST LIFE...
...MY OVERLY CAUTIOUS HERO...
...CRUMBLED TO DUST...
...IN MY ARMS.

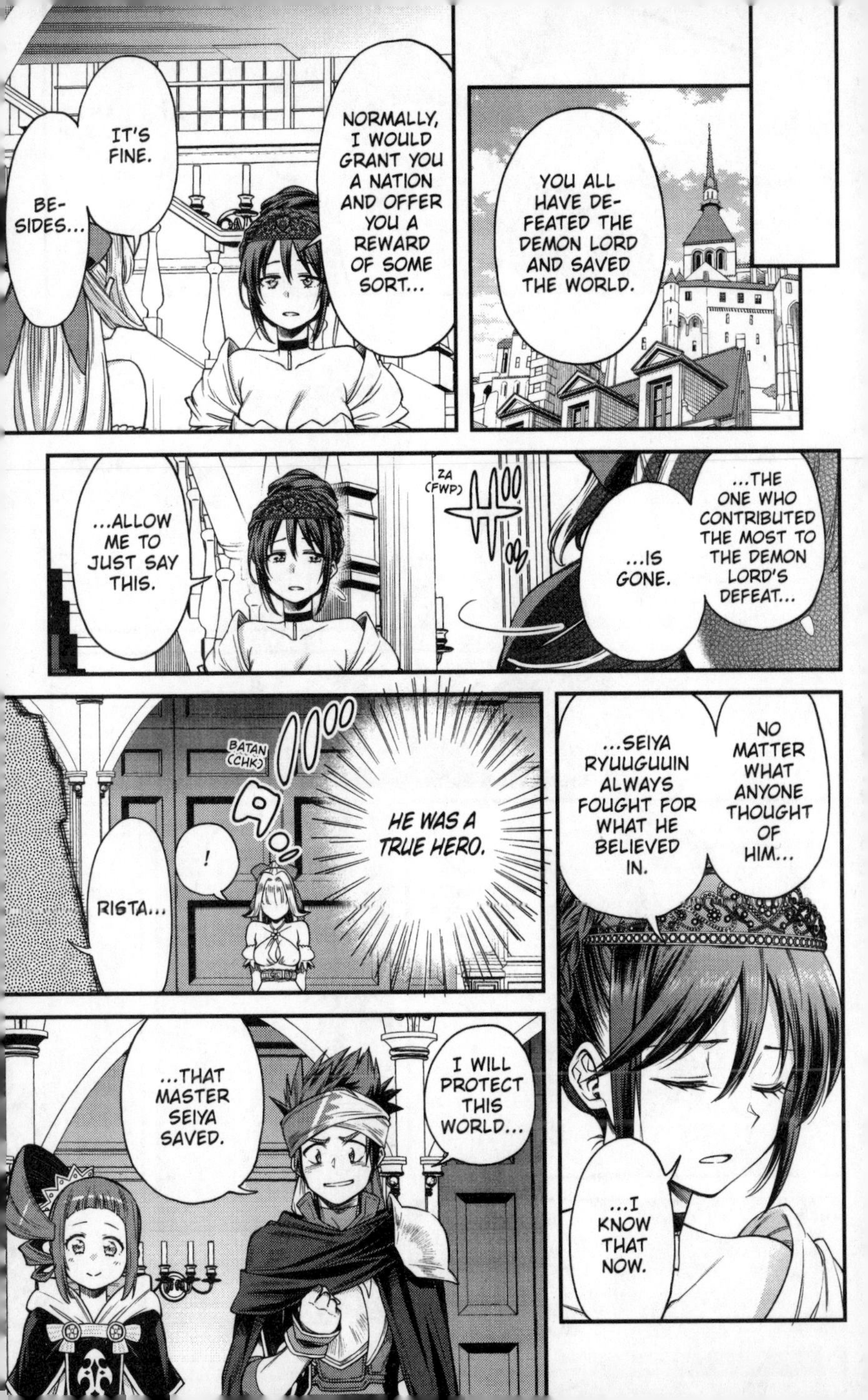
YOU ALL HAVE DEFEATED THE DEMON LORD AND SAVED THE WORLD.
NORMALLY, I WOULD GRANT YOU A NATION AND OFFER YOU A REWARD OF SOME SORT...
IT'S FINE.
BESIDES...
...THE ONE WHO CONTRIBUTED THE MOST TO THE DEMON LORD'S DEFEAT...
...IS GONE.
ZA (FWP)
...ALLOW ME TO JUST SAY THIS.
NO MATTER WHAT ANYONE THOUGHT OF HIM...
...SEIYA RYUUGUUIN ALWAYS FOUGHT FOR WHAT HE BELIEVED IN.
...I KNOW THAT NOW.
HE WAS A TRUE HERO.
BATAN (CHK)
!
RISTA...
I WILL PROTECT THIS WORLD...
...THAT MASTER SEIYA SAVED.

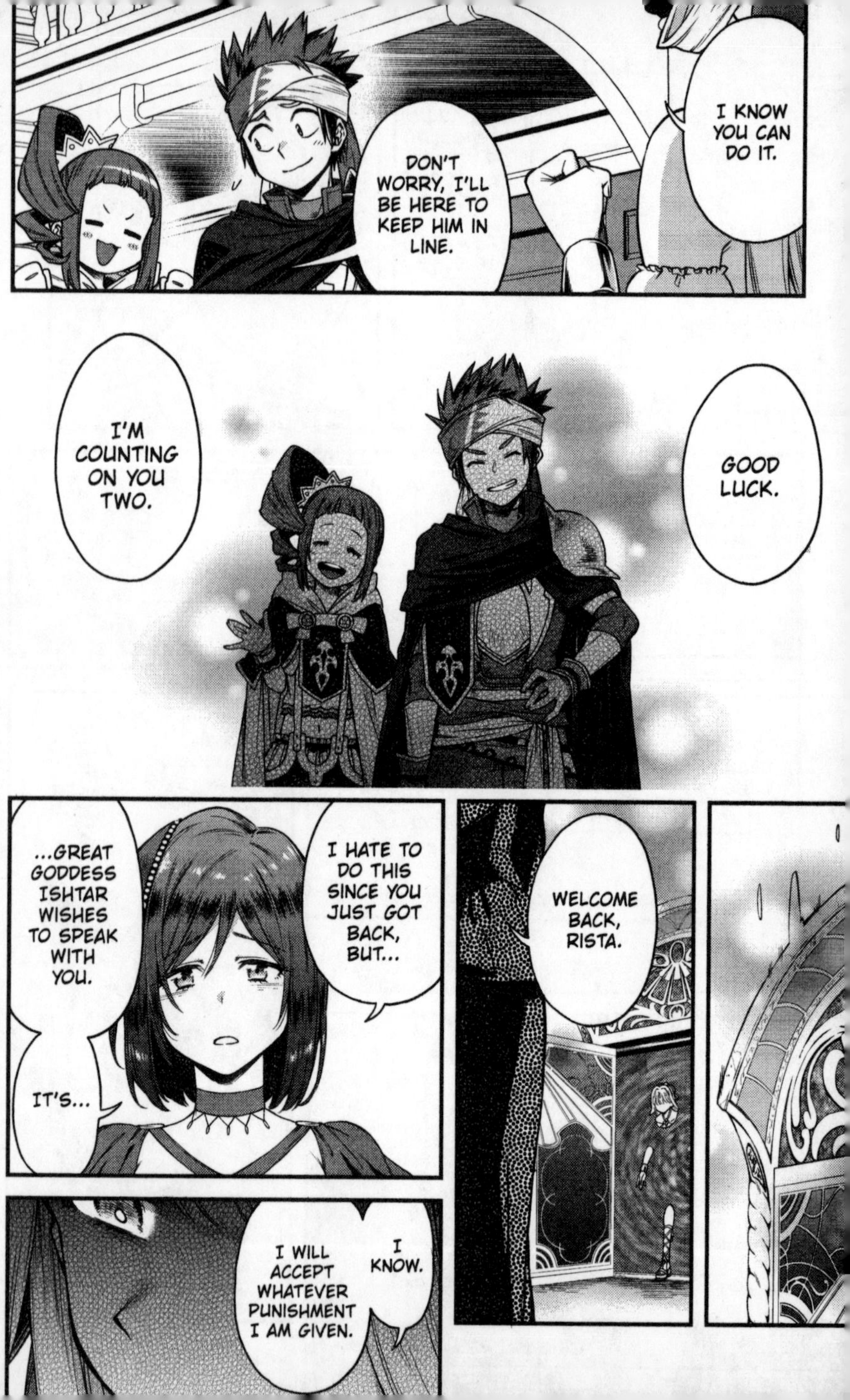
I KNOW YOU CAN DO IT.
DON'T WORRY, I'LL BE HERE TO KEEP HIM IN LINE.
GOOD LUCK.
I'M COUNTING ON YOU TWO.
WELCOME BACK, RISTA.
I HATE TO DO THIS SINCE YOU JUST GOT BACK, BUT...
...GREAT GODDESS ISHTAR WISHES TO SPEAK WITH YOU.
IT'S...
I KNOW.
I WILL ACCEPT WHATEVER PUNISHMENT I AM GIVEN.

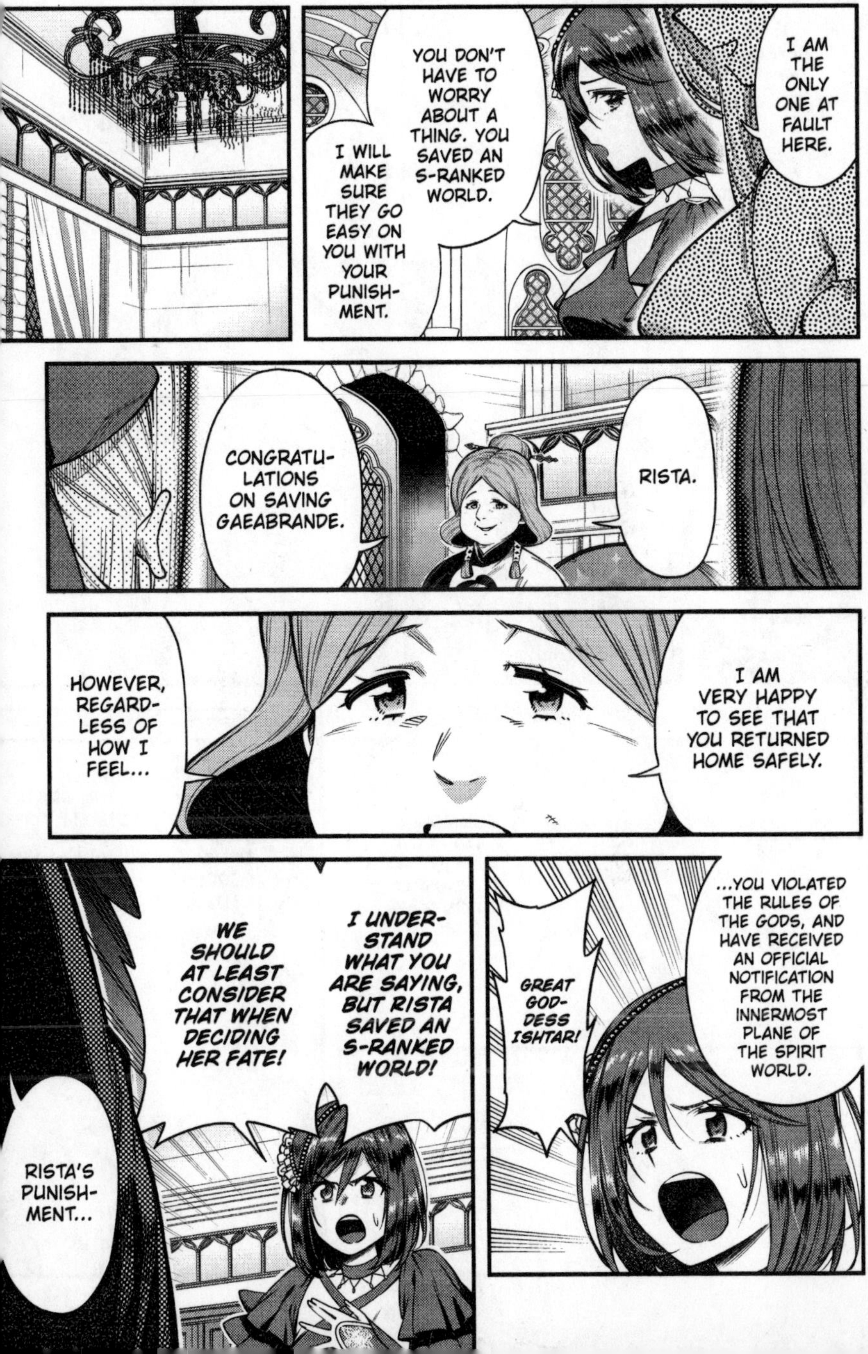
I AM THE ONLY ONE AT FAULT HERE.
YOU DON'T HAVE TO WORRY ABOUT A THING. YOU SAVED AN S-RANKED WORLD.
I WILL MAKE SURE THEY GO EASY ON YOU WITH YOUR PUNISHMENT.
RISTA.
CONGRATULATIONS ON SAVING GAEABRANDE.
I AM VERY HAPPY TO SEE THAT YOU RETURNED HOME SAFELY.
HOWEVER, REGARDLESS OF HOW I FEEL...
...YOU VIOLATED THE RULES OF THE GODS, AND HAVE RECEIVED AN OFFICIAL NOTIFICATION FROM THE INNERMOST PLANE OF THE SPIRIT WORLD.
GREAT GODDESS ISHTAR!
I UNDERSTAND WHAT YOU ARE SAYING, BUT RISTA SAVED AN S-RANKED WORLD!
WE SHOULD AT LEAST CONSIDER THAT WHEN DECIDING HER FATE!
RISTA'S PUNISHMENT...

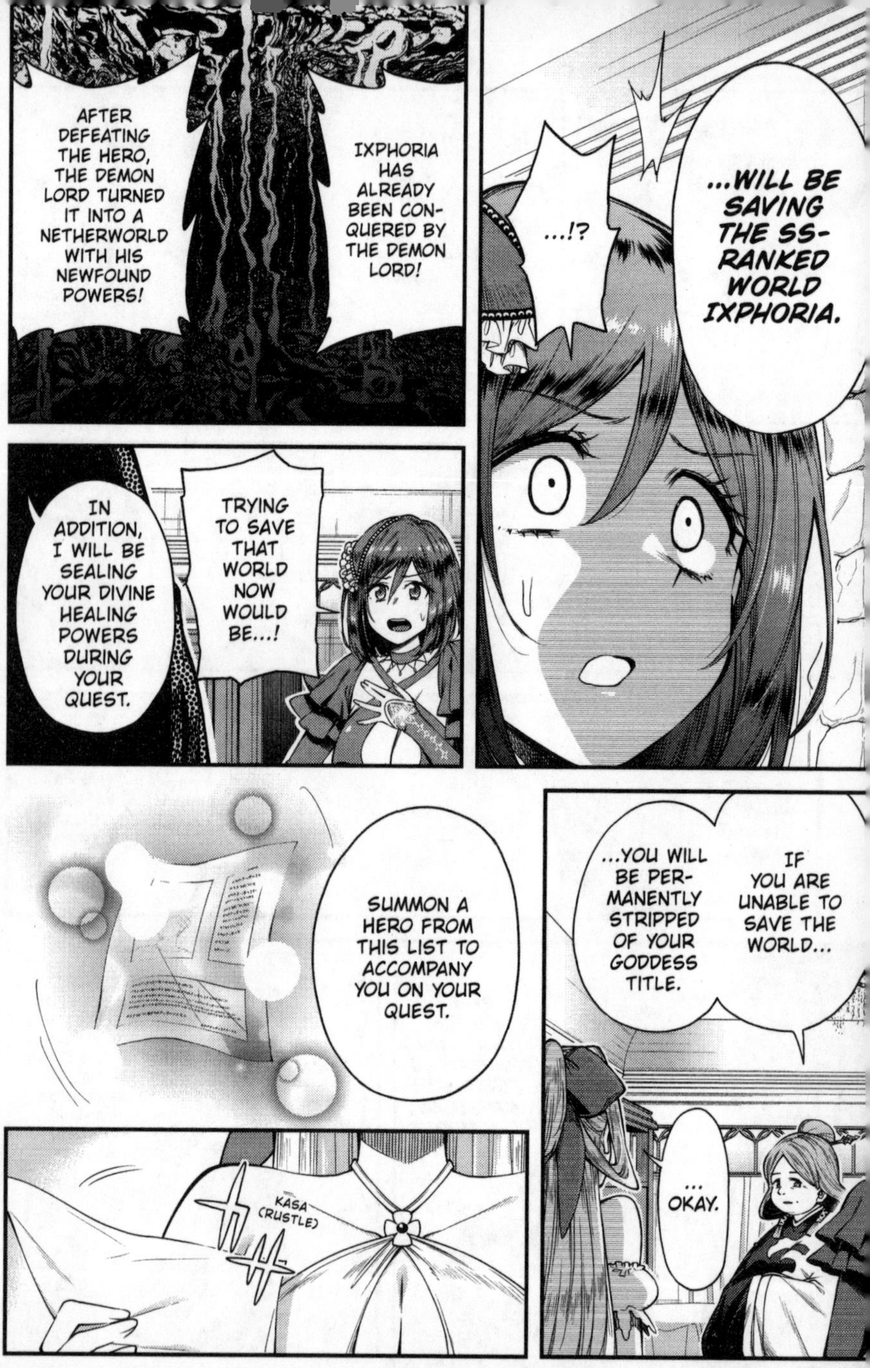
...WILL BE SAVING THE SS-RANKED WORLD IXPHORIA.
...!?
IXPHORIA HAS ALREADY BEEN CONQUERED BY THE DEMON LORD!
AFTER DEFEATING THE HERO, THE DEMON LORD TURNED IT INTO A NETHERWORLD WITH HIS NEWFOUND POWERS!
TRYING TO SAVE THAT WORLD NOW WOULD BE...!
IN ADDITION, I WILL BE SEALING YOUR DIVINE HEALING POWERS DURING YOUR QUEST.
IF YOU ARE UNABLE TO SAVE THE WORLD...
...YOU WILL BE PERMANENTLY STRIPPED OF YOUR GODDESS TITLE.
... OKAY.
SUMMON A HERO FROM THIS LIST TO ACCOMPANY YOU ON YOUR QUEST.
KASA (RUSTLE)

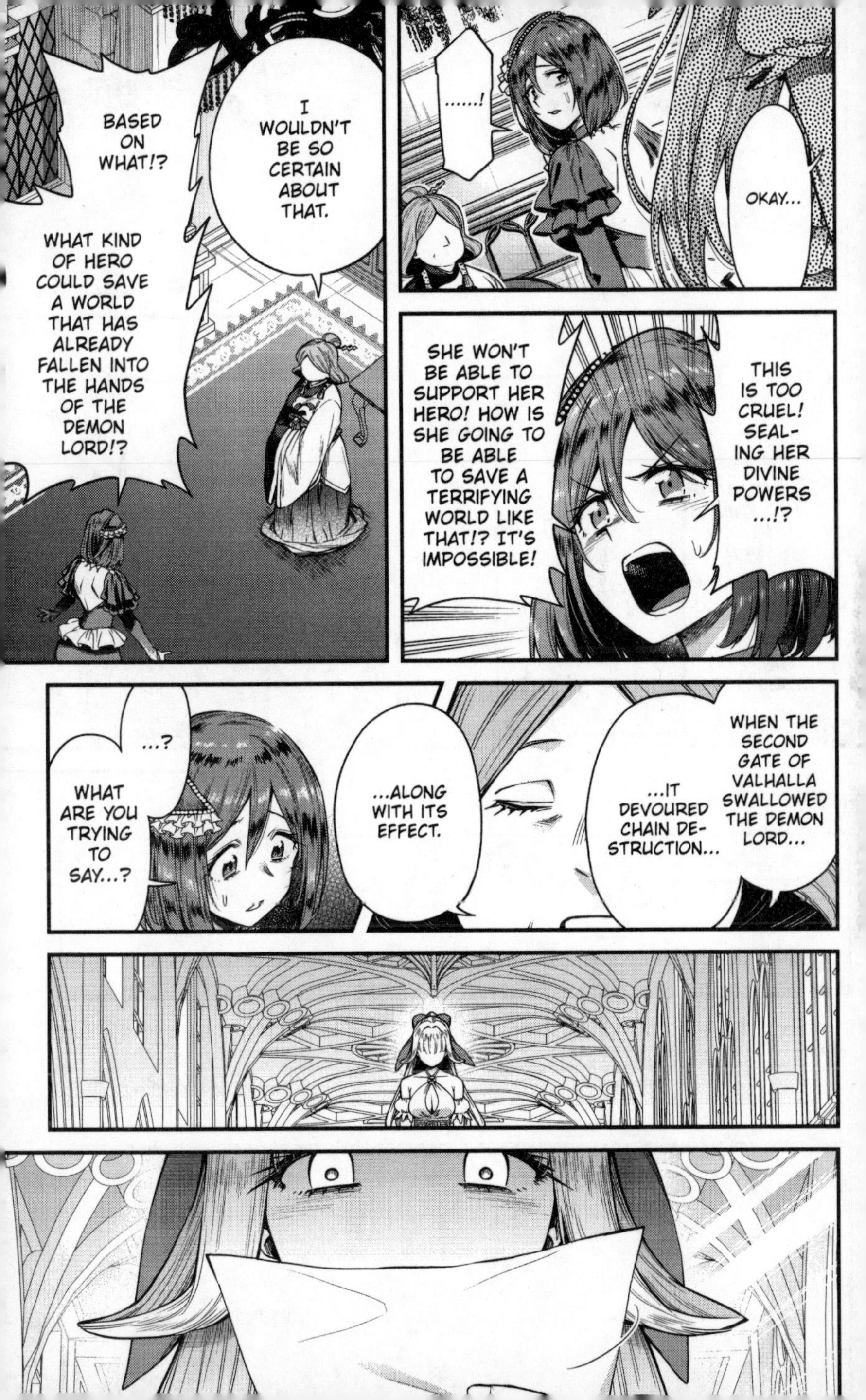
OKAY...
......!
THIS IS TOO CRUEL! SEAL-ING HER DIVINE POWERS ...!?
SHE WON'T BE ABLE TO SUPPORT HER HERO! HOW IS SHE GOING TO BE ABLE TO SAVE A TERRIFYING WORLD LIKE THAT!? IT'S IMPOSSIBLE!
I WOULDN'T BE SO CERTAIN ABOUT THAT.
BASED ON WHAT!?
WHAT KIND OF HERO COULD SAVE A WORLD THAT HAS ALREADY FALLEN INTO THE HANDS OF THE DEMON LORD!?
WHEN THE SECOND GATE OF VALHALLA SWALLOWED THE DEMON LORD...
...IT DEVOURED CHAIN DE-STRUCTION...
...ALONG WITH ITS EFFECT.
...?
WHAT ARE YOU TRYING TO SAY...?

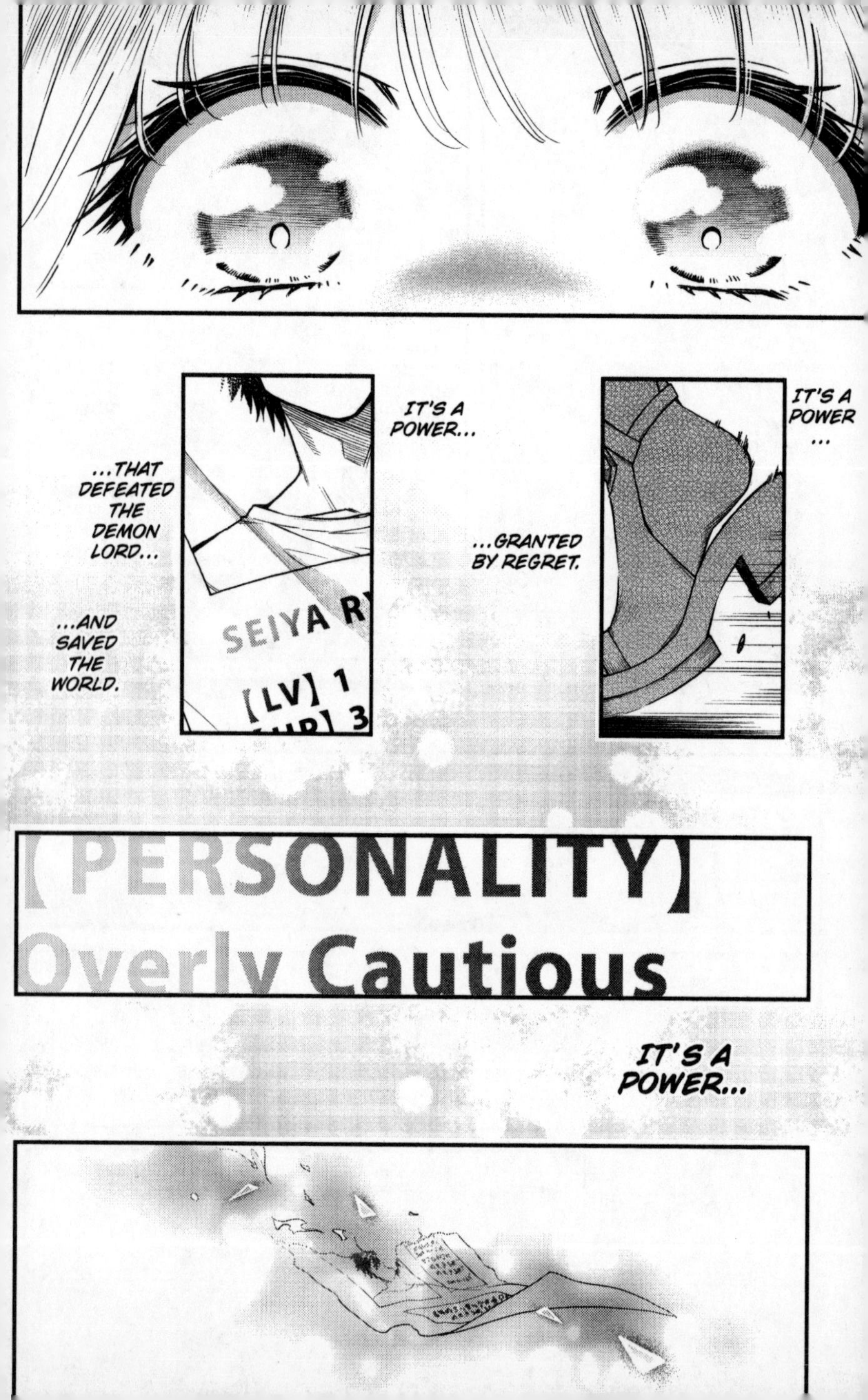
IT'S A POWER ...
...GRANTED BY REGRET.
IT'S A POWER...
...THAT DEFEATED THE DEMON LORD...
...AND SAVED THE WORLD.
SEIYA R
[LV] 1
[PERSONALITY]
Overly Cautious
IT'S A POWER...

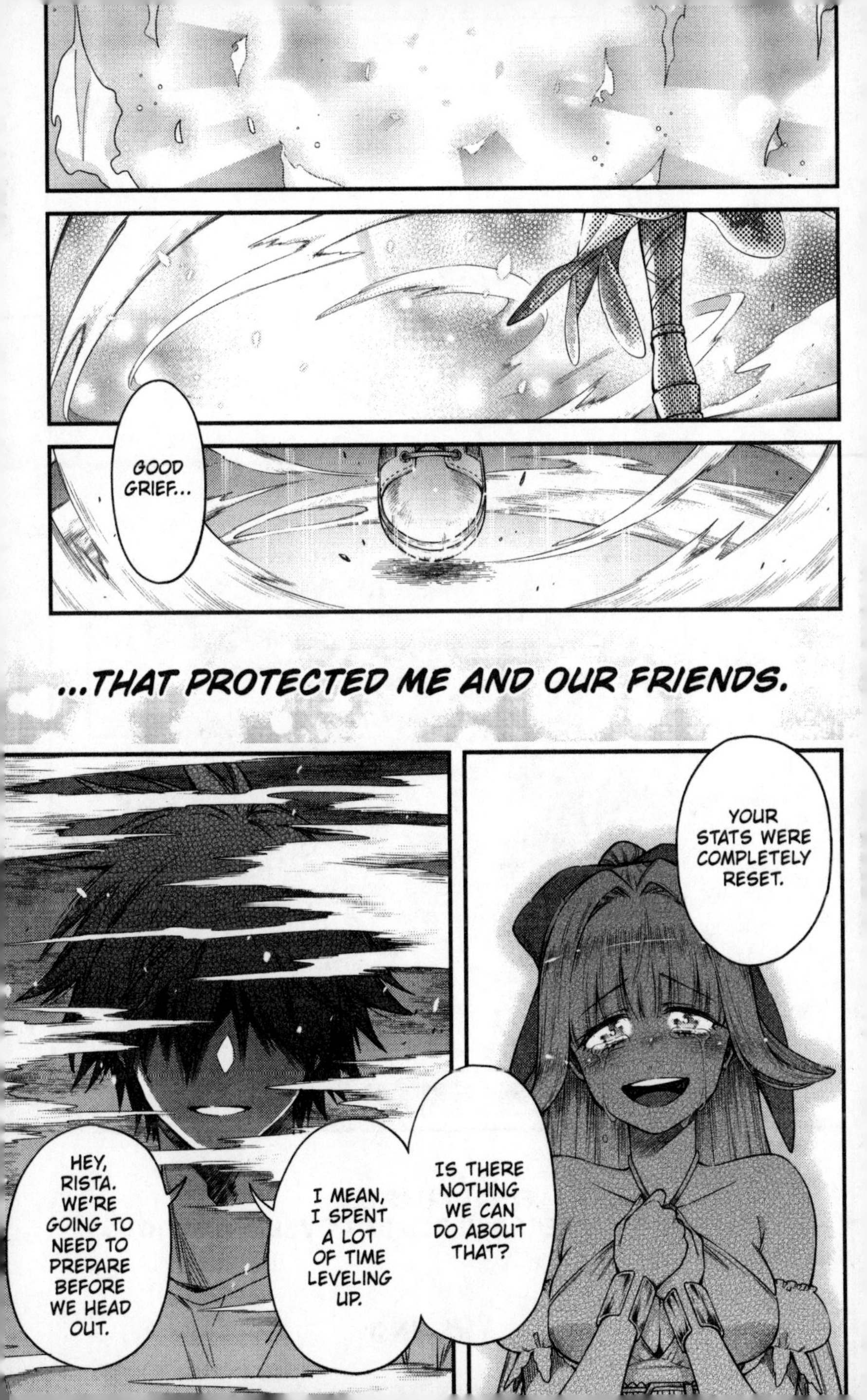
GOOD GRIEF...
...THAT PROTECTED ME AND OUR FRIENDS.
YOUR STATS WERE COMPLETELY RESET.
IS THERE NOTHING WE CAN DO ABOUT THAT?
I MEAN, I SPENT A LOT OF TIME LEVELING UP.
HEY, RISTA. WE'RE GOING TO NEED TO PREPARE BEFORE WE HEAD OUT.

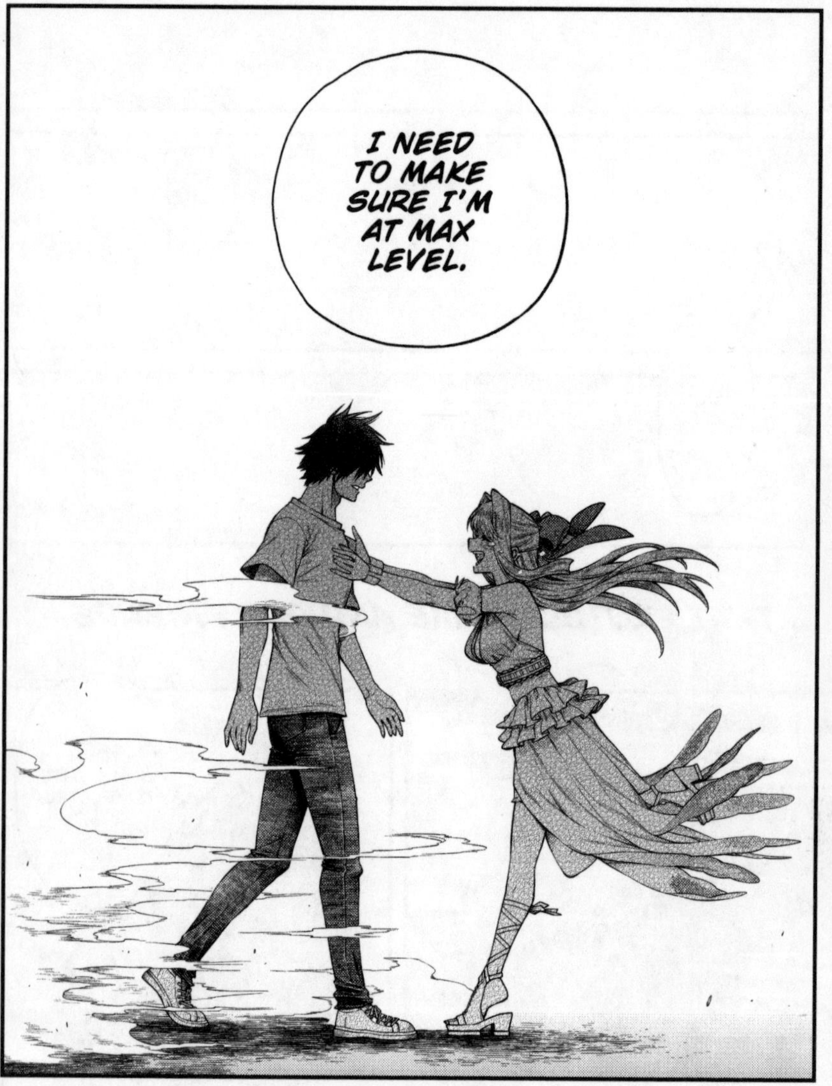
I NEED TO MAKE SURE I'M AT MAX LEVEL.

FINAL CHAPTER:
THE HERO IS OVERPOWERED BUT OVERLY CAUTIOUS

THE END

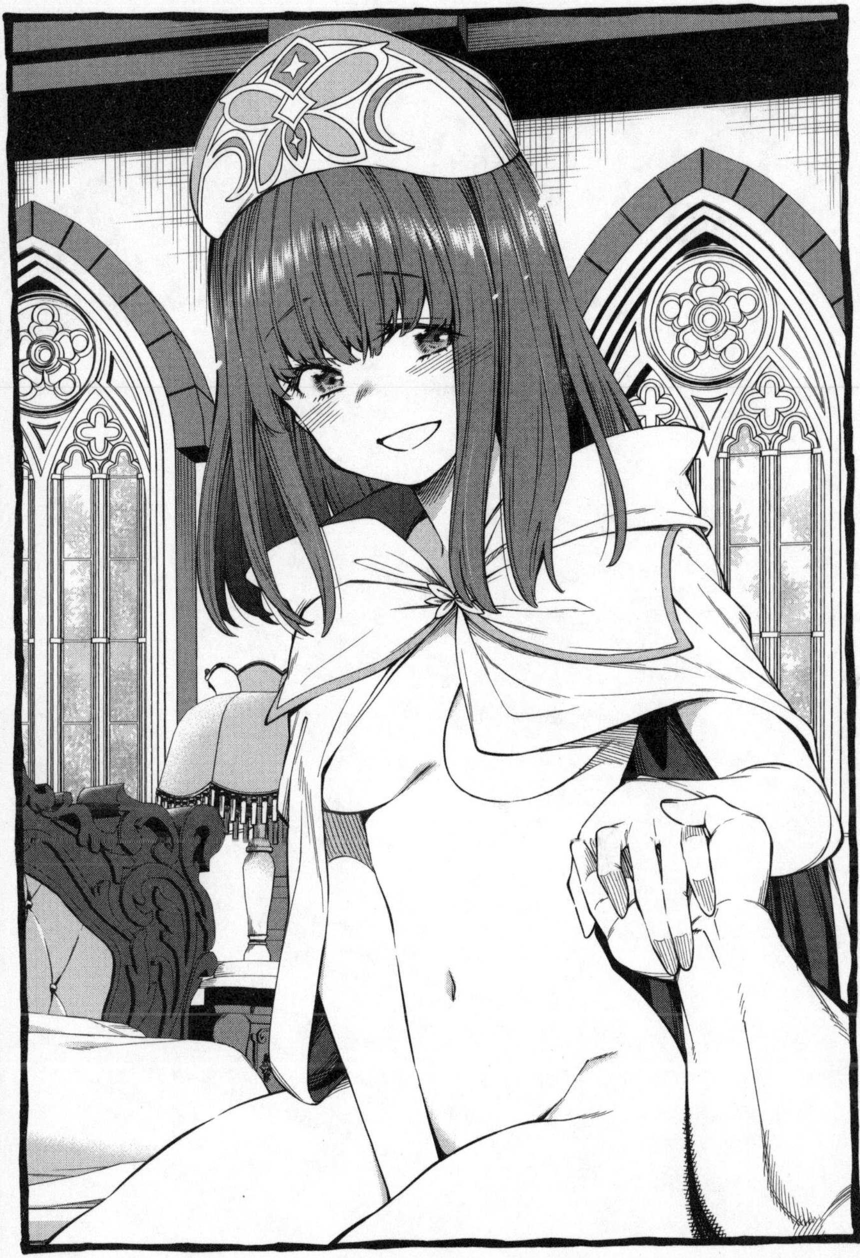

The Hero Is Overpowered but Overly Cautious 6

THE HERO is OVERPOWERED BUT OVERLY CAUTIOUS 6

ORIGINAL STORY: **LIGHT TUCHIHI**
CHARACTER DESIGN: **SAORI TOYOTA**
ART: **KOYUKI**

Translation: **MATT RUTSOHN** ＊ Lettering: **CHIHO CHRISTIE**

This book is a work of fiction. Names, characters, places, and incidents are the product of the author's imagination or are used fictitiously. Any resemblance to actual events, locales, or persons, living or dead, is coincidental.

KONO YUSHA GA ORE TUEEE KUSENI SHINCHO SUGIRU Volume 6
© Light Tuchihi, Saori Toyota 2022
© Koyuki 2022

First published in Japan in 2022 by KADOKAWA CORPORATION, Tokyo.
English translation rights arranged with KADOKAWA CORPORATION,
Tokyo through TUTTLE-MORI AGENCY, INC., Tokyo.

English translation © 2023 by Yen Press, LLC

Yen Press
150 West 30th Street, 19th Floor
New York, NY 10001

Visit us at yenpress.com
facebook.com/yenpress
twitter.com/yenpress
yenpress.tumblr.com
instagram.com/yenpress

First Yen Press Edition: October 2023
Edited by Yen Press Editorial: Conner Worman, Carl Li
Designed by Yen Press Design: Eddy Mingki, Wendy Chan

Yen Press is an imprint of Yen Press, LLC.
The Yen Press name and logo are trademarks of Yen Press, LLC.

The publisher is not responsible for websites (or their content)
that are not owned by the publisher.

Library of Congress Control Number: 2019953328

ISBNs: 978-1-9753-7464-8 (paperback)
978-1-9753-7465-5 (ebook)

10 9 8 7 6 5 4 3 2 1

WOR

Printed in the United States of America

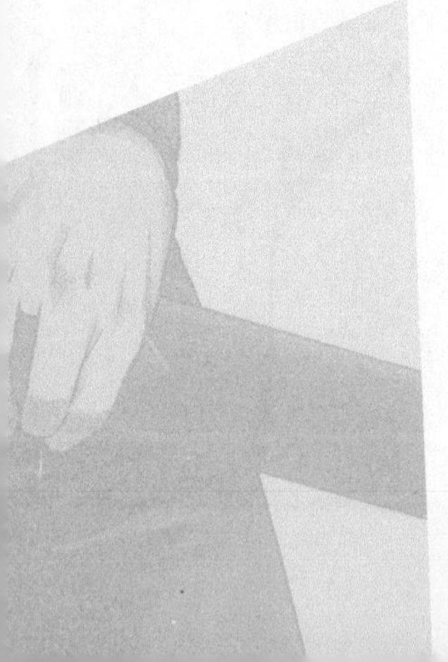